Le Corbusier AND THE MYSTIQUE OF THE USSR: Theories and Projects for Moscow, 1928-1936

JEAN-LOUIS COHEN

Le Corbusier

AND THE MYSTIQUE OF THE USSR

Theories and Projects for Moscow

1 9 2 8 – 1 9 3 6

PRINCETON UNIVERSITY PRESS · PRINCETON, NEW JERSEY

The original edition appeared under the title
Le Corbusier et la mystique de L'URSS: théories et projets pour Moscou 1928–1936
Pierre Mardaga Editeur, Liège, Belgium
© 1987 Jean-Louis Cohen

All works by Le Corbusier copyright Foundation Le Corbusier/SPADEM, Paris

This book has been published with the financial support of the Direction du Livre et de la Lecture, Ministère de la Culture et de la Communication and of the Bureau de la Recherche Architecturale, Ministère de l'Equipement, du Logement, des Transports et de la Mer, Paris.

Translated by Kenneth Hylton
English translation © 1992 by Princeton University Press
Published by Princeton University Press, 41 William Street,
Princeton, New Jersey 08540
In the United Kingdom: Princeton University Press, Oxford

Library of Congress Cataloging-in-Publication Data
Cohen, Jean-Louis, 1949-
Le Corbusier and the mystique of the USSR:
Theories and projects for Moscow, 1928-1936.
Bibliography: p.
Includes index, illustrations.
1. Architecture—Design. 2. Urban Planning. 3. Art history. 4. Russian History.
PL1279.L496   1991   495.1'16   89-6013

ISBN 0-691-04076-1 (alk. paper)

This book has been composed in Adobe Berkeley and Bauhaus typefaces

Princeton University Press books are printed on acid-free paper, and meet the guidelines for permanence and durability of the Committee on Production Guidelines for Book Longevity of the Council on Library Resources

Printed in the United States of America by
Princeton University Press, Princeton, New Jersey

10 9 8 7 6 5 4 3 2 1

CONTENTS

THE PRESENT WORK is the fruit of research that commenced a decade ago with lectures, articles and exhibitions (including *Paris-Moscou*, held at the Centre Georges Pompidou in Paris in 1979), and which I have pursued in the form of further occasional articles and researches. The original French edition, which was published by Pierre Mardaga at the end of 1987, the year of Le Corbusier's centennial, has been significantly revised and expanded for this English-language version. Most of the illustrations have been retained, although some have been replaced by better-quality originals or complemented with photographs discovered since publication of the original edition.

The research leading up to the publication of this work could not have been envisaged without the support of various institutions and individuals. In particular, I should like to express my gratitude to Claude Prelorenzo and Bernard Haumont, directors of the French Bureau de la Recherche Architecturale, whose material support for the research program *Architecture moderne, relations internationales*, some analyses of which are included in the present work, enabled me to achieve a broad overview of architectural relations between France and Russia.

The task would have been impossible without the encouragement of the Fondation Le Corbusier, where I was granted generous access to the source materials that form the basis of this book. My thanks go to President Jean Jenger, Director Evelyne Tréhin, Secretary-General Roger Aujame, Librarian Martine Lasson, and to Holy Raveloarisa, keeper of the fondation's photographic collections. I also wish to express my gratitude to Henry Millon, dean of the Center for Advanced Study in the Visual Arts at the National Gallery in Washington, D.C., for his hospitality while I completed and revised the manuscript.

My thanks go also to institutions whose libraries and archives enabled me to pursue my researches: the State Lenin Library and the Shchusev Architectural Museum (Moscow); the Slavonic Division of the New York Public Library; the Library of Congress (Washington, D.C.); the British Architectural Library (London); the archives of the CIAM at the Eidgenössische Technische Hochschule (Zurich); the Conservatoire National des Arts et Métiers (Paris); and the Getty Center for the History of Art and the Humanities (Santa Monica).

My readings have benefited considerably from contributions by Vigdariia Khazanova, Irina Kokkinaki, Naum Kleiman, Vitia Miziano, Anatoli Strigalev (Moscow); Kenneth Frampton, Mary McLeod (New York); Francesco Passanti (Boston); Rémi Baudouï (Paris); Alan Colquhoun (London, Princeton); Danièle Pauly (Strasburg); Francesco Dal Co (Venice); Jos Bosman, Werner Oechslin (Zurich); Bruno Reichlin (Zurich, Geneva); and Yorgos Simeoforidis (Athens). Raymond Fischer, Lucien Hervé, Charlotte Perriand, and Pierre Vago, witnesses and protagonists of some of the episodes recounted in what follows, have provided invaluable support with their reminiscences and evaluations.

The completion of this book coincided with the preparations for the exhibition *L'aventure Le Corbusier (1887–1965)*, which was held at the Centre de Création Industrielle of the Centre Georges Pompidou in Paris in 1987; it therefore benefited, directly or indirectly, from the support of the exhibition team as a whole, and especially François Burkhardt, director of the CCI, Jana Claverie, Martine Moinot, Guillemette Morel Journel, Jean-Claude Planchet, and Catherine Saint-Martin. I should also like to thank the Studio Littré, whose reproductions of the photographic documents presented in this book were carried out promptly and efficiently.

The present edition was made possible by two generous translation subsidies granted by the Direction du Livre et de la Lecture at the French Ministry of Culture and by the Bureau de la Recherche Architecturale, by the diligence of Elizabeth Powers, its editor at Princeton University Press, and the passion of Kenneth Hylton, its translator.

Finally, I cannot proceed without thanking my first reader, Monique Eleb, for her patience, rigor, and affection.

THE MOSCOW STAKES

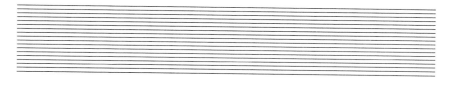

• INTRODUCTION •

MARCH MORNING, 1930. Snow still covers the *izbas* and brick buildings of Moscow. Dressed in a voluminous woolen overcoat and a wide-brimmed, peaked cap (both bought at the GUM), Le Corbusier smiles, a notebook in hand. The notebook has been lost, but in place of the rudimentary scaffolding seen in the background of the photograph, a reinforced-concrete, steel, and glass building stands today. Construction of Centrosoyuz, Le Corbusier's first large public building, began that spring.[1]

The mildly ironic expression of hope that this success had brought to Le Corbusier's eye was to prove unfounded, whereas his resentment at subsequent failures in Russia knew no limits. Yet intense as they were, these two distinct phases of his tumultuous Moscow venture remain largely unknown. Almost twenty years of research have now brought to light the more obscure episodes in Le Corbusier's itinerary, both those he was reluctant to speak of and those whose complex nature critics fond of clear-cut situations have been unable to grasp. As instanced in exhibitions and new publications inspired by the Le Corbusier centennial in 1987, a wealth of new source materials has begun to be exploited, and whole series of repressed critical approaches have begun to emerge, revealing some of the more contradictory aspects of Le Corbusier's life and work and the multiple contours of his personality.[2]

Even without his declared positions and manifestos, the complexity of Le Corbusier's relations with active social forces during the first half of the twentieth century is patent. His career unfolded in the context of traumatic events affecting the entire planet—the First World War and its consequences (the collapse of the central European empires, revolutions in Russia and Germany), the crisis of 1929, and the Second World War, all of which led to new political divisions and to decolonization.

The most intense period of Le Corbusier's theoretical research and creative activity in architecture took place in a world utterly different from the one he had discovered in his youth, during travels to Vienna, Berlin, Prague, and Constantinople. Faced with the formidable threat of violent social change, people suddenly became obsessed with ideas of universal peace guaranteed by international organizations, and the pressing need for a reorganized world economy.

In the tense, creative atmosphere that followed the armistice in 1918, Le Corbusier began to build a public image with a series of campaigns involving publishers, the national press, and exhibitions. In his search for an ever-widening audience—from the 1922 Salon d'Automne to the League of Nations in 1927—he also developed contacts with the Redressement Français, a circle of industrialists firmly anchored to the right of the political spectrum. Yet he continued to take an interest in foreign affairs and in the emergence of new state and social policies—interest, for example, in the new Weimar Republic and Walther Rathenau's early orientations, or events in the newborn Soviet Union.

LE CORBUSIER AND MOSCOW: AN INEVITABLE ENCOUNTER

The "great glow from the East" (in Jules Romains's evocation of the Russian Revolution) was not as dazzling for Le Corbusier as it was for many intellectuals of his generation; he never frequented the circles of friends of the "New Russia." Nonetheless, a number of conditions tended to favor an encounter between the crusader of "machine-age architecture" and forces that, after 1925, constructed "socialism in one country." The pages of *L'Esprit Nouveau* bear witness to the fact that Ozenfant and Le Corbusier paid some attention

1. Le Corbusier on the construction site of the Centrosoyuz, Moscow, March 1930.

[1] Transliterations of Russian places and names mentioned in this book follow the system established by the Library of Congress, with some exceptions, as in the case of ligatures and hard and soft signs, which have been eliminated. Current names have been spelled according to accepted usage.

[2] I will mention here only some of the numerous books published on the occasion of Le Corbusier's centennial: H. Allen Brooks, ed., *Le Corbusier* (Princeton: Princeton University Press, 1987) (collection of all the essays previously scattered in the thirty-two volumes of *The Le Corbusier Archive*); William J. R. Curtis, *Le Corbusier: Ideas and Forms* (Oxford: Phaidon, 1986); Deborah Gans, *The Le Corbusier Guide* (Princeton: Princeton Architectural Press, 1987); Gérard Monnier, *Le Corbusier* (Lyon: La Manufacture, 1986); and Gilles Ragot and Mathilde Dion, *Le Corbusier en France: Réalisations et projets* (Paris: Editions du Moniteur, 1987).

Among the most important catalogues are: Stanislaus von Moos, ed., *L'Esprit Nouveau: Le Corbusier et l'industrie 1920–1925* (Strasburg: Musées de la Ville, 1987); *Le Corbusier: Architect of the Century* (London: Arts Council of Great Britain, 1987); *Le Corbusier et la Méditerranée* (Marseilles: Parenthèses, 1987); Jacques Lucan, ed., *Le Corbusier (1887–1965): Une encyclopédie* (Paris: CCI/Centre Georges Pompidou, 1987).

to Russian intellectual and artistic production, and to the increasing prominence within the avant-garde of the constructivist movement. In addition to his interest in the plastic arts, Le Corbusier was first and foremost struck with the Soviet Union as a "modern" nation, an economy in the making; moreover, his own interests were in line with French public opinion as a whole.

With the launching of the New Economic Policy (NEP) in 1920, the Soviet authorities opened their frontiers to foreign—and especially German—technicians and architects. Yet despite Soviet interest in the culture of Germany and, increasingly, of the United States, the Paris intellectual scene retained pride of place, in that France had long been a country of exile and a training ground for many. Le Corbusier's stature and authority in Paris were such that the Soviets were bound to single him out, in an attempt to reap some of the benefits of his considerable influence throughout western Europe from the mid-1920s on.

When Le Corbusier finally discovered Moscow in October 1928, therefore, there was considerable expectancy on both sides. Tension was resolved briefly with the commissioning of Centrosoyuz—Le Corbusier's largest executed brief until the Unité d'Habitation, which he built only twenty years later. Yet the same tension smoldered on until 1932, when a fatal crisis developed between the two sides, ostensibly on the subject of the Palace of Soviets competition, which constituted an essential turning point in Stalinist architectural policy.

Soviet Russia furnished Le Corbusier with an opportunity to assert his position as an international expert at a crucial stage—crucial both to Russia's economic and cultural development and to Le Corbusier's own career. The most intense phase of Le Corbusier's Russian dream lasted barely three years, from his unhoped-for success in the Centrosoyuz competition in October 1928 to the rejection of his entry for the more spectacular Palace of Soviets in February 1932; and yet his relations with the Soviet Union continued to shift from symbiosis to repulsion and from elation to bitter disillusion for almost fifteen years, in a quite remarkable series of reversals.

A superficial, purely quantitative account of these years would bring to light three highly publicized trips to Russia; two projects for public buildings, of which the first doubtless constitutes Le Corbusier and Pierre Jeanneret's most important joint production of the interwar years; and an urban plan of crucial importance for the "Ville Radieuse." All of these were carried out in an atmosphere of uncommon enthusiasm. On the debit side of the Soviet experiences we may consider not only Le Corbusier's bitter resentment at Russian indifference to his urban planning ideas or the refusal of his Palace of Soviets entry, but also the reactions of right-wing polemicists of the day—such as Camille Mauclair in France or Alexandre de Senger in Switzerland—who were quick to denounce the "Trojan Horse of Bolshevism," and whose attacks could hardly be compensated for by the tenuous prestige that he would enjoy in left-wing opinion.[3]

In the ideal universe that Le Corbusier began to constitute at the outset of the twenties, the focal points were Paris, Rome, Algiers, and Barcelona (the Mediterranean diamond); Athens, Rio, Buenos Aires, and New York; and Moscow. During his formative years, before he adopted the pseudonym Le Corbusier, Charles-Edouard Jeanneret had traveled the "four roads" of Europe from the confines of German cultural hegemony to the limits of Mediterranean culture; yet he had barely rubbed shoulders with the Slavonic world in Bohemia or the Balkans.[4] It was this Eastern world, threatened from the outside and shaken by the Russian Revolution, that would furnish Le Corbusier with one of his most fertile spheres of activity. Perhaps more than elsewhere,

[3] Camille Mauclair, *L'architecture va-t-elle mourir?* (Paris: Editions de la Nouvelle Revue Critique, 1931). Alexandre de Senger, *Le Cheval de Troie du Bolchevisme* (Bienne: Editions du Chandelier, 1931).

[4] On the subject of Le Corbusier's formative "Journey to the East," see Giuliano Gresleri's scientific publication, *Viaggio in oriente* (Venice: Marsilio Editore, 1984). Le Corbusier's text is translated in *Journey to the East*, ed. Ivan Žaknić, trans. Ivan Žaknić and Nicole Pertuiset (Cambridge, Mass.: MIT Press, 1987).

2. Le Corbusier's projects in Moscow, site plan, drawing by Philippe Simon. (1) The Centrosoyuz, 1928–1936. (2) The site of the "Response to Moscow" city plan, 1930. (3) The Palace of Soviets, 1931–1932.

these real or potential Soviet commissions were to become a pretext for an extraordinary and at times frenzied assertion of his ambitions.

THE ARCHITECTURE OF SEDUCTION

Le Corbusier's relations with his clients were invariably of the emotive variety. From the first approaches, which were often timid but sometimes full of bravado, to the paroxysms of fusion and subsequent divorce, he became passionately involved in the task of mobilizing their interest in his projects, and the ensuing relationships were invariably rooted in the time-honored principles of seduction.

At first he would become inflamed, and flatter his clients for the eminent virtues of their social, industrial, or political strategies. This phase of idealization would invariably result in an early project responding to the true origin of the commission. Le Corbusier would then deploy his charms in a more broadly based offensive involving increasingly grandiose and complex schemes: when called on to design a building, he would propose to redevelop a whole district; if asked to furnish a limited study of a district, he would advance ideas for the reorganization of a whole region. The third phase was invariably more disappointing: the client, alarmed by such ardent ambitions, would be drawn into a fatal spiral from which he was incapable of extricating himself except by breaking off or postponing the project with a greater or lesser degree of tact.

More often than not these intrigues culminated in mutual mistrust and resentment. And yet the benefits were not always entirely negligible: Le Corbusier was able to pursue his favorite research themes elsewhere, while at the same time adding one or several fresh projects to his repertory; and the client could think of his momentary deviation as evidence of open-minded benevolence—except where he was tempted to use Le Corbusier as a convenient, *a posteriori* scapegoat for his own failures. This scenario of the seduction process underlay many of Le Corbusier's interwar activities, in parallel with the patient and obstinate search for smaller-scale, less exhilarating ventures of the speculative or breadwinning variety in the Paris urban context. It would, however, be oversimplifying matters to view the intricate web of relations as an opportunistic quest for commissions, given that Le Corbusier's network of affects was shot through with contradictions.

Coherent and articulate in his public relations, Le Corbusier additionally showed a remarkable capacity to adapt to his clients' propositions. He was always careful to grasp their modes of discourse with a view to modulating his own without yielding on the essential point—namely, architectural form. This tactic often took the form of total identification with a given political doctrine or industrial strategy. For instance, he suddenly discovered a pressing vocation as a shoe salesman when consulted for the construction of a chain of shops by the Moravian industrialist Bat'a at the end of the thirties.[5] He proved equally capable of adapting his projects for the transformation of Parisian urban space to the technocratic orientations of the Redressement Français or to the social housing policies that Léon Blum timidly attempted to implement after 1936.[6]

LE CORBUSIER'S IDIOSYNCRATIC BOLSHEVISM

The chronicle of relations between Le Corbusier and Soviet architects and politicians brings to light a comparable process of identification, and one of some considerable intensity, as witness his peculiar reading of Bolshevism. Contesting the Soviet leaders' fidelity to their own doctrines in the wake of the rejection of his Palace of Soviets project, his proposed interpretation of the term (which of course was forged before 1914 in the course of conflicts within the Russian Social-Democratic Workers' party) is tinged with megalomania:

"That word bolshoi . . . what does it mean?"

"Big!"

"So Bolshevism?"

"Bolshevism means: everything as big as possible, the biggest theory, the biggest projects. Maximum. Going to the heart of any question. Examining it in depth. Envisaging the whole. Breadth and size."

Till then, I had understood from our newspapers that bolshevik meant: a man with a red beard and a knife between his teeth.[7]

But if Le Corbusier appears to have integrated his Russian experiences of the years 1928–1932 into his own professional approach, it is equally certain that he was used as a tactical arm in the Soviet architectural debate. It is essentially this aspect of Le Corbusier's relations with Moscow that have hitherto been examined in studies of Soviet avant-garde architecture, such as those by Anatole Kopp,[8] or of the activities of foreign (mostly German) architects working in the Soviet Union at the outset of the thirties, such as those by Christian Borngräber or Marco de Michelis and Ernesto Pasini.[9] Russian historians, such as Irina Kokinakki, have been interested above all in his views on the question of "Soviet architecture's international relations."[10]

[5] See Jean-Louis Cohen, "Nostro cliente è il nostro padrone," in *I clienti di Le Corbusier*, *Rassegna*, Milan, no. 3 (1980): 47–60.

[6] On Le Corbusier's lengthy flirtation with the technocrats, see Mary C. McLeod, *Le Corbusier, from Regional Syndicalism to Vichy* (Princeton: Princeton University Press, forthcoming).

[7] Le Corbusier, "Bolche ou la notion du grand," *Prélude*, no. 4 (1932), reprinted in *La Villa Radieuse* (Boulogne-sur-Seine: Editions de L'Architecture d'Aujourd'hui, 1935), p. 182. English translation: "Bolshoi . . . or the notion of bigness," in *The Radiant City* (New York: Orion Press, 1967), pp. 182–83. Extensive quotation from texts already published in English have been used throughout the book where appropriate, sometimes with slight adaptations.

[8] Anatole Kopp, *Ville et révolution, architecture et urbanisme soviétiques des années vingt* (Paris: Anthropos, 1967); English translation: *Town and Revolution, Soviet Architecture and City Planning, 1917–1935* (London: Thames and Hudson; New York: Braziller, 1970). Idem, *L'architecture de la période stalinienne* (Grenoble: Presses Universitaires de Grenoble, 1978).

[9] Christian Borngräber, "Le Corbusier a Mosca," *I clienti de Le Corbusier*, pp. 79–88. Marco de Michelis, Ernesto Pasini, *La città sovietica 1925–1937* (Venice: Marsilio, 1976).

[10] Irina Kokinakki, "Le Corbusier i Sovetskaia Rossia," *Arkhitektura SSSR* 37, no. 2 (1987): 94–100. The best bibliography of Soviet literature on Le Corbusier has been published in Russia itself, in Irina Ern, *Poslednie raboty Le Corbusier* (Moscow: Stroiizdat, 1975), pp. 104–15.

Other studies have concentrated on a number of late episodes in Le Corbusier's contact with the USSR; these include S. Frederick Starr's analysis of his correspondence with the people's commissar Anatoli Lunacharsky and the future writer Victor Nekrasov,[11] or Thilo Hilpert and Giorgio Ciucci's studies of the contribution of the Moscow adventure to his urban theories.[12] For my part, I attempted some years ago to contribute a global overview of Le Corbusier's Moscow adventures in the cramped space of two somewhat excessively condensed articles.[13]

Despite the existence of some acute but invariably partial investigations, the development of, and crisis in, the relations between Le Corbusier and Moscow and their effect on his discourse and architectural forms have yet to be reconstituted within their political and cultural framework. And although Le Corbusier's expeditions to South and North America, Italy, and North Africa, as well as his initiatory travels in Tuscany and the Balkans, are reasonably well documented, his visits to and interventions in the Soviet Union remain to a large extent clouded in mystery.

TWO MYSTERIOUS EPISODES

The principal cause of these deficiencies is too obvious to require elaboration. For reasons relating to Soviet travel restrictions, it was no easier until the end of the eighties for Western researchers to gain access to Moscow sources than it was for Soviet historians to consult the Fondation Le Corbusier in Paris. But more than these material obstacles, the striking absence of research over the past twenty years can be attributed to Le Corbusier's conspicuous failure to supervise the construction of Centrosoyuz or to gain acceptance either for his scheme to reorganize Moscow or for his entry in the Palace of Soviets competition. The situation has, moreover, been aggravated by the fact that considerable quantities of energy have been spent on detailed and occasionally redundant studies of the minutiae of his great architectural saga.

Global investigations of the Russian experiences have no doubt been hindered by the very nature of characteristic approaches to Corbusian research. Despite the exceptionally rich vein of documentation to be found at the Fondation Le Corbusier, it is important not to neglect cross-referencing, or "perpendicular" research into other sources. The value of this approach is especially obvious in the case of correspondence, which has to be exhaustively reconstituted so that we can place Le Corbusier's own elaborately constructed perceptions of that correspondence in its context. It would be regrettable if we were simply to reproduce his own readings.

Apart from a number of extremely thorough biographical studies concentrating on his Swiss friends or Paris industrialist clients, the first epic narrative accounts have happily given way since 1980 to typological studies pinpointing the breaks and continuities in Le Corbusier's projects and buildings. Kenneth Frampton and Alan Colquhoun consider Centrosoyuz and the Palace of Soviets as part of a series including the League of Nations,[14] while the "Ville Radieuse" is merely seen as one of the great urban projects beginning with the "Ville Contemporaine," and Le Corbusier's interest in constructivist collective housing is seen as participating in a long process of elaboration from the charterhouse of Ema and the immeubles-villas to the unités d'habitation.

Now that these long design continuities have been traced, it becomes possible to consider shorter historical cycles whereby Le Corbusier's consecutive researches are seen to articulate and condition each other. The totality of his relations with Moscow constitutes just one such cycle. Far from representing merely a narrative of difficult or stimulating commissions, as in the case of

[11] S. Frederick Starr, "Le Corbusier and the USSR: New Documentation," Oppositions 23 (Winter 1981): 123–37, and an abridged version of this in Cahiers du Monde Russe et Soviétique 21, no. 2 (1980): 209–21.

[12] Thilo Hilpert, Die funktionelle Stadt. Le Corbusiers Stadtdivision, Bedingungen–Motive–Hintergründe (Braunschweig: Vieweg, 1978), pp. 154–76; Giorgio Ciucci, "Le Corbusier e Wright in URSS," in Alberto Asor Rosa, Manfredo Tafuri, et al., Socialismo Città Architettura URSS 1917–1918. Il contributo degli architetti europei (Rome: Officina Edizioni, 1972), pp. 171–94.

[13] Jean-Louis Cohen, "Cette mystique, l'URSS," Architecture Mouvement Continuité 49 (1979): 75–84, and a more complete version, "Le Corbusier and the Mystique of the USSR," Oppositions 23 (Winter 1981): 84–121. See also my more recent, and shorter, analysis: "Le Corbusier à Moscou," in Lucan, Le Corbusier (1887–1965): Une encyclopédie, pp. 436–44.

[14] Kenneth Frampton, "Le Corbusier's designs for the League of Nations, the Centrosoyus and the Palace of the Soviets," in The Le Corbusier Archive, ed. H. Allen Brooks (New York: Garland, 1982), 3: ix–xxii; reprinted in Brooks, Le Corbusier, pp. 57–70. Alan Colquhoun, "The Strategies of the Grand Travaux," in Modernity and the Classical Tradition; Architectural Essays 1980–1987 (Cambridge, Mass.: MIT Press, 1989), pp. 121–61; originally published as "La composition et le problème du contexte urbain," in Lucan, Le Corbusier (1887–1965): Une encyclopédie, pp. 378–84.

Bat'a, or the staging of architecture against a political backdrop, I have come to view this sum of projects, controversies, and human contacts as a crucial pivot for all Le Corbusier's subsequent activity.

Although condensed into a single edifice, these experiences seem to have retained a certain symbolic power in the Russia of the *perestroika*. Some ideologists of the conservative and xenophobic association Pamiat seem to imply in the present political context that destructions inflicted on Moscow by Stalinist urban planners were based on a plan evolved by Le Corbusier himself; yet we shall see that the relation of Le Corbusier to transformations of the capital of Russia was of a quite different nature.

THE PURPOSE OF THIS BOOK

Although the title of the present work conjures up the "mystique" that Le Corbusier thought he had discovered in Russia (as mentioned in a letter to Anatoli Lunacharsky in 1932), its structure reflects the continual to and fro between Le Corbusier's stated positions concerning Russia and the controversies in which he became involved there, and architectural events relative to the emergence and impact of his architectural and urban projects.

The ensuing enquiry aims both to gauge the shifts in his theories, projects, and strategies as induced by the Soviet "effect," and to assess the consequences of his presence, whether immediate or distant, on the Soviet scene as a whole. This parallel investigation is presented thematically, through the study of the successive sets of circumstances in which Le Corbusier's ties with the Soviet Union were forged, intensified, strained, and broken.

From the rather belated discovery of Le Corbusier's positions by rival Soviet avant-garde movements and the incomprehension with which they were met in 1930 through to the ensuing accusations, this first level of analysis concerns the exchange of doctrinal themes and positions between Paris and Moscow. From the elaboration of the successive projects for Centrosoyuz to its far-from-painless execution, from proposals for the development of Moscow to the hopes crystallized in the Palace of Soviets competition, a second level of study concerns the architectural and urban theoretical approaches whose emergence was hastened by Le Corbusier's contact with the Moscow scene. Finally, it was necessary to pose the question of the mute or dazzling impact of these two series of experiences on Le Corbusier's architecture and his position within the French political spectrum. These two registers are nonetheless presented chronologically, in order that the interaction between exchanges and confrontations "in the field" and ideas and transformations taking place in the design process can be restored in all their subtlety and all their vigor.

Le Corbusier AND THE MYSTIQUE OF THE USSR: Theories and Projects for Moscow, 1928-1936

CHAPTER

L'Esprit Nouveau
and Russia

L E CORBUSIER'S arrival in Moscow in October 1928 to defend his Centro-soyuz project caused something of a stir, given the fact that since the early twenties not only critics but also architects and, more generally, readers of Soviet cultural reviews had become perfectly familiar with his activities.

For reasons of symmetry, Le Corbusier and the Soviet avant-garde could in no wise ignore each other: with *L'Esprit Nouveau*, which had acquired the startlingly immodest subtitle, "Revue internationale illustrée de l'activité contemporaine," Jeanneret and Ozenfant had set up a device for observation and dissemination that could not fail to find an echo among Russian initiatives. At the same time, despite their desire to register a clean break with the West, theorists of the Russian avant-garde had always kept an eye on Paris and had quickly perceived the interest of Le Corbusier's literary and architectural productions.

THE NEW MOSCOW SCENE

The Russians' detailed knowledge of the Paris scene, evidence of which will be furnished, contrasted sharply with French intellectuals' piecemeal perceptions of Russian postrevolutionary production. Parisian views of Russia previous to the Great War had changed radically and new themes emerged against a political backdrop that French public opinion perceived as highly worrying. Mass pro-Russian sentiment was born of the visit to Toulon of the imperial Russian fleet in 1893 and the czar's 1896 visit, which was reciprocated by Félix Faure in the following year.[1] A wave of patriotism, which reached its high point during Russia's 1914 incursions into eastern Prussia, together with military cooperation ranging from the arrival of Russian troops on the western front to Louis Loucheur's inspection of Russian ammunition factories, gave way to prevalent anti-Bolshevik sentiment in the face of Russian interventions in Poland and on the Black Sea, as well as strong resentment among holders of Russian czarist bonds.

In the cultural sphere, the discovery of Russian decorative arts at the Universal Exhibition of 1900[2] and at subsequent Salons d'Automne were clearly minor events when compared with the sensation caused by Diaghilev and his Russian ballet. Russian painting and especially Russian architecture were relatively unknown values for the public and practitioners in France.

In the wake of the revolution, Russian artistic culture underwent profound transformations. Before 1914, the scene had been marked by contacts with the West in general and France in particular, as witness the collections of dealers such as Shchukin and Morozov, affording Muscovite artists direct access to the works of Cézanne and Picasso.[3] Encouraged by the people's commissar for education, Anatoli Lunacharsky, the avant-garde now deployed their activities under the auspices of the new revolutionary authorities, whereas existing professional organizations adopted more or less violently radical positions.

Within the combined spheres of architecture and the fine arts, two groups emerged. Both Zhivskulptarkh (synthesis of painting, sculpture and architecture collective) and Sinskulptarkh (synthesis of painting and architecture) advocated a fusion of artistic disciplines; and in 1920, teaching programs were reorganized within the Vkhutemas.[4] In 1923, new architectural ideas—emerging from the 1918 "plan for monumental propaganda" and from competitions held after the civil war—took concrete shape with the creation of the ASNOVA (or Association of New Architects). Its leading members, Dokuchaev, Ladovsky, and Krinsky, were self-confessed "rationalists"; their projects retained a dynamic dimension which, given their powerful position within the Vkhutemas, could be inculcated on the rising generations.

3. Cover from first issue of *L'Esprit Nouveau*, October 1920.

[1] On popular culture and the political exchanges motivated by rivalry between France and England (and above all with Germany), see Robert Burnand, *La vie quotidienne en France de 1870 à 1900* (Paris: Hachette, 1947), pp. 34–37.

[2] See for example Gabriel Mourey, "L'art populaire russe," *Art et Décoration* 7 (August 1903): 23–246.

[3] On these collections, see Beverly Whitney Kean, *All the Empty Palaces: The Merchant Patrons of Modern Art in Pre-revolutionary Russia* (London: Barrie and Jenkins, 1983).

[4] On the Vkhutemas, see Selim O. Khan-Magomedov, *Vkhutemas, Moscou 1920–1930*, Paris, Editions du Regard, 1990; for specific aspects, see my article focusing on architectural education: Jean-Louis Cohen, "Les 'purs,' les 'appliqués' et les autres, les Vhutemas, Moscou 1920–1930," *Architecture Mouvement Continuité* 45 (May 1978): 13–16.

Two years later, the constructivist movement was consolidated with the founding of the OSA (or Union of Contemporary Architects), united in their belief in the aesthetics of the machine and the necessary subordination of architecture to a new "social determinism." ASNOVA numbered among its ranks El Lissitzky, who had, however, defended the constructivists on his frequent visits to the West. OSA remained in contact with the LEF (or Left Art Front), which insisted on the urgent need for "the art of production."

Foreign observers more often than not saw only the misfortunes of the old elite—"victims," as Serge Stern wrote in 1924, "of the revolutionary upheavals"—and much time would pass before they perceived the various tendencies underlying these different movements.[5] The first opportunity for a dispassionate view of their work was furnished by the 1925 Exposition des Arts Décoratifs held in Paris. Well before this, however, *L'Esprit Nouveau* had begun to present detailed reports on politics and culture inside the New Russia.

L'ESPRIT NOUVEAU AND RECOGNITION OF THE USSR

Although there is little if any evidence of young Charles-Edouard Jeanneret's interest in Russian affairs at this time, the same cannot be said of his associate Amédée Ozenfant. Strongly influenced by the Russian ballet under the direction of the "genius" Diaghilev, Ozenfant had gone a step further and "brought Russia into his life" in 1910 by marrying the Russian artist Zina Klingberg, whom he then accompanied to Russia on four separate occasions before the outbreak of the war.[6]

Over three or so years of peregrinations, Ozenfant painted a series of landscapes which he subsequently brought together in a collection of thirty gouaches entitled *Le voyage de Russie*.[7] When the review *L'Elan* first appeared in 1915, he later claimed that his "painting [was] floating between Russian-Ozenfant and Ozenfant-troubled-by-Cubism."[8] The review incorporated peasant engravings sent by his wife, who had remained in Russia, and published works of Goncharova and Larionov, Russian artists who had settled in Paris.[9]

The attitudes to the Russian scene adopted by the new review founded by Ozenfant, Paul Dermée, and Charles-Edouard Jeanneret were thus at least in part determined by Ozenfant's first-hand knowledge of the Russian artistic milieu and especially of émigré circles in Paris; yet notwithstanding Jeanneret-Le Corbusier's moderate views, as evidenced in his celebrated article "Architecture or Revolution," in which he writes under his pseudonym that "it is possible to avoid the latter," the editors were by no means intimidated by the image of a society in upheaval.[10] This is not to say that *L'Esprit Nouveau*'s views were aligned with those of the Communist party or with explicitly pro-Soviet feelings. Jacques Mesnil, the art critic on the party's daily *L'Humanité* who accompanied one of the first (official) visits to Red Russia in 1921, subsequently made a concerted attack on the ideas expressed in Le Corbusier's article on "La ville contemporaine."[11]

Yet there were overtures of another type, for the review joined forces with those who were in favor of diplomatic relations with the USSR, thus echoing the Treaty of Rapallo, the activities of whose German signatory, Walther Rathenau, were reported on in several issues; in the ninth issue, for instance, the review's foreign affairs commentator, René Chenevier, deplored the attitude of the French government which, by pursuing Clémenceau's anti-Bolshevik policies, was in danger of missing an historic opportunity:

[5] Serge Stern, "Les intellectuels en Russie soviétique: Les architectes," *Les Cahiers Bleus* 1, no. 4 (1924): 232–33.

[6] Amédée Ozenfant, *Mémoires 1886–1962* (Paris: Seghers, 1968), pp. 57–65.

[7] Susan S. Ball, *Ozenfant and Purism: The Evolution of a Style 1915–1930* (Ann Arbor, Mich.: UMI Research Press, 1981), p. 10.

[8] Maurice Raynal, *Anthologie de la peinture en France de 1906 à nos jours* (Paris: Editions Montaigne, 1927), p. 259, quoted by Ball, *Ozenfant*, p. 14.

[9] Ball, *Ozenfant*, pp. 18–19.

[10] On political developments in *L'Esprit Nouveau*, see Roberto Gabetti and Carlo Olmo, *Le Corbusier e "L'Esprit Nouveau"* (Turin: Einaudi, 1975; rev. ed. 1988).

[11] Jacques Mesnil, "Au Salon d'Automne," *L'Humanité*, Paris (11 November 1922).

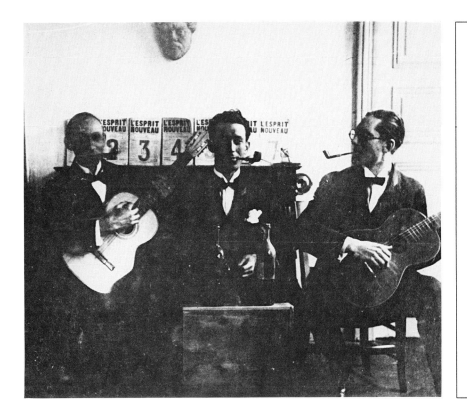

Ce qu'a vu le Docteur NANSEN en Russie.   *Photo Illustration.*

Devant l'immense péril qui menace la Russie, la partie la plus neuve de l'Europe, la mine la plus riche d'espoirs pour la vieille Europe, devant la famine qui menace d'anéantir des millions de jeunes innocents, le COMITÉ FRANÇAIS DE SECOURS AUX ENFANTS (16, Rue des Ecoles, Paris) adresse à tous (sans souci de confession ou de politique) un appel angoissé.
Tous les dons, toutes les idées seront accueillies avec gratitude.
M. Hébertot veut bien prêter gracieusement à l'Œuvre, le Théâtre des Champs-Elysées, pour y organiser une soirée de Gala. Chaque billet d'entrée portera un Numéro susceptible de sortir et de gagner un des lots à la tombola qui se tirera pendant les entr'actes.

LISTE DES DONATEURS AU 18 MARS

AARONSON. — AMAN-JEAN. — BENIKO. — Albert BESNARD. — Nicolas BEAUDUIN. — Germaine BONGARD. — Paul BONIFAS. — BOSSHARDT. — BOURDELLE. — Madame DE BOZNANSKA. — DE BRUNOFF. — Pierre CHARREAU. — DRESA. — Editions de l'ESPRIT NOUVEAU. — Jean EPSTEIN. — Anatole FRANCE. — FRIESZ. — FUJITA. — Albert GLEIZES. — GONTCHAROWA. — GROUPE RUSSE. — JACOB-HEANS. — JAROWLEFF. — Albert JEANNERET. — Charles Ed. JEANNERET. — Pierre JEANNERET. — KISSLING. — LABOUREUR. — LANDAU. — Madame LEMESTRE. — M. LEMESTRE. — LE SIDANER. — André LHOTE. — LURÇAT. — André MARE. — MARCELLO-FABRI. — MARCOUSSIS. — MARVAL. — Madeleine MARX. — MEDGIEY. — MEDJES. — Alexandre MERCEREAU. — MÉTHEY. — METZINGER. — MODIGLIANI. — Luc-Albert MOREAU. — Mela MUTER. — Chana ORLOFF. — OTTMAN. — OZENFANT. — Paul PAINLEVÉ. — POVOLOZKY. — RAVEL. — Madame ROCHE. — SANIT. — Florent SCHMITT. — STEINLEN. — SIGRIST. — SORDONE. — Madame SORDONE. — SORINE. — SUDEIKINE. — Louis SUE. — SWANSON. — VAN DONGEN. — VILDRAC. — VOGEL. — WASSILIEF. — ZADKINE.

Les amis de l'ESPRIT NOUVEAU peuvent remettre leurs dons aux bureaux de l'ESPRIT NOUVEAU (autographes, manuscrits, livres, tableaux, sculptures...) Un reçu sera remis en échange du don.

What role will France play in Russian reconstruction? None whatsoever. For, having speculated on the fall of the Soviets, having compromised its capital with dispossessed landowners and holders of legal but fictitious stocks, France's position is delicate vis-à-vis a government which it has combatted with such severity. The Russia of tomorrow will be a vast field of exploitation and profit, open to the influx of foreign capital. Should France miss the boat, it will be through its own fault, and it will have made the greatest diplomatic blunder since Napoleon III. The damage must be repaired, and negotiations opened.[12]

The review's offices opened its doors to donations ("autographs, manuscripts, books, paintings, sculptures") with a view to helping the starving Russian children;[13] some months later an article by Henri Hertz expressed doubts as to the future of Russia following the death of Lenin, who, "left behind him a struggle for succession which may well result in factions." For Hertz Lenin, "a man of action," had shown evidence of "robust doctrinal training":

Neither a recluse, nor attached only to books, despite the fact that he loved to read, and wrote formidable works, but rather in contact with the avant-garde, which he continually sounded out.
. . . The deliverance of the Russian people resulted in fatalism rather than resolve. . . . Lenin saw the need to master the people both by playing on their fear and by dangling the carrot of dictatorship, without which everything would collapse, and everything revert irrevocably back to the eternal Russian dreamworld. To this cruel task was devoted the whole implacable nature of the man with his squat Asian wrestler's body, his wrinkled face knotted with taut features, whose agile eyes could turn on their object with terrible intensity.[14]

In the last published issue of the review, Vauvrecy (a nom de plume used alternatively by Le Corbusier and Ozenfant) presented, without explicit com-

4. Amédée Ozenfant, Albert Jeanneret, and Le Corbusier in front of the first seven issues of *L'Esprit Nouveau*, Spring 1921.

5. "La famine en Russie," in *L'Esprit Nouveau* 16 (May 1922).

[12] René Chenevier, "Où mène la politique anti-soviétique?" *L'Esprit Nouveau* 9 (June 1921): 1045–51.
[13] "La famine en Russie," *L'Esprit Nouveau* 16 (May 1922): 1970.
[14] Henri Hertz, "Lénine," *L'Esprit Nouveau* 21 (March 1924): n.p.

6. Henri Hertz, "Lénine," in *L'Esprit Nouveau* 21 (March 1924).

ment but in a highly conspicuous layout, the telegrams exchanged between the président du conseil Edouard Herriot and the people's commissar for foreign affairs Boris Chicherin when diplomatic relations between the two states were restored in October 1924.[15]

GLIMPSES OF A NEW CULTURE

At the same time, different areas of artistic activity in Russia were revealed to the readers of *L'Esprit Nouveau*. In the third issue, Emile Fromaigeat reserved an extremely warm reception to the musical policy of the people's commissar for education, Lunacharsky, and underlined the prominent role that "savants" and "artists" hailing from the old intelligentsia were playing in "the scientific and artistic reforms of the Soviets," without, however, attempting to mask the conflicts involved:

The government must sustain battles on all fronts: against outside enemies, right-wing opposition within, and attacks from the extremist Bolshevik party. The latter, the "prolet-kult," wish to abolish all "capitalist art" and institute a new proletarian culture. The régime is obliged to make a number of concessions, and permit them to organize concerts to their liking.

In such an agitated environment, it is hardly likely that durable reforms will be elaborated and gradually implemented. It is also to be feared that the excellent ideas to be found in the Bolshevik effort will be abandoned altogether.[16]

In November 1921, a rather more kaleidoscopic image of Russian research in the field of poetry was furnished by Halina Izdebska in her contribution to the review, in which she attempted to draw up a typology of the poetic and political attitudes of Anna Akhmatova, Ilya Ehrenburg, Alexander Blok, Vladimir Maiakovsky (from whose poem "Order No. 1 to the Army of the Arts" she quotes: "Streets are our brushes, squares our palettes"), Sergei Esenin, and others. In the article she identifies a series of "salient features . . . intrinsic to current Russian poetry":

(1) accessibility and democratic means of expression; (2) the absence of any personal note; (3) the sentiment of cosmic solidarity; (4) a relation of oppositions rather than adoption of values; (5) perverse mysticism.[17]

The third sphere of activity touched on in the pages of *L'Esprit Nouveau* was Soviet theater, in a series of letters by Ilya Ehrenburg that were published in the thirteenth issue. Ehrenburg, who was then living in Berlin, but who had spent a considerable time in France before being expelled and who had known Ozenfant before 1914, confirms the image of poetic diversity evoked by Izdebska; he insists, however, on the marginal aspect of avant-garde experiments, and reacts to the political framework with considerable reticence:[18]

The only theaters in a position to respond to current public tastes are those of the avant-garde. It is essential to rid ourselves once and for all of the myth that avant-

[15] "La reconnaissance des Soviets par la France," *L'Esprit Nouveau* 28 (January 1925): 2321–22.

[16] E.-L. Fromaigeat, "La musique en Russie soviétique," *L'Esprit Nouveau* 3 (December 1920): 297–303.

[17] Halina Izdebska, "La poésie russe des journées bolcheviques," *L'Esprit Nouveau* 11–12 (November 1921): 1231–37.

[18] On Ehrenburg's tortuous literary and political career, see Anatol Goldberg, *Ilya Ehrenburg: Writing, Politics and the Art of Survival* (London: Weidenfeld and Nicholson, 1984). Ozenfant mentions his meeting with Ehrenburg in his *Mémoires*, p. 65.

ÉPHÉMÉRIDES   2322

29 Octobre.

HERRIOT ET TCHITCHERINE S'ÉCRIVENT :

LE PREMIER AMBASSADEUR DE RUSSIE A PARIS

KRASSINE

Le président du Conseil a reçu de M. Tchitcherine, commissaire du peuple aux Affaires étrangères, le télégramme suivant :

Permettez-moi de vous envoyer mes chaleureuses félicitations à l'occasion de l'acte qui ouvre la voie au développement des relations amicales entre nos peuples, voie qui nous dévoile des issues grandes et fécondes vers l'avenir. Je suis heureux de voir que notre amitié personnelle, vieille de quelques années, a contribué à des résultats aussi enviables. Le souvenir de nos entretiens dont les traces sont restées si fraîches dans ma mémoire, m'a aidé durant maintes journées difficiles à attendre patiemment l'heure désirée qui a sonné aujourd'hui.

LE PREMIER AMBASSADEUR DE FRANCE A MOSCOU

M. JEAN HERBETTE

M Herriot a répondu par le télégramme ci-dessous :

Je me réjouis non moins que vous-même de l'acte qui va nous permettre de travailler ensemble au maintien et à l'affermissement de la paix de l'Europe et du monde.

Il n'est pas de peuples mieux faits pour s'entendre que le peuple français si épris de justice et de fraternité et le grand peuple russe dont j'ai moi-même pu apprécier les fortes qualités. Je suis assuré que nos relations personnelles si sincèrement cordiales faciliteront notre commune action dans l'intérêt de nos deux nations...

7. *L'Esprit Nouveau* celebrates the resumption of diplomatic relationships between Paris and Moscow, in *L'Esprit Nouveau* 28 (January 1925).

garde theater is the official art of Russia. Unfortunately, certain influential members of the political and sociological establishment are, as regards aesthetic questions, totally reactionary, and prefer art-with-a-message to constructive art. All claims to the effect that academic drama is persecuted are false. Of the twenty or so theaters in Moscow, only two or three are truly revolutionary. The only element of truth in all this is that, despite the personal preferences of government officials, avant-garde directors have been given the means to carry out their experiments.[19]

Ehrenburg identifies two distinct currents of thought in the "New Theater." Some directors wished to "create, on a stage separated from the public by footlights, a purely theatrical drama conveying the essence of the action," whereas the others "desire to do away with the 'theater box' and to dissolve this essence in life itself, thus dramatizing day-to-day existence." The first of these trends was represented by Tairov's Kamerny Theater, which was familiar to the Parisian public, and which called on the services of several constructivists:

[19] Elie Ehrenbourg, "Le Théâtre Russe pendant la Révolution," *L'Esprit Nouveau* 13 (December 1921): 1515–19.

[Tairov] has suppressed the painted sceneries that make the stage resemble a harem. The actors who constitute one form in three registers, require a set in three registers. The architect has replaced the painter, and it is curious to note that the costumes and decor for *The Annunciation* have been designed by a practicing architect, Vesnin, who, together with Yakulov and Madame Exter, has invented mathematical forms in harmony with modern conceptions. They construct the stage in such a way that the action unfolds vertically rather than horizontally.[20]

The second school of thought was represented by Meyerhold, in whose detailed productions "actors and spectators mix freely":

He has chosen Verhaeren's *The Dawn* as representative of social drama, yet I am convinced that no one could recognize the original. On occasion the actors punctuate their lines with extracts from sensational newspapers, at others the soldiers in the audience climb on stage with their musical instruments. Meyerhold's direction addresses the stage and the auditorium together, and he replaces makeup with masks.[21]

But Ehrenburg (the importance of whose role in Berlin will become clear) was also responsible for the first French publication of Tatlin's project for a "Monument to the Third International" in the form of a relatively poor reproduction for which he was given explicit credit in the next issue of the review, where it was specified that the tower, built in 1919–1921, was to be made of "iron and glass":[22]

It is to be 400 meters high and will be placed in the Mars Field in Petrograd. The model represented here is 15 meters high.

The tower will house vast meeting halls. The spiral leads to a lift. At the top is the radio station.[23]

An identical illustration of Tatlin's tower had been published by Ehrenburg in 1922, in a pamphlet entitled *A vse-taki ona vertitsia* (*Eppur si muove*), containing photographs of machines, industrial artifacts, and paintings. In this little book, Ehrenburg acknowledged his own debt to purism and to *L'Esprit Nouveau*; he included the latter in a "military parade" in which all the avant-garde reviews of Europe stand at attention.[24]

Ehrenburg quoted several paragraphs of "a tract published in *L'Esprit Nouveau*" and cited the "eloquent title" chosen by "the engineer Le Corbusier-Saugnier"—"Des yeux qui ne voient pas."[25] He held up Ozenfant and Jeanneret's review as a sort of mirror to his own self-image; in another chapter, he assimilated the authors of *Après le Cubisme* to the group of "constructors" whose importance for the new Russian scene he then proceeded to underline.[26] His somewhat eclectic view of things was to be criticized in *L'Esprit Nouveau*, not without irony, by the film director Jean Epstein, who nonetheless recognized its utility:

Mr. Ehrenburg has brought together, in a single massive dose, all the novelties of recent intellectual seasons: one is shown locomotives equipped with snowplows, dada, skyscrapers, Charlie Chaplin, a criticism of the Treaty of Versailles, Farman and Van Dongen, Picasso and Caproni, ocean liners and the theater, bridge building and the cinema, the Internationale and the docks.

Clearly, this bird's-eye tour of the world is neither well considered nor particularly well organized. Yet Ilya Ehrenburg has so much to say that he swallows his words and hacks his sentences to pieces. It is these deliria that are touching for me, and I remember the silence of a comrade of mine who, not knowing exactly what he had to say, raised his arms twice in the air and said nothing. And I believe that we can expect a great deal from Mr. Ehrenburg's acolytes. They are already informed—vaccinated so to speak—and, like spendthrifts become indifferent to the riches laid by for their

[20] Ibid., p. 1517.

[21] Ibid., p. 1518.

[22] In fact the model was first exhibited on 8 November 1920 in Petrograd, and then in Moscow. See Anatoli Strigalev, "O proekte pamiatnika III Internatsionala khudozhnika V. Tatlina," in Vigdariia Khazanova, ed., *Voprosy sovetskogo izobrazitelnogo iskusstva i arkhitektury* (Moscow: Sovetsky Khudozhnik, 1973), pp. 408–52; Anatoli Strigalev, "From Painting to the Construction of Matter," in Larissa Zhadova, ed., *Tatlin* (New York: Rizzoli, 1988), pp. 13–43; John Milner, *Vladimir Tatlin and the Russian Avant-Garde* (New Haven: Yale University Press, 1983), pp. 151–80.

[23] "La tour de Tatline," *L'Esprit Nouveau* 14 (January 1922): 1680. The model was in fact only seven meters high. See Strigalev, "O proekte," p. 437. Ehrenburg also publishes later the same drawing in Germany: Elias Ehrenburg, "Ein Entwurf Tatlins," *Frühlicht* 3 (Spring 1923), pp. 92–93.

[24] Ilya Ehrenburg, *A vse-taki ona vertitsia* (Berlin; Moscow: Gelikon, 1922), pp. 40–42. For this little manifesto, large numbers of photographs were acknowledged to have been borrowed from various issues of *L'Esprit Nouveau*.

[25] Ibid., p. 63. Initially used by Jeanneret and Ozenfant for their joint publications, the pseudonym Le Corbusier–Saugnier was referred to by many critics when discussing the architect's early writings of the 1920s.

[26] Ibid., p. 85.

LA TOUR DE TATLINE

A LA TROISIÈME INTERNATIONALE

faite par Wladimir Tatline *en 1919-1921 en verre et fer. Elle doit avoir 400 mètres de haut et être placée sur le Champ de Mars de Pétrograd. Le modèle reproduit ici mesure 15 mètres de haut.*

Elle renfermera de vastes salles de réunion. La spirale sert de chemin à un ascenseur. Au sommet station de radio.

(Documents remis par M. Elie Ehrenbourg).

benefit, rather than voicing their astonishment in a thousand charming ways, will ruin themselves at once with beautiful constructions.[27]

Apart from comments on music, drama, and poetry, *L'Esprit Nouveau* published articles on the art scene in Russia in two separate issues, with observations by the painter Ivan Puni and reproductions of his work; in a later issue, when Puni, who lived in Paris before the war, had left Russia for good, Ozenfant devoted a further article to his work—not to his suprematist period but to those of his works that reflect the attitudes of the purists:

Puni has understood the necessity of organized, created art; he perceives that art "without an object" necessarily leads to ornamentalism, and that painting reduced to a mere combination of forms, with no reference to the world of feelings, lacks humanity. He has retained cubist construction in his canvases, yet he also admits of "the object," and introduces pictorial composition.[28]

Puni's own analysis of constructivism, whose "intuitive" and utilitarian tendencies he criticized, corroborates Ozenfant's and bears witness to the fact that he had, verbally at least, rallied the cause of purism (which, he assures us, he favored even before he left Russia):

Russian constructivism, some examples of which have been seen in France during performances of the Kamerny Theater (with sets by Vesnin), and which is also well known through reproductions of the Tatlin tower (*L'E.N.* no. 14), is *not* a purely plastic movement; rather, its theories are rooted in sociology. The interest that the use of heterogeneous materials (iron, cardboard, paper, wood, etc.) aroused in France in 1913–14 had repercussions in Russia during the same period; yet Russian ideas concerning such experiments took the form of a sort of fetishism, a cult of "true materials." Marxism thus influenced the theory of constructivism, for at this time (1917) power in Russia passed into the hands of the Marxist communists.

. . . Marxism has brushed aside the intellectual element and emphasized the spirit of matter. Constructivism has stripped art of its symbolic significance, inasmuch as all art is fundamentally symbolic.

8. "La tour de Tatline," in *L'Esprit Nouveau* 14 (January 1922).

9. Ilya Ehrenburg, front cover of *A vsetaki ona vertitsia*, drawing by Fernand Léger, 1922.

[27] Jean Epstein, "Les livres," *L'Esprit Nouveau* 16 (June 1922).
[28] A. Ozenfant, "Ivan Puni," *L'Esprit Nouveau* 23 (May 1924).

Faced with the arguments of constructivism, Puni joined ranks with the purists and underlined common aspects of his own position:

> As a logical consequence, it is generally thought desirable to have done with art as an end in itself; it has ceased to be necessary, in that it is no longer the source of intellectual emotions. It now pursues a goal—that of satisfying supposedly proletarian tastes by means of the technically well-executed object (strange as it may seem, intuition is still at the heart of the constructivist object, for Russian art theory has made no new discoveries concerning the logic or rhythms of art). . . . The art of creating paintings, which are useless objects, has no place in the new society, whose guiding principle is economy and strength of materials, and also the usefulness of effort. Tatlin's tower, which I, not being an engineer, am in no position to judge, is a typical instance of this. . . . Above all I must say that the Purist's attitude to useful objects—industrial products for example—is quite different, for he considers merely that the form of such objects is determined by criteria of maximum utility. Utilitarian objects are neither better, nor more useful, for being the creations of artists as opposed to engineers. This opinion has been defended in Russia by a number of painters, of whom I am one.
>
> Strange to say, machine-age romanticism still holds sway in Russia, and the machine has neither been thrown down from its pedestal, nor confined to the museum along with classical models.[29]

In a relatively vehement analysis, Puni also attacked the suprematism of Malevich, who had in turn kept his distance vis-à-vis the constructivists. However, readers of *L'Esprit Nouveau* lacked visual means of judging the matters under discussion, since there was only one reproduction of constructivist work in the issue in question: Konstantin Medunetsky's metal-rod construction published in the twenty-first issue, doubtless in honor of his visit to Paris with the Kamerny Theater in 1923 when an exhibition of the sculptor's work was held at the Galerie Paul Guillaume.[30]

In the magazine's twenty-fifth issue, Le Corbusier finally gave expression to his own view of Russian constructivism, which, clearly influenced by Puni's remarks, he contrasted with Hermann Finsterlin's expressionism. His perception of the phenomenon was doubtless still somewhat vague, since he illustrates his critical miscellany with the photograph of a student exercise executed by Mikhail Turkus at the Moscow Vkhutemas under the direction of Ladovsky, a "Rationalist" hostile to the constructivists.[31]

Love of the machine, keen affection for the pure, convincing drawings of mathematicians and engineers (since geometrical drawings are in fact supposedly demonstrations of certainty). And therein resides the mirage: the poetic attitude to truth, as perceived on the geometer's drawing board, is not so easily transformed into plastic truth. Russian constructivism transposes too quickly, too often without re-forming a pure, plastic fact; there is a confusion here. Yet how convincing it is! How incomparably superior to the horrors of a Finsterlin! Constructivism rings so true, while the others ring so false. Poles apart. Constructivism is poles apart from neurasthenia.[32]

Some pages later, a text on the "Lesson of the Machine," which would subsequently be reprinted in *L'art décoratif d'aujourd'hui*, hammers the point home and reveals an interest in Russian architectural production that is in no way fortuitous, in that it originates in part from the attempts of certain Russians to come into contact with the review:

Art has nothing to do with the machine (the error of constructivism). Yet we are enchanted. But our eyes have been robbed of pure form. The means to art (whose end is an emotion that is constant, humane, eternal) have been emancipated, illuminated with clarity.[33]

[29] Ivan Puni, "Russie," *L'Esprit Nouveau* 22 (April 1924). Puni (1892–1956) was in Italy and France from 1910 to 1912; he moved to Berlin in 1921, and lived in Paris from 1923 to his death. See the *catalogue raisonné* of his early work, Hermann Berninger and Jean-Albert Quartier, *Jean Pougny (1892–1956), catalogue de l'oeuvre*, vol. 1, *Les années d'avant-garde, Russie-Berlin, 1910-1923* (Tübingen: Ernst Wasmuth, 1972).

[30] On Konstantin Medunetsky (1899–ca. 1935), see Christina Lodder, *Russian Constructivism* (New Haven: Yale University Press, 1983), p. 253. The construction published in *L'Esprit Nouveau* was first exhibited in Moscow in 1921 during the third exhibition of the OBMOKhU (Society of Young Artists), a key moment for the assertion of constructivism in the sphere of art: ibid., pp. 66, 69. It should also be noted that Medunetsky's work was exhibited at the *Erste russische Kunstausstellung* held in Berlin in 1923.

[31] "Russian Constructivist study," illustration for Le Corbusier, "Coupures de journaux," *L'Esprit Nouveau* 25 (July 1924). The model in question was constructed by the student (and future teacher) Mikhail Turkus in 1923, as an "expression of dynamics, rhythm, relations and proportions (on a given surface)." See Selim O. Khan Magomedov, *Pioneers of Soviet Architecture: The Search for New Solutions in the 1920s and 1930s* (New York: Rizzoli, 1987), p. 113. The circumstances surrounding the acquisition of this photograph, which also appeared in *ABC*, no. 2 (1924), are unclear; Le Corbusier may have come into possession of it through the good offices of the ASNOVA, or else have received it along with a consignment of illustrations for an article by El Lissitzky (see subsequent discussion).

[32] Le Corbusier, "Coupures de journaux."

[33] Le Corbusier, "La leçon de la machine," *L'Esprit Nouveau* 25 (July 1924).

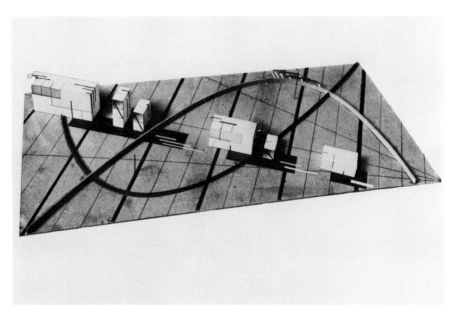

10. Mikhail Turkus, "Expression of Dynamism, Rhythm, Relations and Proportions (on a Surface)," exercise done at the Vkhutemas under the direction of Nikolai Ladovsky, Moscow, 1923; published by Le Corbusier with the caption "Russian Constructivist Study," in *L'Esprit Nouveau* 25 (July 1924).

EL LISSITZKY'S PARISIAN VENTURES

The readers and, *a fortiori*, the editors of *L'Esprit Nouveau* had at their disposal a fairly complete view of the Russian art scene; and yet they appear to have been almost totally ignorant of the architectural situation in the USSR. The closing down of the review in 1925 certainly prevented the publication of at least two articles that had, moreover, been envisaged by the Russians themselves. Le Corbusier had been initially approached by the leaders of ASNOVA, who suggested that they should take a common stand against the "pseudoclassical architects":

We know you well, dear colleague, your name is known not only in France, but also abroad; your indefatigable search for new architectural forms attracts our deepest sympathies.

. . . We wish, dear Sir, to find moral support in you. Should you consent to become our associate, public opinion would be easily conquered.[34]

Apart from this official correspondence, contact of a more personal nature was established by El Lissitzky, who was undergoing treatment at a sanatorium in Orselina, near Locarno. Lissitzky declared himself the association's "representative plenipotentiary" for Europe and America and, as such, responsible for contacting "the forces of the world." He described the organization's objectives as follows:

Their aim is to unite all rationalist architects and all those close to them in the field of construction, in order to raise architecture, as an art, to a level corresponding to modern techniques and sciences.[35]

Lissitzky charms Le Corbusier with the multiple possibilities of contact with Moscow. Reminding the architect that his work was familiar to him, since he had already published examples in the short-lived Berlin review *Veshch, Gegenstand, Objet*, of which he and Ilya Ehrenburg had shared the editorship in 1922, Lissitzky now asks him to furnish documentation for ASNOVA, with particular reference to three distinct projects. Would Le Corbusier be willing

[34] ASNOVA, letter to Le Corbusier, Moscow, 3 March 1924, FLC. Some weeks later, the association sent Le Corbusier a series of photographs showing its "theoretical and experimental" work: Vitali Lavrov (for ASNOVA), letter to Le Corbusier, Moscow, 23 June 1924, private collection. On ASNOVA, see Kirill Afanasev and Vigdariia Khazanova, eds., *Iz istorii sovetskoi arkhitektury 1926–1932 gg., dokumenty i materialy* (Moscow: Nauka, 1970), pp. 39–64.

[35] El Lissitzky, letter to Le Corbusier, Orselina, 23 March 1924, FLC.

11. Opening illustration for the article submitted by El Lissitzky to *L'Esprit Nouveau* in 1924. The original caption is: "This is not Dada. It's not the ruins of the Roman forum nor the reconstruction of Pompeii; it's the architecture of the First Agricultural Exhibition in the Soviet Union, in 1923, created by the degenerate pupils of Palladio and impotent architects."

to assist in the preparation of an "International Congress of Modern Architects" to be held in Moscow—a project that, if Lissitzky is to be believed, had already received a favorable response from architects in Germany and Holland? Might he not put down on paper some suggestions to this effect? Was he aware of the international conference on architectural education to be held in London, invitations having reached them in Moscow?[36]

Le Corbusier seized the opportunity furnished by this correspondence with El Lissitzky to ask him for an article, informative but "in telegraphic style," on the architectural situation in Russia;[37] at the same time, the secretary of ASNOVA addressed to Le Corbusier six photographs of work by students of the Vkhutemas, including possibly the one he published in the twenty-fifth issue of *L'Esprit Nouveau*.[38]

El Lissitzky had in fact been aware of the review's activities for some time. In his correspondence with Sophie Küppers, he insisted that she send him copies at his therapeutic retreat in Switzerland. Also, he was determined to learn French, since "it really is stupid that I have to be content with looking at it." He confided to Küppers his intention of writing "to Le Corbusier *alias* Jeanneret regarding Moscow matters."[39] Lissitzky makes no attempt to conceal his indignation at Puni's article when, in May 1924, he tells his wife of the request for an article for *L'Esprit Nouveau* and the need to "wait for the photos, whereas our people are so passive":

Thank you for the translation of the article by Puni. Don't get yourself too worked up. It is the fault of the editorial staff of *L'Esprit Nouveau* that they publish an appraisal *before* they publish the facts. And for good measure it's by a painter who left Russia four years ago, and whose whole way of thought is completely foreign. I wrote to tell Ozenfant this today. I am supposed to write the article on Russian architecture, as you already know. There will be little chance there for me to argue with Puni. It's just the old story, Puni bows to the viewpoint of Ozenfant–Jeanneret, and then everything is all right.[40]

[36] Ibid.

[37] Le Corbusier, letter to El Lissitzky, Paris, 6 May 1924, published in El Lissitzky, *Proun und Wolkenbügel, Schriften, Briefe, Dokumente* (Dresden: VEB Verlag der Kunst, 1977), pp. 180–81.

[38] Vitali Lavrov, letter to Le Corbusier, 23 June 1924.

[39] El Lissitzky, letter to Sophie Küppers, Orselina, 21 March 1921, in Sophie Lissitzky-Küppers, ed., *El Lissitzky, Life, Letters, Texts* (London: Thames and Hudson, 1968), p. 47.

[40] El Lissitzky, letter to Sophie Küppers, Orselina, 11 May 1924, ibid., pp. 49–50.

Some days later, Lissitzky wrote to Le Corbusier to tell of his indignation in almost identical terms:

I have just had translated Puni's article on Russia in no. 22 of *L'Esprit Nouveau*. I regret that such a respectable and serious review, which we at home hold in such high esteem, should publish, *before* setting out the available material, an article that doesn't give the facts but merely an evaluation, by a painter who left Russia four years ago and knows nothing of our development.

This increases the difficulties of my task, which I will nonetheless attempt to resolve.[41]

The demise of *L'Esprit Nouveau*, whose twenty-ninth issue was transformed by Le Corbusier into an *Almanach de L'Architecture Moderne*, precluded immediate publication of Lissitzky's text; the fact that it had been sent to Paris, along with seven illustrations, in a somewhat crude French translation may also have weighed in the balance. Finally, Lissitzky sent his article to the Berlin review *Das Kunstblatt*, which in February 1925 published an abridged version, although it included the same documents that Lissitzky had earlier sent to Le Corbusier.[42]

The article itself was in no way an unambiguous apology of the progress made since 1917, but rather a chronicle of the major events in the architectural debate, together with a series of caustic assessments of the different positions involved and an outline of Lissitzky's own position. The article opened with a collage, a "catalogue of horrors," of the buildings shown at the 1923 Moscow Arts, Crafts and Agriculture exhibition; these were built by "the degenerate pupils of Palladio and by impotent architects." Here Lissitzky's target was essentially the architect in chief Ivan Zholtovsky:

Modern architecture in Russia?

There isn't any. There is a struggle for modern architecture. Like everywhere else in the world. As yet there is nowhere a new architectural CULTURE. The only truly new constructions are those designed by anonymous builders, engineers head and shoulders above the qualified architects, to meet the needs of the time. It is in this sense that modern architects in several countries have been struggling for years to achieve a new tectonics. The watchwords are everywhere the same: functionality, truth to materials, constructive sense.[43]

Lissitzky compares the main trends on the Soviet scene from the Sinskulptarkh of 1917–1918 to ASNOVA, via the work of Tatlin and the productions of the workshops of Ladovsky, Krinsky, and Dokuchaev at the Vkhutemas; he also outlines the principles of his own production:

My aim was to bring to architecture all the energy crystallized in modern painting. Not recent forms such as the square, but those forces that are revealed in the construction of new volumes. One ought not to be distracted by the original element in painting, color. The problem is to articulate space by means of line, plan, volume. Not isolated bodies, impermeable to the outside, but relations and relationships. The outside, bodies that are the products of movement, born *of* and *in* circulation. New constructions. Awareness of the fifth view (from above). An insistence on the use of new materials, yet without fetishism in the rigorous application of this notion: functionality. (This is what I have aspired to in my work, which I consider the "stage of transformation from painting to architecture" [PROOUN].[44]

Beyond this personal and collective program, Lissitzky makes no mystery of his concern for professionalization of the new architecture, which, preempting Emil Kaufmann's analyses by almost a decade, he places in ironic parallel with the great projects of the French Revolutionary period:

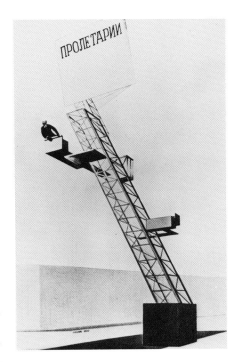

12. El Lissitzky, speaker's tribune, 1920, version drawn in 1924; illustration for the article submitted by El Lissitzky to *L'Esprit Nouveau* in 1924.

[41] El Lissitzky, letter to Le Corbusier, Orselina, 15 May 1924, FLC.

[42] El Lissitzky, "SSSR's Architektur," *Das Kunstblatt*, no. 2 (February 1925): 49–53.

[43] El Lissitzky, "Architektur SSSR," article typewritten in French, unpublished, FLC. (New translation from the published German article cited in n. 42, which appears to have been the original version.) Capitals by Lissitzky. The French text contains various handwritten annotations and revisions by Le Corbusier—evidence that publication had indeed been envisaged.

[44] Ibid. The words in brackets, which give the French text a more personal dimension, are absent from the version published in *Das Kunstblatt*.

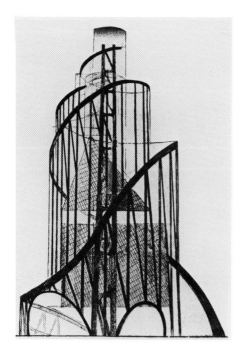

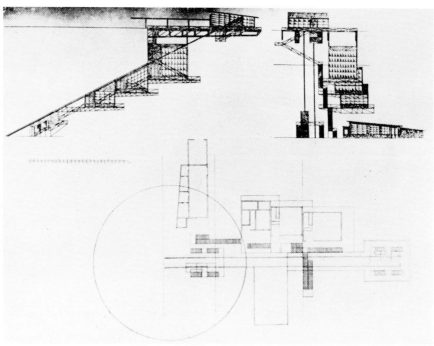

13. Vladimir Tatlin, Monument to the Third International, Moscow, Petrograd, 1919–1920, elevation; illustration for the article submitted by El Lissitzky to *L'Esprit Nouveau* in 1924.

14. Anonymous, Landing Platform and Restaurant Hanging under a Cliff at Sea, exercise on mass and equilibrium conceived at the Vkhutemas under the direction of Nikolai Ladovsky, Moscow, 1922; illustration for the article submitted by El Lissitzky to *L'Esprit Nouveau* in 1924.

Professionalism, which has made possible the rise of the new Russian pictorial culture, should from now on be the aim of architecture. It would be appalling to view the modern spirit as merely that which "is devoid of ornament and molding." And it would be dangerous to build everything in concrete. Rodin perverted sculpture to the extent that it had become possible to cast everything in bronze. We are not here talking of the interplay of cubes, but of constructional and spatial ideas. A century ago, after the French Revolution and during the Napoleonic era, the energies that had been liberated also focused on the problem of architecture. In most cases, the projects remained on paper and can be described in a single word: problems. The monument to Newton, stripped of all ornament and molding, is merely a giant half sphere. Or the work of Ledoux. But in the North, such problems became realities, in Zakharov's Admiralty and Thomon's Stock Exchange at Petersburg. Today's connoisseurs of art view these works as the products of megalomania. They are right, of course: everything that transcends the average is maniac. I hear echoes of the judgment of Russian production—mechanomania. But patience. We are in the midst of our labors, and happy to perform them for our own time.[45]

Lissitzky was clearly aware of the negative reactions of the mid-1920s to the new architecture, which anathematized its "romanticization" of the machine and its unjust rejection of the "lessons" of classicism—both of which assessments later Parisian critics would indulge to the full.[46] It should be added that the year 1925, in which *L'Esprit Nouveau* ceased publication just as Russian avant-garde architecture was on the point of finding its voice, nonetheless furnished the occasion for a rapprochement between Le Corbusier's work and that of his Soviet counterparts, at the Exposition Internationale des Arts Déco-

[45] Ibid. This text appears to have escaped the attention of Adolf Max Vogt in his early inventory of parallels between architectural production in the wake of 1789 and 1917 respectively: Adolf Max Vogt, *Russische und französische Revolutions—Architektur 1917–1789. Zur Einwirkung des Marxismus und des Newtonismus auf die Bauweise* (Cologne: M. DuMont Schauberg, 1974).

[46] E.g., Jean-Claude Vigato, *Doctrines architecturales dans l'entre-deux-guerres: Le jeu des modèles, les modèles en jeu* (Nancy: CEMPA, 1980).

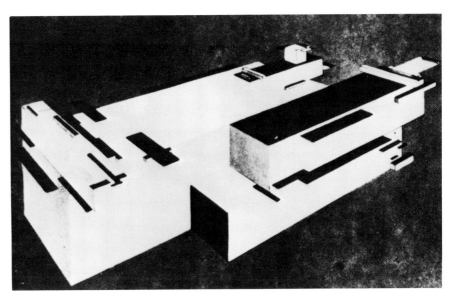

16. Kazimir Malevich, Suprematist *Arkhitekton*, 1924 (?); illustration for the article submitted by El Lissitzky to *L'Esprit Nouveau* in 1924.

15. Iosif Grushenko, Tower for the Production of Chemicals, exercise on volume and space conceived at the Vkhutemas under the direction of Nikolai Ladovsky, Moscow, 1922, model photo; illustration for the article submitted by El Lissitzky to *L'Esprit Nouveau* in 1924.

ratifs et Industriels Modernes, where more than one visitor noted the disparity between the Melnikov and Le Corbusier/Pierre Jeanneret *L'Esprit Nouveau* pavilions and practically all the others.

It is nonetheless significant that Soviet critics measured the impact of their own display by comparing it with Le Corbusier's building, which Ehrenburg considered "the only pavilion worth looking at in the whole exhibition."[47] Yakov Tugendhold, who before the war had published articles in *L'Art Décoratif*,[48] and who was especially attentive to the Western art scene in general and Le Corbusier's work in particular, celebrated the virtues of the Soviet pavilion and perceived its echo in that of *L'Esprit Nouveau*:

In the *L'Esprit Nouveau* pavilion, as in some others that have been completed behind schedule, it is impossible not to perceive resonances with its Soviet counterpart, which has unleashed a veritable storm of criticism and mockery in the popular Parisian press (which is nothing—there are people who pay for that!), but which has also aroused the attention, and sometimes the admiration, of the French artistic intelligentsia.

In their view, the Russian pavilion has become a symbol of "L'Esprit Nouveau." It is in fact the most powerful construction in the whole exhibition, an example of "func-

[47] Ilya Ehrenburg, "Vsemirnaia vystavka," *Ogonek* 30 (1925): 289. On the Soviet representation at the Decorative Arts exhibition, see S. Frederick Starr, *K. Mel'nikov, le pavillon soviétique, Paris 1925* (Paris: L'Equerre, 1981; original ed., Rome: Officina Edizioni, 1979); Jean-Louis Cohen, "Il padiglione di Mel'nikov a Parigi, une seconda ricostruzione," *Casabella* 529 (November 1986): 40–51.

[48] Jacques Touguenhold, "L'illustration russe," *L'Art Décoratif* 179 (September 1912): 125–44; "L'imagerie russe," *L'Art Décoratif* 197 (November 1913): 11–12. During the twenties, Tugendhold (1882–1928) was one of the driving forces at the Museum of New Western Art based on the collections of Shchukin and Morozov, and an attentive commentator on the Parisian scene.

17. Konstantin Melnikov, Pavilion of the USSR at the Exposition des Arts Décoratifs et Industriels Modernes, Paris, 1925, view of construction site.

18. Architecture exhibition of the Soviet representation at the Exposition des Arts Décoratifs et Industriels Modernes, Grand Palais, Paris, 1925.

tional" architecture, in this case well adapted—with its broad staircase and public galleries, and its mast inscribed with the initials of the Republic—to the search for a maximum effect of agitation. To paraphrase Le Corbusier, one might say that our pavilion is a "machine for agitation."[49]

The ironic reference to a celebrated Corbusian notion bears witness to the widespread dissemination, whether direct or indirect, of his ideas in Soviet Russian intellectual culture. These had in fact followed several distinct channels, be they early translations of articles in *L'Esprit Nouveau* or reports concerning Le Corbusier's own publications, town-planning projects, and architectural realizations; and they reached both radical milieux and the more prosaic professional circles.

[49] Yakov Tugendhold, "Stil 1925 goda," *Pechat i Revoliutsiia* 5 (October–November 1925): 42; republished as "Stil nashego vremeni," in *Khudozhestvennaia kultura zapada* (Moscow: Gos. Izdat., 1928), pp. 160–90.

CHAPTER

•2•

Moscow Observes
the Distant Star

SOVIET PRESENCE at the 1925 exhibition in Paris was manifested in Melnikov's pavilion, Rodchenko's workers' club, and a series of architectural projects presented on the first floor of the Grand Palais. The hundred and twenty or so projects by twenty-three individual or group exhibitors give a relatively positive image both of Russian architectural training and of the competitions held during the years immediately preceding the exhibition. Besides forty projects from the various workshops of the Vkhutemas, exhibits included competition sketches for the Paris pavilion and the Moscow Palace of Labor; housing projects by the Vesnins, Melnikov, and Ilya and Panteleimon Golosov; and a selection of pavilions from the 1923 Arts, Crafts, and Agriculture exhibition.[1]

Amid the panels of exhibits rose two spiral constructions, Yakulov's monument to the twenty-six commissars of Baku and Vladimir Tatlin's monument to the Third International; two Soviet commentaries furnish explanations of these projects. In the pages of the official catalogue, Nikolai Dokuchaev highlights the divergences between the ASNOVA, of which he was a member, and the two rival schools, "symbolists—the epigones of academicism—and the constructivists—the romantics of contemporary technique," both of which he assimilates to Le Corbusier's positions despite the fact that they had been lauded by the ASNOVA only a year earlier:

They are the romantics of technology, passionately idealizing engineer-ism, parents of the constructivist architects of Western Europe (e.g., Le Corbusier–Saugnier). Their "technicism" seems marked with mystical power and self-importance. Their architectural images are those of the engineer. . . . The left-wing representatives of this faction—the constructivists—who share these general traits with the others—nonetheless differ, at least in their declarations, by their absolute negation of all aesthetics. Art for them is engineer-ism plus utilitarianism plus economic considerations.[2]

Moisei Ginzburg's analysis of architectural orientations in the Soviet Union, which he published in *L'Amour de l'art*, furnishes implicit yet positive evidence of a convergence of views between the constructivists and Le Corbusier. Ginzburg underlines the emergence within the Soviet Union of a "new social consumer" who "has replaced the isolated individual of prerevolutionary times"; but above all, he insists on the foundations of the new aesthetics:

Another element is clearly manifested in the architecture of Soviet Russia, and reflects the desire to direct its efforts exclusively toward present necessity: the exceptional development of European technology, which has led to the creation of a whole gamut of complete organisms—machines, automobiles, aircraft, etc., which are concrete, new and beautiful in themselves, in which perfection is obtained without the aid of aesthetic fancy. The very notion of "Aesthetics" appeared to us in a completely new light, and this has also had repercussions on architecture. In contrast with prerevolutionary architects, whose eyes were closed to this whole new world, the young practitioners have at last caught sight of the unlimited vistas opened up by a rational and sincere application of current constructions, and the power of expression of new building materials: concrete, reinforced cement, iron, glass.[3]

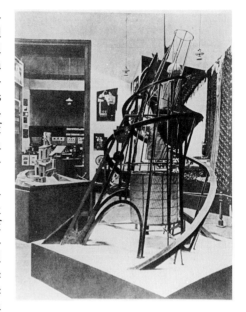

19. Vladimir Tatlin, Monument to the Third International, Moscow, Petrograd, 1919–1920, and Georgi Yakulov, Monument to the Twenty-six Baku Commissars, 1923, models exhibited at the Exposition des Arts Décoratifs et Industriels Modernes, Paris, 1925.

[1] A largely incomplete list of exhibits is given in the official catalogue of the Soviet section: *Exposition internationale des arts décoratifs et industriels modernes, Union des Républiques Socialistes Soviétiques, Catalogue* (Paris: Editions de la représentation de l'URSS à l'Exposition de Paris, 1925), pp. 66–69. The list differs radically from that given in the French catalogue, *Catalogue Général Officiel,* *Exposition internationale des arts décoratifs et industriels modernes* (Paris: Imprimerie de Vaugirard, 1925), p. 684. To date, the most accurate account has been furnished by Anatoli Strigalev, "Sovetskaia arkhitektura na parizhskoi vystavke," in *Problemy istorii sovetskoi arkhitektury* (Moscow: TsNIIP Gradostroitelstva, 1980), pp. 30–31.

[2] N. Dokuchaev, "Les trois directions de l'architecture russe," in *L'art décoratif et industriel* (Paris: Editions du Comité de la Section de l'URSS à l'Exposition Internationale des Arts Décoratifs et Industriels, 1925), pp. 80–85.

[3] M. L. Ginzburg, "L'architecture, l'art industriel, l'art du livre et l'art de la mise en scène dans l'URSS. I. L'architecture," in *L'amour de l'art* 6 (1925): 389–92.

20. El Lissitzky, title page of *Veshch*, no. 3 (Berlin, 1922).

If the "eyes which do not see" to which Ginzburg alludes had finally been opened, it was in large measure due to the ideas of Le Corbusier that, even before 1925, had without question been more favorably received in Russia than in Western Europe.

VESHCH, A SHORT-LIVED PLATFORM

A major factor in the dissemination of Le Corbusier's positions was the avantgarde review *Veshch/Gegenstand/Objet*, two issues of which were published in Berlin by Soviet intellectuals whose respective roles have already been discussed, Ilya Ehrenburg and El Lissitzky. The title of the review was inspired by an anecdote recounted by Albert Gleizes and cited in the last pages of *Eppur si muove*: at a Paris salon, the painter asked a plumber which of the works on display he liked best; the plumber pointed to a sculpture by Lipschitz and commented, "Now, *that's* an object."[4]

Although both editors strove to introduce documents on Russian artistic production in *L'Esprit Nouveau*, this effort was nothing compared with Ozenfant and Jeanneret's *involuntary* contribution to *Veshch*. Practically half its pages were filled with translations and illustrations of texts taken from *L'Esprit Nouveau*. The editors' initial ambitions—to inform the Russian public of the Western art scene and vice versa—were unequally achieved, and Western material clearly predominated.[5]

The issues dated March–April and May 1922 contain four articles taken from *L'Esprit Nouveau*. The combined first and second issues include the article on Jules Romains by Jean Epstein and Albert Jeanneret's text on "La musique et la machine"; the third issue has an unsigned article on Cézanne, Louis Delluc's commentaries on the photogenic, and a translation of an article by Amédée Ozenfant and Charles-Edouard Jeanneret, "A propos du purisme," with two paintings by Ozenfant. It also gave pride of place to Le Corbusier's positions by publishing, in its first double issue, "Les Maisons en série" and a previously unpublished text, "L'état actuel de l'architecture," which appeared under the title "Sovremennaia arkhitektura" ("Contemporary Architecture"). In this article, Le Corbusier celebrates the German contribution to European architecture, but insists on the French engineers' contribution to the "constructive method":

In architecture it is not as apparent as it might be, but with surprising continuity painting and sculpture has left an imprint on the landmarks of that country's strong traditions, now associated with cubism and its consequences. Cubism and its sequel are based on the physics of painting and on the psychology of perception; German expressionism rejects the physical qualities of things and appeals to sentimental and violent feelings, nearly always sickeningly unhappy.

Health is in France. Architectural health is in principles; for architecture, physics is one of the basic conditions; for architecture, the psychology of perception is the very process of creation; proportions are the result of correlating mass and line, as registered by the senses.

Construction is the basis of any architecture, but architecture is more than construction—it is creatively correlated to a higher order. It considers *plasticity*, which is formed *purposely by deriving sound conclusions from plastic conditions and from technical data.*[6]

Both editors of *Veshch* strove to nurture direct relations with Paris. In 1923, Ehrenburg wrote to Le Corbusier to assure him that he was doing "all in [his] power for the propaganda of your review," and to inform him that the Russian

[4] Ehrenburg, *A vse-taki ona vertitsia*, p. 136.

[5] For an overall analysis of the review, see Kestutis Paul Zygas, "*Veshch/Gegenstand/Objet*, Commentary, Bibliography and translations," *Oppositions* 5 (Summer 1976): 115–28.

[6] Le Corbusier–Saugnier, "Sovremennaia arkhitektura," *Veshsch*, no. 1–2 (1922): 20–21, English text in *Oppositions* 5 (Summer 1976): 123–24. Le Corbusier sent this text, from which the French original is lost, in March: Le Corbusier, letter to Ilya Ehrenburg, Paris, 3 March 1922, FLC. Ehrenburg sent a warm letter of thanks: Ilya Ehrenburg, letter to Le Corbusier, Berlin, 12 March 1922, FLC.

21. El Lissitzky, title page of *Veshch*, no. 1–2 (Berlin, 1922), containing Le Corbusier's article "Contemporary Architecture."

review *Krasnaia Niva* was "highly interested" in the "city of three million inhabitants."[7] In October of the same year, Ehrenburg reiterated his appreciation of *L'Esprit Nouveau*, "the only interesting review in Europe"; above all, he asked Le Corbusier to communicate his conditions for a translation of *Vers une architecture*, since the publishers Gosizdat were looking for "a book on architecture."[8]

The familiar tone of this correspondence was certainly epistolary rather than based on direct contact, for Ehrenburg subsequently declared that he did not meet Le Corbusier until 1925, on the occasion of the Exposition des Arts Décoratifs—his first opportunity to encounter both the man and his architecture (in this case, the studio built for Ozenfant on the avenue Reille):

The first houses in the new industrial style were being built. Here was constructivism, not on Rodchenko's drawing-board but in reality. The artist Ozenfant invited me to his house. It had been built by Le Corbusier: light, austerity, the whiteness of a hospi-

[7] Ilya Ehrenburg, letter to Le Corbusier, Moscow, undated (1923), FLC. *Krasnaia Niva* was an illustrated weekly published by *Izvestia*.

[8] Ilya Ehrenburg, letter to Le Corbusier, Berlin, 31 October (1923), FLC. In 1970, Jean Petit wrote that "Immediately on publication of *Vers une architecture*, the state publishers in Moscow asked for translation rights; but the planned Russian edition never materialized." Jean Petit, *Le Corbusier lui-même* (Genève: Éditions Rousseau, 1970), p. 57.

22. Le Corbusier, "Eyes which do not see," page of *Vers une architecture* (Paris, 1923).

[9] Ilya Ehrenburg, *Truce 1921–1933* (London: McGibbon and Kee, 1963), p. 93. (This was the third volume of Ehrenburg's memoirs, published under the collective title *Men, Years—Life.*)

[10] Edgar Norvert, "Obzor zhurnalov," *Arkhitektura*, no. 1–2 (1923): 42–44. This was the review of the MAO (Moscow Architectural Society), which had just resumed its activities in the city.

[11] Le Corbusier, "Ochi nevidiashie," *Khudozhestvenny Trud* no. 2 (1923): 26–27.

[12] Nikolai Tarabukin, *Ot Molberta k mashine* (Moscow: Izd-vo Rabochnik Prosveshcheniia, 1923).

[13] Nikolai Tarabukin, "*L'Esprit Nouveau*, Ezhemesiachny zhurnal, Parizh, no. 16," *Pechat i Revoliutsiia* 2, no. 7 (1922): 349–50.

[14] N. Tarabukin, "*L'Esprit Nouveau*—Parizh, 1922 g., no. 17," *Pechat i Revoliutsiia* 3, no. 2 (1923): 250.

[15] N. Yavorskaia, "Le Corbusier–Saugnier, K voprosam arkhitektury," *Pechat i Revoliutsiia* 4, no. 55 (1924): 296–97.

tal ward or of a laboratory. I thought of Tatlin's constructions, of the enthusiastic Vkhutemas crowd. It was the same, and yet different.[9]

Yet *Veshch* was far from being the only vehicle for Le Corbusier's ideas in Russia—if we assume that such a vehicle existed, since the readers of Lissitzky and Ehrenburg's review were after all primarily Russian émigrés. Several other periodicals carried on what *Veshch* had begun; for instance, *Arkhitektura*, a review for Moscow architects, also reported on the activities of *L'Esprit Nouveau*.[10] The review *Khudozhestvenny Trud* went a step further by publishing extracts from "Des yeux qui ne voient pas" at the outset of 1923,[11] while *Pechat i Revoliutsiia*, a review published "with the direct participation" of the people's commissar Lunacharsky, included several reviews of *L'Esprit Nouveau* by the painter Nikolai Tarabukin, whose 1923 book, *From the Easel to the Machine*, was the source of one of the fundamental theories of constructivism.[12]

Tarabukin focused on articles both by the "artists" Ozenfant and Jeanneret and by the "architect Le Corbusier-Saugnier," in particular his analyses of the Parthenon, together with photographs of its architectural elements.[13] Speaking some months later of Le Corbusier as "one of the more original authors of the review," Tarabukin nonetheless evoked the ambiguities of his analyses:

> The article, devoted almost entirely to an apology of the self-taught architect whereby the author contrasts spontaneous talent with an artificial polishing of skills, creates an odd impression. The accompanying illustrations, instead of reinforcing the author's arguments, seem rather to contradict them[14]

THE DEBATE OVER *VERS UNE ARCHITECTURE*

To judge from the list of subscribers included in the seventeenth issue of *L'Esprit Nouveau*, the 1923 appearance of *Vers une architecture*, a collection of published and unpublished essays, must soon have come to the attention of the Moscow critics. September 1924 marked the publication of an early review by Nina Yavorskaia, one of the administrators of the Museum for Western Contemporary Art, who makes a sharp distinction between Le Corbusier's positions and those of the constructivists:

> Browsing through this book—seeing juxtaposed on the same page an automobile and the Parthenon, followed by an extract from the review *L'Esprit Nouveau*: "There is a new spirit; it is a spirit of construction"—one might be tempted to infer that the author's ideas are those of a constructivist. Yet this conclusion would be erroneous. The great value of the book resides precisely in the fact that its author has transcended the romanticism of the machine which is so characteristic of the late 19th and early 20th centuries, and which is still so clearly perceptible among the Russian constructivists.[15]

In fact, it is the notion that architecture is necessarily a "plastic art" that Yavorskaia finds most convivial, although she considers this reflects "neither a formulation of the grounds of architecture, nor evidence of historical research," but rather a partial manifesto together with a reiteration of ideas that are well known but are lacking all justification. Some weeks later, a sharp debate broke out on the pages of a review more technical than cultural in its orientations, *Stroitelnaia Promyshlennost (The Building Industry)*, regarding the positions expressed in *Vers une architecture*. These were strongly applauded by Boris Korshunov, who considered that "several such ideas are already in the air" in Russia, and that Le Corbusier's great merit resided in his having been the first to "articulate them in writing":

This book is of great psychological interest to us; it is important to see how the best minds in their own domains are shackled by the inertia and reactionary attitudes of the society of his contemporaries. With all the passion at his command, the author criticizes his colleagues for their ignorance of contemporary society and their failure to understand new modes of living, which imply new forms, for the rapid evolution of technology inexorably brings with it new conditions and forms that the inertia of contemporary society, and in particular that of its architects, makes it impossible to master.[16]

Korshunov set out and approved Le Corbusier's theses one by one, and then attempted to consolidate a common front with the modern architects of the West:

It should be noted that the author's fundamental positions are correct. . . . They may yet be a far cry from urban reform, but the principles that he sets forth, and the manner in which he poses the problem, require attentive reading on our part. It can only be deplored that, despite the evident interest that Le Corbusier's book has generated among our architects, the links with this young French movement should still be so weak.[17]

These encomiums provoked a detailed reply from Alexei Shchusev, an adept of the neo-Russian style before 1914, an attenuated form of modernism in the twenties, and, later, eclectic academicism. Shchusev advocated skepticism concerning all forms of architectural prediction and, recalling that since the outset of the nineteenth century the average life expectancy of stylistic movements had been a mere fifteen years, refused to believe that the new style was to be found in the "grain elevators of Buffalo." Shchusev remained open to Western architecture and technique, agreed with Le Corbusier's condemnation of U.S. architects—and his positive assessment of U.S. engineers—yet insisted that a line must be drawn:

Yes, one must look to the West, not because of the poverty of our own ideas, but because we have, for the moment, but few possibilities and resources at our disposal, and because we cannot yet draw from our own experience. Architecture is not as flexible as painting, music or the dramatic arts, if only because experimental plans are unconvincing; the clear expression of constructive principles can only be achieved in practice, on a large scale.

In order to correctly predict the architectural productions of the new era, it is essential to define the bases of the new constructive principles, in such a way that the new generation of architects is not confused as to elementary notions of style, beauty and construction. It is important to differentiate between new architectural types and mere stylistic exercises on constructive themes.[18]

Shchusev also attacked the position of Korshunov (and Le Corbusier) on the aesthetics of the machine, and emphasized the ephemeral character of technical problems and their solutions:

Let us examine the machine and its influence, as a powerful principle of rationality and dynamics, on architectural creation.

The principles of machine construction are powerful, but they aren't eternal. We know that a relatively outdated locomotive no longer seems particularly beautiful to us, despite the logic of its construction, and the latest model of the phonograph to be had in America resembles nothing so much as a can of food in a traveling bag—it no longer expresses the extraordinary mastery of technology, infinitely more expressive, of the original model with its trumpet. One might make a similar comparison between the steam locomotive and its diesel counterpart, which resembles a passenger car equipped with an engine.

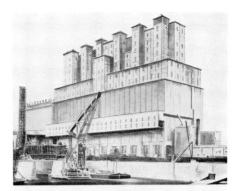

23. Le Corbusier, "3 Reminders to Mssrs. the Architects," page of *Vers une architecture* (Paris, 1923).

[16] Boris Korshunov, "O printsipakh arkhitekturnogo stroitelstva," *Stroitelnaia Promyshlennost* 2, no. 12 (1924): 760–62. Boris Andreevich Korshunov (1885–1961), a teacher at the Polytechnic Institute of Moscow, joined forces with Moisei Ginzburg in the 1926 competition for the Palace of Labor at Ekaterinoslav, and was thus close to constructivist views, but subsequently became an ally of the rationalists. The magazine in question was essentially technical, but it also published large numbers of articles by architects; it was organically related to the building syndicates, and advocated a rationalization of construction procedures and of the urban economy.

[17] Ibid., p. 760.

[18] Akad. Arkh. Alexei Shchusev, *Stroitelnaia Promyshlennost* 2, no. 12 (1924): 760–62. This response to Korshunov's article is untitled. For Shchusev's career, see N. B. Sokolov, *A. V. Shchusev* (Moscow: Gos. Izd. Literatury po Stroitelstvu i arkhitekture, 1952).

24. Le Corbusier, "Voisin Plan" for Paris, 1925, perspective with Paris skyline, FLC 29721.

Expressiveness is more inherent to art than to the machine; as a result, the machine can only constitute a principle, and not a type, of architecture.[19]

LE CORBUSIER'S URBAN IDEAS DISCUSSED

The debate that emerged during the first half of the 1920s about the future of the Russian city was largely inspired by the experiments carried out by the Garden City movement, on whose principles the "Novaia Moskva" plan adopted in 1924 was based to a large extent, as Catherine Cooke has shown.[20] Plans for the reshaping of large cities oscillated between cosmetic programs and grandiose theoretical schemes based on the satellite-cities of English or German inspiration. Set against this background, Le Corbusier's projects quickly assumed the sensational proportions of absolute novelty.

In 1925, Boris Korshunov reiterated his approbation of Le Corbusier's theses, especially those regarding the layout and height of skyscrapers and his denunciation of the "corridor street," which he had illustrated in his "city for three million inhabitants"; Korshunov underlined the contrast between this scheme and Auguste Perret's 1922 project for skyscrapers in Paris.[21] Once more, he insisted on the validity of Le Corbusier's model for Soviet technicians:

Like every new contribution to town planning, Le Corbusier's ideas are of great interest to those working on the development of our cities, and a sharp incentive to apply them to the conditions obtaining in our own country.[22]

Some weeks later, Korshunov cited the proposals of the "Plan Voisin de Paris" as possible solutions to the problems of socialist Moscow:

Paris, like our Moscow, is a product of the Middle Ages, with streets 9 to 11 meters wide and crossroads every 30 to 50 meters. Although it is difficult for us now to comprehend the problem of traffic in Paris, we will have to face the same problem in two or three years' time. And then we shall not be able to avoid "surgical" solutions within the city. Le Corbusier proposes replacing the medieval "paths" with avenues 50 to 80 meters wide, housing blocks 400 meters long with a density of 5%, and all this at the heart of the city, where activity is at its most intense.

Apparently, the problem has become so acute, and the solution so problematic, that Le Corbusier's proposals can no longer be considered mere utopias, given also the fact that he attempts to answer the "characteristic question of today: where will you find the money?" What is important for us is the boldness and simplicity of his ideas; as I have already said, our own cities are "fallow ground" compared with Paris, and the cost of demolition and reconstruction is almost nothing in comparison with the West!

The question of the future planning of our cities, and of the specific problem of Moscow, has become a pressing one. It would be a grave error to apply partial reme-

[19] Ibid., p. 761.
[20] Catherine Cooke, "The Garden City Idea, the Russians," *The Architectural Review* 163 (June 1978): 353–63, and "Le mouvement pour la cité-jardin en Russie," in Jean-Louis Cohen, Marco De Michelis and Manfredo Tafuri, eds., *URSS 1917–1978: L'architecture, la ville* (Paris: L'Equerre; Rome: Officina Edizioni, 1979), pp. 200–233.
[21] "Goroda blizkogo budushchego," *Stroitelnaia Promyshlennost* 3, no. 2 (1925): 125–26. The review's editors made no further mention of the exchange of views between Korshunov and Shchusev, and implicitly declared the latter victorious in as much as they did not counterbalance his positive evaluation of Le Corbusier's projects. See also F. Davydov, "Proekty frantsuskogo arkhitektora Le Corbusier," *Krasnaia Niva*, no. 13 (1924): 318.
[22] B. Korshunov, "Noveishie vzgliady na gorodskoe stroitelstvo," *Stroitelnaia Promyshlennost* 3, no. 12 (1925): 874.

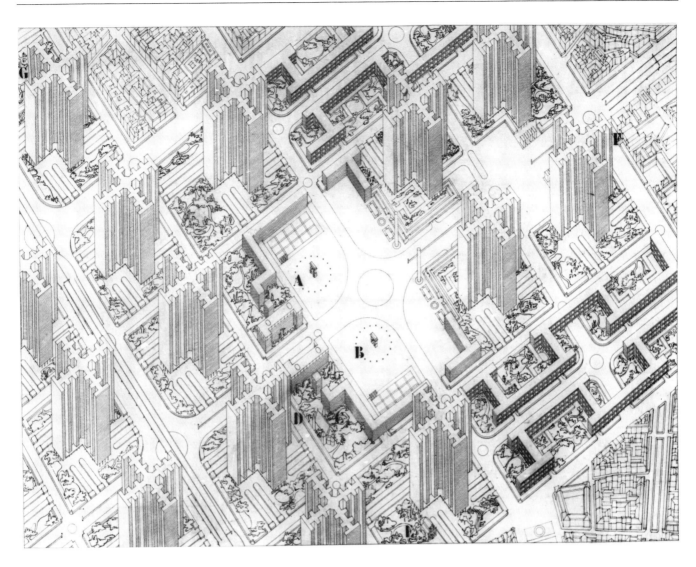

25. Le Corbusier, "Voisin Plan" for Paris, 1925, partial axonometric view, FLC, 29723.

dies on the assumption that the city will continue to vegetate as it has over the past centuries. We must learn from the tragic experience of Western cities and draw the appropriate conclusions.[23]

This somewhat simplistic transposition was not the only extrapolation of large-scale urban projects that Le Corbusier had based on ideas developed in *Urbanisme*. An article by Yakov Tugendhold, published posthumously in 1928, offered a more dialectical view. Tugendhold denounces Le Corbusier's "quasi-fetishist veneration of machine forms, of *technicism*," and considers the most positive aspect of his work to be his apology of "technical progress." He appreciates the "judicious geometrical construction" of the 1922 "city for three million" project, and, citing Le Corbusier's "lyrical description," considers his analysis of the skyscraper "a positive aspect of his teaching when compared with Americanism." Tugendhold, who merely paved the way for many subsequent attacks of a far more perfidious stamp, reserves his most vigorous criticisms for the supposedly "bourgeois individualistic ideas" of Le Corbusier, whose city—that of "bureaucracy and the small proprietor"—is designed "with the private-car owner in mind."[24]

Apart from these spectacular projects that, on occasion, were compared with the theoretical proposals of other Western architects, Soviet commenta-

[23] B. Korshunov, "Noveishie vzgliady na gorodskoe stroitelstvo, Le Corbusier, *Urbanisme*," *Stroitelnaia Promyshlennost* 4, no. 2 (1926): 147–48.

[24] Iakov Tugendhold, "*Urbanisme* Le Corbusier," *Revoliutsiia i Kultura*, no. 23–24 (December 1928): 87–91.

26. "The City of the Future according to the Project of the Architect Le Corbusier–Saugnier," in *Stroitelnaia Promyshlennost* 3, no. 2 (1925).

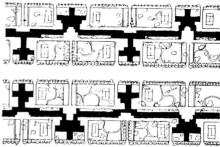

27. Le Corbusier on a roof terrace of the Quartiers Modernes Frugès, Pessac, 1926.

tors also paid some attention to the garden cities and housing schemes elaborated by Le Corbusier and Pierre Jeanneret from the outset of the twenties.[25] Early in 1927, the civil engineer Volfenzon cited the workers' housing project for Peugeot at Audincourt and above all at Pessac as "isolated experiments, to be viewed as anticipations of the future which, moreover, are better appreciated abroad than in France itself." Volfenzon clearly views Le Corbusier as a loner:

> The principles which he expresses with his Gallic feeling for clarity, logic and beauty carry conviction. In Le Corbusier's theoretical work, the theses and ideology of the new architecture are clearly articulated for the first time.
>
> His practical experiments, especially in the field of housing construction, are extremely interesting; yet at the same time they reveal the complexity of the problem of implementing new principles.
>
> The photographs of his buildings give the impression of inventions as yet unmastered. These forms, so recently imagined, doubtless furnish an inkling of the architecture of the future[26]

AN ARCHITECTURE THAT SHOOK MOSCOW

Little by little, the image of the theorist was gradually coupled with early representations of Le Corbusier's executed designs; in addition to the young doctrinaires of the avant-garde and critics of the Paris art scene, he now began to interest experienced practitioners such as Nikolai Markovnikov, the architect of Sokol, the first garden city to be built in Moscow following the revolution. Markovnikov's comprehensive 1927 study of Le Corbusier's housing designs cites the Danish critic Steen Eiler Rasmussen's 1926 article on the

[25] Vygodsky, for instance, compared the "Ville Contemporaine" with propositions by Werner Hegemann and the Luckhardt brothers. See L. Vygodsky, "Novye tipy ukrupnennoi zastroiki na Zapade," *Stroitelnaia Promyshlennost* 6, no. 2 (1928): 128–30.

[26] Gr. Inzh. Volfenzon, "Poselkovaia arkhitektura Zapada," *Stroitelnaia Promyshlennost* 5, no. 1 (1927): 50–53.

28. Le Corbusier Church villa, view through the glass wall, Ville-d'Avray, 1928–1929.

relations between purist theory and Le Corbusier's early projects.[27] Markovnikov considers the qualities of Le Corbusier's 1922 "mass-produced houses for artisans," and insists with some considerable vehemence on the flimsiness of the constructions at Pessac (whose formal combinations he describes in detail) or the villa La Roche–Jeanneret;[28] like Bruno Reichlin in recent years, he emphasizes Le Corbusier's ultimate neglect, under the influence of De Stijl, of the expression of structure:[29]

Le Corbusier completely ignores notions of constructional solidity and stability. His motto is "What is not indispensable must be eliminated." His supports are of minimal thickness. Thus he has abandoned the time-worn rule of architecture which states that the thickness of a pillar must give an idea of the mass that it has to hold up. His furniture consists of a tenuous framework of steel tubes. His staircases, too, are constructed from slender metal elements, the steps being nothing more than sheets of metal without vertical supports. Ramps are rounded strips of iron resting on rare shafts. Wherever possible, he strives to dissimulate the thickness of the walls. His windows stretch along the walls in continuous bands; the lintels are invariably flush with the walls to mask their thickness. The same principle applies to the doors, which are cut into the walls without imposts or frames.[30]

It would be tedious to catalogue all the references to Le Corbusier in the Soviet press; suffice it to say that the successive stages of his work were reviewed, so to speak, in real time; the critics were only a few weeks behind their French colleagues. However, in order to grasp the role that the Soviets assigned to Le Corbusier in contemporary European culture, it is useful to examine their reaction to two fundamentally important events in his international career, the Weissenhof exhibition at Stuttgart and the competition for the League of Nations project at Geneva, both occurring in 1927.

"Le Corbusier's creations" were immediately hailed as the most "original"[31] of the Stuttgart *Siedlung*, which Tugendhold himself judged to represent, all in all, the triumph of his ideas concerning the ribbon window and the roof

[27] Steen E. Rasmussen, "Le Corbusier, die kommende Baukunst?" *Wasmuths Monatshefte für Baukunst*, no. 9 (1926): 378–93.

[28] The Pessac development was considered by many authors to be evidence of Le Corbusier's interest in housing for the "masses." See L. Vygodsky, "Sovremennaia arkhitektura na Zapade," *Stroitelnaia Promyshlennost* 5, no. 5 (1927): 27. This was the second of a vast panorama in three installments on Western architecture, including coverage of Auguste Perret, Tony Garnier, and Eugène Freyssinet.

[29] Bruno Reichlin, "Le Corbusier vs. De Stijl," in *De Stijl et l'architecture en France*, ed. Bruno Reichlin and Yve-Alain Bois (Liège: P. Mardaga, 1986), pp. 91–108.

[30] N. Markovnikov, "Zhiloi dom v traktovke Le Corbusier," *Stroitelnaia Promyshlennost* 4, no. 10 (1926): 732–34. In a broader context, see by the same author *Zhilishchnoe stroitelstvo za granitsei i v SSSR* (Moscow: Centrozhilsoyuz, 1928), pp. 44–64.

[31] L. Vygodsky, "Vystavka *Die Wohnung* v Stuttgarte," *Stroitelnaia Promyshlennost* 5, no. 11 (1927): 751.

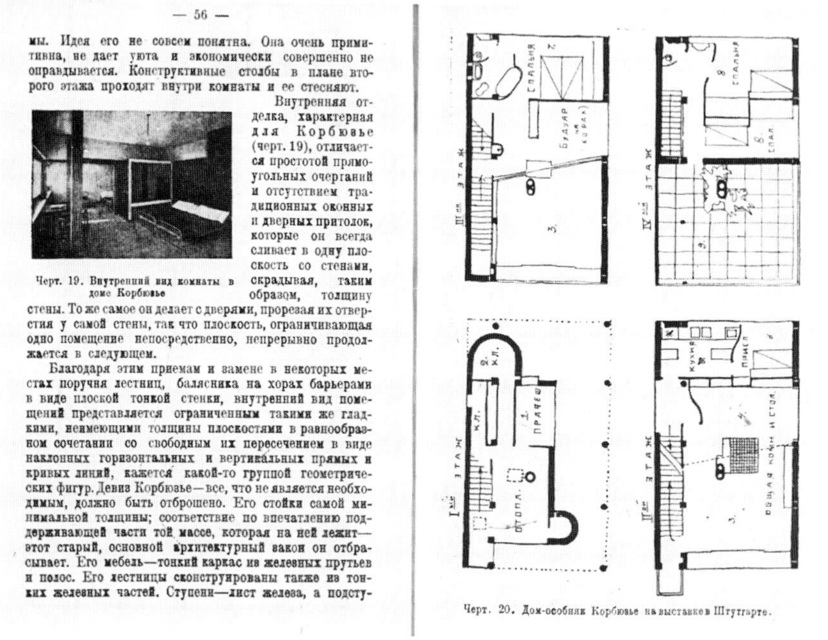

29. Le Corbusier, house in the Weissenhof *Siedlung*, Stuttgart, 1927; in N. V. Markovnikov, *Zhilishchnoe stroitelstvo za granitsei i v SSSR* (Moscow, 1928).

— 56 —

мы. Идея его не совсем понятна. Она очень примитивна, не дает уюта и экономически совершенно не оправдывается. Конструктивные стойки в плане второго этажа проходят внутри комнаты и ее стесняют.

Внутренняя отделка, характерная для Корбюзье (черт. 19), отличается простотой прямоугольных очертаний и отсутствием традиционных оконных и дверных притолок, которые он всегда сливает в одну плоскость со стенами, скрадывая, таким образом, толщину

Черт. 19. Внутренний вид комнаты в доме Корбюзье.

стены. То же самое он делает с дверями, прорезая их отверстия у самой стены, так что плоскость, ограничивающая одно помещение непосредственно, непрерывно продолжается в следующем.

Благодаря этим приемам и замене в некоторых местах поручня лестниц, балясника на хорах барьерами в виде плоской тонкой стенки, внутренний вид помещений представляется ограниченным такими же гладкими, неимеющими толщины плоскостями в разнообразном сочетании со свободным их пересечением в виде наклонных горизонтальных и вертикальных прямых и кривых линий, кажется какой-то группой геометрических фигур. Девиз Корбюзье—все, что не является необходимым, должно быть отброшено. Его стойки самой минимальной толщины; соответствие по впечатлению поддерживающей части той массе, которая на ней лежит—этот старый, основной архитектурный закон он отбрасывает. Его мебель—тонкий каркас из железных прутьев и полос. Его лестницы сконструированы также из тонких железных частей. Ступени—лист железа, а подсту-

Черт. 20. Дом-особняк Корбюзье на выставке в Штутгарте.

terrace, and which for him resembled "a sort of oriental city with its white cubic houses"; this image was also later to be used by the traditionalist opponents of *neues Bauen*.[32] The most detailed critique of Le Corbusier and Pierre Jeanneret's two Stuttgart houses came from the architect Nikolai Shcherbakov who, like practically all Soviet observers, formed his judgment on the basis of documents published in magazines, and who admired the solutions adopted for the exteriors.[33]

The double house built by Le Corbusier may be considered an extraordinary instance of individual housing, one that transcends habitual proportions. To judge from the photographs, one is struck by the remarkably simple external aspect which is Le Corbusier's hallmark, and which we associate with "classical" calm and poise. This simplicity is, so to speak, both dense and eloquent. . . . Le Corbusier uses reinforced concrete (for his posts and beams), glass, roofing and stairs in a way that no one before him has done. He is totally committed to his search for improved forms of human habitation. His experiments reflect hitherto undreamt-of possibilities whose influence extends to all international architecture.[34]

Shcherbakov was critical (and he was far from being alone in this) of the narrow first-floor corridor, the poor arrangement of the study, and the distances separating the servant's room from the kitchen and the kitchen from the stairs. He also considered Le Corbusier's house to be the most extravagant of the exhibition, in terms of building and maintenance costs. In conclusion, Shcherbakov criticized the emphasis placed on the building's exterior "to the detriment of logic, comfort, functionality and economy," and viewed the house more as an isolated object than as a veritable *type* for mass production, as in the projects of Mart Stam or Mies van der Rohe.

On the other hand, the painter Kazimir Malevich's appraisal of the Stuttgart experiment was wholly positive. In an article published in *Novaia Generatsiia*, Malevich presents the "five points for a new architecture" as formulated in Stuttgart—"the fruit of long experience"—and congratulates Le Corbusier and Jeanneret for "having borne in mind the needs of contemporary man in their treatment of dimensions, order, stairs, the form and distribution of the cupboards and that of the furniture, which is organically integrated into the structure."[35]

The second major event, the Geneva competition, was viewed with a certain degree of irony in the Soviet Union, which had not yet joined the League of Nations. David Aranovich echoes "Western critics" in his assertion that the "failure" of the competition, marked by the victory of academicism, was due to the difficulty of the project; at the same time, all-glass or wholly "cubic" projects are the butt of his irony. Aranovich expresses doubts as to the value of the monumental, eclectic, or neoclassical entries and clearly views Le Corbusier and Jeanneret's entry as the highlight of the competition:

Under these circumstances, it is particularly interesting to examine what the "genius" of French architecture, Le Corbusier, has submitted (in collaboration with Pierre Jeanneret). Le Corbusier has remained perfectly true to himself on this occasion. The facades are treated in his habitual manner, by means of sharply emphasized and highly visible surfaces. This principle is greatly enhanced by the enormous scale of the building, which here enables it to escape a resemblance with ocean-going liners. But the most significant aspect of the project is the plan that, over and above what is or is not acceptable, reveals Le Corbusier as a great artist of architecture. Some position their buildings in linear fashion, others organize them into banal horseshoe configurations; but Le Corbusier posits a novel solution for all the volumes concerned. Quite apart from Le Corbusier's remarkable faculties of urban design, he here exploits to the

[32] Tugendhold, "*Urbanisme* Corbusier," p. 89.

[33] Catalogues of the exhibition also circulated in the country, since they were still to be found at Moscow "bukinisty" (used-book stores) in 1974.

[34] V. Shcherbakov, "Vystavka po zhilishchnomu stroitelstvu v Stuttgarte v 1927 godu," *Stroitelstvo Moskvy* 5, no. 1 (1928): 10–13.

[35] Kazimir Malevich, "Teoriia sovremennoi zapadnoi arkhitektury," *Novaia Generatsiia*, Kiev, no. 6 (1928): 116–24; English translation in Troels Andersen, ed., *K. S. Malevich: Essays on Art* (Copenhagen: Borgen, 1971), vol. 2 (1928–1933), pp. 155–57.

30. Le Corbusier, project for League of Nations, Geneva, 1927, general axonometric view of second design, FLC 23185.

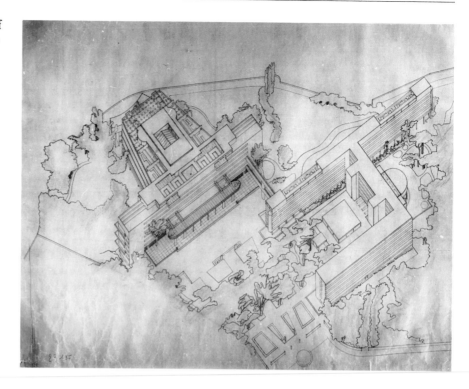

full his ability to integrate architecture and landscape. Moreover, unlike the other entrants Le Corbusier has aligned his project not with the river but rather with the shores of the lake, with the idea that the different facades of the building would thus offer varied views of the different aspects of the park. Finally, he has discovered an original way of accentuating monumentality in the main block, which takes the form of a trapezoid inscribed in a bend in the lake.[36]

It is well known what energies Le Corbusier deployed at the end of 1927 in his attempt to sway the jury, with testimonies from the most "advanced" architects from Paris and other European nations and with the arguments that he developed in *Une maison—un palais*.[37] The absence of Russian signatures in the petition is easily explained by the fact that the Soviets refused to recognize the existence of an international body that they considered the illegitimate product of "imperialist warmongering." But the Russian boycott took no direct part in a debate that was of such fundamental importance to Le Corbusier himself and to the fate of the "Modern Movement" as a whole (since it was to a large extent responsible for the creation, in the following year, of the CIAM, and the members of the different groups of the new Soviet architecture did not hesitate to follow Le Corbusier's example in their own work and in the animated debates that marked Moscow throughout the twenties.

THE NEW ARCHITECTURE CONFRONTS LE CORBUSIER

The attitudes of Soviet architectural organizations toward Le Corbusier reveal differences between the various schools of thought of the day. Alexei Shchusev, who, after 1925, began to assume the language of a watered-down modernism, adopted a highly critical yet relatively courteous position.[38]

We have already witnessed the early attempts of ASNOVA, the first organization to acquire a name for itself, to convert Le Corbusier to its cause. In the

[36] D. Aranovich, "Iz novostei arkhitektury Zapada," *Stroitelnaia Promyshlennost* 5, no. 8 (1927): 538–39.

[37] Le Corbusier, *Une maison—un palais, à la recherche d'une unité architecturale* (Paris: G. Crès et Cie, 1928).

[38] Akad. arkh. Alexei Shchusev (see n. 18).

first—and only—issue of the review *Izvestia ASNOVA*, published in 1926 by El Lissitzky and Nikolai Ladovsky, Le Corbusier figures prominently among the "foreign representatives" of the association, along with Adolf Behne, Mart Stam, Emil Roth, and Karel Teige.[39] Yet the articles themselves make no explicit mention of Le Corbusier's positions; they are devoted first and foremost to an analysis of "Soviet" skyscrapers and the work of students at the Vkhutemas.

El Lissitzky himself, who can hardly be considered representative of the association, given that they fell out over the publication of *Izvestia ASNOVA*, gave some indication of Le Corbusier's European and Russian activities in a work published in 1925 and cowritten with Hans Arp, *Les -ismes de l'art*, which documents several constructivist productions, proposes a definition of purism, and includes a reproduction of a canvas by Jeanneret.[40] Kazimir Malevich, with whom El Lissitzky had collaborated in his suprematist phase, also focused his attention on purism, even before his discovery of the Stuttgart houses, in an article in which he considered the relations between painting and architecture; in Malevich's view Le Corbusier, like van Doesburg, Rietveld, and Gropius, was "well on the road toward Suprematist architectonics."[41]

Those who advocated a transformation of architecture based on new functional or formal principles were not the only ones to be interested in Le Corbusier; his work was also reviewed by the theorists of "left-wing art," who were aiming to subordinate the orientations of modern art to the requirements of production. When Korneli Zelinsky reproached Le Corbusier for his lack of ideological clarity in *LEF*, a review of the "Left Front of the Arts," he sounded a critical chord that would find widespread echoes when the architect's credit came to be contested in Moscow. Zelinsky saw in Le Corbusier's cult of primary volumes "organically adapted to our psychology" a position that, unhappily, was "equally acceptable [to] the Academician Shchusev and comrade Lunacharsky."[42] Yet he took pains to emphasize the documentary value of *Vers une architecture*:

If we strip Le Corbusier-Saugnier's book of all its petit-bourgeois and metaphysical components, we shall find there a mass of precious materials concerning contemporary architecture. Above all it describes magnificently well the situation of Western architecture since the war, and unmasks its ideology.[43]

The nuances in Zelinsky's position were echoed in the attitudes of practitioners of the constructivist movement who, in 1926, identified explicitly with Le Corbusier in the first issues of their official magazine *Sovremennaia Arkhitektura* (*Contemporary Architecture*).

CONSTRUCTIVIST SUPPORT FOR MACHINE AESTHETICS

As early as 1922 in *Konstruktivizm*, a manifesto that may be considered the first theoretical formulation of the movement, Alexei Gan evoked "Western constructivism" and *L'Esprit Nouveau*. Like Nina Yavorskaia, Gan cites the watchword, "There is a New Spirit; it is a spirit of construction," but insists that the Russian aim is to evacuate the very notion of art:

Our constructivism has set itself a clear aim: to find the communist expression of material structures.

In the West constructivism flirts with politics, declaring that the new art is outside of politics, but that it is not apolitical.

Our constructivism is aggressive and uncompromising; it wages a severe battle with

[39] *Izvestia ASNOVA*, no. 1 (1926): 1.

[40] El Lissitzky and Hans Arp, *Les -ismes de l'art* (Erlenbach-Zurich, Munich, Leipzig: Eugen Rentsch Verlag, 1925), pp. x and 15. The painter Jeanneret is christened "Pier."

[41] Kazemir Malevich, "Zhivopis i problema arkhitektury," *Novaia Generatsiia*, Kiev, no. 2 (1928): 116–24; English translation in Andersen K. S. Malevich: Essays on Art, 2: 7–18.

[42] Korneli Zelinsky, "Ideologiia i zadachi sovetskoi arkhitektury," *LEF*, no. 3 (1925): 77–108.

[43] Ibid., p. 79.

parasites, with painters left and right, in a word with all those who defend, even half-heartedly, speculative aesthetic activity of art.

Our constructivism is fighting for the intellectual and material production of a communist culture.[44]

Alexander Vesnin's view was less explicitly political. A trained engineer who left his profession in order to collaborate with his brothers, Vesnin had, from 1917 on, worked on futurist painting and theater before joining the initial "hard core" of constructivists. In the "Credo"—the term was borrowed from Van de Velde (as well as some others!)—that he composed for the INKhUK (the Institute of Artistic Culture), Vesnin's stated aim was to establish an architectural analogy with the attempts of his friend Liubov Popova and the theater director Vsevolod Meyerhold to create a "biomechanics" by "Taylorizing" the theater:

Just as every part of an engine represents an active force, essential to the functioning of the given system and embodied in its appropriate shape and material, and these may not be willfully altered without damaging the working of the entire system, so in every object constructed by an artist each component element represents a materialized force and cannot be discarded or altered without impeding the efficient functioning of the given system, i.e. the object.

The modern engineer has created works of genius: the bridge, the steam locomotive, the aircraft, the crane. . . .

The modern artist must produce objects equal to them in strength, tension and potential, as organizing principles in terms of their psychophysiological impact on human consciousness.[45]

In 1924, Moisei Ginzburg gave a broader, more political edge to these considerations when he published *Stil i epokha*, a book and manifesto combined, whose method and organization owed a considerable debt to *Vers une architecture*. The book's conceptual and visual strategies certainly owe a debt to Corbusian ideas despite the absence of any reference to him in the text or illustrations. Ginzburg's approach is inspired by Wölfflin and other European art historians: if each historical epoch carries with it a specific "style" that travels a determined trajectory, it ought to be possible to trace that of the contemporary style, based on the machine.

Even more than Vesnin in his "Credo," Ginzburg roots the criteria for the new aesthetics in the internal articulations of the machine and, like Vesnin, echoes Alberti in asserting that "there is no part or element of the machine that does not occupy a particular place, position, or role in the overall scheme and that is not the product of absolute necessity."[46]

In the machine, there are no elements that are "disinterested" from the standpoint of elemental aesthetics. There are no so-called "free flights of fancy." Everything in it has a definite and clear-cut constructive task. One part provides support, another rotates, a third produces forward motion, and a fourth transfers that motion to the pulleys.

This is why the machine with the most actively functioning parts, with an absolute lack of "nonworking" organs, quite naturally leads to an utter disregard of decorative elements, for which there is no longer room, and leads precisely to the idea of constructivism, so prevalent in our time, which must by its very being absorb the "decorative," its antithesis.

. . . Under the influence of the transformed conditions of life and the significance of modern economics, technology, and the machine and its logical consequences, *our aesthetic emotion, its character, has been transformed as well.*

. . . *The most desirable decorative element for us is precisely the one that is unvarnished*

[44] Alexei Gan, *Konstruktivizm* (Tver: Tverskoe Izd-vo, 2ia Tipografia: 1922), p. 70; English translation in Lodder, *Russian Constructivism*, p. 238.

[45] Alexander Vesnin, "Kredo," speech before the INKhUK, the Institute of Artistic Culture, April 1922, private collection, Moscow; in Mikhail Barkhin and Yuri Yaralov, eds., *Mastera Sovetskoi arkhitektury ob arkhitekture* (Moscow: Iskusstvo, 1975), 2: 14; English translation in Khan-Magomedov, *Pioneers*, p. 548.

[46] Moisei Ginzburg, *Stil i epokha, problemy sovremennoi arkhitektury* (Moscow: Gosudarstvennoe Izdatelstvo, 1924), p. 93. English translation in Moisei Ginzburg, *Style and Epoch*, ed. and trans. Anatole Senkevitch, Jr., with a preface by Kenneth Frampton (Cambridge, Mass.: MIT Press, 1982), p. 86. Some chapters of the book had previously been published in the form of isolated articles in *Arkhitektura*, the MAO magazine of which Ginzburg was editor. For the genesis of the book and its theoretical context, see Senkevitch's introduction to the American edition: ibid., pp. 10–33.

31. Alexander Vesnin, dust jacket for Moisei Ginzburg's *Stil i Epokha*, 1924.

in its constructive aspect; thus, the concept of the constructive has absorbed within itself the concept of the "decorative."[47]

Although Ginzburg's attempts to extrapolate an (as yet comparatively elementary) design method based on observations of the machine and the analysis of certain contemporary projects (such as that of the Vesnin brothers for the Palace of Labor competition of 1923) are more systematic than Le Corbusier's, he exploits a similar, if not an identical, visual repertoire.

As in the *L'Esprit Nouveau* articles that would make up *Vers une architecture*, Ginzburg's book contains reproductions of airplanes, ships, and industrial buildings, although Ginzburg took care not to use the same photographs; like Le Corbusier, he included the Caproni triplane but now viewed on the ground rather than in a nose dive;[48] like him he showed the test circuit at the Fiat factory at Lingotto, but with no cars in sight;[49] and, like him, he included a series of views of American grain elevators, but whereas Le Corbusier's were taken from Walter Gropius's 1913 *Jahrbuch* of the Deutsche Werkbund, Ginzburg, as Reyner Banham points out, took his from other sources—in all probability Russian technical reviews.[50]

[47] Ginzburg, *Stil i epokha*, pp. 121–22; p. 101 of the English text.

[48] See *L'Esprit Nouveau* 9 (June 1921): 978, and Ginzburg, *Stil i epokha*, p. 10. The predominance in Ginzburg's book of illustrations from northern Italy is no doubt attributable to the fact that he spent some years at the Academy of Fine Arts in Milan before the war.

[49] See *L'Esprit Nouveau* 19, and Ginzburg, *Stil i epokha*, pp. 139, 141.

[50] Reyner Banham, *A Concrete Atlantis: U.S. Industrial Building and European Modern Architecture* (Cambridge, Mass.: MIT Press, 1986), pp. 231–32. The photos in question are found in Ginzburg, *Stil i epokha*, pp. 111, 131, 137, 143, 153.

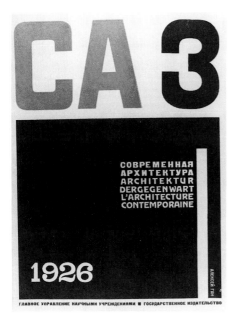

32. Alexei Gan, cover of *Sovremennaia Arkhitektura* 1, no. 3 (1926).

33. Page of *Sovremennaia Arkhitektura* 1, no. 3 (1926).

The link between Le Corbusier's theses and those of Ginzburg was emphasized in 1925 by V. Zgura, who claimed that "although he is more able from the scientific and literary points of view, M. Ginzburg nonetheless reiterates several of Le Corbusier-Saugnier's essential ideas."[51] In November 1924, Ginzburg dispatched his book to "Monsieur Le Corbusier–Saugnier" with the "Hommage cordial de l'auteur";[52] in the theses that he set out in his report to the First Congress of Construction, held in Moscow in May 1926, he insisted on Le Corbusier's contribution to "new trends in the field of architecture at home and abroad."[53]

The idealization of airplanes, ships, and grain silos was not the only trait that Le Corbusier and Ginzburg shared. The role of nineteenth-century French rationalist culture—with which Le Corbusier was so familiar—in the formation of Russian theory must not be underestimated. Just as Moscow had published Viollet-le-Duc's curious work *L'art russe* in 1879, the year of his death,[54] so Russia was the only nation to have undertaken a translation of Auguste Choisy's, *Histoire de l'architecture.*[55] In *Ritm v arkhitekture*, written before *Stil i epokha* in 1923, Ginzburg explicitly invoked the heritage of Choisy and even redrew his analytical sketches of the Acropolis.[56] Ginzburg and Le Corbusier shared other common references such as John Ruskin's positions, the dissemination of which in Russia was due in part to the good offices of French-born Robert de la Sizeranne.[57] From 1926, under Ginzburg's ideological hegemony, the constructivists who had formed OSA in 1925 began to give pride of place to Le Corbusier's work in their review, *Sovremennaia Arkhitektura*, and took pains to use his productions as a prop for their manifestoes.[58]

"THE VERY FIGURE OF THE NEW MAN"

Urbanisme was warmly recommended by the editors in the magazine's second issue, in which Ginzburg cites Le Corbusier on several occasions in a programmatic text (couched in kominternist terminologies) that presents the "international front of the new architecture."[59] Contrasting Le Corbusier with the "ulti-

[51] V. V. Zgura, "M. Ia. Ginzburg, *Stil i epokha, problemy sovremennoi arkhitektury,*" *Pechat i Revoliutsiia* 5, no. 2, (1925): 289.

[52] Moisei Ginzburg, inscription in the copy of *Stil i epokha* sent to Le Corbusier, Moscow, November 1924 (FLC). Le Corbusier cut out some illustrations, especially those at the end of the book, which show new Soviet production; this fact testifies, at the very least, to Le Corbusier's familarity with the early work of the constructivists.

[53] Moisei Ginzburg, "Noveishie techeniia v oblasti arkhitektury u nas i za granitsei," in *Trudy Pervogo Vsesoiuznogo sezda po grazhdanskomu i inzhenernomu stroitelstvu* (Moscow, 1926), p. 188; reprinted in Khazanova, *Iz istorii*, p. 37.

[54] Eugène-Emmanuel Viollet-le-Duc, *L'art russe, ses origines, ses éléments constitutifs, son apogée, son avenir* (Paris: Vve A. Morel et Cie, 1877); translated by N. Sultanov, with an introduction by Viktor Butovsky as *Russkoe*

Iskusstvo, ego istochniki, ego sostavnie elementy, ego vysshee razvitie, ego buduchnost (Moscow: Izd. Khud.-promyshlannogo Muzeuma, 1879). See the analysis by Robin Middleton, "Viollet-le-Ducsky," *Architectural Design* 40 (1970): 67.

[55] Auguste Choisy, *Istoriia arkhitektury*, 2 vols., trans. N. S. Kudriukov (Moscow: P. S. Uvarov, 1906–1907).

[56] Moisei Ginzburg, *Ritm v arkhitekture* (Moscow: Sredi kollektsionerov, 1923).

[57] Robert de la Sizeranne, *Reskin i religiia krasoty* (St. Petersburg: V. M. Sablin, 1900).

[58] For the history of this organization, see S. Frederick Starr, "OSA: The Union of Contemporary Architects," in George Gibian and H. W. Tjalsma, eds., *Russian Modernism, Culture and the Avant-Garde, 1900–1930* (Ithaca, N.Y.: Cornell University Press, 1976), pp. 188–208.

[59] "Le Corbusier *Urbanisme*," *Sovremennaia Arkhitektura* 1, no. 2 (1926): 37.

mate bad taste" of other architectural productions of the 1925 exhibition, he situates his work in the tradition of changes ushered in by the Perret brothers:

Le Corbusier-Saugnier alone has succeeded, not only in revealing the inventiveness that is specific to the national character of his work, but also in giving it a new, contemporary form.

Le Corbusier is above all the very figure of the new man, full of energy and perseverance in the propaganda that he deploys in defense of his ideas. In the space of two or three years, he has succeeded in creating a truly contemporary review, *L'Esprit Nouveau* (which unfortunately has not survived), and has written three books, *Vers une architecture, Urbanisme* and *L'art décoratif d'aujourd'hui*—all three full of characteristically French flashes of intelligence and slogans precisely launched. But Le Corbusier's innovative personality finds its fullest expression in his architectural works. He is the author of a reasonable project for the contemporary city, a city of skyscraper offices, a city concentrated in one spot yet impregnated with air, light and green spaces—an alternative to the disorders of Paris, New York and other cities of the present. He has designed different types of urban construction, in each case radically reconsidering the problem posed. Finally, his villa designs reflect an organization of the habitat that is at once simple, clever and new.[60]

In this same issue, Vasili Kalish's review of *L'art décoratif d'aujourd'hui* again contrasts Le Corbusier's positions with the productions of the Exposition des Arts Décoratifs, which the reviewer sees as an instance of "that sentimental cult of the intimate object . . . which the author categorically rejects."[61] Kalish fully endorses Le Corbusier's ideas as expressed in the book, which he paraphrases on occasion, and attempts to demonstrate the validity of his search for new standards in everyday objects in the context of the conditions "for a general leveling of social classes"—conditions obtained in the Russia of the day.

Some months later, a somewhat technical contribution, this time by Le Corbusier himself, was published as part of a survey of the roof terrace taken from *Bauwelt*; in this text, he extols the virtues of internal rainwater falls.[62] From this moment on Le Corbusier was presented as a "collaborator" on the review, along with Gropius, Mies van der Rohe, Krejcar, and a few others.[63] Le Corbusier and Pierre Jeanneret's participation at the 1927 Werkbund exhibition in Stuttgart was given double coverage, with extensive publication of the "Five Points of a New Architecture"[64] and an almost imperceptibly ironic reading of their two houses.[65]

Le Corbusier's regular presence on the pages of *Sovremennaia Arkhitektura* makes the absence of any evidence of his work at the inauguration of the "First Exhibition of Contemporary Architecture" rather strange. The exhibition opened at the Vkhutemas on 18 June, showed projects selected to a large

34. Le Corbusier, "Five Points of a New Architecture," in *Sovremennaia Arkhitektura* 3, no. 1 (1928).

[60] Moisei Ginzburg, "Mezhdunarodny front sovremennoi arkhitektury," *Sovremennaia Arkhitektura* 1, no. 2 (1926): 42. This article is illustrated for the most part by views of the villa La Roche-Jeanneret.

[61] Vasili G. Kalish, "Le Corbusier–Saugnier Dekorativnoe Iskusstvo Sovremennosti," *Sovremennaia Arkhitektura* 1, no. 2 (1926): 46–48.

[62] Dimitri S. Markov, "Anketa o ploskoi kryshe," *Sovremennaia Arkhitektura* 1, no. 4 (1926): 102–3; El Lissitzky, "Ploskie kryshi i ikh konstruktsii," *Stroitelnaia Promyshlennost* 4, no. 11 (1926): 820–22. The original survey

was carried out by Walter Gropius: "Das flache Dach (Umfrage, veranstaltet von Walter Gropius)," *Bauwelt* 14 (1926): 162–68, 223–27, 361.

[63] See the advertisement in *Sovremennaia Arkhitektura* 1, no. 4 (1926): 32.

[64] Le Corbusier, "Piat tezisov," trans. I. Gurevich, *Sovremennaia Arkhitektura* 3, no. 1 (1928): 23–27.

[65] I(osif) Gurevich, "Sovremennoe Zhile, vystavka-poselok Weissenhof okolo Stuttgarta," *Sovremennaia Arkhitektura* 3, no. 1 (1928): 28–36.

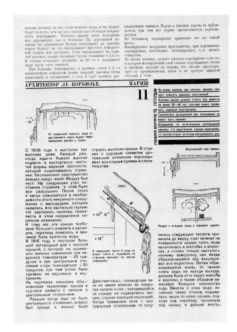

ВИЛЛА в ГАРШ
ЛЕ КОРБЮЗЬЕ • П. ЖАННРЕ

35. Le Corbusier, answer to *Bauwelt*'s "inquiry on the flat roof," published in *Sovremennaia Arkhitektura* 1, no. 4 (1926).

36. Le Corbusier, Stein-de Monzie villa, Garches, 1926–1928; in *Sovremennaia Arkhitektura* 4, no. 5 (1929).

37. Alexei Gan, poster for the First Exhibition of Modern Architecture, Moscow, 1927; in *Sovremennaia Arkhitektura* 2, no. 6 (1927).

extent by the constructivists. The Paris architects represented were Mallet-Stevens and André Lurçat. They had been approached by the Brussels architect Victor Bourgeois, who appears to have been the Soviets' go-between for France and Belgium.[66] Le Corbusier's absence from this dazzling demonstration of the convergences between Soviet avant-garde architects and their Western counterparts is all the more puzzling since the first traces of his influence were to be detected both in a number of housing projects presented

[66] Irina V. Kokinakki, "Iaia vystavka sovremennoi arkhitektury v Moskve," in *Problemy istorii sovetskoi arkhitektury*, pp. 39–54; English translation in *Architectural Design* 53 (1983): 50–59. The absence of Le Corbusier is lamented by Aranovich: David Aranovich, "Vystavka sovremennoi arkhitektury," *Stroitelnaia Promyshlennost* 5, no. 6–7 (1927): 153.

there in the context of a "friendly competition" organized by OSA on the theme of new housing types, and in the sets designed by Andrei Burov for Eisenstein's film, *The General Line.*

Two interpretations can be placed on this absence, which was remarked on by some contemporary observers. The first is local and involves the constructivists' self-conscious reluctance to reinforce Le Corbusier's influence on the Russian scene even further, given its already considerable effect on the press and on architectural production; Ginzburg's subsequent criticisms lend weight to this interpretation. The second concerns the manner in which the invitations were handed on by Bourgeois, whose relations with Le Corbusier were not especially cordial and who might well have "forgotten" to include him in the enterprise.

In fact, Le Corbusier's architecture had no need of such publicity to be well known within the Soviet Union, whether in avant-garde circles or in the profession as a whole, which had already had ample opportunity for study. In formal terms, Le Corbusier's influence was already perceptible to the young art historian Alfred H. Barr, who detected its presence during a visit to Moscow in 1927, in Ginzburg's building on the Malaia Bronnaia.[67]

One ought also to emphasize the fact that Le Corbusier was far from being unknown to the Soviet leaders themselves. Trotsky, who was expelled from the Communist party in this year, had had occasion, at the outset of the twenties, to remark on the interest of *L'Esprit Nouveau*,[68] as had Lunacharsky,[69] and coverage of Le Corbusier's most recent productions in the cultural press would certainly not have escaped the attention of those in charge of policy, industry, and culture, for whom the Paris scene remained of central importance.

It is, therefore, hardly surprising that in May 1928, Le Corbusier received an invitation to participate in a competition for the building of the headquarters of the people's cooperatives in Moscow; like German architects, such as Erich Mendelsohn,[70] who had already been invited to take part in the Soviet construction effort, Le Corbusier was already considered a foreign "technician" well enough established for the authorities to risk consulting him.

[67] Alfred Hamilton Barr, Jr., "Russian Diary 1927–28," *October*, no. 7 (1978): 13; and "Notes on Russian Architecture," *The Arts* 15 (February 1929): 103–7.

[68] In a letter to Le Corbusier dated 31 October 1923, Ilya Ehrenburg stated that "in one of his latest articles, Trotsky has spoken in highly sympathetic terms of the trends reflected in *L'Esprit Nouveau*." I have as yet been unable to locate the article in question.

[69] Anatoli Lunacharsky, "Iskusstvo i ego noveishie formy," in *Iskusstvo i revoliutsiia* (Moscow: Novaia Moskva, 1924), pp. 193–229 (report submitted to the university of Moscow on 2 December 1923). In "Promyshlennost i Iskusstvo," another text in the same collection, Lunacharsky makes explicit reference to Le Corbusier who, according to I. A. Shats, Lunacharsky's secretary and translator of a text published in *Khudozhestvenny Trud*, sent copies of *L'Esprit Nouveau* directly to the people's commissar.

[70] Erich Mendelsohn was invited in 1926 to build the "Krasnoe Znamia" textile mill in Leningrad. For the first interventions of Western architects in the USSR, see de Michelis, Pasini, *La città sovietica*, pp. 18–32.

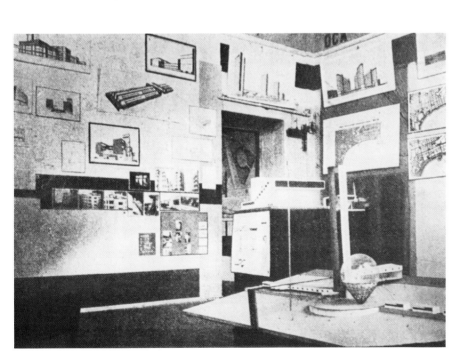

38. Works by the architects of the OSA at the the First Exhibition of Modern Architecture, Moscow, 1927; in *Sovremennaia Arkhitektura* 2, nos. 4–5 (1927).

CHAPTER

3

1928: Le Corbusier Discovers Moscow

AMÉDÉE OZENFANT'S early visit to Moscow had been an experience of fundamental importance; in his eyes, Russia would long remain an exemplary world. And just as the journey marked his beginnings as a painter, so another trip made in 1913 marked the beginnings of the semifictitious poetry of Le Corbusier's fellow countryman Freddy Sauser, alias Blaise Cendrars, who treated his own travels as a pretext for his *Prose du Transsibérien*:

At the time I was an adolescent
I was barely sixteen but I had forgotten my childhood
I was 16,000 leagues from my place of birth
I was in Moscow, the city of a thousand and three bell towers and seven stations
And I could not get enough of the seven stations, the thousand and three towers
For my adolescence was so ardent and so crazy
That my heart burned in turns like the temple at Ephesus or the Red Square in
Moscow
Against a setting sun.[1]

39. Alexander Rodchenko, "In the Streets of Moscow," photograph, 1929.

Le Corbusier's aims in setting out on this, for him, crucial journey were initially somewhat more prosaic: he simply wished to be there, in the fall of 1928, to defend his designs of the Centrosoyuz project—for which he had received a brief in May of that year and which he had sent to Moscow in July—and to make the on-the-spot modifications that the Soviets desired. To judge from the correspondence, from as early as 1924, between Le Corbusier and ASNOVA, this trip was a long-expected one, although it was not the first visit to the USSR by a leading Western architect—Bruno Taut and Erich Mendelsohn had already been warmly received in 1926.[2]

Although no Paris architect had visited the USSR before, a large number of French intellectuals and politicians had had occasion to discover Bolshevik Russia during the 1920s, attempting to make direct contact with the Soviet scene and establishing the "return from Russia" as one of the major literary genres of the interwar period. Whether alone or in groups, these French errants, from Edouard Herriot to Anatole de Monzie, from Georges Duhamel to Ernest Mercier, and from Louis-Ferdinand Céline to André Gide, followed a route through Russia that was strictly controlled by the authorities; their accounts reflect presuppositions ranging from strong anti-Soviet feeling to revolutionary ardor.[3]

Questions of architecture and town planning play a relatively marginal role in these accounts. Three distinct types of analysis emerge in fact, more often than not as annexes to political observers' descriptions of state policy or journalists' and writers' descriptions of everyday life in the large cities. These analyses focus on urban policy, the state and its management of residential facilities, and the architectural debate proper.

Avant-garde architectural productions occasionally received notice in these accounts. Emile Schreiber went into raptures over a communal dwelling that bore a strong resemblance to that built by Moisei Ginzburg for the Narkomfin in 1928–1929,[4] while Marc Chadourne appears to have seen, in Melnikov's Rusakov club, "a baroque studio set for German cinema."[5] In the year of Le Corbusier's first visit to Moscow Georges Duhamel, however, reacted cautiously to the new architecture:

Browsing through some German books on art in Bolshevik Russia gives one a fallacious impression of Russian cities. They show all the most austere samples of constructivist art, the child of the revolution; one also finds remarkable examples of modern poster art. In this way, once one has closed the book, one imagines a red Russia

[1] Blaise Cendrars, "Prose du Transsibérien et de la petite Jeanne de France," in *Œuvres complètes* (Paris: Denoël, 1963), 1: 20. For where the poet and the architect born in the same year and the same city crossed paths, see Jacques Gubler, "LC et BC: paragone difficile," *Le Corbusier à Genève 1922–1932: Projets et réalisations*, exhibition catalogue (Lausanne: Payot, 1987), pp. 143–52.

[2] On this visit, see "K priezdu innostranykh gostei," and Bruno Taut, "Arkhitektura kak vyrazitel vlasti," *Stroitelnaia Promyshlennost* 4, no. 7 (1926): 464, 465–69; Bruno Taut, "Novaia arkhitektura v SSSR," *Stroitelnaia Promyshlennost* 4, no. 8 (1926): 562–64.

[3] Fred Kupfermann, *Au pays des Soviets, le voyage français en URSS 1917–1939* (Paris: Gallimard/Julliard, 1979).

[4] Emile Schreiber, *Comment on vit en URSS* (Paris: Librairie Plon, 1931): 24–27.

[5] Marc Chadourne, *L'URSS sans passion* (Paris: Editions Mornay, 1932): 53–54.

composed essentially of buildings with harsh industrial silhouettes, covered with fu-turist billboards inviting the whole world to rise up. The cumulative effect of these documents concerning an art without grace, if not without greatness, inspires the reader to poignant melancholy. But let him not be deceived: Russian cities do not have this disquietingly severe aspect.

. . . With a hundred or so children playing around an austere housing block, all comes right again and its harsh lines seem to soften. Constructivism, a rigorous art, is without hypocrisy. No vain ornamentation. Let the iron framework be seen in all its naked glory, let the building reveal its skeleton, the logical reasons for its power. Setting aside a certain languid grace, our Eiffel tower might be viewed as a "pre-constructivist" monument. And if, as Claudel asserts, the Chinese make "écorché landscapes," the architects of the new Russia seem desirous of making "écorché monuments."[6]

Few travelers, however, had interests as real as Le Corbusier, whose task it was to negotiate a project of considerable scale when compared with his previ-ous realizations. Le Corbusier's curiosity about the "New Russia," which Ana-tole de Monzie had discovered as early as 1923,[7] was manifested in his pres-ence at receptions held at the Soviet Embassy in 1925,[8] and became intensified even before the Centrosoyuz brief. Opening these new horizons, Le Corbusier asked the film critic on *L'Humanité*, Léon Moussinac, to supply him with membership cards for the "Amis de Spartacus" film club in Paris, which pro-jected films of the Soviet avant-garde; public showings of some of these—including Eisenstein's *Potemkin*—were banned at the time.[9]

Even before his departure, the objectives of the trip were clearly fixed in his mind. The problem above all was to get the Centrosoyuz brief and, in order to do so, to build up a movement around his ideas; but he also wanted to ac-quaint himself with architectural production, test the atmosphere of Moscow, and to profit from this occasion with a "scoop" back in France. Before his arrival in Moscow, he negotiated a contract with *Paris-Midi*, which agreed to publish his travel impressions "in the form of a series of front-page articles dealing with economic, artistic and intellectual life, changes in mores, archi-tecture."[10]

The journey was not, as was the rule, organized by VOKS, a Soviet state institution created in 1925 for the purpose of organizing cultural exchanges and visits, from the most illustrious to the most modest (although it did organ-ize part of his schedule), but by the Centrosoyuz itself, which financed the trip and took Le Corbusier under its wing.[11]

AN ARRIVAL THAT ATTRACTED NOTICE

On 1 October 1928, Le Corbusier left Paris for Prague, where he gave an invited lecture to the Club of Architects at the "Free Theater" and met, among others, Vítěslav Nezval, Jaromír Kejcar, and Karel Teige; he undertook to send the latter copies of the plans for the Mundaneum and Centrosoyuz projects.[12] He left Prague on 6 October and reached Moscow via Warsaw on 10 October, accompanied by his mother's good wishes:

And now there you are in great mother Russia, full as she is of "terrifying" legends. There, too, I trust in your lucky star, and that the Russians, intelligent people in the vanguard of modern ideas, will find your own ideas to their taste and will entrust you with this great architectural project. Be prudent in your speech, don't make politics, and remain an artist who has come to speak solely of his art.[13]

[6] Georges Duhamel, *Le voyage de Moscou* (Paris: Mercure de France, 1928): 170–71.

[7] Anatole de Monzie, *Du Kremlin au Luxem-bourg* (Paris: A. Delpeuch, 1924), and *Petit manuel de la Russie nouvelle* (Paris: Firmin Didot et Cie, 1931).

[8] This was confirmed by Pierre-André Emery, then a draftsman in Le Corbusier's firm, in a conversation with Francesco Passanti.

[9] Le Corbusier, *Diary VI*, beginning 3 Feb-ruary 1928, FLC.

[10] P. Germon (*Paris-Midi*), letter to Le Cor-busier, 28 September 1928, FLC.

[11] For the aims of this organization, which published a newsletter for distribution in the West, see Olga Kameneva, "VOKS," in *Bol-shaia Sovetskaia Entsiklopediia*, vol. 12 (Moscow: A-Obshch. Sovetskaia Entsiklope-diia, 1928), pp. 670–71.

[12] Le Corbusier, *Diary VII*, beginning Octo-ber 1928, p. 4, FLC, and letter from Karel Teige to Le Corbusier, Prague, 15 October 1928, FLC. This letter deals first and foremost with the question of Le Corbusier's fees for his lectures in Prague.

[13] Marie-Amélie Jeanneret, letter to Le Cor-busier, Corseaux, 10 October 1928, FLC.

On 13 October, an article by David Arkin in *Pravda* announced Le Corbusier's arrival in terms that were both critical and flattering:

To Moscow has come Le Corbusier, the most brilliant representative of today's advanced architectural thought in Europe. The name Le Corbusier has long been synonymous with the struggle for new forms in architecture and the art industries. His ideas have exercised an unquestionable influence on young Soviet architecture and on the advanced circles of our artistic youth.[14]

Arkin went on to describe the manifold register of Le Corbusier's activities and cited the theoretical positions of *Vers une architecture* concerning the "aesthetics of the engineer"; yet he made no attempt to hide his reserve as to Le Corbusier's political convictions and evoked the impossibility of implementing the ideas expressed in *Urbanisme* in a country where private landholding was the rule:

The reflections of Le Corbusier and a host of other advanced architects are balked by these difficulties which are in fact fatal for Western architectural production. Are Le Corbusier's solutions in this domain as revolutionary as those concerning aesthetics? His critical thought, sharp and original, stops short of decisive conclusions. And Le Corbusier poses the question in reverse: he is inclined to grant to architecture the role of a revolutionary factor, and expects from it a "revolution in life-styles" that would make the social revolution superfluous! At this point, the hardy profaner of aesthetic idols of bourgeois society closes himself off in an impasse of aesthetic phrasing.

Le Corbusier is not only a most brilliant theoretician and a polemicist, but also a practicing builder. This combination accounts for his force as a pioneer of new architectural ideas. Although constrained in his building activities by the conditions of "social demand," Le Corbusier has furnished a whole series of interesting examples of the new "artistic and functional" architecture—the geometrical simplicity of its lines and the combination of volumes and surfaces clearly define the spaces of his constructions.

The influence of this "Le Corbusier style" has already crossed the borders of France. Together with the work of the Germans Gropius, Mendelsohn and Taut, the French

40. Le Corbusier in the offices of VOKS, together with Olga Kameneva (on his left) and Andrei Burov (on his right), Moscow, October 1928.

41. Le Corbusier lecturing at the State Academy of Artistic Sciences, Moscow, October 1928.

[14] David Arkin, "K priezdu Le Corbusier," *Pravda,* 13 October 1928. David Efimovich Arkin (1899–1957) was certainly the Soviet critic most open to French architecture and its interpretations. From the outset of the thirties he was to find himself at the heart of the network of international links with Soviet architecture. In 1948 he would be accused of being a propagandist of "cosmopolitanism" and "Americanism" in architecture.

42. Le Corbusier in a group of Soviet architects, Moscow, October 1928; left to right: Le Corbusier, Andrei Burov, Alexander Vesnin.

[15] Ibid.

[16] A. V. Shchusev (MAO), letter to Le Corbusier, Moscow, 11 October 1928, FLC. Some days later, Shchusev dedicated to "M. Le Corbusier, l'éminent architecte français" the issue of the *MAO Yearbook* devoted to projects since 1917: *Ezhegodnik MAO,* Moscow, 5 (1928), FLC.

[17] Le Corbusier, *Diary VII*, p. 36. The notes taken during his stay in Moscow begin at the end of the diary and are frequently disordered, since the numbers in fact correspond to two pages. They have been transcribed here for the first time.

[18] Tugenhold, "*Urbanisme* Le Corbusier," p. 87. On 24 October, the newspaper *Nasha Gazeta,* which on 18 October had announced the arrival of "the talented representative and one of the founding fathers of Constructivism," published a photograph of Le Corbusier and Lunacharsky during the lecture. As for Kameneva, she was replaced at the head of VOKS by M. F. Petrov, an old Bolshevik dilettante.

[19] Some of the drawings that Le Corbusier executed during his lecture are kept in the Shchusev Architectural Museum in Moscow.

[20] Mogues, "La ville future, la conférence faite par l'architecte Le Corbusier au Musée Polytechnique sur l'architecture et l'urbanisme," Moscow, 26 October 1928, FLC. This summary account was written by one of the managers of the electrical company that had approached Le Corbusier.

[21] Ibid.

[22] I. Rakhmanov, "Urbanizm (doklad frantsuskogo arkhitektora Le Corbusier," *Iskusstvo v shkole,* no. 11 (1928): 22–23.

architect Mallet-Stevens and the Dutch professional Oud, these constructions mark the outset of a new epoch for architecture. And they have inspired the work of a whole group of young Soviet architects.[15]

LE CORBUSIER'S MOSCOW AUDIENCES

In his article, Arkin announced for that evening the reading by Le Corbusier of a "report" on "contemporary architecture" under the aegis of OSA and the State Academy for Artistic Sciences, to be held at the academy itself. Two days beforehand, A. V. Shchusev, president of the MAO (Moscow Society of Architects), had written a letter to Le Corbusier expressing his "joy" at his arrival in Moscow and inviting him to give a lecture under the auspices of his society.[16] In the notes that he prepared then and there, in the final pages of his diary, Le Corbusier could scarcely conceal his satisfaction on learning of his influence within Moscow and at the warm welcome that he had received there:

My works have passed the blockade. I am very well known, very popular. My lectures are held before a packed assembly.[17]

A week after his first conference, on 20 October, Le Corbusier gave a second lecture in the great hall of the Polytechnic Museum, the headquarters of the Association for the Promotion of Political and Scientific Knowledge. Entitled "Urbanism," this was the key lecture of Le Corbusier's stay, chaired by Anatoli Lunacharsky and delivered in the presence of Olga Kameneva, president of VOKS and Trotsky's sister. This meeting came off as brilliantly as the first.[18] As confirmed by a Soviet observer, the lecture was devoted essentially to presenting the main lines of Le Corbusier's "contemporary city."[19]

The architect Le Corbusier conducted his audience on a guided tour of the city of the future. The formidable sixty-story skyscrapers have simple, geometrical lines and are made of iron-concrete and glass. They resemble American office buildings and represent the business center.

. . . All the railway stations, subway stations and garages, together with the immense airfield, are to be found in the business quarter. Yet these technical perfections do not have the monotonous appearance of iron constructions: future town planning involves the exploitation of the tiniest spaces with greenery.[20]

As soon as he discovered the Soviet capital, Le Corbusier was tempted by an initial application of his ideas to Moscow:

At the end of his report M. Le Corbusier informed us that Moscow was still an Asian city, which it is necessary to care for by building new pavements and demolishing old houses, yet leaving old monuments in place. It is also important to enlarge our parks and gardens, shift the business center elsewhere and, by surgical elimination of all side streets, lay out new ones beside existing main streets and line them with skyscrapers.[21]

Le Corbusier's lecture was not simply a summary of urban renewal techniques as proposed in the "Plan Voisin"; far from limiting his declarations to the issue of necessary demolitions, he also raised the problem of preserving existing Muscovite monuments, an intervention that appears to have generated some interest:[22]

I have heard that it is intended to demolish the churches of the Kremlin.

The New Spirit . . . is rooted in the greatness of the sages who lived before us. There is a confusion. It is a question of city planning. You in Moscow also have this problem. Why have you not elaborated a great plan for the city of the new world?

43. Le Corbusier's lecture at the Poly-technical Museum, Moscow, 20 October 1928; left to right: Anatoli Lunacharsky, Le Corbusier, Andrei Burov, ?, ?, Nikolai Kolli, ?, Alexander Vesnin.

44, 45, 46. Sketches executed by Le Corbusier during his lecture at the Polytechnical Museum, Moscow, 20 October 1928.

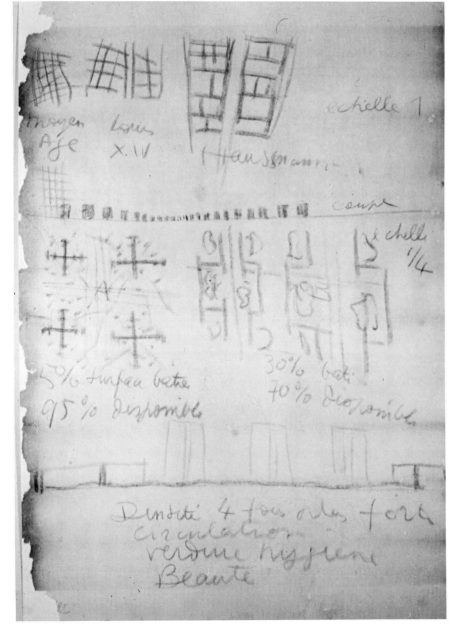

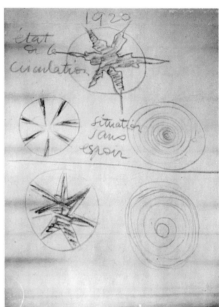

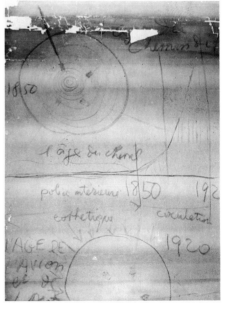

I have been lucky enough to study the Vesnin brothers' plans for the Lenin library. Magnificent, alive, gay, laughing, happy. A truly serene house of work and meditation.

Here's the rub: instead of this modern approach, a classical one is preferred. Moscow is repeating the Palace of Nations adventure in Geneva. And in Geneva, two years on, a solution has yet to be found. The power of the modern idea is such that the academics are simply incapable of keeping step.

There it is: I find Moscow in the same trance as our Western nations.

I say: an epoch that is wholly modern.

It is a criminal mistake to resuscitate things of the past, for the result is not living organisms but papier mâché ghosts.

But it is essential to preserve the testimony of works that in their time were "contemporary," that they might serve as a lesson and provoke admiration among people of quality.[23]

This sums up Le Corbusier's unvarying attitude toward the architectural past: he condemns all servile reproductions of historical testimony, yet abhors their destruction.

STUNNING DISCOVERIES

As well as giving his public lectures, Le Corbusier made visits both within and outside the city. Above all he became absorbed with a small team of "unpaid" helpers, including "highly competent, technically gifted architects," in finalizing his project "in a large office at Centrosoyuz." In this way he became acquainted with the atmosphere of Moscow company life:

I visited the Centrosoyuz warehouses, a veritable anthill where everyone works indefatigably. In the entrance halls, posters interesting for their multiple imagery. The fight against alcohol, the fight against the church = ignorance and capital. Every morning the "journal" of the Institute is posted up, typewritten, with watercolors, ideas and suggestions, propositions to the bosses, discussions regarding the steps to be taken.[24]

Le Corbusier was acutely interested in urban life and its rhythms and cadences: one of the most significant fields of observation for him was the organization and duration of work. He applauded the "tightly organized, active, clean" work that he encountered at the "cinema union" (*centrale du cinéma*) and the "lunchtime buffet" for the purposes of continuity of work, and showed interest in the way free time was organized:

The working day is over at 3:30 P.M., after which Soviet workers or employees meet together in premises reserved for them or in clubs. The bosses themselves decide and discuss in peace and quiet.[25]

The program of workers' clubs, a keystone of the "cultural revolution" whose implementation dated from the outset of the 1920s, was one of the manifestations of Soviet sociocultural policy that most astonished Le Corbusier:

The consequence of the day ending at 3:30 P.M. is the creation of clubs.

Initially, the clubs were set up with the idea of night school in mind.

. . . There are no cafés in Moscow. Impossible to get a drink. The people take things seriously. They appear to know how to organize things.

And in clubs! The great idea.

. . . 1 club = cinema, theater (with a covered and open-air stage), gymnasium, library, common room! These are typical.[26]

[23] Le Corbusier (untitled) notes for the lecture of 20 October 1928, FLC. (Translator's note: the last phrase of this extract translates "ceux qui sont bien nés," literally, "those well-born"; yet it seems scarcely credible that Le Corbusier would use such a phrase before a Marxist-Leninist audience.)

[24] Le Corbusier, *Diary VII*, p. 46.

[25] Ibid., p. 38.

[26] Ibid., pp. 36–37.

47. Le Corbusier in a group of Soviet architects, Moscow, October 1928; left to right: Andrei Burov, Le Corbusier, Nikolai Sobolev, Alexander Vesnin, Georgi Golts.

48. Le Corbusier in a group of Soviet architects, Moscow, October 1928; left to right: Andrei Burov, Le Corbusier, Georgi Golts, Nikolai Kolli.

He was also happy—following his misadventures in Geneva—to find the Centrosoyuz management well disposed toward him and open to new ideas in their discussions of the project. Given the fact of such stimulating clients, Le Corbusier became particularly interested in the structure of the architectural profession and its organization into "cooperative establishments," and in the fact that the "best architects have independent status and negotiated contracts by mutual agreement in Minsk, Batum or Nizhny-Novgorod"; he was also attentive to the procedures used in architectural competitions, which were standard practice:

At any moment there are competitions for factories, institutes, clubs.
   . . . The state delegates the task of organizing the competitions and of nominating the juries to the associations themselves (I have myself attended a meeting in which, on the proposition of the committee, individual members were voted on by a show of hands. The assembly itself can also make their own propositions).[27]

Given such democratic procedures, the architects themselves had to work under conditions of considerable urgency—faced with "gigantic tasks," they were "constantly pressed for time." Le Corbusier was struck by the fact that they seemed nonetheless able to work together:

The architects collaborate constantly (unlike us). Individual quality?? Certainly. But of another, more collective nature, for there is already a unified tendency that brings all the young practitioners together, and even obliges the older ones to cooperate.[28]

The proliferation of competing organizations in favor of the new architecture could hardly mask the continuing presence of conservative elements, who nonetheless knew how to manipulate the jargon of the day. Le Corbusier noted that "the academy has followed suit, and copies the 'modern' style without understanding it," and that "there are too many false moderns."[29]

He held out high hopes for the industrialization of a nation that "is everywhere equipped with model factories and clubs, and armed with (pure) Taylorism," and for the constant presence of organized teaching programs. Wherever he went he was struck by the rise of the Rabfak, or workers' faculties. He noted that "teaching, and more teaching, is the constant preoccupation: laboratories, schools, clubs," and that "there is a classroom in every factory."[30] In the artistic disciplines, the Vkhutein, which had replaced the revolutionary Vkhutemas, was now open to large numbers of pupils who had not had secondary education. Le Corbusier was introduced to this new generation in the company of Alexander Vesnin and Dean Novitsky, who viewed him as "the greatest architect-thinker in Europe":[31]

The teaching at the Higher School of Architecture is an extraordinary demonstration of the modern credo. Here a new world is being rebuilt, constructed like the mystique that gives rise to a pure technology.
   Constructivism is a banner that flaps well in the wind.
   The packed crowd of students, always poorly dressed. One is crushed, one is stifled. Alexander Vesnin smiles eternally.[32]

The ease with which the young architects, who reflected "the same mentality as that of the 19th-century iron age," discovered "pure, extraordinary solutions" and obtained commissions enabling them to express new ideas was the object of Le Corbusier's astonishment, if not of a certain amount of jealousy:

Office buildings are being built in the very latest modern styles. Categorical formulas, occasional good taste.

[27] Ibid., p. 39.
[28] Ibid., p. 40.
[29] Ibid., p. 35.
[30] Ibid., p. 38.
[31] Pavel Novitsky, dedication to Le Corbusier in the anthology *Raboty arkhitekturnogo fakulteta Vkhutemasa* (Moscow: Vkhutemas, 1927), copy preserved at the Fondation Le Corbusier.
[32] Le Corbusier, *Diary VII*, p. 37.

49. Le Corbusier, sketch of the Kremlin wall, the Nikolskaia Tower, and the Red Square, Moscow, October 1928.

50. Le Corbusier, with Sergei Eisenstein (center) and Andrei Burov (right), Moscow, October 1928 (Sergei Eisenstein Archive, Moscow).

. . . Everywhere they build clubs in the most modern styles, factories ditto, farms, hydraulic plants.

They build enormous commissions at thirty.

EISENSTEIN AND LE CORBUSIER'S "NEW CLIENTS"

Although he associated with Vesnin, Ginzburg, and a few other architectural celebrities, Le Corbusier also spent time with students and young practitioners. Together with Sergei Kozhin, a former assistant to Ivan Zholtovsky who was helping with modifications to the Centrosoyuz project, he visited a village sixty-five kilometers from the capital, where he discovered the "constructive soundness" of the izbas built, as he hastened to note, "on *pilotis.*"[33] Above all, he was accompanied everywhere by Andrei Burov, one of Alexandr Vesnin's former pupils at the Vkhutemas whose architectural designs contained large numbers of elements borrowed from Le Corbusier's own work. Dressed like Le Corbusier's model, the young Soviet architect is invariably to be found in the foreground of the photographs of the trip—so much so that his colleagues nicknamed him "Burov–Le Corbusier."

Yet Burov was not just a "groupie"; he also introduced Le Corbusier to Sergei Eisenstein, for whom he had produced some set designs for a film shot in the fall of 1928: *The General Line*. The encounter with Eisenstein and his films was a major event for Le Corbusier, who did not hesitate to rechristen the film *The Straight Line* in his notes. As a mark of his sympathy for the Soviet film director, he gave him a copy of *L'art décoratif d'aujourd'hui*, which contained the following dedication:

[33] The photographs taken in the course of this excursion are to be found in Starr, "Le Corbusier and the USSR," pp. 122–37.

To M. Eisenstein this dedication after *Potemkin* and *The Straight Line*. I seem to think as M. Eisenstein does when he makes films. Spirit of truth, a coat of whitewash, two chapters that express the same conviction. With my deepest sympathy and highest regard.[34]

On 16 October, Le Corbusier attended a private showing, organized by VOKS on the architect's request, of *The Battleship Potemkin*. He also saw four reels of a film in progress on the question of industrialization and agriculture—a film that would be modified on several occasions before being authorized for general viewing under the title *Old and New*. The weekly *Sovetsky Ekran* subsequently reported Le Corbusier's reactions to these early takes:

He was especially interested in the part devoted to propaganda for the architecture of "machines for living" (as Le Corbusier himself has it) which he originated. There is a *sovkhoz* specially designed for *The General Line* by the architect Burov, one of Le Corbusier's most ardent followers. Le Corbusier was greatly satisfied with the architectural form given to the *sovkhoz*, and confessed himself quite astonished to discover the existence in our country of a radically different application of Western architectural forms and principles.[35]

In the only interview that Le Corbusier gave during his stay in Moscow, he expanded on his dedication and evoked the common ground between his own work and that of Eisenstein:

Architecture and the cinema are the only two arts of our time. In my own work I seem to think as Eisenstein does in his films. His work is shot through with the sense of truth, and bears witness to the truth alone. In their ideas, his films resemble closely what I am striving to do in my own work.

I should like to take this opportunity to express all my admiration for Eisenstein's principle of freeing events from all that is uncharacteristic or insignificant. This insistence on essentials not only raises his work above mere narrative, but also raises the everyday events that escape our superficial attention (be it running milk, women scything, or piglets) to the level of monumental images. For instance, the procession of *The General Line*, with its "dynamic porticoes" of the advancing icons and the sculptural quality of its figures, can only be compared with the sharpness of Donatello's characteristic figures.

As for Burov's "sovkhoz," whose tall cylinders, recalling the grain elevators in Buffalo, combine with ribbon windows and the *pilotis* of an imaginary Corbusian dwelling, he invoked the specter of a new clientele:

In this society for workers and farm laborers, the buildings that we habitually see in the West, such as suburban villas and town houses, are built with the practical needs of agriculture in mind. It is infinitely more agreeable to view splendid herds of cattle and Yorkshire pigs than a bourgeois clientele!

In the notes that he wrote on his return to Paris, Le Corbusier again referred to his impressions on seeing the film:

Armed with the *Almanach d'architecture moderne* (Paris, Crès), Eisenstein sought out an architect capable of building reinforced concrete constructions that attest to the New Spirit. And he had a model farm built near the Caucasus, the setting for his film: cows, pigs, and horses circulate in the middle of the scientific instruments of a pasteurization laboratory; the farm's personnel, both men and women, are dressed in white tunics like the staff of a clinic. The *muzhik* must certainly be dumbfounded.[36]

Still, the affinities between Le Corbusier's theory of the "lyricism" of the

51. Andrei Burov, Model Sovkhoz, stage set for Sergei Eisenstein's film *The General Line*, 1926–1927.

52. Andrei Burov, Model Sovkhoz, stage set for Sergei Eisenstein's film *The General Line*, 1926–1927 (with cattle).

[34] Le Corbusier, dedication in *L'art décoratif d'aujourd'hui* Moscow (25 October 1928), copy in the Eisenstein archives, Moscow. Eisenstein also owned a copy of *Kommende Baukunst*, the 1926 German edition of *Vers une architecture*.
[35] V. S. (Vladimir Solev), "Novaia klientura arkhitektora Le Corbusier," *Sovetsky Ekran*, no. 46 (13 November 1928): 5. The version cited here is the original manuscript, extracts of which are given in Khazanova, "Rabota Arkhitektora A. Burova v Kino," *Voprosy sovetskogo izobrazitelnogo iskusstva i arkhitektury*, pp. 466–71.
[36] Le Corbusier, "L'architecture à Moscou," *L'Intransigeant*, Paris (24 and 31 December 1928). Quotation from the FLC manuscript, p. 5.

machine and Eisenstein's "pathos of the machine" remained less explicit than latent in the course of this first contact.

THE EYE OF THE ARCHITECT

Despite Le Corbusier's interest in the forms and colors of the city—for example, the "fantastic, artificial green" of the "copper roofs"—he took away few graphic impressions from his first trip to Moscow, for "it is forbidden to draw in Moscow: puerility." He waited in vain for permission to draw in the streets, a restriction doubtless imposed for military reasons:

As in Geneva, committees are the home ground of the authorities. The bureaucracy rules. I waited three weeks for permission to draw, and still it didn't come! Despite the fact that highly placed individuals, including a people's commissar, intervened on my behalf. I began to feel like a conspirator.[37]

In fact, a few sketches drawn literally under his overcoat give evidence of his having seen the Kremlin, Red Square, and of the interest that he showed in an early example of postrevolutionary architecture, Sergei Chernyshev's new Institute of Marxism-Leninism, built on the Tverskaia street in 1926. In order to draw this building he hid in the doorway of the Moscow Soviet headquarters across the street. As he was forbidden to sketch the city, he filled his notebooks with purist still lifes.[38] In the margins, his observations on Moscow—"the old carcass of an Asiatic village"—compare well with those made by Walter Benjamin, who had visited Moscow from early December 1926 till the end of January 1927, and for whom the Soviet capital was at once "a summer vacation colony" and "an improvised metropolis that has fallen into place overnight":

The village character of Moscow suddenly leaps out at you undisguisedly, evidently, unambiguously in the streets of its suburbs. There is probably no other city whose gigantic open spaces have such an amorphous, rural quality, as if their expanses were always being dissolved by bad weather, thawing snow, or rain.[39]

For Benjamin, "nowhere does Moscow really look like the city it is, rather it more resembles the outskirts of itself." Russia's artistic past lived on in several salient aspects of this "embryo of a new world" as Le Corbusier discovered it in 1928. Like Walter Benjamin and Alfred H. Barr, Le Corbusier retraced the history of Russian art in the activities of the avant-garde.[40] His second "Journey to the East" thus furnished the occasion for a sort of inner return to the scene of the first, of which he now heard echoes:

I hear a Turkish concert just as I heard one given by the Sultan's dervishes 20 years ago—marvel of the invisible thread.

But above all, it was the places and paintings that reminded him of Turkey and Italy. At first he found "a clue I fumbled for in the dark . . . Venice, St. Mark's Square, Campanile, Fond. dei Turchi." Later, having frequented the museums and visited the studio where Igor Grabar restored ancient icons, his comparisons would embrace broader horizons:

An International Style, Byzantine throughout Europe and Asia. Giotto was not alone, for at the same time in Moscow, Kiev or Yaroslavl, they produced pure masterpieces. The Russian school is nobler (Greek painted vases, 3rd period). Italian screen paintings are the same as the prestigious icons of the Kremlin.[41]

He also viewed the icons as bearing a direct relationship to ancient Greece:

[37] Le Corbusier, *Diary VII*, p. 33.

[38] See for example drawing no. 120, FLC, dated Moscow, October 1928.

[39] Walter Benjamin, *Moskauer Tagebuch* (Frankfurt: Suhrkamp, 1980); English translation: "*Moscow Diary,*" *October* 35 (Winter 1985): 112 (preface by Gershom Scholem, translated by Richard Sieburth, edited by Gary Smith).

[40] Barr, "Russian Diary," p. 13.

[41] Le Corbusier, *Diary VII*, p. 38. Le Corbusier subsequently wrote to Grabar of how happy he would be "to help Europe to get to know his work": Le Corbusier, letter to Igor Grabar, Moscow, 21 October 1928; quoted by Kokkinaki, "Le Corbusier i Sovetskaia Rossia," p. 100.

53. Le Corbusier, sketch of Ivan the Great's tower and the Archangel Mikhail cathedral in the Kremlin, Moscow, October 1928.

54. Le Corbusier, sketch of the Marxism-Leninism Institute and of the monument to the Revolution on Sovetskaia Square, as seen from the entrance of the Mossovet, Moscow, October 1928.

55. Sovetskaia square with the Marxism-Leninism Institute, built by Sergei Chernyshev (1926), and the monument to the Revolution built by Dmitri Osipov and Nikolai Andreev (1918), Moscow, photograph taken in 1928.

56. Osip Bove's Triumphal Arch at
Tver Gate, commemorating the victory
of 1812 over Napoleon (1827–1834),
Moscow; postcard, before 1914.

57. Le Corbusier, pencil-and-ink
sketch of Osip Bove's Triumphal Arch
with the cupolas of the Old Believers' cathedral, as seen from the sidewalk of the
Bielorussian Station, Moscow, October
1928.

[42] Le Corbusier, *Diary VII*, p. 41.

Russian art has its roots in Byzantium, with its antique painted vases and frescoes. The
impression of Greek antiquity is sharper in Russian icons of the 12th century than in
the decadent paintings of Pompeii.[42]

58. Miasnitskaia Street at the corner of the main post office, Moscow; photograph taken in 1928.

In the "monastic quiet" of the Shchukin and Morozov museums, which housed the city's Western art collections and which were "kept with rare good taste by M. Ternovets, who has inherited the task from their former owners," Le Corbusier noted that "there are few such places of tranquillity in the world."[43] On the occasion of his visit to the Kremlin, the absence of visitors surprised him:

For the Kremlin visit, Lunarcharsky intervened. . . . Meticulous cleanliness. View of the churches containing very special icons. The door sealed shut.

A woman is sent for to break the seals. Blue sky.

Delightful urbanism. Charming Turko-Italian style. Everywhere the frescoes and icons are being cleaned (but no retouching).

Veritable revelations. Thanks to Lunarcharsky. I say the Soviets show Russia her art, unlike the tsars whose restorations were scandalous, black allowed to blacken till nothing was seen, absolute blackness (candles, processions). The soldier is delighted (we translate for him). At the Kremlin museum, weaponry, gold and silverware, sparkling cleanliness. Exhibition layout remarkable. Yet no one has come here for the past seven years.[44]

A "MYTH" IS DISCOVERED

Although he appreciated the "dignified, unhurried, efficient, careful, serious" atmosphere of the meeting at which he presented his Centrosoyuz project, and noted the refreshing absence of certain traits characteristic of French public administration (noting for example that there were no "pen pushers" in the offices of the Mossovet), Le Corbusier nonetheless felt the presence of Soviet bureaucracy. The company meetings and the show of democracy left him cold when it came to discussing his projects. He was unhappy about having to submit his project to the "lower" ranks of the Centrosoyuz personnel, especially since they "muttered objections to the *pilotis*, saying, 'we'll be toppled over by the wind!'" He was, moreover, shaken by his friends' "faith" in and passion for their work, as witness the fact that "the term *rabota* (labor) is always present in Muscovite conversation":

[43] Boris Ternovets (1884–1941) was director of the Museum of New Western Art. For the activities of the museum in general, see Lilia Aleshina and Nina Yavorskaia, eds., *B. N. Ternovets pisma dneviki stati* (Moscow: Sovetsky Khudozhnik, 1977); Lilia Aleshina and Nina Yavorskaia, *Iz istorii khudozhestvennoi zhizni SSSR, internatsionalnie sviazi v oblasti izobrazitelnogo iskusstva* (Moscow: Iskusstvo, 1987); Nina Yavorskaia, *Iz istorii sovetskogo iskusstvoznania* (Moscow: Sovetsky Khudozhnik, 1987).

[44] Le Corbusier, *Diary VII*, p. 40.

Nothing can be explained without the presence of faith, of a myth. Faith in the "great experiment."

Le Corbusier well appreciated the social cost of this "experiment," especially in terms of manufactured goods, regarding which he noted that "the shop windows are empty, for there is nothing to sell except food," or of living conditions in shared accommodation with its "communal kitchens":

The sharing of apartments. No one was thrown out; instead, new inhabitants were allotted to every room.

No furnishings are stolen or confiscated, but milk and eggs are bought with doors, curtains, etc., of which the peasants are especially fond.[45]

Such objects were certainly attractive to the "all-powerful peasant," who took away "whatever struck his fancy" in an "exchange that perhaps improves the household and poisons the *izba*." Yet Le Corbusier approved the contempt for material conditions that he perceived all around him, and noted that "enormous faith is required to compensate for the suppression of the desire for money":

The "thirst for gold" has been quenched: 200 roubles for party members; 400, 500 for specialists.

And massive taxes for all.

Thus the demon has been crushed.[46]

But if "the blockade galvanizes, creates a state of mind," Le Corbusier was well aware of the limits of asceticism and wondered "if the human carcass will respond":

The Diogenic state of mind, indeed! For the fanatics of shelter.

The system lacks a stimulus, a dynamic factor, this for the masses, who are in no way Diogenic. Lethargy is present.

Lenin had intended to abolish money: payments in kind were to be handed out, shoes, clothes, housing, etc. . . . ! 1921. And then the same Lenin reintroduced the monetary system, the only means of exchange.[47]

As soon as he arrived in Moscow, Le Corbusier noted that "clothing is threadbare" and that "there's money to be made in the clothing business," a subject to which he returned on several occasions. Doubtless as his personal contribution to the fight against "the clothing crisis," he sold his "overcoat (raincoat) to Burov for 300 rubles."

But apart from his intense interest in both everyday affairs and architectural production, Le Corbusier seems to have paid scant attention to the political intrigues of the day, despite the defeat of the opposition to Stalin, the exclusion of Trotsky and Zinoviev from the party, and the beginnings of the repression of their partisans. Olga Kameneva, who had welcomed Le Corbusier in the name of VOKS, would be relieved of her duties in the following year. Le Corbusier's indifference to Soviet politics stands in stark contrast with the attitude of most visitors; but the glowing description that he wrote to his mother in a letter announcing that he had obtained the Centrosoyuz project left her incredulous, such was the contradiction with her own vision of the "horrors" of Bolshevism:

I was positively shaken on reading your letter from Moscow. In all the newspapers here, Russia has invariably been depicted as quite devoid of values, its morals deplorable, the family swept away, and above all the persecution of the intellectuals; children on the streets; thus it is that I have read and reread your epistle, in which you give a completely different picture with seeming impartiality.

45 Ibid., p. 41.
46 Ibid., p. 34.
47 Ibid., p. 33.

59. Boris Velikovsky, Gostorg building, Miasnitskaia Street, Moscow, 1925–1927; photograph taken in 1928. Le Corbusier saw in it an "ideal vertical beehive."

. . . You have been understood and accepted; I share the joy you must feel at having your plans rewarded. Well done! Educated Russians have always given the impression of strong-headedness and a lively intelligence. They have always revolted (nihilism) against autocratic régimes which seemed monstrous to them. But the Bolshevik leaders are generally Jews, of relatively low extraction, and their pogroms have rendered them odious. What is one to believe?[48]

To the astonishment of his mother, Charles-Edouard reflected on the justifications for the revolution, whose excesses he seemed to forgive in the notes that he wrote on the train home—notes inspired by the reading of a novel by

[48] Marie-Amélie Jeanneret, letter to Le Corbusier, Corseaux, 28 October 1928, FLC.

Victor Margueritte, *Prostituée*, which he had found in the International Bookshop in Moscow:

Our world is neat and well ordered, but its sharp contours throw dark shadows. And in these shadows? Only Christ and the Salvation Army take a look. Is there something awry?

Looked at from this angle, one has to admit that revolt, revolution is justified.

And is our own social system not as definitive as all that?

I am confused, worried, saddened, moved at the fact that the people suffer because it has had an idea.[49]

In the train, after having been seen off by Alexander Vesnin and one of his brothers, Ginzburg, Burov, Kolli, and Nakhman, Le Corbusier decided to broaden his knowledge by reading the analyses of the USSR in the bulletin of Le Redressement Français.[50] He also sketched, in the margins of a map of the world, a series of communicating vessels to illustrate the manner in which East and West might profitably conjugate their resources. One system (Europe), in which "the movement of capital" and "the force of action" combines with "indifference to the hierarchy of production," and another (Russia), in which the "ordering of production in terms of motivated hierarchy and equity" combines with "the absence of a spirit of quality, that is to say, of the higher . . . aim."[51]

LE CORBUSIER THE REPORTER

On his return from Moscow, equipped with few if any sketches and a jumble of relatively disorganized notes, Le Corbusier wrote a text on "Architecture in Moscow" from which he excised his most acid reflections on Soviet society. *Paris-Midi*, however, was apparently unsatisfied with Le Corbusier's "turn of phrase": Germon had wanted "color and picturesque above all, a sort of physiognomy," whereas Le Corbusier had concentrated on a reading of the Russian architectural scene.[52] In the end the article was first published in *L'Intransigeant*; some months later, through the good offices of Sigfried Giedion, it appeared in German in the *Neue Zürcher Zeitung*.[53]

In this article, a spirited rewriting of his travel notes, Le Corbusier gives an enthusiastic account of "what one feels stirring about one in Moscow (whether this sensation be artificial or deeply motivated) as the precursors of a new world."[54] He perceives a twofold lesson to be learned from this. First, in a city "abounding with projects of the boldest sort," he had encountered the "ardent, passionate, determined, numerous cohorts" of the constructivists and had at once realized the gulf that separated them from the German functionalists. Second, he had been able to take the measure of an impressive building effort on a scale justifying the greatest hopes for commissions:

This country builds, and needs to build. Everywhere, from one end of the country to the other, but principally in Moscow and Leningrad, a whole nation stands in need of amenities. Thus there can be no question of building palaces to the greater glory of an aristocracy that has disappeared, but rather the buildings required for the day-to-day running of the country: factories, workshops, dams, then clubs (places for meetings, discussions and study), and finally, rented accommodation required in order to resolve finally the acute housing crisis, whether in Moscow or elsewhere. To build in Russia is an immense undertaking, for the frontiers of the nation defy the imagination.[55]

[49] Le Corbusier, *Diary VII*, p. 31.

[50] Le Redressement Français was a group of industrialists concerned with the rationalization of French society; its spiritual guide, Ernest Mercier, visited the USSR in 1936 and returned a determined advocate of the Franco-Russian alliance against Nazi Germany. See Ernest Mercier, *URSS, réflexions* (Paris: Centre Polytechnicien d'Etudes Economiques, 1936).

[51] Notes and sketches in the margin of a "Mirovaia Karta" (map of the world) priced thirty kopecks, Moscow, Gosizdat, 1928, FLC.

[52] Germon, letter to Le Corbusier.

[53] Le Corbusier, "Die Baukunst in Moskau," *Neue Zürcher Zeitung*, Zurich (9–10 April 1928). This German translation was again published in the *Berliner Tageblatt* (15 June 1929), and cited in *Das neue Russland* (June 1929): 7.

[54] Le Corbusier, "L'architecture à Moscou," typewritten manuscript, p. 4, FLC.

[55] Ibid., p. 2.

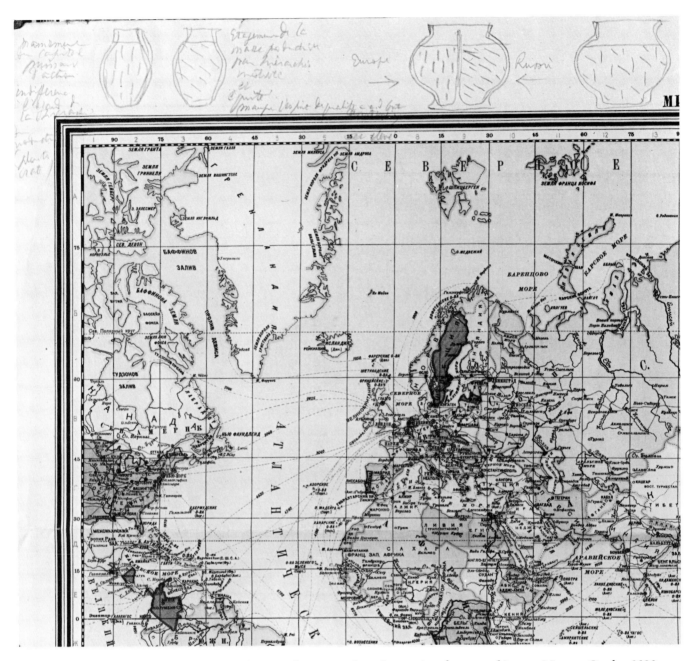

60. Le Corbusier, the fusion of Europe and Russia; drawing made in the margins of a geographic map, Moscow, October 1928.

Yet despite his enthusiasm, Le Corbusier failed to respond to an invitation from Francis Jourdain, an active member of "The Friends of the Soviet Union," to publish an account of his travels in the association's newssheet, *L'Appel des Soviets*:

It appears that you will be building over there? They stand in great need of you. The effects and repercussions of your work will doubtless be considerable in this new country where everything has to be built up from scratch, a nation that has its eyes riveted on a future that is the future.

May I promise my comrades a few lines from you (a letter or an article)? Or would you agree to receive an interviewer? We should be extremely proud and happy to record your kind words in favor of a great but maligned nation which has the whole world against it. This quite apart from political considerations, naturally, since our association is independent of all parties.

. . . Modern Russian—or specifically Soviet—architecture does not exist—as yet. But that the USSR is a magnificent sphere of activity for the architects (owing to the problems posed, the presence of general goodwill, the absence of routine, and even of tradition, by which I mean the possibility of calling everything to account, "to start again on a fresh basis")—I should be happy for a man like you to say this.[56]

THE LURE OF NEW COMMISSIONS

[56] Francis Jourdain, letter to Le Corbusier, Paris, 26 November 1928, FLC. Jourdain had visited Moscow in 1927, and had furnished an account of his stay in *Les dents sans couteau*; he was a contributor to *L'appel des Soviets,* "a review for the illustration and defense of Soviet Russia," founded in 1928. For the life and work of Francis Jourdain, see Arlette Barré-Despond and Susanne Tise, *Jourdain (Frantz 1847–1935, Francis 1876–1958, Frantz-Philippe 1906)* (Paris: Editions du Regard, 1988), pp. 211–344.

[57] Le Corbusier, *Diary VII*, p. 33.

In this "new country" it seemed likely that, in addition to the finalization of his second Centrosoyuz project, Le Corbusier would find other commissions. When called on to carry out studies for a new power station at Bobriki, he again came up against the problem of negotiating projects in open general meetings:

They are to build the largest plant in the world. I was asked to design the buildings. But first it was felt useful to be introduced to the mass of engineers. A meeting was improvised for the next day, in front of the plant. There were a hundred engineers present, women and men. The president declared, "Now the link has been made between the engineer and the architect." But alas, what is the usual case? The engineer minds the architect's business.[57]

61. A. Kuznetsov with Gennadi and Vladimir Movchan, Anatoli Fisenko, Ivan Nikolaev, et al., Electrotechnical Institute, Moscow, 1927; photograph taken in 1928. Le Corbusier notes *a propos* this building: "Here, in the purest theory, is the modern world reshaped."

These real or potential commissions reveal that, barely a year after his failure to secure the League of Nations project, Le Corbusier was at last being taken seriously as an expert on architectural and city-planning issues, a role he had adopted ever since his first talk on "urbanism" at Strasburg in 1923.[58] Le Corbusier's initial satisfaction at this would strongly determine his subsequent relations with Moscow; but for the moment, he could not resist the temptation to offer a preliminary study of Moscow's urban form, doubtless with a view to an as yet somewhat vague future intervention on a grander scale:

The plan for Moscow (here, too!) refers directly to the age of the horse. . . . They say for instance, that the Sadovaia boulevard is lined with large numbers of trees and it might be transformed into a broad thoroughfare; we'll widen the streets leading out toward Leningrad and Yaroslavl. What have Leningrad and Yaroslavl to do with it? We'll have the subway under the Sadovaia boulevard; circular road, circular subway!!![59]

Three short weeks had thus been enough for the "surgeon of the contemporary city" to envisage large-scale interventions in a city whose atmosphere he had barely—and yet how avidly!—taken in.

[58] Le Corbusier, "Le centre des grandes villes," in Société Française des Urbanistes, *Où en est l'urbanisme en France et à l'étranger (Strasbourg 1923)* (Paris: Eyrolles, 1923), pp. 247–57.
[59] Le Corbusier, *Diary VII*, p. 32.

CHAPTER
4

The Centrosoyuz Adventure

THE BUILDING for which Le Corbusier was to win the commission in October 1928 quickly became the focus for intellectual and professional debate. Only a few months after the battle triggered by the rejection of his project for the League of Nations had died down, Le Corbusier could at last demonstrate the validity of his ideas with the execution of a large-scale program. The most striking evidence of the great hopes that Le Corbusier placed in the Centrosoyuz project is doubtless to be found in the pages of the *Œuvre complète* published in 1930, where his stated aim is "to constitute in Moscow a veritable demonstration of contemporary architecture, based on the lessons of modern science."[1]

THE COOPERATIVES AND THE NEP

The occasion for this "demonstration" was linked to the role of the cooperatives—of which Centrosoyuz or Central Union of Consumer Cooperatives was a key element—in the construction of Soviet society.[2] The cooperative movement first made its appearance in Russia in the 1860s—that is, only twenty years after the founding of the Rochdale Equitable Pioneers Society—and had undergone rapid growth, culminating in the creation in 1898 of the MSPO or Moscow Union of Consumer Cooperatives, of which Centrosoyuz was the direct descendant.

Essentially a rural phenomenon before 1914, the cooperative movement was shot through with conflict between Menshevik and Bolshevik factions within the Social-Democratic party. At the outset of 1917, it numbered twenty-four million members and sixty-three thousand different societies. These were integrated into the state apparatus during the period of War Communism, but implementation of the New Economic Policy (NEP) and Lenin's repeated insistence resulted in a large degree of autonomy for these societies and the freedom to pursue their development.[3] The NEP-inspired expansion of the cooperatives was in no way limited to internal trade, and they began to play a key role in Soviet export activities.[4]

The 1920s were marked by keen competition between the declining private sector and the cooperative system. For the period 1920–1923, retail trade still accounted for almost 80 percent of the circulation of goods. This figure dropped to 44 percent for 1925–1926 and to 24 percent for 1927–1928, whereas the cooperatives raised their share in the market from 33 to 54 percent over the same period.[5] In 1932, when the fields were collectivized and private-sector trade was abolished, the cooperatives' share in the market started to dwindle, at least in the cities, and state-run stores began to dominate the retail sector—in 1935 they represented 62 percent of the total as against 38 percent for the cooperatives. Building of Centrosoyuz's new headquarters thus began shortly before it reached the high point of its power and influence in Russia.[6]

The activities controlled and initiated by the Soviet Centrosoyuz after 1926, under the direction of its newly appointed president Isidor Liubimov, were not restricted to retail trade and included cooperative housing and finance, both well developed by the end of the decade.[7] The financial resources of the cooperative system were a mark of its economic importance and resulted in the implementation of an active architectural program of rural and urban shopping and warehousing facilities. From 1926–1927, Centrosoyuz integrated a small group of architects and engineers under the leadership of Pavel Nakhman.[8]

62. Headquarters of the Moscow region's Union of Cooperatives, photograph taken in 1928.

[1] Willi Boesiger and Oscar Stonorov, eds., *Le Corbusier et Pierre Jeanneret, Œuvre complète 1910–1929* (Zurich: Girsberger, 1930), p. 206.

[2] For a full description of Centrosoyuz, see G. Litvak, "Centrosoyuz," *Malaia Sovetskaia Entsiklopediia*, vol. 9 (Moscow: OGIZ, 1931), pp. 675–77.

[3] Alexandra S. Merkulova, *Istoriia potrebitelskoi kooperatsii* (Moscow: Ekonomika, 1970).

[4] *Allrussischer Zentralverband der Konsumgenossenschaften* (Berlin: Verlag Centrosoyuz, 1923).

[5] Ilya Vatenberg, *Le mouvement coopératif en URSS* (Paris: Editions Sociales, 1947), p. 12. See also the amusing illustrated statistics published in *Potrebitelskaia Kooperatsiia SSSR, Albom diagramm* (Moscow: Izd. Centrosoyuza, 1928).

[6] *Socialist Construction in the USSR, Statistical Abstract* (Moscow: Soyuzgouchet, 1936), pp. 408–9.

[7] Born in 1882 of lowly peasant extraction, Isidor Evstingeevich Liubimov began to militate in Jaroslavl and Kostroma from 1902. A "professional revolutionary" and delegate at the 1907 congress held in London, he shouldered increasing responsibilities in the Bolshevik group. After 1917 he was president of the Minsk Soviet, fought the civil war, and became assistant president of the Moscow Soviet in 1924. Appointed president of Centrosoyuz in 1926, Liubimov became assistant to the peoples' commissar for trade Anastasi Mikoian and trade delegate at Berlin in 1930–1931 and peoples' commissar for light industry in 1932. He disappeared in the purges of 1937. I. E. Liubimov, *Malaia Sovetskaia Entsiklopediia* vol. 4 (Moscow: A/O Sovetskaia Entsiklopediia, 1929), pp. 122–25.

[8] N. V. Markovnikov, "Konkurs Centrosoyuza v MAO," *Stroitelnaia Promyshlennost* 6, no. 2 (February 1928): 122–25. For an example of the designs by the in-house technicians, see: "Kholodilnik Centrosoyuza," *Stroitelstvo Moskvy* 4, no. 12 (December 1927): 7–9.

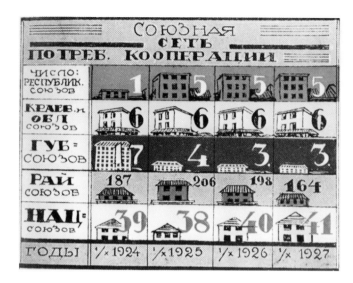

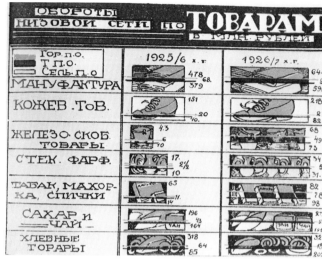

63. The development of the Consumer Cooperatives' network in the USSR, 1924 to 1927; in *Potrebitelskaia Kooperatsiia SSSR, Albom diagramm* (Moscow, 1928).

64. The revenue of the Consumer Cooperatives' network in the USSR by types of goods, 1925 to 1927; in *Potrebitelskaia Kooperatsiia SSSR, Albom diagramm* (Moscow, 1928).

THE FIRST CENTROSOYUZ COMPETITION

Early in 1926 the Mossovet allocated to Centrosoyuz, whose headquarters were then located in the Bolshoi Cherkassky Pereulok, a plot of land stretching from 35 to 43 Miasnitskaia Street (a busy radial link between the city center and the railway stations to the northeast) for the purpose of constructing "an extremely large office building" there.[9] The street already contained the new Central Post Office by Oscar Munts and the Vesnin brothers, and the Gostorg, a glass and reinforced concrete edifice built by Boris Velikovsky and his team in 1925–1927.

The Society of Civil Engineers was given the responsibility of organizing a competition for the development of the twelve thousand square-meter site, whose irregular contours were bounded by the existing Miasnitskaia together with two thoroughfares that had been envisaged in the plan for "Greater Moscow": a new Miasnitskaia running parallel with the old, and an arterial link perpendicular to these two radial axes.[10]

Since 1923–1924 the construction of office buildings for the new industrial and commercial institutions created by the NEP had been a major vector for the new architecture in Moscow. But although the competition for ARKOS (the Anglo-Russian Trading Society) attracted entries from the Vesnins and Vladimir Krinsky, and the *Leningradskaia Pravda* competition was marked by projects by Melnikov, Golosov, and the Vesnins, in neither case was the program realized. Effective constructions, such as the Gostorg building overlooking the Centrosoyuz site, which Le Corbusier described as "an ideal vertical beehive,"[11] were not always built as a result of competitions. Even with competitions, procedures were sometimes so muddled that by 1926 they had become the focus of sharp controversy in the press, especially regarding the question of openness and publicity.

The majority of competitions launched within the city were in fact organized by the MAO, whose recourse to closed consultations was called into question during the first Congress on Civil Construction and Engineering in 1925. In the following year, ASNOVA claimed the right of entrants to participate in the elaboration of briefs, demanded that juries be neutral, and recommended that the process of selection take the form of public trials in which it would be possible for "defendants" to respond to the "charges."[12] In reality,

[9] "Sooruzhenie doma Centrosoyuza," *Stroitelstvo Moskvy* 5, no. 3 (March 1928): 31. Centrosoyuz earmarked 500,000 rubles for the construction of housing with a view to relocating the two hundred people then living on the site.

[10] "Konkurs na sostavlenie proekta doma Centrosoyuza," *Stroitelstvo Moskvy* 5, no. 5 (May 1928): 24.

[11] Le Corbusier, *Diary VII*, p. 37, FLC.

[12] "V zashchitu konkurentov," *Izvestia ASNOVA*, no. 1 (1926): 7.

however, the profession as a whole was concerned with the way in which consultations were handled.

In 1928, at the time of the Vesnin brothers' defeat in the competition for the Lenin library (which was won by Vladimir Shchuko), Grigori Barkhin emphasized the importance of establishing open, two-phase competitions and of the obligation to involve the winner in the construction phase. He even proposed that a watch committee be created, with the specific task of ensuring that competitions remained above board—regardless of the organizers.[13] Barkhin also criticized the unvarying composition of the juries, and advocated mobility and the election of some members by the entrants themselves.

In May 1928 the MAO was forced to respond by implementing tighter regulations concerning its own competitions, although it did not follow Barkhin's recommendation that the winner be automatically hired for the construction phase.[14] It was thus amid some controversy that Centrosoyuz launched a competition open to all architects, with 19 June 1928 as the deadline for submissions. A jury of ten, including six architects or engineers, was to be presided over by Isidor Liubimov, with the civil engineer E. A. Tatarinov as its "director."

The brief required entrants to locate "the building's principal entrance, studied in a spirit of monumentality," on the Miasnitskaia, "one of the busiest commercial thoroughfares in Moscow." It also also stipulated that "load-bearing walls and floors" be of reinforced concrete, while leaving to the entrants' discretion the "character and materials of the facades." Finally, given the absence of shops, it was permitted "to raise the ground floor above street level so as to create a wall base."[15] The brief recommended dividing the site into four units of different sizes, with a view to accommodating two thousand employees in all. Unit A was to house the executive, accounts and departments for the planning, forecasting, and organization of Centrosoyuz; B would contain the various commercial departments; C was for the club, restaurant, library, and dispensary; finally, the workshops, garages, apartments, and ancillary services were to be grouped together in D.

Thirty-two different teams submitted projects within the stipulated two-month deadline, which Tatarinov himself described as "rather tight." No less than twelve prizes and three distinctions were attributed. The first prize went to B. M. Velikovsky (who had designed the nearby Gostorg building) and V. M. Voinov, for a building with a dense perimeter organized around two trapezoidal courtyards. A. T. Kapustin and M. Savelev received the second, I. A. Zvevdin and I. A. Zaporozhets the third, and N. A. Trotsky, S. N. Kazak, and T. Ia. Zelikman the fourth prizes respectively.[16] At the same time a "closed" competition was organized, and invitations sent out to the Berlin architect Max Taut, to Thomas S. Tait of the firm of Sir John Burnet in London, to an architects' collective from the Centrosoyuz Warehousing Department, and to Le Corbusier and Pierre Jeanneret.

LE CORBUSIER'S EARLY PROJECT

In May 1928 Le Corbusier received a written invitation to participate in the competition from Nikolai Popov, director of Centrosoyuz Paris office. On 19 May he accepted, and two days later he had in his possession a reasonably good translation of the general brief, a description of the building regulations then in force in Moscow and applicable to the project,[17] and a note written in extremely approximate French indicating Soviet requirements for the building's general appearance:

[13] G. Barkhin, "K voprosu ob arkhitekturnykh konkursakh," *Stroitelnaia Promyshlennost* 6, no. 4 (April 1928): 304–6.

[14] MAO, "Polozhenie o konkursnykh sorevnovaniiakh," dated 23 May 1928, document conserved at the TsGALI. Cf. Khazanova, *Iz istorii*, pp. 22–24.

[15] *VOGI obiavliaet otkryty konkurs na sostavlenie proekta doma Centrosoyuza, Moscou* (Moscow: Centrosoyuz, 1928), p. 3.

[16] E. Tatarinov, "Dom Centrosoyuza v Moskve," *Stroitelnaia Promyshlennost* 6, no. 9 (September 1928): 646–52, and "Dva konkursa na dom Centrosoyuza," *Stroitelstvo Moskvy* 5, no. 11 (November 1928): 2–6.

[17] UPGI, *Vremennye stroitelnye pravila dlia g. Moskvy* (Moscow: Mospoligraf, 1928).

65. Le Corbusier, Centrosoyuz, outline of land allotted to the site between the old and the new Miasnitskaia streets and the two rings of Moscow's boulevards, May 1929 FLC 15955.

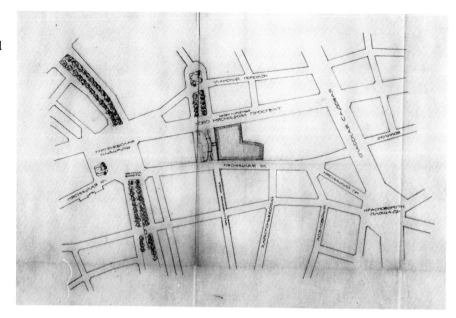

66. Le Corbusier, Centrosoyuz, draft for locating the project on the site, spring 1928, FLC 16239.

The architecture should be in the pronounced style of an official central administrative building. Most attention should be paid to the silhouette and relief. The beauty and grandeur of the edifice will depend on the simplicity of its forms. Decorative detail should be avoided wherever possible. . . . The Centrosoyuz building is to be located on a raised square overlooking three broad thoroughfares, and can thus constitute a notable architectural unity.[18]

Based on an analysis of the building's functional requirements, the early studies using axonometric sketches by Pierre Jeanneret reveal a series of combinations of three and sometimes four long rectangular blocks, together with a variable shape intended for the club building. Initially a floating, angular fragment in which no single element predominated, the building began to take shape as the entrances became more clearly marked. The L-shaped theme gradually evolved into a broad vertical plane running parallel with the Miasnitskaia, thus permitting a wide entrance for vehicles and a roof terrace at the top of the same block.

At the same time the club building acquired a more distinct formal identity, and ceased to be a somewhat indistinct irregular solid. Two early alternatives can be noted: on the one hand there was the idea of a closed block, even if

[18] Untitled document, 1928, FLC.

some of the facades were to be permeable, and on the other, in defiance of the brief, the principal front was to be located along the new boulevard, and the main entrance was treated as a rectangle within a block punctuated with balconies and strip windows throughout its length. In one of the sketches a charming red flag with a somewhat ironic, solitary star, works to reinforce the relatively weak vertical axis.

The version sent to Moscow in July 1928 took the form of three distinct blocks running perpendicular to the Miasnitskaia, along which a fourth element is positioned. The block flush with the boulevard thus found an echo in the curious combination of a short linear block, the club building perpendicular to this, and a third rectangular element completing the whole; a covered passageway forged a link between the first two blocks, thus evoking the image of a courtyard.

Far from being based on continuous variations on a constant scale, as was the case in the League of Nations project, here the volumes are autonomous, with articulations reinforced by the introduction of passages. It should also be noted that, whereas all the different elements are accessible at ground level via a central area from which elevators and ramps lead to the other floors, the buildings themselves are solidly implanted on the ground. The note that Le Corbusier attached to the twelve plans he sent to Moscow made no attempt to conceal the indeterminate hierarchical layout of the buildings, which were "topped with roof gardens" and with "a basketball ground and a running track":

We have sought to avoid large-scale blocks with courtyards. Our buildings are arranged in such a way that light will penetrate everywhere.

. . . Given that Miasnitskaia Street is extremely noisy and relatively narrow, we have set back the commercial services block behind a tree-lined garden.

There is, in fact, no predominant facade. The block along Miasnitskaia Street and the one on the future boulevard are of one and the same architectural value. Nonetheless, we have chosen the Miasnitskaia entrance for those departments having the largest numbers of staff, while the executive and administrative services will be located along the new boulevard.[19]

The note drew attention to the choice of ramps leading off to the different floors, a theme that Le Corbusier was to reiterate on his return from Moscow in the Villa Savoye,[20] and furnished an extremely precise description of the internal distributions specific to personnel, visitors, social amenities, and automobiles:

In a building designed for the comings and goings of over 2,000 people, the question of circulation is of capital importance. We have approached the problem as urban planners, that is, we have considered that corridors and stairs are, so to speak, enclosed streets. In consequence, these streets are 3.25 meters wide, and are always well lit. Moreover, we have replaced tiring flights of stairs with gently sloping (14%) ramps that allow for free and easy circulation. The Centrosoyuz palace does not, therefore, contain any stairs, although we have placed at the ends of the corridors 4 small staircases that allow for rapid links between floors.[21]

Like many of the conceptual elements, the technical solutions reflect a degree of continuity with the Geneva competition entry, whether it be in terms of the "closed-circuit central heating, refrigeration and ventilation plant," the "club hall based on modern acoustic principles, such as have been applied to the Salle Pleyel in Paris or the Great Assembly Hall at the League of Nations," or the glass facades and the "rigorous application of the 'strip window,' thus ensuring maximum lighting." It should be added that extracts from the League

[19] Le Corbusier and Pierre Jeanneret, "Plan pour l'édification des bâtiments du Centrosoyuz de Moscou," Paris, July 1928, handwritten document, p. 1, FLC.

[20] Tim Benton, *The Villas of Le Corbusier 1920–1930* (New Haven: Yale University Press, 1987), pp. 191–204. The systematic use of ramps in Centrosoyuz was condemned on economic grounds by Roger Ginsburger in *Frankreich: Die Entwicklung der neuen Ideen nach Konstruktion und Form* (Vienna: Anton Schroll Verlag, 1930), pp. 81–82. On Ginsburger, see my article "Roger Ginsburger and the Construction of Modernity in France (1920–1930)," in *Neues Bauen in der Welt, Rassegna*, no. 38 (June 1989): 26–35.

[21] Le Corbusier and Jeanneret, "Plan pour l'édification," p. 3.

67. Le Corbusier, Centrosoyuz, alternatives for locating the project on the site, spring 1928, FLC 15923.

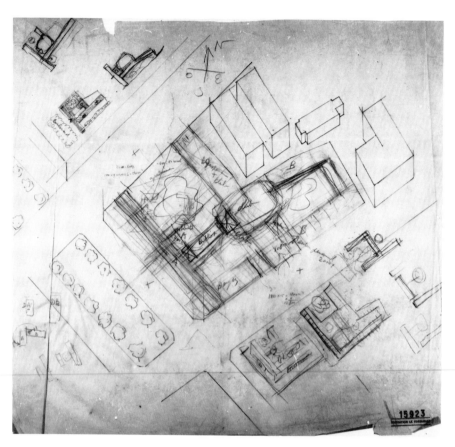

68. Le Corbusier, Centrosoyuz, six alternatives for locating the project on the site, spring 1928, FLC 16248.

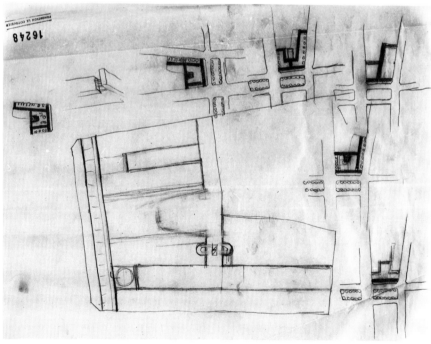

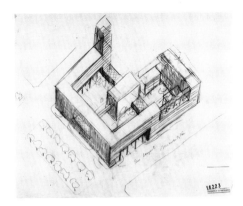

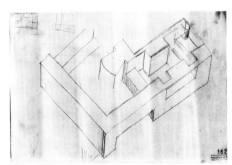

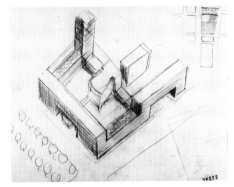

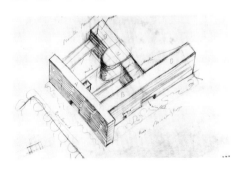

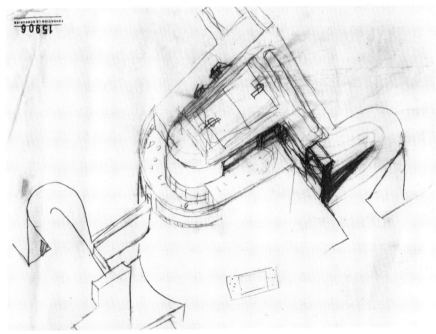

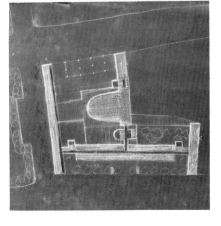

69. Le Corbusier, Centrosoyuz, preliminary sketch, spring 1928, FLC 16223.

70. Le Corbusier, Centrosoyuz, preliminary sketch, spring 1928, FLC 16222.

71. Le Corbusier, Centrosoyuz, preliminary sketch, spring 1928, FLC 16245.

72. Le Corbusier, Centrosoyuz, preliminary sketch, spring 1928, FLC 16246.

73. Le Corbusier, Centrosoyuz, groundfloor plan, spring 1928, FLC 16023.

74. Le Corbusier, Centrosoyuz, sketch of club roof, with ramps and sports ground, spring 1928, FLC 15906.

75. Le Corbusier, Centrosoyuz, typical floor plan, spring 1928, FLC 16249.

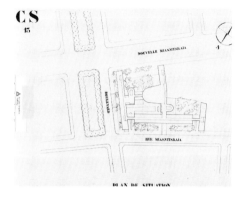

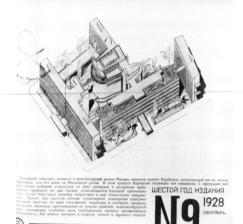

76. Le Corbusier, Centrosoyuz, site plan, spring 1928, first project sent to Moscow.

77. Cover of *Stroitelnaia Promyshlennost* 6 (September 1928) presenting Le Corbusier's first project for the Centrosoyuz as the "sensation of the present moment," Moscow.

78. Le Corbusier, Centrosoyuz, "ground-plan" plan, spring 1928, first project sent to Moscow FLC 15676.

---

of Nations project were sent to Moscow with the Centrosoyuz dossier. In Geneva Le Corbusier had "conducted the development of [his] buildings toward a single skyline, smooth and pure," asserting that "at the very top, on the immense roof terrace, all hatred [could] cease."[22] This time the defense of the the flat roof was largely superfluous, since few or none of the other entrants had recourse to sloping roofs:

The idea of these roof terraces was born of conclusive experimentation carried out by us more than 15 years ago, in an extremely hostile climate (the Jura, at an altitude of 1,000 meters). The theory of the flat roof drained within the building is the direct consequence of the introduction of central heating in countries with extremes of cold and heavy snowfall in winter. It is in fact the only solution for such climates.

Moreover, so as to eliminate the dilation of reinforced concrete in summer, we complete our roof terraces with a system of gardens whose effect is to maintain above the concrete, and underneath the cement course that rests on a bed of sand, a constant humidity that precludes all dilation effects. We have experimented with this theory of the flat roof in all our buildings over the past 15 years, with resounding success. It has, moreover, been adopted by most contemporary, modern architects.[23]

That Le Corbusier's initial project was (to say the least) warmly received by his fellow professionals in Moscow even before the results of the competition were announced is clearly evidenced in the choice of cover for the September issue of *Stroitelnaia Promyshlennost*:

The current sensation in the life of architecture in Moscow is the project elaborated by Le Corbusier at the request of Centrosoyuz for its new headquarters on Miasnitskaia. With his astonishing capacity to shake off the influence of all conventional and old-fashioned architectural traditions, he has produced a design remarkable for its simplicity and above all for the absence of technological bias. The plan is simple and entirely practicable, with passageways and glass arcades, ramps instead of stairs and a club building in the shape of a horseshoe—an original yet highly practical solution. The project may be classed without reserve as a product of reason and the most sensible reflection.[24]

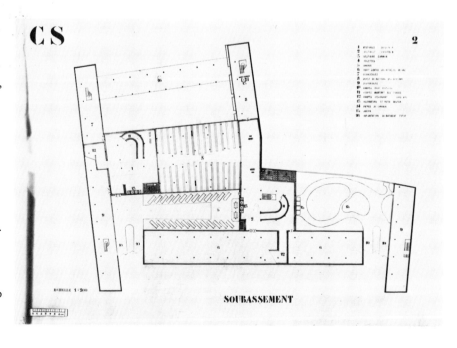

[22] Le Corbusier, *Une maison—un palais*, pp. 152, 155.
[23] Le Corbusier and Jeanneret, "Plan pour l'édification," pp. 5–6.
[24] *Stroitelnaia Promyshlennost*, cover for the September 1928 issue. *Stroitelstvo Moskvy* also dedicated to the project its November 1928 cover story.

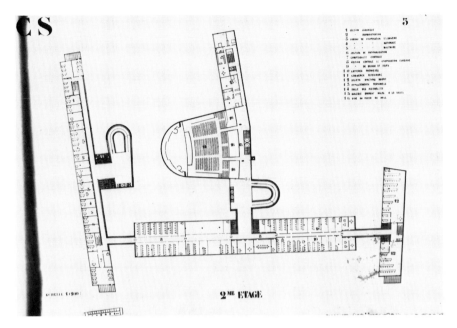

79. Le Corbusier, Centrosoyuz, second-floor plan, spring 1928, first project sent to Moscow, FLC 15679.

80. Le Corbusier, Centrosoyuz, general axonometric view, spring 1928, first project sent to Moscow.

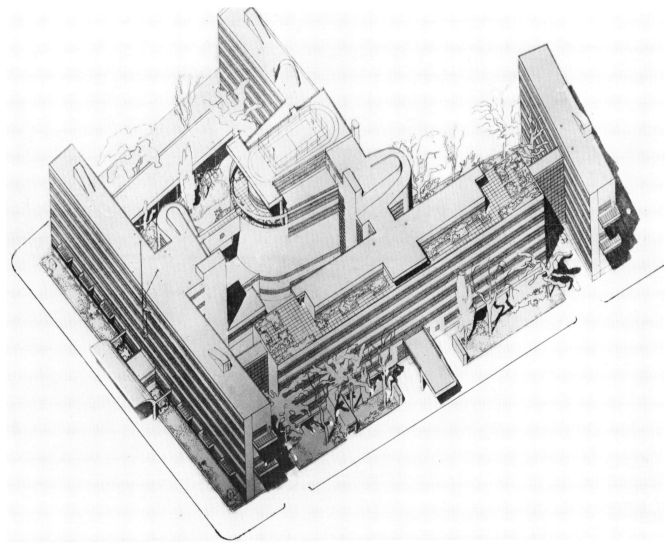

81. Le Corbusier, Centrosoyuz, sketch for the west facade on the projected boulevard, spring 1928, FLC 15965.

82. Architects' team of the Centrosoyuz warehouse building directory, project for the Centrosoyuz competition, second turn, Moscow, summer 1928; in *Stroitelnaia Promyshlennost* 6 (September 1928).

83. Victor and Leonid Vesnin, competition project for the Centrosoyuz, third turn, Moscow, summer 1928; in *Stroitelstvo Moskvy* 5, no.11 (November 1928).

84. Boris Velikovsky, competition project for the Centrosoyuz, first prize at the first turn, Moscow, summer 1928; in *Stroitelnaia Promyshlennost* 6, no.9 (September 1928).

Like the "open" competition entries, Le Corbusier and Jeanneret's designs were examined along with the other "closed" submissions by a technical commission chaired by L. A. Serk and composed of Victor Vesnin, M. Ia. Ginzburg, I. I. Kondakov, Ia. A. Kornfeld, G. B. Krasin, M. V. Kryukov, I. P. Mashkov, and Ia. O. Raikh. Tait and Burnet's designs were rejected as "primitive," and Max Taut's were judged "insufficient." The commission selected the

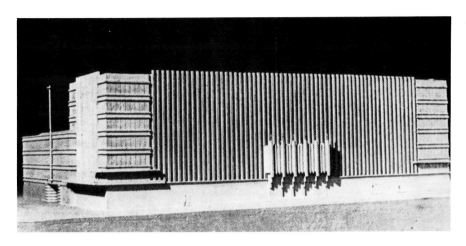

85. Peter Behrens, competition project for the Centrosoyuz, third turn, Moscow, October 1928.

86. Max Taut, competition project for the Centrosoyuz, third turn, Moscow, October 1928.

in-house architects' entry (designed by Centrosoyuz's warehousing department) as "well thought out and well executed" but excessively dense, and the French entry, which it commented on as follows:

The clarity of the plan from the viewpoint of Centrosoyuz's administrative, operational, and social components, the successful treatment of the entrances and vestibules, the fact that the Miasnitskaia Street front is set back, the ingenious locations of the cloakrooms and car parks, the original treatment of the club building, together with the fact that Le Corbusier's designs are full of new solutions creatively handled, all justify the selection of this project for further elaboration.

Among the project's failings is its excessive density in relation to the neighboring plot, the complexity of the assembly hall's superstructure and insufficient lighting in the cloakrooms. The club building is not sufficiently distinct from the other elements of the project.[25]

Having performed its task the technical committee recommended the holding of a third competition with entries by A. A and V. A. Vesnin, I. V. Zholtovsky, I. I. Leonidov, A. S. Nikolsky, A. A. Ol, A. V. Samoilov, and P. M. Nakhman, a team from OSA led by A. L. Pasternak and V. Vladimirov, and the German master Peter Behrens. At the same time, Le Corbusier and the in-house collective were asked to submit new versions of their projects before 20 October.[26]

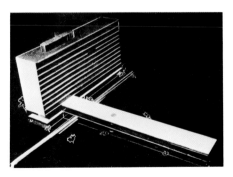

87. Ivan Leonidov, competition project for the Centrosoyuz, third turn, Moscow, October 1928.

[25] Tatarinov, "Dom Centrosoyuza v Moskve," pp. 649–50.
[26] *Diary VII*, p. 41.

88. OSA team led (Alexander Pasternak, Viacheslav Vladimirov) competition project for the Centrosoyuz, third turn, Moscow, summer 1928; in *Stroitelstvo Moskvy* 5, no. 11 (November 1928).

89. Le Corbusier, Centrosoyuz, "Proposal for the organization of the surrounding blocks," 20 October 1928, project drawn in Moscow, FLC 16111.

90. Cover of *Stroitelstvo Moskvy* 5, no.11 (November 1928), with two views of Le Corbusier's first Centrosoyuz project, designed by Elkin and Gustav Klucis.

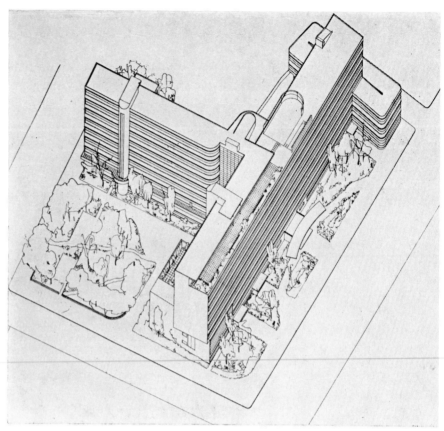

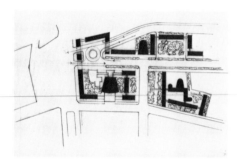

THE VICTORY OF 1928

The weeks spent in Moscow in October 1928 meant that Le Corbusier could modify his designs "on the spot" with Kozhin (although he had first envisaged working with Leonidov). He then submitted the revised project to Isidor Liubimov and the different groups in charge of the competition:

In October I was called on to make some modifications (museum added). All Moscow and Leningrad were working on modifications or preparing new designs. I therefore had to produce a variant project with unpaid help. For two weeks I occupied an office at Centrosoyuz, to which I had free access.[27]

Only a few months after the Geneva conflict, Le Corbusier now entered into negotiations with the Soviet authorities with a certain feeling of apprehension; but when he came face to face with "Liubimov assisted by a Centrosoyuz council, one of Kerensky's ministers, another director, the president of the building commission and a number of engineers (dressed *à la russe* in black shirts)," he was pleasantly surprised:

Clear-cut, courteous, easygoing, quick, efficient discussion! I am a good judge of this, since I was the object of the debate.
They are all men of today.[28]

And he indeed encountered "sympathy" for his ideas at this "highly dignified, unhurried, efficient, serious" meeting where he had expected "heavy opposition to the relatively bold solutions that failed in Geneva." The emotional intensity of the moment is reflected in the sketched transcription of a dream

[27] Ibid., pp. 36–37. Le Corbusier noted, "phone Burov or Colly re. Leonidov," ibid., p. 9.
[28] Ibid., p. 41.

91. Le Corbusier, "Victory without brutality," drawing based on a dream made during the final competition for the Centrosoyuz, Moscow, 30 October 1928.

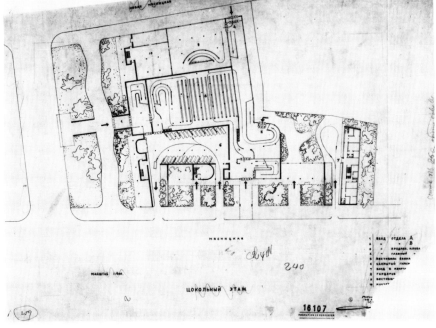

92. Le Corbusier, Centrosoyuz, ground-floor plan with first appearance of *pilotis*, 20 October 1928, project drawn in Moscow, FLC 16107.

93. Le Corbusier, Centrosoyuz, general axonometric view, 20 October 1928, project drawn in Moscow, FLC 16113.

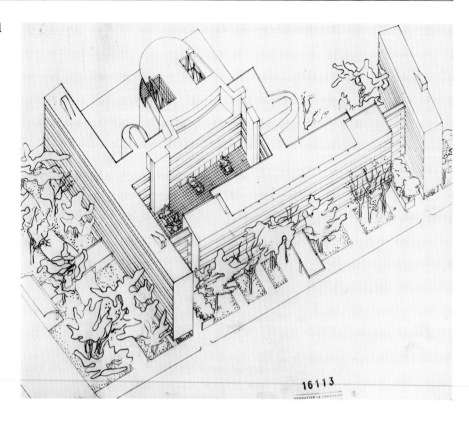

[29] Le Corbusier, drawing 5541, Moscow, 30 October 1928, FLC.

[30] Le Corbusier, "Osnovnye printsipy proekta postroiki doma Centrosoyuza," *Stroitelnaia Promyshlennost* 6, no. 11 (November–December 1928): 849–50.

[31] Le Corbusier, letter to Sigfried Giedion, Paris, 16 April 1932, FLC.

[32] Isidor Liubimov, ed., *Bolshie Goroda Zapadnoi Evropy, Berlin Parizh London, po dannym zagranichnoi delegatsii Moskovskogo Soveta* (Moscow: Izd. MKKh, 1926).

[33] Boesiger and Storonov, *Œuvre complète,* p. 170. The most exhaustive analyses of the Geneva project to date are Patrick Devanthéry and Inès Lamunière, "La SdN—un Palais moderne," in Isabelle Charollais and André Ducret, eds., *Le Corbusier à Genève 1922–1932: Projets et réalisations* (Lausanne: Payot, 1987), pp. 17–34; and Werner Oechslin, ed., *Le Corbusier et Pierre Jeanneret: Das Wettbewerbsprojekt für den Völkerbundspalast in Genf* (Zurich: gta/Ammann, 1988). This book publishes the German translation of Devanthéry and Lamunière's article and many other interpretations and documents.

he had on 30 October, which he entitled "Victory without brutality" and which shows a solid, well-developed female figure emerging from the water and shaking herself off.[29] As testified in the Russian transcription of the meeting to which the dream image refers, his recent experiences at the League of Nations and the Mundaneum were still very much in his mind; in fact he used them as reference material to justify his Centrosoyuz designs.[30]

The presence of Liubimov certainly had something to do with Le Corbusier's agreeable impressions; they were to remain on direct terms for over a decade, regardless of Liubimov's political future. All in all, Le Corbusier regarded him as "a lover of architecture," as he commented in a letter to Giedion.[31] Well versed in metropolitan planning issues, which he had studied at length on field trips to Paris, London, and Berlin,[32] the president had, moreover, toyed with the idea of having an apartment built over the Centrosoyuz, as his colleague Nikolai Miliutin had done over the Narkomfin building designed by Ginzburg.

In a brief note addressed to Liubimov, Le Corbusier gave reasons for the modified plans, which set the buildings back from the limits of the site and now included a "museum" as required. He also announced the decision to use *pilotis,* which had been conspicuously absent from the first project, as they had been from the initial League of Nations entry. But whereas in Geneva the "High Secretariat" had declared, "We cannot accept the notion of working over automobiles,"[33] this time the Soviets made no objections:

I have removed the small wing overlooking the new Miasnitskaia and modified the services in the block on the old Miasnitskaia. I have also rotated the club building ninety degrees on its axis.

I feel we must exploit the precious terrain at our disposal and have placed the vast system of vestibules at the *raised ground-floor level.* This space represents a highly efficient solution to the problem of distributions and will afford visitors to Centrosoyuz a truly majestic impression. It will, moreover, contain the required museum.

. . . I plan to raise the building on *pilotis*. This approach represents the most brilliant solution to the problem of multiple access, allows for unchecked circulation in the cloakroom areas, and presents the optimal solution to the demand for a *closed* parking facility.

. . . The floor plans remain unchanged except, very obviously, for the relocation of the services housed in the suppressed new Miasnitskaia wing.

Moreover, in order to give a clear picture of these new solutions I am having a series of interior and exterior perspective views drawn up.[34]

In the same note, Le Corbusier indicated his intention to have the so-called "anatomical details"—that is, the "window types," insulating wall types, ceilings and floors—drawn up in Paris where he had "ten skilled draughtsmen" at his disposal, and, while raising explicit questions concerning his fees, stated his determination to pursue the project to its conclusion:

I wish to make it clear that I should be extremely happy to carry out the Centrosoyuz project. I shall bring to this task all that I have learned in architecture. It is with great joy that I shall contribute what knowledge I possess to a nation that is being organized in accordance with its new spirit; personally speaking, moreover, I have never followed any other line of conduct[35]

The new project left intact the basic layout of the earlier design. Following its ninety-degree rotation, the club building was now perpendicular to the Miasnitskaia on its longitudinal axis, thus highlighting the entrance. The opposition between the curved walls of the club and the rectangular prisms in which it was set, the thickest of which was now disposed along the Miasnitskaia, created all the urban tension of a more compact design. Significantly, the ground level, closed off from the two main blocks, was henceforth open to the street thanks to the *pilotis*, which created at least partial transparency. This response to the demand for "grandeur" stands in stark contrast to Peter Behrens's entry, whose monumentality was grounded in "unity and massiveness."[36]

THE "LYRICAL" PATH

In his *Voyage de Moscou*, Georges Duhamel had evoked the "odiferous dough" of the crowds, which "ooze out onto the pavements and streets"—a "sticky wave" through which the trams "elbow their way."[37] In his lecture at Buenos Aires a year later, Le Corbusier would justify the use of *pilotis* by claiming that "technology is the very basis of lyricism"; and he, too, would describe the crowds that had impressed him during his stay:

These are the buildings of the Centrosoyuz in Moscow. Offices of the food cooperatives, with 2,500 civil servants. The need to sort the crowds that enter and leave all at once; the need for a forum space at such times, when the employees' galoshes and fur coats are full of snow; a well-regimented system of cloakrooms and distributions is required. Finally, the service vehicles cannot circulate in Miasnitskaia Street, which is too narrow. The system of *pilotis* completely covers the ground (or almost). These raise the office buildings to the first-floor level, thus allowing for the free flow of traffic beneath them, either in the open air or in enclosed zones that flow into the great forum to which the two principal entrances give access. "Paternoster" elevators (continuous lifts on the "bucket-and-chain" principle) and immense helicoidal ramps lead off from

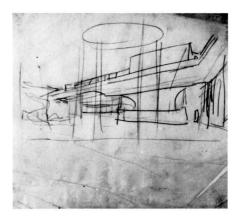

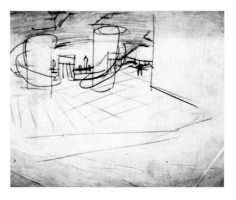

94, 95, 96. Le Corbusier, Centrosoyuz, sketches of ground-floor hall, beginning of 1929, FLC 16333 (details).

[34] Le Corbusier, handwritten note to Isidor Liubimov, Moscow, October 1928, p. 1, FLC.
[35] Ibid., p. 2.
[36] Peter Behrens, "Verwaltungsgebäude des Konsumverbandes in Moskau," *Die Baugilde* 11, no. 9 (1929): 679–82.
[37] Duhamel, *Le voyage de Moscou*, pp. 155–58.

97. Le Corbusier, Centrosoyuz, perspective view from Miasnitskaia Street, 20 October 1928, project drawn in Moscow, FLC.

98. Le Corbusier, Centrosoyuz, perspective view of *pilotis* parallel to Miasnitskaia Street, 20 October 1928, project drawn in Moscow, FLC.

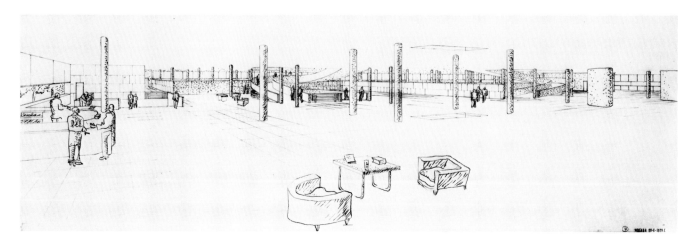

99. Le Corbusier, Centrosoyuz, perspective of ground-floor hall, 20 October 1928, project drawn in Moscow, FLC.

the forum, thus eliminating the need for stairs and making for rapid dispersal. Doors are placed where necessary, under the buildings, in the facades, away from the buildings. Window openings (lights) can be positioned at will.

This classification has in fact been implemented. This type of building reflects two distinct phases: the first is the disordered influx of people on a vast horizontal plane situated at ground level; this is a lake. The second is fixed, quiet work, sheltered from the noise and hubbub, with everyone in his allocated place and easy to monitor—offices, with rivers as the means of communication between them.

Circulation is a term I used all the time in Moscow, so much so in fact that some

Soviet delegates became distinctly ill at ease. *Architecture is circulation.* Think what this means. It condemns academic methods and sanctions the principle of *pilotis.*[38]

Above the grid of *pilotis*, which assumed ever greater importance for Le Corbusier, the building thus resembled a picturesque assembly of "prisms":

Faced with the problem of Moscow, what did architecture do? We were required to use all the technical advances of the time, and we furnished the quintessence as regards the building's functional organization. Here is what we did with the new architectural terminologies: I drew the first, central office block: its in-depth dimensions were divided up so as to afford maximum lighting. This block contains large areas for collective work and is enclosed within plate-glass facades at either end. The opaque side walls consist of two layers of thin volcanic stone.

I then positioned the two other office buildings: a glass facade on one side, and a mixed (glass and stone) wall for the corridors; at the ends, completely opaque walls of the same stone. These three prisms constitute the major elements of the composition; they are disposed in plan and section so as to create specific impressions, here a vertical cliff wall, there a welcoming basin. The central block is a story lower than the two flanking buildings—this was important. All three are raised on *pilotis*, in the air, detached.

Appreciate the entirely new and formidable virtues of this architecture; the impeccable line of the substructure. The building resembles an object in a window display, and it is perfectly legible.

The *pilotis* are rich in their cylindrical forms; they bring light to the shade or half-shade and, to the mind, a striking impression of tension. On the ground the play of light affords highly imaginative effects. On the skyline are the impeccable lines of this crystal prism circled with a band of volcanic stone that mark the parapet of the terraces. The sharp break with the sky is one of the most adorable conquests of modern technique (the elimination of the roof and the cornice).[39]

More than just a means of channeling the "sticky wave," Le Corbusier's new device is a picturesque architectural landscape seen, not in the architectural promenade of the ramps, but rather from the *outside*—the only viewpoint capable of furnishing the images of "cliff face" and "basin," which are so evocative of the Alpine skyline.

As Alan Colquhoun has remarked, the combination of three prismatic volumes and a hall harks back to the League of Nations project and looks forward to the Cité de Refuge studies of the following year.[40] Yet as Le Corbusier indicated in a sketch which he included in his *Précisions*, it also invites comparison with the Cook and Loucheur houses, the interplay of whose flexible forms within a grid of *pilotis* and posts here becomes that of a single, freestanding element—the hall—within a flexible framework of rectilinear office blocks.[41] In his villa designs, Le Corbusier went beyond the traditional organization of the closed, compact building; with Centrosoyuz, he broke with the traditional office building organized around a courtyard, and instead proposed a new type of edifice capable of engendering a series of angular planes; this is made clear in a drawing executed in Moscow, which shows the principle at the level of a whole district.[42]

THE THIRD COMPETITION: HAPPY ENDING

All in all, the designs submitted for the third competition were simpler and more radical than those of the first phase, and to a certain degree reflect the influence of Le Corbusier's solutions—so much so in fact that the Vesnin

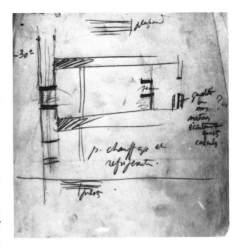

100. Le Corbusier, Centrosoyuz, study sketch of the section across the offices, beginning of 1929, FLC.

[38] Le Corbusier, "Les techniques sont l'assiette même du lyrisme; elles ouvrent un nouveau cycle de l'architecture," in *Précisions sur un état présent de l'architecture et de l'urbanisme* (Paris: G. Crès et Cie, 1930), pp. 46, 48.

[39] Ibid., pp. 59–60.

[40] Colquhoun, "Strategies of the *Grand Travaux.*"

[41] Le Corbusier, *Précisions*, figs. 17, 19, p. 47.

[42] Drawing executed by Le Corbusier in Moscow, FLC no. 16111.

101. Le Corbusier, Centrosoyuz, perspective of an office, 20 October 1928, project drawn in Moscow, FLC.

102. Le Corbusier, graphic comparison of the Centrosoyuz, the Cook house and the Loucheur house ground plans; published in *Précisions* (Paris, 1930).

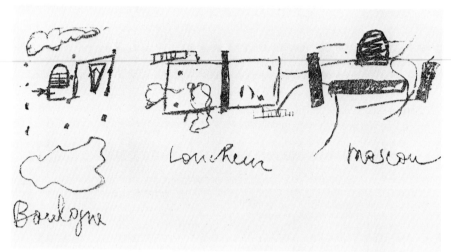

[43] A. Pasternak, L. Slavina, V. Vladimirov, and N. Vorotyntseva, "Pererabotki proekta Le Corbusier doma Centrosoyuza," *Stroitelstvo Moskvy* 5, no. 11 (1928): 4–5. This rather clumsy scheme hardly justifies the claim made by Pasternak's niece that he had worked for Le Corbusier in Moscow: Ann Pasternak Slater, introduction to Alexander Pasternak, *A Vanished Present* (New York: Harcourt Brace Jovanovitch, 1984), p. xxii.

[44] A. Mestnov, "Zakliuchitelny konkurs na dom Centrosoyuza," *Stroitelstvo Moskvy* 6, no. 1 (1929): 20–24.

brothers' designs look like rearticulated versions of Le Corbusier's fundamental propositions, while the OSA team contented itself with a rather uninspired rearrangment of his initial scheme.[43] The most traditional entries came from Peter Behrens—a simple, down-to-earth block with forceful treatment of the facades—and Ivan Zholtovsky, whose designs were not made public. The most laconic project was by Ivan Leonidov, who condensed the whole brief into one extremely refined and elongated slab.[44]

The technical commission acknowledged Le Corbusier's modifications but considered that a number of ambiguities persisted, and even that certain modifications were for the worse:

The variant here presented has not brought the slightest improvement to the initial design, unless it be the rotation of the club building and a repositioning of the blocks so as to respect regulations concerning the limits of the terrain. It should, moreover, be noted that in their schematic form, the variant plans pose a whole variety of questions, such as the siting of the gymnasium, how the kitchens are to be supplied, the evacuation of exhaust fumes from the garage, etc.

. . . In general, however, one is forced to recognize the ingenious layout of the office buildings along the new Miasnitskaia, the clear demarcation between the executive and commercial blocks, the sufficiently imposing character of the former, the interesting and original functional treatment of the various elements and of the composition as a whole and, finally, the attractive character of the project's architectural forms.[45]

In short, Le Corbusier's "formidable talent" led the commission to ask him to submit a last project, one that respected the needs of Centrosoyuz and the constraints of the site, but which also "retained the original features of this architect's creation." Meanwhile, with Le Corbusier's continuing presence in Moscow, the other contenders began to press for a decision by means of two texts addressed to the Centrosoyuz executive. On 27 October, considering that "conservative traditions still held sway within the leadership" and that "in the interests of the development of architecture, these must be rooted out with all possible speed," Pavel Nakhman, Andrei Ol, Anatoli Samoilov, Alexander Nikolsky, and Leonid Galperin formulated a wish as constructive as it was disinterested:

To entrust one of the leading exponents of Western architectural thought with Moscow's most important commission is, to our minds, a great step toward the liberation of architecture from stagnation.

We therefore welcome the idea of giving Le Corbusier the task of finalizing the Centrosoyuz project, and are convinced that his edifice will be a clear and efficient reflection of current architectural ideas.[46]

Two days later the OSA, represented in two different competition entries, intervened in the persons of Moisei Ginzburg and Alexander Vesnin, who expressed their conviction that "the Centrosoyuz building, if executed to Le Corbusier's designs, will not only make a magnificent contribution to the new Moscow, but also constitute a powerful incentive to reconsider buildings under construction that are out of phase with contemporary life-styles."[47]

Despite this somewhat surprising movement of opinion, whereby all those participating in the final phase (with the exception of Behrens, who was in Berlin, and Zholtovsky, who was never in the running) now pleaded in favor of a fellow competitor, the technical commission's reluctance to hand over a clear-cut commission was still reflected in the jury's final remarks, even if it recommended that "all the fundamental principles of Le Corbusier's project be accepted, that all further modifications be merely the expression of economic or technical constraints, and that these should in no way undermine the composition as a whole."[48]

Nikolai Markovnikov's concluding remarks on the competition procedure reveal differences of opinion between the technical commission and the architectural profession as a whole. Markovnikov mentioned "the desire expressed by others that Le Corbusier should play a direct role in the execution of the project and that it should be built, if not to his own designs, then at least in accordance with his indications," but made no attempt to conceal his misgivings about the use of *pilotis* "in our climate and living conditions." For Markovnikov, however, to call into question the idea of *pilotis* would be to "reduce Le Corbusier's idea to nothing," as would the notion of building only one "experimental" ramp.

[45] "Otzyv tekhnicheskoi komissii," Moscow, 30 November 1928, FLC.

[46] A. Ol, A. Samoilov, A. Nikolsky, and L. Galperin, "V pravlenie Centrosoyuza," Moscow, 27 October 1928, FLC. This declaration was read to the technical committee on the same day.

[47] OSA, M. Ginzburg, and A. Vesnin, "V pravlenie Centrosoyuza," Moscow, 29 October 1929, FLC. Le Corbusier's project had already appeared in "Plan sooruzheniia stroenii Centrosoyuza v Moskve, sostavlenny Le Corbusier i Pierre Jeanneret," *Sovremennaia Arkhitektura* 3, no. 6 (1928): 177–81.

[48] "Postanovlenie Komsto po proektu 'Doma Centrosoyuza,'" Moscow, November 1928, FLC.

On Opposite Page:

104. Le Corbusier, Centrosoyuz, comparison of the four most important stages of the project; drawing by André Lortie. (1) Competition project, Spring 1928. (2) Project drawn in Moscow, October 1928. (3) Project drawn in Paris, beginning of 1929. (4) Final project, 1929–1930.

105. Nikolai Kolli, Yvonne Gallis, Le Corbusier, and Pierre Jeanneret at the dinner table, rue Jacob, Paris, beginning of 1929 (?).

106. Le Corbusier, Centrosoyuz, general axonometric view on the old Miasnitskaia Street, beginning of 1929, FLC 16918.

107. Le Corbusier, Centrosoyuz, general axonometric view on the new Miasnitskaia Street, beginning of 1929, FLC 16052.

Markovnikov attacked the commission's narrow-minded view that the great hall produced a "disagreeable, cluttered impression," and compared the project's spatial qualities with those of the mosque at Cordoba and the great cistern at Constantinople with its "thousand and one columns." Expressing his disdain for the "petty and anemic advice" of those for whom the prospect of losing a few thousand rubles was appalling, he considered that the price to pay was a small one when compared with the project's "colossal significance" for building technology in the USSR:

It must be said that, even if Le Corbusier's project is not executed, his conferences and his work on the project for Centrosoyuz's headquarters have made a strong impression and are of such value to Russian architecture and technology that we owe a debt of gratitude to Centrosoyuz. We ought if possible to seize on this opportunity to associate foreigners with our work and to enter into communication with Western culture.[49]

Another opportunity was given Le Corbusier when he was asked by MOGES, the Electricity Authority for the Moscow Region, to design a project for a power station in Bobriki. Initial discussions concerning this, "the largest coal-burning power plant in the world," were held in October,[50] and in January 1929 Le Corbusier sent in a proposed contract for the sum of fifty thousand francs, although nothing appears to have come of it.[51]

THE DETAILED PROJECT

103. Victor Vesnin, Nikolai Kolli, Georgi Orlov, et al., Dnieper power plant, 1928.

On his return to Paris, Le Corbusier immediately set to work on drawing up a contract with the Russians who, for their part, secretly envisaged an alternative solution in case his final project should prove unsatisfactory. A minute of 5 December raises the idea of entrusting the Vesnin brothers with a further study should this prove to be the case.[52] In the meantime, the contract concerned "the preliminary project for the architecture of the building" and stipulated that this must follow the instructions of the technical commission. The project had to be finished at the latest one month after the arrival in Paris of "two architectural assistants" from Centrosoyuz.[53]

At the same time, the brief was extended to accommodate 2,500 rather than 2,000 employees. As Moshe Lewin remarks, the cooperation was then profiting from the bankruptcy of small shops and small and medium-sized companies in the private sector;[54] but although it planned to continue growing in this way, collectivization put an end to the process. A fairly precise plan for the gradual occupation of the building had already been discussed in Moscow.[55]

In December Pavel Nakhman, the author of the in-house project for Centrosoyuz who had remained in close contact with Le Corbusier during his stay, arrived in Paris with the architect Nikolai Kolli who, among other things, spoke French. In accordance with the contract that they had just signed, Le

[49] N. Markovnikov, "Le Corbusier i ego novye eskizy doma Centrosoyuza," *Stroitelnaia Promyshlennost* 6, no. 11 (November–December 1928): 850–54.

[50] Le Corbusier, *Diary VII*, p. 33.

[51] The document in question was passed on by the Russian Embassy in Paris: E. Falk and

B. Smirnoff, letter to Le Corbusier, Paris, 6 February 1929, FLC.

[52] "Postanovlenie no. 12 obedinennogo zasedaniia pravleniia C-za SSSR," 5 December 1928, FLC.

[53] "Contrat entre le Centrosoyuz et Le Corbusier et Pierre Jeanneret," 30 November 1928, handwritten, FLC. The contract was signed by Le Corbusier on 10 December; the architects' fees were fixed at 2.5 percent.

[54] Moshe Lewin, "The Immediate Background of Soviet Collectivization," *The Making of the Soviet System* (New York: Pantheon, 1985), p. 111.

[55] "O razmeshchenii chastei apparata Centrosoyuza v novom dome," Moscow, October 1928, handwritten, FLC.

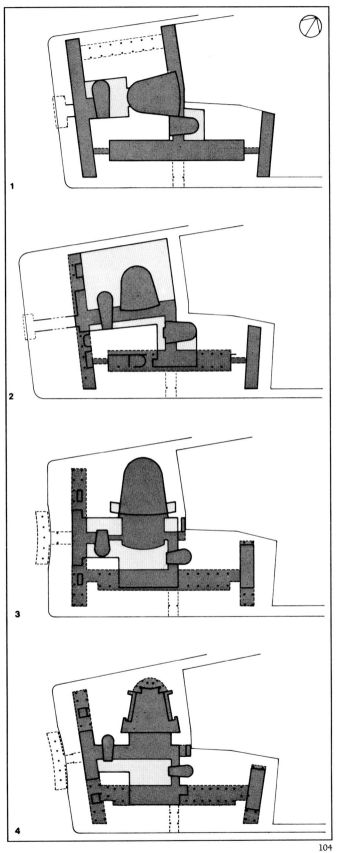

1

2

3

4

104

105

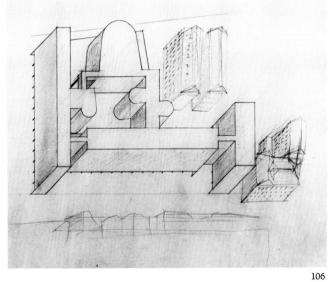

106

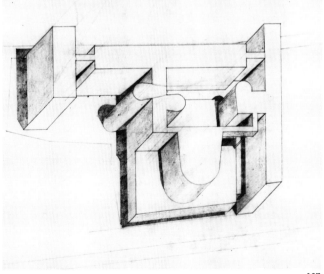

107

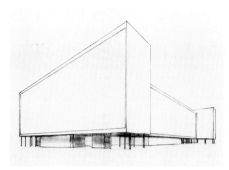

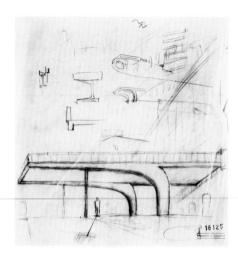

108. Le Corbusier, Centrosoyuz, general perspective, beginning of 1929, FLC 16033.

109. Le Corbusier, Centrosoyuz, sketch of entrance porch on the old Miasnitskaia Street, beginning of 1929, FLC 16125.

Corbusier and Pierre Jeanneret undertook to "inform them of the latest advances in French architecture." An active member of the design team and a crucial element in the supervision of the site until the building's completion, Kolli established close relations with Pierre Jeanneret in particular.[56] Work on the new project went ahead briskly, a fact that Le Corbusier mentioned in a letter to Ginzburg in January 1929:

MM. Nakhman and Kolli seemed well satisfied, and I believe we have achieved a result after all our efforts; I hope it will meet with your approval.[57]

Owing to problems related to the acquisition of the plot, the geometry of the project underwent a radical transformation and the earlier, trapezoidal layout, open to the new Miasnitskaia, now took the form of a rigid rectangular matrix. The theme of the *pilotis* was further developed and its significance was easier to appreciate: the garage that had occupied part of the ground floor was removed and replaced by the great hall, now at street level. A model highlighting these alterations was made. Sent to Moscow in 1930, where it was shown at the "Style of the Industrial Bourgeoisie" exhibition, it appears to have been subsequently lost.[58]

From this point on, Le Corbusier was particularly concerned with the elaboration of a system of *respiration exacte* for the heating and refrigeration of his glass prisms, and with *aération ponctuelle* for the interiors. The idea of using this system came to him during his stay. He then made thorough enquiries as to the characteristics of materials available in Moscow but, in a note to his cousin, he voiced serious doubts concerning the possible solutions:

Pierre, rework the whole window system. We might perhaps use double glazing and heat between the panes. See G. Lyon and laboratory.

Study one hot-water heating for offices; one hot-air heating per double-glazed partition to keep out the cold.[59]

This alternative was adopted in the early 1929 project. When the public was subsequently invited to inspect the plans in rue de Sèvres on 30 January, the card sent out emphasized that "this considerable edifice designed to house the work and recreation of 2,500 persons contains entirely new solutions to the problem of lighting, heating, and ventilation, and to that of horizontal and vertical circulations."[60] When he at last presented the project to the press, Le Corbusier emphasized its technical aspects:

The instructions given to the architects by the Muscovite authorities were as follows: "We wish to benefit from all the advances in construction that modern technique has

[56] Le Corbusier later noted that he took Kolli and Nakhman to see Gustave Lyon at Orly, and that they visited the Citroën works together, in *Diary VIII*, begun 1 December 1928, p. 6, FLC.

In 1918 Nikolai Dzhemsovich (Iakovlevich) Kolli (1894–1966) built the "Red Wedge," a propaganda monument on Moscow square. A graduate from the Vkhutemas in 1922, he received a prize at the Moscow Agricultural Exhibition in Moscow for a "peasant's house" design in the following year, when he also began teaching and worked on the prefabrication of housing components. In 1927, designs of his were shown at the "First Exhibition of Contemporary Ar-

chitecture," and between 1927 and 1932 he worked with Victor Vesnin on the construction of an electrical power station on the Dnieper. Between 1933 and 1941 Kolli was director of Architectural Studio no. 6 in Moscow; and built the Kirovskaia subway station, the Izmailovo stadium, and the *Izvestia* complex. Even before the end of the Second World War, Kolli worked on the reconstruction of Minsk, Riga, and Kalinin; at this time he was also director of the Public and Industrial Building Research Institute. He designed a large number of housing developments in Moscow. See "Nikolai Dzhemsovich Kolli," *Arkhitektura SSSR* 17, no. 1 (1967): 49; "Nikolai Dzhemsovich Kolli," in Barkhin and Yara-

lov, *Mastera Sovetskoi Arkhitektury*, 2: 349–64.

[57] Le Corbusier, letter to Moisei Ginzburg, Paris, 22 January 1929, FLC.

[58] A photograph of the exhibition as held at the Museum of New Western Art, where Le Corbusier's designs were shown as well as paintings by Léger and by Ozenfant, appears in Yavorskaia, *Iz istorii*, pl. 3.

[59] Le Corbusier, note written in Moscow, October 1928, FLC.

[60] Invitation card, FLC. As indicated in the *Carnet noir*, in which the office's plans were recorded, the new portfolio of nineteen plans was drawn up between 9 and 25 January 1929. There is no previous reference to Centrosoyuz. See *Carnet noir*, p. 24, FLC.

110. Le Corbusier, Centrosoyuz, ground-floor circulation plan, beginning of 1929, FLC 16083.

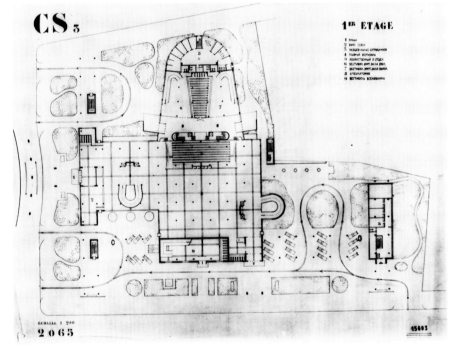

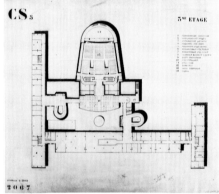

111. Le Corbusier, Centrosoyuz, ground-floor plan (with the caption "1er étage" or "second floor"), beginning of 1929, FLC 15693.

112. Le Corbusier, Centrosoyuz, "3e étage," fourth-floor plan, beginning of 1929, FLC 15695.

made possible." The problem was thus posed in a highly characteristic and intelligent manner.

The architects therefore designed an edifice in which, thanks to the liberties afforded by reinforced-concrete techniques, the idea of interiors that breathe . . . leads to a striking example of the modern office building. And it is precisely the struggle against intense cold (as low as −40° C. in Moscow) that led to the creation of isothermal buildings that are indifferent to both heat and cold, building types applicable everywhere, whether in the tropics or in polar regions. The combination of two patented methods, that of Gustave Lyon (*aération ponctuelle)* and that of Le Corbusier and Pierre Jeanneret (*murs neutralisants*) has brought about a complete transformation in traditional methods of heating.

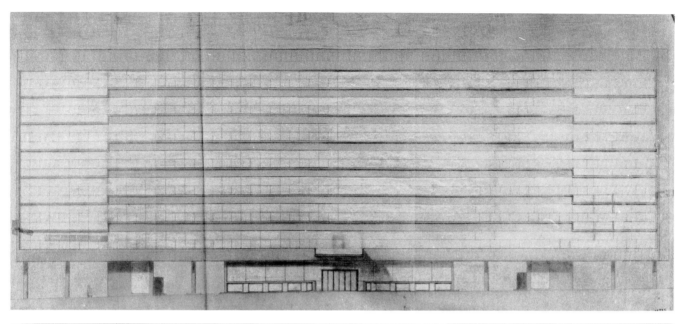

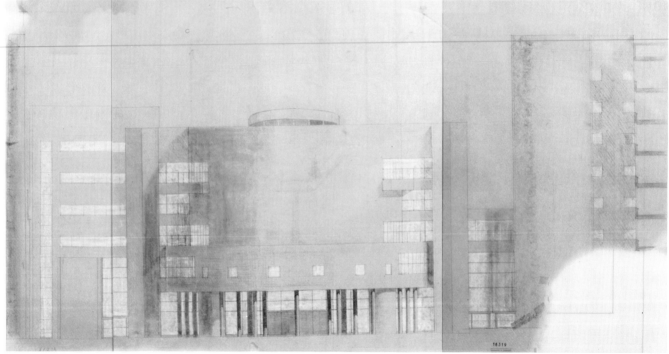

113. Le Corbusier, Centrosoyuz, study for the side facade, beginning of 1929, FLC 16235.

114. Le Corbusier, Centrosoyuz, study for the rear facade, beginning of 1929, FLC 16319.

Le Corbusier went on to explain the formal implications of these choices, which constitute "the very basis" of the shapes of his building:

Such methods entail the following unavoidable architectural consequences: the buildings become *types*—office types, assembly-hall types, etc. The facades are reduced to smooth surfaces (double membranes). These surfaces can be all glass, all stone or a combination of the two, depending on the function required. The roofing is flat; melted snow and rainwater are evacuated in the warmth the building. . . . The blocks are placed on *pilotis*, thus permitting cars and people to circulate underneath them. It is a good thing to dissociate (oblique) vertical elements such as stairs (or preferably ramps) from the horizontal ones—the offices.

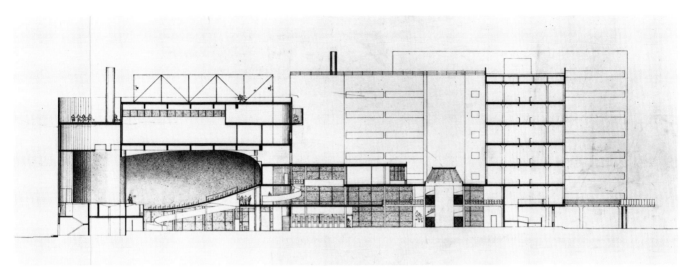

115. Le Corbusier, Centrosoyuz, transverse section, beginning of 1929, FLC 15701.

116. Le Corbusier, Centrosoyuz, section on one of the office wings, beginning of 1929, FLC 16203.

Thus emerges an unprecedented, complex architectural plan, one requiring a new aesthetic approach on the part of the architect.

The architecture consists of moving relations. The elements that make it possible to perceive these relations are its volumes and surfaces and its limpid, clearly readable lines. What makes it artistically moving is the quality of the relations between the various geometrical elements.[61]

The recourse to novel ventilation systems was also emphasized in an article for *Sovremennaia Arkhitektura*[62] by Nikolai Kolli, who was now back in Moscow with the plans and, apparently, the model of what he considered the definitive project. He wrote to Le Corbusier and Jeanneret of the positive impressions he had taken away with him from Paris:

I must admit in all sincerity that in the course of my two months in Paris, the fact of laboring [*raboter*] daily in your office became a truly agreeable routine, and I keenly feel the absence of your most friendly assistance.

The project that we have brought back with us from Paris is considered with quite exceptional interest. The CS executive finds that it corresponds exactly to all their

[61] Le Corbusier, "Maison de l'Union des Coopératives à Moscou," *Cahiers d'Art*, no. 4 (1929): 162–68.

[62] Nikolai Kolli, "K proektu doma Centrosoyuza," *Sovremennaia Arkhitektura* 4, no. 4 (1929): 135–41.

117. Le Corbusier, Centrosoyuz, study model, beginning of 1929, view from above.

118. Le Corbusier, Centrosoyuz, study model, beginning of 1929, overall view.

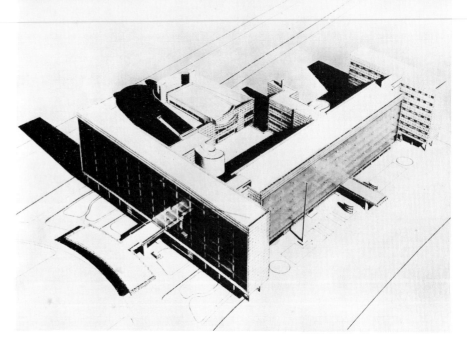

desires. No fault has been found with the architectural composition. They fear, however, that the heating you have proposed will be the source of major economic difficulties.[63]

At the end of April, the executives of Centrosoyuz finally resolved to entrust the building of the project to the Paris team. During the presentation of the project to the municipal authorities, however, a further geometrical modification was adopted owing to problems with the site—it had proved impossible to acquire one of the plots of land—and the project now reverted to the earlier, trapezoidal configuration, as Kolli, now recognized by the Soviets as Le Corbusier's assistant, reported:

[63] Nikolai Kolli, letter to Le Corbusier and Pierre Jeanneret, Moscow, 7 March 1929, FLC. It should be remembered that "rabotat" means "to work" in Russian but that a "rabot" is the French name for "plane," a carpenter's tool.

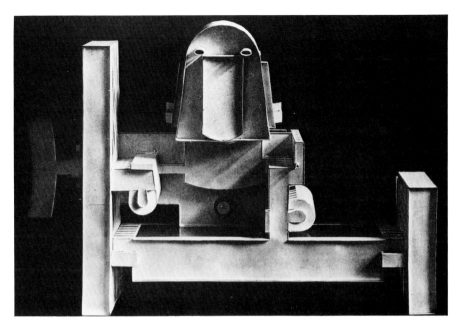

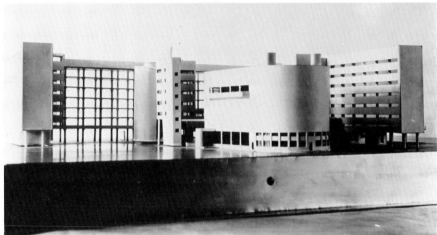

119. Le Corbusier, Centrosoyuz, study model, beginning of 1929, view from above.

120. Le Corbusier, Centrosoyuz, study model, beginning of 1929, view from the rear.

121. Le Corbusier, Centrosoyuz, study model in a vitrine at the "Style of the Industrial Bourgeoisie" exhibition, Moscow, 1930.

The Centrosoyuz office has reworked the plans that we brought back from Paris. I was mostly absent when this was done, having returned to my work on the dam, but I did tell them to be careful, since in my view there would be modifications that you would not approve. . . . The problem of the improvement of the site (right angles) has proved insurmountable, and the earlier variant has been adopted for the moment.

I trust you will consider this as an insignificant yet indispensable phase for the submission of the project for state approval.[64]

Although Le Corbusier considered the "right-angled" solution superior, he sent back word of his "good" opinion of the revised plans and of his view that a return to the earlier layout was "tolerable," while at the same time emphasizing the need for Kolli's regular presence in Paris so as to fix the "spirit" of the project clearly in his mind.[65] It is amusing to note the influence of the shape of the plot on the project, in a country that had, to use Le Corbusier's own terms, effectively achieved "mobilization of the ground."[66] On 1 June, Le Corbusier at last signed the contract relative to the working drawings, including a detailed study of the finishings and part of the planning of the interior. The contract, based on fees (expressed in American dollars) representing 2 percent of building costs, or $25,000, specified that the architects must visit the site at least twice a year, "whenever Centrosoyuz should so desire," and at its expense.[67]

THE FAILURE OF "RESPIRATION EXACTE"

From 6 to 17 June 1929, Le Corbusier was in Moscow supervising the construction drawings. This was in fact to be his penultimate visit, for he would only return on one other occasion, from 5 to 17 March 1930. The atmosphere of this second trip, which did not generate the same public interest as the first, can be judged from a postcard of a cactus, countersigned by Kolli and Nakhman, which he sent to Yvonne Gallis:

This is Russia: Eskimos playing among the cacti. The *pilotis* further the revolution, vodka is used for soap, the speeches work off one's thirst and the ideals persist.[68]

On his return to Paris he inspired Sigfried Giedion to write an article celebrating the scale of the enterprise in the *Neue Zürcher Zeitung*:

This is the sign of a certain boldness on the part of a regime that defends a building of this scale in the face of popular opinion, and which thus opens up new paths for the future. Clearly, the people's representatives have not given in without a struggle. Le Corbusier recounts that they were critical of the use of *pilotis* in the project. The same prejudices hold sway in Russia, France and Switzerland. And the same arguments can be used both here and everywhere. Here one speaks of the lakeside dwellings and barns of the Valais, and the President of the Soviet invokes the peasant dwellings of the Volga, which are built on the same sound principles as those that allow for a transparent ground floor, such that, given increased future traffic, one will have a clear view across the neighborhood.[69]

Yet as Bruno Taut's own position testifies, the advocates of the new architecture in western Europe were far from unanimous. Although Taut was critical of the persistence of monumental projects by the pre-Bolshevik retrenchment, and in particular of the rejection of the Vesnins' project for the Lenin Library, he nonetheless rejected the alternative as represented by the Centrosoyuz project:

[64] Nikolai Kolli, letter to Le Corbusier, Moscow, 2 May 1929, FLC.
[65] Le Corbusier, letter to Nikolai Kolli, Paris, 9 May 1929, FLC.
[66] It is no less curious that, four years later, the "right-angled" version of the project was published without comment as "Une maison sans escaliers," in *L'Architecture d'Aujourd'hui*, no. 10 (1933): 105–8.
[67] "Contrat entre l'Union Centrale des Coopératives . . . et les architectes," Paris, 1 June 1929, FLC.
[68] Le Corbusier, postcard sent to Yvonne Gallis, Moscow, 13 June 1929, FLC. Le Corbusier married Yvonne Gallis in the following year.
[69] Sigfried Giedion, "Le Corbusiers 'Zentrosoyus' in Moskau," *Neue Zürcher Zeitung*, Zurich (19 July 1929).

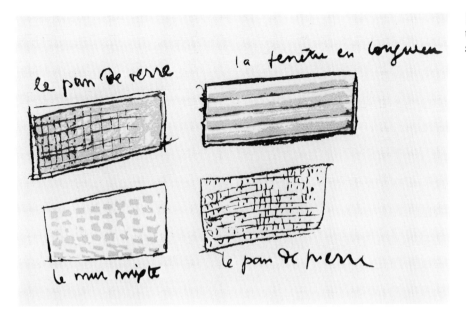

122. Le Corbusier, the four facade types of Centrosoyuz; published in *Précisions* (Paris, 1930).

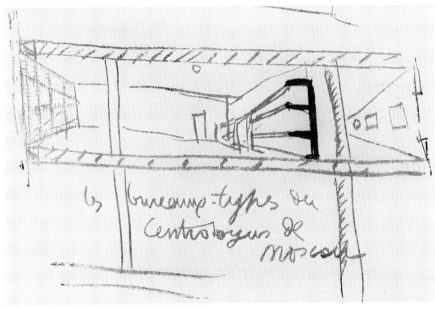

123. Le Corbusier, the "typical offices" of Moscow's Centrosoyuz; published in *Précisions* (Paris, 1930).

Instead of monumentality we are faced with a pseudorational artistry; one, however, that is the fruit of such talent that Moscow is quite taken aback[70]

The detailed project raised questions concerning the interior and the surrounding buildings. To the discreet atmosphere of the offices, which he had designed in 1928 as laboratories for planners with reassuringly optimistic production curves on the walls, Le Corbusier now contributed architectural "silence" by means of the sliding cabinets that he had already used in his villas:

These methods can be applied to the model offices of the Palace of the Cooperatives in Moscow: the walls separating the offices from the corridors are constituted in this way: throughout the building's length, the partition becomes a model filing system. This solution was, moreover, the one envisaged for the Palace of Nations in Geneva.

Offices or living room, study or boudoir; always and everywhere, standard, highly

[70] Bruno Taut, "Russlands Architektonische Situation," *Moderne Bauformen*, no. 2 (1930): 59.

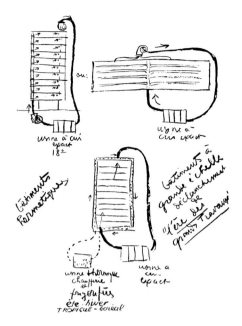

124. Le Corbusier, the "machines for *air exact*"; published in *Précisions* (Paris, 1930).

precise functions are carried out and satisfy, ordering the objects around common, human dimensions. It's farewell to the old office cabinets.[71]

Although Le Corbusier did not succeed in convincing the Soviets of the relevance of his proposals for the district as a whole, he nonetheless paid careful attention to the building's exterior, which was to be lined with trees and art works, as outlined at another conference in Buenos Aires:

Completing the architectural symphony, positioned in front of the building in the familiar posture of organs of human dimensions, here are the concrete, stone faced awnings that serve to protect vehicles in the street as they arrive. Here you see a number of objects arranged so as to create strong horizontal and vertical relations: the Cooperative flagpole and a number of pedestals on which I should like to see some examples of contemporary statuary (Lipschitz, Brancusi, Laurens) playing a dazzling role in the architectural symphonies. There are mathematical places that resemble the centers of gravity of the composition. These places dominate space. It is no longer, as in the time of Mansart, "the engraver who in the tympanum sculpts trophies"; rather, it is the plastician [*sic*] who, through his work which resembles a shooting star or lighthouse, must keep these pure, silent crystal or stone prisms at a respectful distance.

This winter we shall transplant along the vast, limpid facades a number of beautiful trees whose arabesques will enrich the composition and whose presence will be more and more welcome to us as we study architecture and city planning. One of iron and concrete architecture's most authentic claims to the public's gratitude will be the fact of having introduced trees into the urban landscape.[72]

A reading of Le Corbusier's later writings reveals, however, that the basic conflict with the Soviets concerned the question of heating and ventilation. He later pronounced an irrevocable condemnation of "the Russian authorities, who refused to agree" to carry out his plans,[73] while he was absorbed in the partial and highly problematic implementation of the same system in his Salvation Army's Cité de Refuge project, where its limitations first became evident.[74] In order to define the system further, Le Corbusier did not hesitate to mobilize transcontinental expertise. His journey to Argentina and Brazil revealed the vast potential for projects in Latin America—a potential that he flashed before the American Blower Corporation when, faced with persistent Soviet skepticism and conscious of the prestige of American engineering in the Russia of the first Five-Year Plan, he asked them for a written estimate:

I am taking this opportunity to ask you for a dossier concerning Moscow, *which in my view constitutes the focus of architecture and city planning in the world.*

It is imperative that Moscow be a resounding success. I should be in despair if our building (which everyone is talking about) were equipped with age-old heating systems. It would be a defeat. I intended to see you in New York in March. But things are moving fast in Moscow: the decision is imminent!

I am convinced that (the new system) represents a formidable solution for the future. Technical support from the Americans would be decisive in Moscow.

. . . Your immediate answer is absolutely indispensable. All I wish from you is *an approximate estimate,* but one precise enough to permit a decision either way.[75]

As quickly as he could have wished, the Americans, who were in fact more hardware producers than consultant engineers, furnished a lucid yet reticent analysis but one that was brutal in its conclusions as to the failings of the system, which they judged extravagant, noisy, and potentially smelly:

Our hasty and somewhat superficial calculations indicate that the method proposed would require, in order to heat and ventilate the building, four times as much steam

[71] Le Corbusier, "L'aventure du mobilier," *Précisions,* p. 116.

[72] Le Corbusier, "Les techniques," pp. 60–61.

[73] Willi Boesiger, ed., *Le Corbusier et Pierre Jeanneret, œuvre complète 1929–1934* (Zurich: Girsberger, 1935), p. 35.

[74] Brian Brace Taylor, *Le Corbusier: The City of Refuge, Paris 1929–1933* (Chicago: Chicago University Press, 1987).

[75] Le Corbusier, letter to F. R. Still, Paris, 3 January 1931, FLC. A detailed file on Centrosoyuz and the proposed systems accompanies this document.

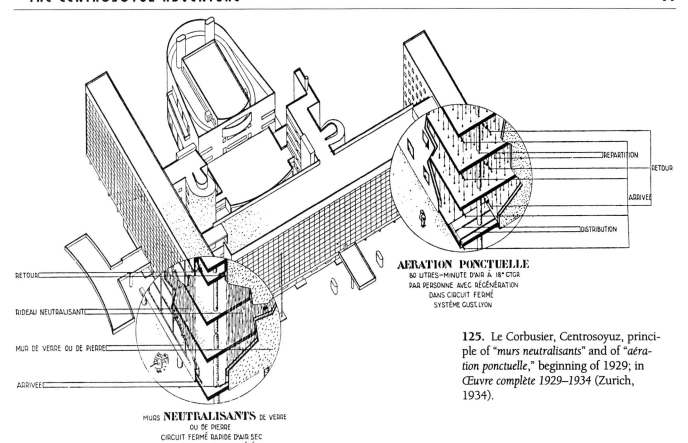

RETOUR

RIDEAU NEUTRALISANT

MUR DE VERRE OU DE PIERRE

ARRIVEE

REPARTITION
RETOUR
ARRIVEE
DISTRIBUTION

AÉRATION PONCTUELLE
80 LITRES-MINUTE D'AIR À 18° CTGR
PAR PERSONNE AVEC RÉGÉNÉRATION
DANS CIRCUIT FERMÉ
SYSTÈME GUST. LYON

MURS **NEUTRALISANTS** DE VERRE
OU DE PIERRE
CIRCUIT FERMÉ RAPIDE D'AIR SEC
CHAUD (HIVER) OU FROID (ÉTÉ)
SYSTÈME L.C.–P.J.

125. Le Corbusier, Centrosoyuz, principle of "*murs neutralisants*" and of "*aération ponctuelle*," beginning of 1929; in *Œuvre complète 1929–1934* (Zurich, 1934).

126. Le Corbusier, Centrosoyuz, sketch of the proposed heating system, beginning of 1929, FLC 16049.

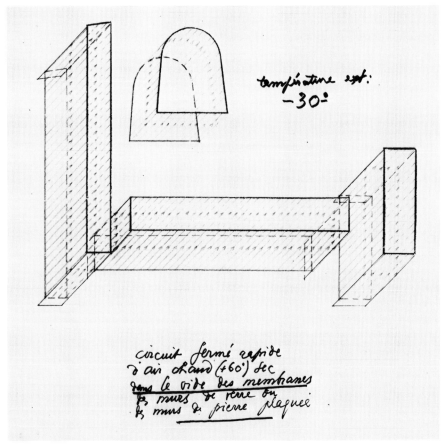

température ext:
–30°

circuit fermé rapide
d'air chaud (+60°) sec
dans le vide des membranes
des murs de pierre ou
des murs de pierre plaquée

127. Survey of the Centrosoyuz's site and its surroundings, FLC 16346.

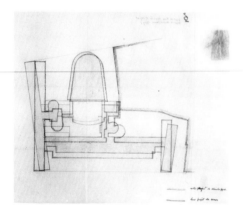

128. Le Corbusier, Centrosoyuz, modifications of the building's contours between December 1928 and March 1929, May 1929, FLC 15952.

and twice as much mechanical power as would be necessary with methods currently employed in our country under comparable atmospheric conditions.[76]

The Americans highlighted the system's high running and maintenance costs, the need to plan for far more air for refrigeration than for heating, and the fact that the figure for the replenishment of air in the building had been underestimated. Clearly, the absence of all technical support for Le Corbusier's proposals made his defense a desperate affair—all the more so since the Soviets, who had by then been reduced to selling the czars' art collections to the Americans through the intermediary Armand Hammer in order to pay for their factory construction programs,[77] were to say the least extremely reluctant to use high-technology heating equipment, especially if it was experimental.

FRUSTRATIONS ON THE CONSTRUCTION SITE

The problems encountered in the finalization of the project did not, however, discourage Liubimov, who, having been relieved of his responsibilities at Centrosoyuz, was now in Berlin.[78] In February 1930 he asked Le Corbusier to submit a housing project for Soviet employees working in the capital of the Reich. The latter, who claimed he would be "enchanted" to study the problem, proposed one of his "housing blocks equipped with communal amenities (hotel services) based on researches carried out since 1922," and cited the Wanner apartment block at Geneva as evidence of the realism of his ideas:

The fact of [our] building in Berlin would not be looked upon with an evil eye in Germany, where our work is well known and well regarded—where, in fact, we already have a following. We have worked for the City of Stuttgart. The City of Frankfurt has commissioned a considerable body of work by Dutch and Swiss architects. Moreover, we might for instance ask our colleague Walter Gropius, with whom we are on the best possible terms, to collaborate or suggest an assistant.[79]

Contact was duly made with Gropius; Le Corbusier requested a meeting on the platform of Berlin-Friedrichstrasse station for discussions.[80] But the initiative appears to have fallen flat, doubtless owing to Russian cheeseparing in their foreign investment programs. Meanwhile, Kolli labored on the drawing board and on site to mediate between Le Corbusier's high-technology ambi-

[76] American Blower Corporation, letter to Le Corbusier, 24 January 1930, FLC.

[77] Robert C. Williams, *Russian Art and American Money, 1900–1940* (Cambridge, Mass.: Harvard University Press, 1980); Armand Hammer (with Neil Lyndon), *Hammer* (New York: G. P. Putnam's and Sons, 1987).

[78] See the glowing speech by the Centrosoyuz management on the occasion of his departure at the end of December 1929: *Postanovleniia 3 (XXI) Sessii Sovetov Centrosoyuza SSSR i Centrosoyuza RSFSR* (Moscow: Centrosoyuz, 1930), pp. 121–22.

[79] Le Corbusier, letter to Isidor Liubimov, Paris, 25 February 1930, FLC.

[80] Le Corbusier, letter to Walter Gropius, Paris, 26 February 1930, FLC.

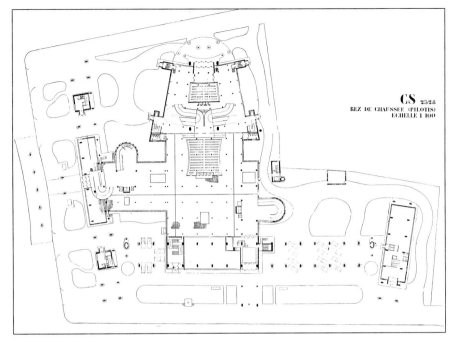

129. Le Corbusier, Centrosoyuz, ground-floor plan of the final project, May 1929; in *Œuvre complète 1929–1934* (Zurich, 1934).

130. Le Corbusier, Centrosoyuz, position of the building on the site, May 1929, FLC 16346.

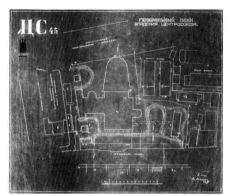

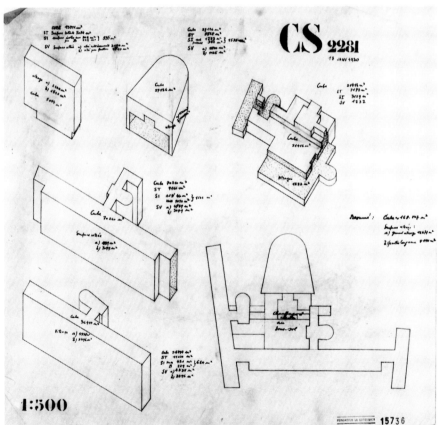

132. Le Corbusier, Centrosoyuz, ramps of A wing, October 1929; drawing by Anke Komter, FLC 15795.

131. Le Corbusier, Centrosoyuz, graphic calculation of surfaces and volumes; drawing by Ernst Weissmann, January 1930, FLC 15736.

[81] The plans recorded in the *Carnet noir* testify to the more or less continual intervention of Weissmann and Maekewa from July 1929 to February 1930. Kolli joined the team between 30 January and 14 February 1930, from which time Sert played a diminished role. The work carried out in Paris during this second phase of the study focused mainly on general views of the building and a number of details. In the third phase, which lasted until May 1931, Rice, McClellan, Geiser, Saporta, Safran, Renner, Sedlak, and Bursztin made their appearance in the finalization of incidental details sent to Moscow.

[82] Nikolai Kolli, "Dom Narkomlegproma," *Arkhitektura SSSR* 4, no. 10 (1936): 28.

[83] The subsequent adventures of Sammer (1907–1973), who assisted Kolli on some stations of Moscow's subway, took him as far afield as Japan and Pondicherry, where he worked with Antonin Raymond: Jindřich Krise, "Zemrel František Sammer, architekt urbanista e filosof," *Architektura ČSR*, no. 3 (1974): 140–43.

[84] Centrosoyuz, letter to Le Corbusier, Moscow, 12 July 1931, FLC.

[85] "Hannes Meyer über Sowjetrussland," *Die Baugilde*, no. 30 (1931): 1602.

[86] Hannes Meyer, "Bauen, Bauarbeiter und Techniker in der Sowjetunion," *Das neue Russland*, nos. 8–9 (1931): 49. This is a transcription of the lecture given at the Berlin Marxistische Arbeiterschule on 13 October; English translation: Hannes Meyer, "Construction, Construction Workers and Technicians in the Soviet Union," in an appendix to El Lissitzky, *Russia: An Architecture for World Revolution* (Cambridge, Mass.: MIT Press, 1970), p. 216.

[87] Nikolai Kolli, letter to Le Corbusier, Moscow, 26 March 1932, FLC.

tions and the somewhat rudimentary methods of the Moscow construction industry. In Paris, more detailed plans were drawn up by Kunyo Maekewa, Ernst Weissmann, and Jose Luis Sert, who were joined by Kolli in January or February 1930.[81] In Moscow, Kolli liaised with Soviet technical teams: first with the Mosstroi's concrete office, directed by the engineer Z. Ia. Sheiman assisted by the engineers Tsirlin and M. S. Ozernov, and afterward with Mosproekt, where the same Ozernov was assisted by the architects A. N. Fedorov and T. I. Tarasov.[82]

Kolli supervised the group of technicians responsible for the adaptation of the project to Soviet norms, and a system of radiators was finally chosen. At the same time the shortage of quality materials made it necessary to modify details incessantly. In this work he entertained distant but privileged relations with "Monsieur Pierre," and never failed to mention him in his letters of the period. Charlotte Perriand went to Moscow on two occasions, in 1932 and 1934, and the Czech architect François (František) Sammer, who had worked in the rue de Sèvres office, took charge of the final phase of construction with Kolli.[83] In the course of his third stay, Le Corbusier was present at the launching of the first operations on the site, but in July 1931 work was suspended as a direct result of the first Five-Year Plan, which granted absolute priority to industrial programs. Centrosoyuz had thus momentarily to sacrifice its headquarters "in order to participate in the accomplishment of the grand design," which "made it absolutely necessary to mobilize all available forces and construction materials."[84]

The interruption of building work found a sardonic advocate in the person of Hannes Meyer, former director of the Bauhaus who, following his purge from Dessau, offered his services to the Soviet architectural and city-planning institutes together with a "brigade" of *Bauhaüsler*. During a lecture he gave in Berlin in October, Meyer judged the destiny of Le Corbusier's Centrosoyuz "characteristic" and guaranteed that "this orgy" of concrete and glass would never be finished, but that it would be abandoned, if only because of the materials":[85]

We even abandon buildings that have been started and whose foundations have been finished, simply because waste of materials has to be avoided at all costs. An example of this is the building of the Centrosoyuz (designed by Le Corbusier). At the moment we lack the capability to carry out such projects. They are beyond the scope of the present Five-Year Plan. We abandon such unfinished projects, like a cake half-eaten, so we can have our daily bread.[86]

On his return to Berlin in the spring of 1932 Liubimov—who had since been appointed people's commissar for light industry, and who thus had at his disposal resources that the cooperatives, whose activities were declining in the face of the forced expansion of the state sector, doubtless lacked—succeeded in getting construction work restarted, a fact that certainly tempered some of the bitterness felt by Le Corbusier following his failure to win the Palace of Soviets competition. Liubimov's renewed "patronage" armed Kolli with "firm hopes" for the building's completion—if only Le Corbusier would condescend to offer his "help" and "advice."[87] The latter's initial response to this was both warm and affirmative:

For me it is *a great joy*. The Centrosoyuz will live at last! The suspension of work was for us an occasion of much sadness. The resumption of construction under your direction is a guarantee of success.

Another joy: the return of *M. Liubimov*. Between us friendship has developed; between us, confidence and esteem. M. Liubimov is *a man of architecture*. He under-

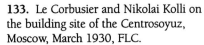

133. Le Corbusier and Nikolai Kolli on the building site of the Centrosoyuz, Moscow, March 1930, FLC.

134. Le Corbusier and Nikolai Kolli on the building site of the Centrosoyuz, Moscow, March 1930, FLC.

135. Reinforcement of a ramp, Centrosoyuz, Moscow, 1932.

136. Reinforcement of a floor, Centrosoyuz, Moscow, 1932.

stands, more than that, he loves. With such a man, Russian architecture is built on rock. Please tell him that I shall do my utmost to make him proud, *extremely proud*, of the work in hand.[88]

But at the same time, "following studies carried out by the Saint-Gobain laboratories," Le Corbusier made a new attempt to introduce an advanced version of his *respiration exacte*. This again resulted in failure. It was no longer a time for outbidding tactics, and he had to fight tooth and nail to have as many elements of the original project built as possible. Soviet architecture was turning toward "socialist realism," and, in the eyes of the Muscovites, the

[88] Le Corbusier, letter to Nikolai Kolli, Paris, 6 April 1932, FLC.

building's empty shell reflected discredit on the principles of its construction. A German observer noted that in the neighboring Gostorg building, which was also largely glass-faced, "the people take their work off to the shady side in summer and take refuge in the warmer parts of the building in winter, if, that is, they manage to survive at all in these offices":

The reinforced concrete skeleton of Le Corbusier's design was left unfinished for two years, and the gloomy framework with its protruding rusty steel reinforcing was left staring into the sky along the busy street while the people prayed for sanity. This has changed now, and people passing the building on the street notice with amazement that the exterior shell (in order to free the walls, even the columns have been pushed into the interior, true to Dessau fashion) has been filled in with red cut stone (Artik tuff from the Caucasus), while the upper part of the protruding wing along the future street alignment has begun to look like the stone wall of a refrigeration plant. The smooth stone surfaces of the other walls are pierced by small, square, prisonlike openings. It is true that previously published designs of the elevations call for similar stone surfaces in these areas, and thus the horror of glass walls in other parts of the building (which have been temporarily sheathed with plywood to protect the interior work) may yet become reality.

One can only wonder what kind of stylistic accomplishment the finished building will eventually represent.[89]

In December 1933 the skeleton and metalwork were finished, and construction of the club block was started after a number of modifications, including the decision to sacrifice the planned top-floor gymnasium.[90] Some weeks later, while Le Corbusier was himself envisaging a trip to Moscow, Charlotte Perriand visited the site. Perriand, who had been working with the firm on furniture design since 1927, realized that "the problem is not to inaugurate the building but rather to ensure that it is correctly finished"[91]—a view corroborated by photos taken by Jose Luis Sert when he inspected the site in May.[92] One of the problems that Charlotte Perriand had to resolve was that of color. Le Corbusier had sharply criticized the "psychophysiological decadence of the shades" on receiving a seventy-three-point chromatic study with samples attached:

The colors are those of the boudoir, and not of the Soviet Union! . . . They do not match the psychological state of the USSR—such, at least, as we would like to imagine it, that is, fully active, and not asleep or immersed in drawing-room discussion.

The conflict with Kolli over color enabled Le Corbusier to reaffirm his own views on the question, but also to emphasize how much he would like to visit the distant site:

Colors do not have to be prepared in such a pedantic, professorial manner. Chromatic treatment should intervene once the building is finished, when the plasterwork has been completed, the scaffolding has been removed and light can penetrate the build-

137. Le Corbusier, Centrosoyuz, photograph of the building site, taken by Jose Luis Sert, Moscow, May 1934.

138. Le Corbusier, Centrosoyuz, installation of the stone cladding, Moscow, 1934.

139. Le Corbusier, Centrosoyuz, photograph of the building site, Moscow, 1934.

[89] Anonymous, "Zwischen Klima, Stil und Zweck," *Bauwelt* Berlin, no. 7 (1933): 172. English translation: "Climate, Style and Function," in an appendix to Lissitzky, *Russia*, p. 224.

[90] Nikolai Kolli, letter to Le Corbusier, Moscow, 9 December 1933, FLC.

[91] Charlotte Perriand, letter to Le Corbusier, Moscow, 18 January 1934, FLC.

[92] Jose Luis Sert, letter to Pierre Jeanneret, Barcelona, 18 June 1934, FLC

ing. Only then can one appreciate the reciprocal value of the different walls, which one decorates in accordance with the specific laws of color: red to enliven, blue to give depth to a wall, yellow dangerous and quite localized or as a complement to the other two. Either strong or delicate shades can be used. In short, chromatic treatment should give expression to a building, and not destroy it.

To sum up. Personally, I view this study as premature and, if I had anything to say in the matter, it would be this: when the time comes to bring painters into the building, I wish to be called to Moscow in order to discuss what is to be done with the Moscow authorities. You know that I place my experience entirely at your disposal.[93]

In the context of the new Soviet political line, however, the struggle for the building took on far greater proportions at a time when, as we shall see, even André Lurçat launched attacks on Le Corbusier in Moscow. The correspondence with Liubimov shows that this criticism had become a cause for concern:

The Palace of Industry will not be old-fashioned as some wish to claim; on the contrary, it will find its true place, above all in a Russia that has burst its old bonds. The plans were drawn up in a completely responsible frame of mind. The building will be neither a barracks nor a box. If it is well built, it will be a work of great architectural quality and dignity. This is my innermost conviction. I am also convinced that with your profound understanding of architectural matters, you have not let us down.

The battle I have fought for so long has its ups and downs. My ideas are misrepresented in the USSR. Those responsible for this are either people who do not understand me, or else people with a vested interest (these I know).

I am impatient for the building to be finished and the object of fair criticism such as was planned. I also hope to visit Moscow then, and I shall not close this letter without expressing how much I regret having been prevented from doing so for almost four years.[94]

As the months went by, the attacks on the building on Miasnitskaia Street

140. Le Corbusier, Centrosoyuz; drawing by D. Rubinstein in *Literaturnaia Gazeta*, Moscow (December 1934).

141. Le Corbusier, Centrosoyuz, detail of the facade in construction, Moscow, 1934.

142. Le Corbusier, Centrosoyuz, overall view of the finished building, Moscow, 1936.

[93] Le Corbusier, letter to Nikolai Kolli, Paris, 13 April 1934, FLC.

[94] Le Corbusier, letter to Isidor Liubimov, Paris, 25 September 1934, FLC.

143. Le Corbusier, Centrosoyuz, view of the auditorium's facade, Moscow, 1973.

144. Le Corbusier, Centrosoyuz, view of the rear facade, Moscow, 1973.

[95] Nikolai Kolli, "Proizvedenie mastera," *Arkhitektura SSSR* 2, no. 12 (1934): 7–8.

[96] Viktor Kokorin, "Chuzhoi dom," *Arkhitekturnaia Gazeta* (24 January 1935).

[97] S. N. Kozhin, "Oshibki zamysla," *Arkhitektura SSSR* 2, no. 12 (1934): 9. For the subsequent development of the district bordering on Centrosoyuz, see B. M. Velikovsky, "Novaia Miasnitskaia ulitsa," *Arkhitektura SSSR* 1, no. 11 (1933): 57.

(renamed Kirov Street, following the assassination of the Leningrad party-secretary) indeed increased in intensity at the very time when it took its place on the Moscow skyline.

UNDER ENEMY FIRE

The criticisms became apparent at the end of 1934 when, in his report on the state of advancement of the Narkomlegprom (as the building was now called), Kolli stressed that it would be premature to judge an unfinished structure and that, in any case, it was important to consider it in the context of the time of its design (1929–1930).[95] Like Viktor Kokorin, for whom the building was an "unholy" object, a number of architects who had been close to Le Corbusier during his 1928 visit were now more aloof.[96] This is also true of Sergei Kozhin, who was critical of the "cold, monotonous, disagreeable" nature of the walls behind which "people must work under tension, like automatons, without joy"—in a word, "in the American way." "Simplistic, and even primitive," for Kozhin the building was "devoid of all artistic sense," and he considered the *pilotis* "of an unusual character" in a street that was to play a major role in the new plan for Moscow.[97]

On the other hand, the judgment of the convinced traditionalist Ivan Fomin was more complex; he took pains to highlight the "insufficiencies" of the building's "qualities." But, although he criticized the capitalist architect for failing to express the joy of living in an architecture of contrasts between the expanses of glass and the walls of tuff, whose "poverty" inspired doubt as to his capacity to build anything except villas, he nonetheless recognized the building's simple, laconic character, the quality of its lighting and even the *pilotis,* which he thought reasonable. Above all, Fomin emphasized that Le Corbusier's "architectural forms [did] not run counter to the principles of construction":

It is true that Le Corbusier's architecture does not constitute an ideal for us, nor a model for the new architecture whose role is to express the qualities of this remarkable epoch. Nonetheless, this production merits serious study. It is one of the most ad-

145. Le Corbusier, Centrosoyuz, view of finished *pilotis*, Moscow, 1936.

146. Le Corbusier, Centrosoyuz, overall view from the Miasnitskaia Street, 1973.

vanced buildings of the school that was so influential during the first decade of Soviet architecture.[98]

For Alexander Vesnin, a notable member of this school, Centrosoyuz was quite simply "Moscow's best building in the last hundred years," and he invoked the remarks of the workers on the construction site as clear evidence of mass support for the new architecture as compared with the criticisms of "amateurs" who disliked its "simplicity" and "primitivism":

This building is characterized by clarity of architectural thought, precision in the construction of masses and volumes, the purity of different elements reflecting con-

[98] I. Fomin, "O prostote i bogatsve," *Arkhitektura SSSR* 2, no. 12 (1934): 8. In the twenties Fomin, a St. Petersburg architect, practiced and advocated the "proletarian Doric."

147. Le Corbusier, Centrosoyuz, tangential view from the Miasnitskaia Street, 1989.

148. Le Corbusier, Centrosoyuz, view of the auditorium's entrance, Moscow, 1936; in *Arkhitektura SSSR* 4, no. 10 (1936).

trast and nuance, overall scale and attention to detail, a lightness associated with monumentality, simplicity and architectural unity.[99]

In July 1935 Le Corbusier learned "while in the train between Warsaw and Vienna that Centrosoyuz was in use." He asked Sammer for photographs of the building,[100] but the Czech architect was leaving for Japan and entrusted Kolli with the task of passing on the latest news of the site when he visited Paris in September of the same year.[101]

As soon as he arrived in Rome, Kolli succeeded in thwarting the censor and what he called "the mail mystery"—none of the books sent by Le Corbusier had reached him for three years—and wrote that he was "doing everything in his power to supervise construction in accordance with the plans drawn up in Paris," despite the fact that "ideas had changed" in Moscow, where the search was now on for "architecture in conformity with the desires of the people." Kolli had survived "intense struggles and concerted attacks that, more often than not, were directed against the building's design conception." At the moment of writing, only the club had yet to be completed.[102] When Kolli reached Paris, however, Le Corbusier was in the United States, and they were unable to meet to discuss the building.

Because he could not influence the building's progress from a distance, Le Corbusier now made a final attempt to "finish the architectural symphony" of Centrosoyuz. Since 1934 Le Corbusier had repeatedly asked Liubimov for permission to go to Moscow. Before his ultimate disappearance, he pleaded with him to hire the services of the sculptor Jacques Lipschitz for two sculptures that he had intended for the entrance front.[103] Lipschitz, who had made two sculptures for Madame de Mandrot's house at Le Pradet, attempted during a trip to Moscow to secure the commission for the statues but failed to meet either Liubimov or Kolli, who was in Paris at the time:

What I have discovered here far exceeds my expectations. I am filled with enthusiasm by the scale and audacity of everything that is happening in all domains, and you can imagine how happy I should be to participate in the construction of this new world. Only we can invent the forms adapted to its grandeur and novelty. From the first day, whenever I have spoken of Centrosoyuz—despite all the imperfections due to the construction and to a number of modifications of your plans, the fact that the building is not sufficiently set back, etc.—I have done nothing but repeat that it is the most significant building in Moscow. . . . Thus you can comprehend how excited I am at the prospect of making the two sculptural masses that you envisaged in your plans, and which frankly, if they are a success, will strike a highly significant note relative to the building as a whole.[104]

In the summer of 1936 the Narkomlegprom building began to take definitive shape both inside and outside; on the exterior, the folds of the curtains brought a hint of disorder to the patterned expanse of glass. Kolli, who assumed "complete responsibility for the artistic quality of the interiors," at last had photographs of the building's most significant spaces published in an article that he wrote for the official review *Arkhitektura SSSR*.[105]

In his guided tour of the building from the ground floor to its summit, Kolli explained that in the first months of the building's use the free space of the "colonnade"—the term he now applied to the *pilotis*—had functioned to the satisfaction of all. The posts in the great hall had attained the dignity of columns faced with reconstituted gray marble and, to compensate for the lack of capitals, pale-colored oak moldings and black marblite plinths. The walls were of yellow Crimean marble, and the floor was composed of large squares of light-gray marble with a crisscross pattern of darker gray lines. The ramps

[99] Aleksandre Vesnin, "Legkost, Stroinost, Iasnost," *Arkhitektura SSSR* 2, no. 12 (1934): 8.

[100] Le Corbusier, letter to František Sammer, Paris, 31 July 1935, FLC.

[101] František Sammer, letter to Le Corbusier, Moscow, 17 September 1935, FLC.

[102] Nikolai Kolli, letter to Le Corbusier, Rome, 24 December 1935, FLC.

[103] Le Corbusier, letter to Isidor Liubimov, Paris, 7 October 1935, FLC.

[104] Jacques Lipschitz, letter to Le Corbusier, Moscow, 21 October 1935, FLC. In his memoirs, Lipschitz's impressions are less lyrical: Jacques Lipschitz (with H. H. Harnason), *My Life in Sculpture* (New York: Viking Press, 1972), p. 131.

[105] Kolli, "Dom Narkomlegproma," pp. 27–33.

149. Le Corbusier, Centrosoyuz, view of the hall, Moscow, 1936; in *Arkhitektura SSSR* 4, no. 10 (1936).

were carpeted in black rubber and paneled with oak. The walls of the landings were of gray marble. The office partitions were also largely decorated in various pale-colored woods.[106]

Kolli, who was highly satisfied with the luminous quality of the interiors, also described the system that had finally been selected to protect the building from the cold and the heat: for the former, radiators lined the glass facades, and for the latter, the engineer P. N. Sabarov, who had designed the "grandiose" metal frames for the double glazing, had the traditional curtains replaced with roller blinds. Different types of glass had been used: sanded glass for the exterior and translucent glass inside. Kolli did not fail to mention the technical problems met, especially those developed in the preparation of the curved formwork and metalwork. But he also felt obliged to include a short but significant anti-Corbusian comment when he emphasized that "the nakedness and simplicity of the forms, and the primitive proportions fail to give this building complete artistic expression."[107]

Yet Kolli's reticent remarks proved overindulgent, and David Arkin, who had welcomed Le Corbusier in 1928 in *Pravda*, now expressed strong reservations concerning the building "to which no passerby could be indifferent" and which was "the object of criticism and debate not only among architects but throughout the city." Arkin emphasized the fact that "Le Corbusier had practically been deprived of the right to experiment" in the West, a fact that made this instance of the new architecture's "mortally oversimplistic character" all the more remarkable. Arkin attacked the building's "lack of proportion," in that it "fronts the street with blind gables and the dumb glass walls" and, more perversely, accounted for this in terms of the absence of "regulating lines"

[106] Kolli described the building in similar terms in one of his last letters to Le Corbusier, Moscow, 25 March 1936, FLC.

[107] This did not prevent Kolli from sending a copy of the article to Le Corbusier "with regards" at the outset of 1937, as witness the signed copy dated 21 January 1937, FLC.

150. Le Corbusier, Centrosoyuz, view of a ramp in the hall's mezzanine, Moscow, 1936; in *Arkhitektura SSSR* 4, no. 10 (1936).

151. Le Corbusier, Centrosoyuz, view of a staircase, Moscow, 1936; in *Arkhitektura SSSR* 4, no. 10 (1936).

152. Le Corbusier, Centrosoyuz, view of a ramp from above, Moscow, 1936; in *Arkhitektura SSSR* 4, no. 10 (1936).

153. Le Corbusier, Centrosoyuz, view of a ramp from below, Moscow, 1957.

154. Le Corbusier, Centrosoyuz, view of an office, Moscow, 1936; in *Arkhitektura SSSR* 4, no. 10 (1936).

(*tracés régulateurs*) for the facades. Arkin was highly critical of the extensive use of glass, and congratulated Kolli for his treatment of the hall while at the same time deploring the building's incapacity to fit in with the urban "whole" of the surrounding district.[108]

In short, Le Corbusier's building, which in 1928 had been thought well in advance of its time, was now considered one of the "youthful errors" of the new régime, a regrettable instance of the erring ways of early "socialist" architecture. Such, in any case, was the position that Roman Khiger, a half-repentant constructivist, took up in 1935:

The Narkomlegprom building on Kirov Street. A long while ago, its author was the idol of our constructivists. His innovative radicalism seemed revolutionary. His literary pathos had made large numbers of conquests. And now the project of this glorious master is half-completed. Can it be considered to have embellished the city, in the best sense of the term? With great difficulty. In architecture, as in all creative spheres, simplicity is obviously preferable to tiresome luxuriance. Yet the Narkomlegprom's lapidary geometries are not rendered attractive by their simplicity. The building is not joyous. It is severe and sad. Its transparent expanses of glass seem monotonous and out of place. The artistry of the interiors, the tenuousness of its facades, the purity of its proportions, the abstract quality of its volumes and the dazzling display of its windows are here so impersonal that they do not appear to constitute an expressive architectural language for the observer. It is as yet no more than a skeleton, and not the flesh and blood of an architectural body.[109]

ENDGAME: THE QUESTION OF FEES

Although the Narkomlegprom building was now practically finished and a part of the past, this did not put an end to Le Corbusier's contractual relations with the Soviets. The balance of his fees as expressed in American dollars in 1930, which Centrosoyuz had promised to pay when building was suspended some months later, was slow in coming. As early as 1934 Le Corbusier had complained to Liubimov of the delay in payment. Apart from this direct channel, he was to use a whole range of strategies to achieve his goal. In the following year he approached Potemkin, the Soviet ambassador in Paris, and pressed Alexis Léger, secretary-general at the French Ministry of Foreign Affairs, to intervene on his behalf:

When, in 1928, I was called to Moscow following an international competition . . . my ideas were the object of lively curiosity and considerable sympathy in the USSR. I was welcomed with open arms and entrusted with a large commission which was to console me for my sad adventure of the previous year in Geneva.

. . . It is certain that, before 1930 (the year of the great academic reaction in Russia), I had been an effective tool of French propaganda in the USSR.

. . . It is important to understand that the reaction against me was so violent in Russia that, in an indirect way, I was considered somewhat undesirable, and since 1930 I have been unable to have myself called to Moscow in order to supervise construction work.[110]

In this letter Le Corbusier claimed to be acting as a "wronged French citizen" and stated that "the People's Commissars had acknowledged" that Centrosoyuz was "the best thing that had been done so far." In the same year Le Corbusier asked Boris Iofan, then in Paris, to plead his cause for him in Moscow;[111] in a letter to Sammer, whom he had also rallied to the cause, he

[108] David Arkin, "Dom na ulitse Kirova," *Arkhitektura SSSR* 4, no. 10 (1936): 34–35.

[109] Roman Ia. Khiger, "Arkhitektura revoliutsionnikh let," *Arkhitektura SSSR* 3, no. 10–11 (1935): 65. Khiger found the Vesnins' Palace of Culture for the ZIL factory and Ginzburg's Narkomfin building acceptable as instances of a more complex, expressive architecture.

[110] Le Corbusier, letter to Alexis Léger, Paris, 9 May 1935, FLC. Alexis Léger, whose notorious Anglophilia influenced the French policy of nonintervention in the Spanish civil war, is better known under his *nom de plume*, Saint-John Perse.

[111] Le Corbusier, letter to Boris Iofan, Paris, 28 July 1935, FLC. In his reply, Iofan assured Le Corbusier of his devotion: Boris Iofan, letter to Le Corbusier, Moscow, 20 November 1925, FLC.

subsequently expressed his amazement that an architect whose ideas were so different from his own should have received his request so warmly:

I have seen Iofan, who has come to see me here in Paris. He has promised to see about the problem of my fees for Centrosoyuz. You will admit how curious it is that Iofan should be the one to defend my interests in Moscow. But the world is everywhere turned on its head, and nothing ought now to surprise us.[112]

Having sent a whole series of pressing demands, in 1937 he asked Francis Jourdain, who had been invited to the Congress of Architects, to make enquiries. The balance was finally paid in 1939, a few weeks before the German-Soviet Pact was signed and diplomatic relations between France and the USSR were broken off.

Despite large-scale modifications to some internal details, it may be said that the finished building was a relatively faithful reflection of Le Corbusier's original designs, to the extent that its volumes and internal distributions had been carried out in accordance with his instructions. Its limitations were linked to his incapacity to integrate the lessons of a construction program that he could only follow by proxy; and although Centrosoyuz doubtless constitutes an important moment in Le Corbusier's conceptual development, it did not improve his building strategy. But the failure of part of the building's technical brief, the *respiration exacte* and the *murs neutralisants*, should in no way obviate its real successes—namely, the extension of the idea of the "architectural promenade" and the implementation of the "erudite interplay" between "the crystal prisms circled with bands of volcanic stone"—in this, the largest institutional edifice yet built by Le Corbusier.[113]

[112] Le Corbusier, letter to František Sammer, 31 July 1935, FLC.

[113] The building is now the headquarters of the Goskomstat, or Soviet State Committee for Statistics.

CHAPTER

5

Le Corbusier and Soviet
Avant-Garde Theory

DIRECT RESULT of the impact of Le Corbusier's ideas and forms on Soviet architectural culture, Centrosoyuz not only constituted a dazzling success that largely compensated for the failure of the League of Nations project but also revealed new convergences and, above all, divergences between his own positions and those of the Soviet avant-garde. These convergences and divergences cannot be considered from the point of view of purely bilateral relations between Le Corbusier and Moscow; they are part and parcel of a new theoretical distribution, which coincided with a new phase of the "modern movement," and which affected almost all European nations in the last years of the 1920s.

At this time, Le Corbusier already stood out from the main body of "new pioneers" cited by Henry-Russell Hitchcock in his *Modern Architecture*.[1] He was no longer the young pamphleteer of *Vers une architecture* or the painter Jeanneret but rather an architectural theorist and practitioner of international standing. As Bruno Reichlin has shown in his analysis of the successive transformations of the La Roche project, Le Corbusier's debt to artistic movements of the immediate postwar era, such as De Stijl, had remained as mute as it was dazzling;[2] yet now he had to situate his work in the much vaster European context. In the wake of the Weissenhof exhibition at Stuttgart and the campaign in favor of his League of Nations design (both in 1927), the creation of the Congrès Internationaux d'Architecture Moderne in 1928 provided not merely a platform for Le Corbusier's ideas, but also an occasion to do battle *in camera* with various brands of German functionalism, and with certain architects from Austria (and France).[3]

A twofold adjustment followed Le Corbusier's visit to Moscow in 1928. On the one hand, the different forces of the Soviet avant-garde openly adopted attitudes that were less adulatory, more incisive, and fraught with consequences for the Russian scene; on the other, Le Corbusier tried to rally his new constructivist friends to do battle with the Germans. Some Soviet attacks on Le Corbusier were uncommonly virulent. In the case of El Lissitzky, who, in addition to his own artistic involvement, was relatively well known as an architectural critic in the Soviet press, it was perhaps a question of avenging Le Corbusier's refusal to publish his 1924 article.

155. El Lissitzky, Sophie Küppers (top, left to right) and Piet Mondrian (leaning on the stairs) on the terrace of Le Corbusier's Stein-de Monzie villa, Garches, 1928.

EL LISSITZKY STRIKES BACK

Four years after *L'Esprit Nouveau* had refused to publish El Lissitzky's article, just as Le Corbusier was on the point of obtaining the Centrosoyuz commission, Lissitsky launched an attack in the Muscovite press—as cruel as it was well argued—on the Mundaneum project and Le Corbusier's attitude as a whole. Lissitzky called on Soviet architects to "make a precise appraisal" of Western culture, in which architecture was merely a "buffer between the producer/entrepreneur and the consumer/inhabitant." In terms not dissimilar to those that Bruno Taut was to use a year later, he pointed to Le Corbusier as the "clearest example" of this state of affairs:

Le Corbusier has blinded the idolaters of constructivism and functionalism with the pronounced *artisticité* of his own brand of functionalism. Le Corbusier is first and foremost an artist, and contemporary art is a particularly effective instrument—so effective in fact, that it triumphs even where its manifestos are belied by the facts. The painter Charles Jeanneret who, together with the painter Ozenfant, invented the school of purism—that is, an attempt to transcend cubism—has written a series of provocative articles for the magazine *L'Esprit Nouveau*, couched in the most brilliant

[1] Henry-Russell Hitchcock, *Modern Architecture: Romanticism and Reintegration* (New York: Payson and Clarke, 1929), pp. 163–71.
[2] Bruno Reichlin, "Le Corbusier vs. De Stijl," in *De Stijl et l'architecture*, pp. 91–108.
[3] On the controversy surrounding the creation of the CIAM, see Jacques Gubler, *Nationalisme et internationalisme dans l'architecture moderne de la Suisse* (Lausanne: L'Age d'Homme, 1975), pp. 145–61; and Jean-Louis Cohen, "L'architecture d'André Lurçat (1894–1970): autocritique d'un moderne," (Ph.D. thesis, Paris, Ecole des Hautes Etudes en Sciences Sociales, 1985), pp. 271–314.

of literary styles, on the subject of a new aesthetics of architecture. His excellent training in the analysis of painting gives Le Corbusier an advantage over other modern architects of the West. His aesthetics first invoke the power of elementary geometrical shapes—the cube, the square, the cylinder, the pyramids and the changeless beauty of the Pantheon—that participate in the process of evolution; second, by taking into account new techniques, new materials and new means of construction (reinforced concrete), Le Corbusier proposes revolution. The artist's discoveries are to revolutionize engineering.[4]

Citing earlier analyses published by Sigfried Giedion in *Bauen in Frankreich*,[5] Lissitzky considered Le Corbusier as an inheritor of the nineteenth-century French building tradition—and thus no more than "an isolated branch suspended in the air"—and also in relation to his clients or "patrons":

The Bohemianism, isolation and inverted snobbery [*déclassement*] of today's artists have reached their apogee in France. Given that Le Corbusier is an artist, he is a case in point. Like all Western artists, he feels compelled to be an absolute individualist, and to recognize nothing outside of himself, because otherwise one might doubt his originality, and because originality is the sensation that gives the measure of what is "new."

. . . Up till now, Le Corbusier has built for patrons in France. This summer, we visited his latest work in the suburbs of Paris. The owner of the villa, an American of German extraction, said, "It is certainly more interesting for you to *visit* our house than it is for us to *live* in it."

. . . Thus it is that Le Corbusier the artist (and not the constructor, the builder, the engineer) was commissioned to build a house that is designed to be a sensation, a piece of magic, and the finished product is published in women's magazines, along with the latest in fashion (cf. *Vogue*, August 1928).

At present, in a beautiful old park on the outskirts of Paris, Le Corbusier is building a villa for American clients on the site of an old palace. The ground floor will "hide" the old plan: an example of "camouflage," to use Le Corbusier's own expression.[6]

Lissitzky mentions Stuttgart and Pessac—the latter was commissioned by "a capitalist who had read *Vers une architecture*"—and comments that "these individualistic, antisocial origins are what characterizes the work of the talented master"; according to him, "the result is not a building to be *lived in*, but rather, a *showpiece*." On the subject of the term *freedom*, which figures in the famous "Five Points of a New Architecture," Lissitzky becomes pointedly ironical: "equipped with these five points, the architect's lyrical *expression* is freed from all constraint." Like Filippo Marinetti, with his "words at liberty," he can "abandon the old grammar and syntax." As regards functionalism, Lissitzky insists that the mathematical term *function* denotes a relation of "dependence," and that "the functionalist architect merely formulates a series of relations in a novel manner":

Le Corbusier, on the other hand, proposes new housing conditions—a variant on the houses at Pompeii: he abandons horizontal extension for verticality, with generous rooms for public use, large open-air "rooms" on the roof, but tiny recesses for sleep and work. . . . Given the fact that the society for which he builds has long since lost its traditional housing culture—without proposing a new one—Le Corbusier invents a nonexistent culture in his studio; in his role as the artist in isolation, he has designed houses that are disorienting to the user, and which he himself would never inhabit. The reason for this is the architect's antisocial nature, the great distance that separates him from the expectations of the vast mass of people. He has affinities neither with the proletariat, nor with industrial capital.

[4] El Lissitzky, "Idoli i idolopokonniki," *Stroitelnaia Promyshlennost* 7, nos. 11–12 (1929): 854–58. This article was published in the same issue as Le Corbusier's second project for the Centrosoyuz, on which it constitutes a commentary.

[5] Sigfried Giedion, *Bauen in Frankreich, Eisen, Eisenbeton* (Leipzig: Klinkhardt and Biermann, 1928).

Another text by Giedion, on the "luxury of the volume of air" in the villa Stein, also appears to have had an influence—in this case, negative—on El Lissitzky's analysis: Sigfried Giedion, "Le problème du luxe dans l'architecture moderne," *Cahiers d'Art*, no. 5–6 (1928): 254–56.

[6] El Lissitzky, "Idoli," pp. 854–58. Sophie Lissitzky-Küppers, who recalls the Weissenhofsiedlung at Stuttgart in positive terms, evokes this visit to the villa Stein with a "young Armenian"—Le Corbusier's "assistant"—and Piet Mondrian. See the illustrations published here and Lissitzky-Küppers, *El Lissitzky*, p. 84.

Giedion had communicated Le Corbusier's address to El Lissitzky. See El Lissitzky, letter to Sigfried Giedion, St. Johann in Pongau, 1 August 1928, Giedion archives, gta/ETH, Zurich.

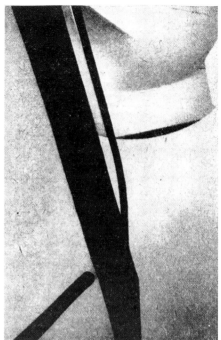

But Lissitzky also criticizes Le Corbusier's formal working methods, on the basis of what "he has shown on the drawing board":

Le Corbusier is a classicist, his formal world is that of the geometry of Euclides, a finite universe composed of the three coordinate axes. Within this framework he manipulates, with a high degree of sensitivity, the spatial relations that he creates by means of explicit intersections between the three dimensions. In order to achieve this, he uses reinforced concrete, since this material is infinitely flexible—and to this end he sacrifices the elementary requirements of functionality and usage.

... Le Corbusier has not formulated clear principles for the construction of his architectural forms. He talks of lyricism, and all his work is essentially intuitive, and lacks general rules. Yet if there is a single rule, one that is borrowed from history, it is that of the Golden Section, although this cannot be consistently applied to space—it is absolutely precise in two dimensions, but becomes meaningless in three. In the work of Le Corbusier, the eye of the painter is everywhere present—not only in his use of color, which he manipulates as a painter, but also at the level of architectural design: he does not materialize his designs, but merely colors them in. His system of composition involves the construction of a frame—a fact that explains why photographs of his buildings give an impression of unity even when they are upside down.

Lissitzky is here alluding to an experiment carried out during his visit to Stuttgart, when he photographed a fragment of staircase with his eyes closed; the result evokes an abstract painting. But Lissitzky's reservations as to Le Corbusier's architecture are small beer compared with those concerning the principles of his town planning and large-scale projects—reservations based above all on a political assessment that leads him to condemn Le Corbusier's "city of nowhere," a city that is "neither capitalist, nor proletarian, nor socialist ... a city on paper, extraneous to living nature, located in a desert through which not even a river must be allowed to pass (since a curve would contradict the style)."

For Lissitzky, the emphasis on automobile traffic is excessive in projects whose essential value is that of "agitation." Lissitzky criticizes both the Palace

156. El Lissitzky, Sophie Küppers, and Piet Mondrian (left to right) on the terrace of Le Corbusier's Stein-de Monzie villa, Garches, 1928.

157. El Lissitzky, photograph of the stairs in one of Le Corbusier's houses in the Weissenhof *Siedlung*, Stuttgart, 1927.

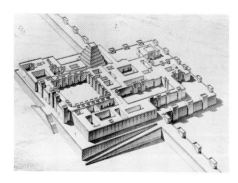

158. Georges Perrot and Charles Chipiez, reconstruction of Sargon's palace in Khorsabad, axonometric view.

of Nations project, and the fact that Le Corbusier "lost" the battle for its acceptance by the League. Citing the assessment of Hannes Meyer, another unsuccessful candidate, he refutes Le Corbusier's explanation concerning the shape of the auditorium, which was supposedly based on the "laws of acoustics." But it is the Mundaneum project, from the "encyclopedic poem of the brief" to Le Corbusier's architectural response, that Lissitzky singles out for his most pointed irony (he terms it a curious "fruit of functionalism"):

The heart of the composition is a Babylonian pyramid with a spiral ramp winding up to its summit. This pyramid is taken directly from history, although its structure is neither the granite of the Egyptians, nor the brick of Assyria, but rather glass and metal. At the heart of the pyramid's interior, instead of the tomb of some Pharaoh, one finds an even more venerable center—the "sacrarium," a temple to all the gods and idols that humanity has invented in the course of its history.

When confronted with this project of Le Corbusier's, I see myself reopening volume 2 of Perrot and Chipiez's *Histoire de l'art dans l'antiquité* (Chaldea and Assyria), and studying their reconstruction of the palace of Sargon in Khorsabad. But the original differs from the copy in that the former was more functional, as has always been the case.

But Lissitzky is not content to refer Le Corbusier's project back to some of its sources;[7] he also compares it to another spiral, one that has "engendered the pathos of the new class that is in the vanguard of history": Tatlin's tower. Thus for Lissitzky, the "beginnings of Soviet architecture" would appear to coincide with "an end to idolatry." Warding off all accusations of chauvinism, and claiming that "there is henceforth only one social and class front on this planet," he invites his fellow citizens to adjust to the experience of Soviet architecture. Le Corbusier, who was making last-minute revisions to his Centrosoyuz project, did not deign to answer this attack, although he could not ignore it. Yet he abandoned his reserve some months later, when Karel Teige reiterated a number of Lissitzky's arguments in the Prague review *Stavba.*

[7] Georges Perrot and Charles Chipiez, *Histoire de l'art dans l'antiquité* vol. 2, Chaldée et Assyrie, pp. 422–48. (Paris: Hachette, 1884).

159. Le Corbusier, Mundaneum, Geneva, 1928, overall perspective.

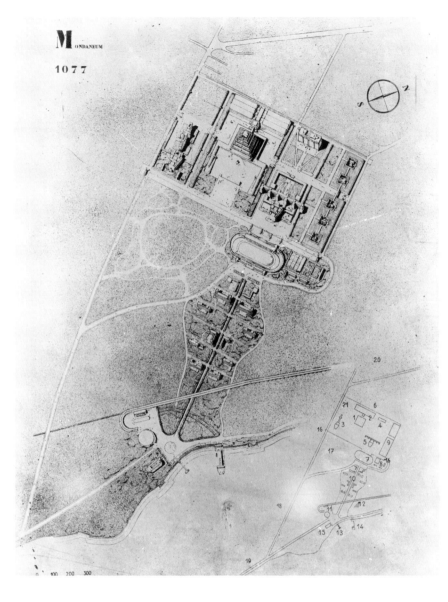

160. Le Corbusier, Mundaneum, Geneva, 1928, general axonometric view.

[8] Teige reviewed *Vers une architecture* as early as 1923: Karel Teige, "K nové architektuře," *Stavba*, no. 11 (1923): 179–83. Following a brief period of literary studies in Prague, Teige (1900–1951) quickly became known for his paintings, collages, and typographic compositions, but also for his art criticism. In October 1920 he cofounded Devĕtsil, an iconoclastic movement, for which, in 1924, he wrote his "Manifesto of Poeticism." As much interested in sculpture and the cinema as in poetry and architecture, to which much of his writing is devoted, Teige was an active participant in left-wing Communist organizations before finally breaking with the party at the end of the thirties. A prolific contributor to *Stavba,* Teige was interested in the social implications of architecture; at the invitation of Hannes Meyer, he taught at the Bauhaus in Dessau. His writings on architecture include: *K sociologii architektury* (Prague: Odeon, 1930); *Moderní Architektura v Československu* (Prague: Odeon, 1930); *Nejmenší byt* (Prague: Vaclav Petr, 1932); *Architektura pravá a levá* (Prague: Leva Fronta, 1934); *Vývoj sovĕtské architektury* (Prague: Prokop, 1936).

[9] Karel Teige, letter to Le Corbusier, Prague, 15 October 1928, FLC.

[10] On the genesis of the Mundaneum and the relations between Otlet and Le Corbusier, see Giuliano Gresleri and Dario Matteoni, *La città mondiale Andersen Hébrard Otlet Le Corbusier* (Venice: Marsilio, 1982); Pierre Saddy, "La pyramide du Mundaneum," in Pierre Saddy and Claude Malécot, eds., *Le Corbusier le passé à réaction poétique* (Paris: Caisse Nationale des Monuments Historiques et des Sites, 1988), p. 44; Alena Kubova, "Le Mundaneum, erreur architecturale," ibid., pp. 48–50.

KAREL TEIGE AND THE "DEFENSE OF ARCHITECTURE"

On his first visit to Moscow in October 1928, Le Corbusier had traveled by way of Czechoslovakia. The fact that Le Corbusier was well known to the Czechs was largely due to energetic interventions on his behalf by the young intellectual Karel Teige.[8] Yet although Teige spared no effort to be the first to publish the Centrosoyuz project, he entered into sharp disagreement with Le Corbusier on the subject of the Mundaneum.[9] Like Lissitzky, Teige criticized the mystifying illusions of Paul Otlet's brief and the "puzzling, archaic impression" given by the project, although he ascribed Le Corbusier's "metaphysical architecture" more to sources in "American 'antiquity'" than in Mesopotamia.[10] Teige begins by condemning the project's monumental proportions and, not surprisingly, the use of the Golden Section as its *tracé régulateur*:

Le Corbusier's proposal is the error of monumentality (a monumentality different from and less brutal than the German monumentality of the architecture of megalo-

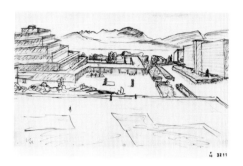

161. Le Corbusier, Mundaneum, Geneva, 1928, sketch of the museum and its ramps, FLC 32114.

mania), the error of the "palace." It reveals the dangers (exposed already in Le Corbusier's book *Une maison, un palais*) of the definition that a palace is a house, a "machine for living in" that is endowed with certain dignity and architectural potential. . . . It shows the failure of Le Corbusier's aesthetics and formalistic theories, which we, from the point of view of Constructivism, have always fought against: the theories of the Golden Section and of geometrical proportion. In short, all these *a priori* aesthetic formulas that have formalistically been deduced from historical styles in our times are unproved and unsupported.[11]

For Teige, as for Hannes Meyer (from whose 1928 manifesto *bauen* he quotes at some length), the use of such systems of proportion is a sure sign of the return to notions of composition—to the "expression of an ideological and metaphysical imagination" which he ascribes to the academic tradition, and of which he hopes to rid the whole field of modern architecture:

The prisms of individual buildings in their proportions, and the whole Mundaneum in its rhythm, are dominated by the Golden Section, the measurements of which, as current history still believes, determined the harmony of the most famous works. Thus the Mundaneum is *Reissbrett-Ornamentik*, a project born, not from real and rational analysis of the program (because this program would not be capable of such an analysis and solutions), but from *a priori* aesthetic and abstract geometric speculation, following a historical stereotype. It is not a solution for realization and construction, but a composition. *Composition*: with this word it is possible to summarize all the architectural faults of the Mundaneum.[12]

In fact, Teige contests Le Corbusier's insistence on the idea that the architecture of the "machine age" is still an art, and that it contributes "something more" than a building's use value:

The criterion of purposefulness, the only reliable criterion of quality in architectural production, has led modern architecture to discard "mammoth bodies of monumentality," and to cultivate its brain: *instead of monuments architecture creates instruments.* If aesthetics intervene in the production of use values, there follow imperfections in architectural creation, and this is its mark. . . . Only where no ideological-metaphysical-aesthetic intentions but only the dictates of practical life direct the architect's work, does the affection for art stop.[13]

Le Corbusier wrote his reply to this article at the end of May or beginning of June 1929, in a train rolling across the plains of Poland toward Moscow, although it was not to be published in France before the end of 1933.[14] In this seminal text, Le Corbusier invokes "Alexander Vesnin, the founder of 'constructivism,'" in a vehement yet ironic attack on the utilitarian vision of architecture as exemplified in Karel Teige's and Hannes Meyer's celebration of *Sachlichkeit*, and in El Lissitzky's remarks. Le Corbusier outlines his own vision of the Mundaneum, but he also counters theory with anecdote:

Yet let us be quite clear on the question of *Sachlichkeit*. In its fundamentally equivocal character, the postulate "what is useful is beautiful" is as dubious as it is assertive (and we've heard it before). You will not contradict me if I inform the uninitiated reader that this is one of the supreme commandments of the *neue Sachlichkeit*.

Last year, during the final stages of designing the Mundaneum, a breath of revolt blew through our offices: the pyramid (which is one of the elements of the project) bothered our young architects. On other drawing boards, the final plans for the Centrosoyuz at Moscow were the object of unanimous approbation. These plans were reassuring, for the brief posed the purely rational problem of office buildings. Yet both Mundaneum and Centrosoyuz had been born in our heads in this same month of June. Suddenly, the peremptory argument was heard: "What is useful is beautiful." At

[11] Karel Teige, "Mundaneum," *Stavba*, no. 4 (1929): 145–55. English translation in *Oppositions* 4 (October 1974): 89.

[12] Teige, in *Oppositions* 4 (October 1974): 90.

[13] Ibid., p. 91.

[14] Le Corbusier, "Défense de l'architecture," *L'Architecture d'Aujourd'hui*, no. 10 (1933): 38–61. It had been published in Czech two years earlier: Le Corbusier, "Obrana architektury, Odpověd K. Teigovi," *Musaion*, no. 2 (1931): 42–53.

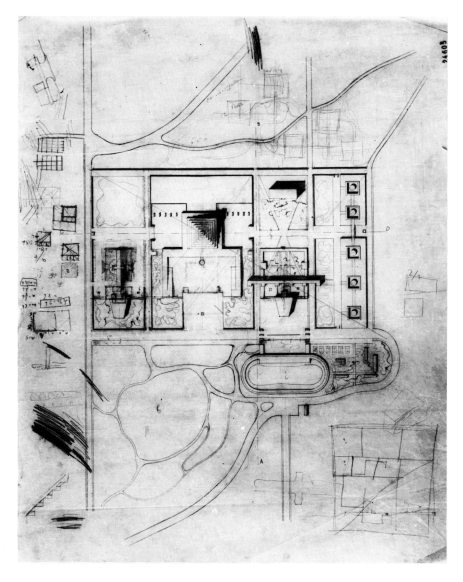

162. Le Corbusier, Mundaneum, Geneva, 1928, overall plan with proportion grid ("tracé régulateur"), FLC 24605.

the same moment, Alfred Roth (a fiery temperament) gave his wire-mesh wastepaper basket, which refused to accommodate the mass of old drawings that it was his task to destroy, a violent kick. Under Roth's energetic treatment the wastepaper basket, which was, technically speaking, perfectly *sachlich* (a direct expression of the wire mesh) assumed the shape which you see in the drawing.

Everyone burst out laughing. "It's hideous!" said Roth. "Pardon me," I replied, "but this basket now contains far more; it is more useful, therefore it is more beautiful! Be consistent with your principles!"[15]

In his 1931 reply, Teige reaffirmed his "Socratic conception," whereby "what is functionally perfect is beautiful," and claimed that architecture was "neither a composition, nor an art, but a science." Yet he also made attempts to shift the debate onto new ground, on the one hand by stressing that Le Corbusier was already out of his depth, and on the other, by emphasizing more important political differences:

Your work represents a beginning, a landmark in modern architecture, and it is the cue for the appearance of new departures; you have played a historic role comparable

163. The wire-mesh wastepaper basket in the rue de Sèvres atelier before and after Alfred Roth kicked it, as published in Le Corbusier's "Défense de l'architecture."

[15] Le Corbusier, "Défense de l'architecture," pp. 43–44.

to that of Picasso in the development of painting. The new generation, which has taken your work as its starting point, is already opposed to it on several points, and especially on that of your theory; it no longer accepts your aesthetics or your social attitudes, but considers your work the starting point of a new architecture. Thus the discussion of your own conceptions may enable one to measure the ground covered in architectural thought these past few years. I would add that I would never have wished on you the sad fate of the great reformers who are venerated merely on the basis of dogmatic, conservative criteria.[16]

For Teige, the "heart of the problem" resided in the "*tracés régulateurs*, Golden Section, axes"—that is, in "mathematical formulations that are alien to the execution of concrete tasks." The projects for Centrosoyuz and the Mundaneum furnished a convenient contrast:

The Mundaneum is easily outmatched by other works of a constructive character, such as those of Perret, or with another work by the same author, such as Centrosoyuz, which was not designed with the aid of *tracés régulateurs* or the Golden Section.

I shall not hark back to the futile Muscovite debate concerning Functionalism and Constructivism, to the extent that the two terms are synonymous, and are merely two different definitions of a single notion. And yet the Soviet movement, with its Functionalism and its Constructivism, is not a manifestation of the soul; rather, it is a true reflection of the building of socialism. The problem is how to apply dialectic materialism to architecture, and Leninism to building. Other than this idea, there is no modern architecture, and all aesthetic and formalist speculation stems from the academicism of an age that is past and gone.[17]

Teige continued to criticize Le Corbusier, albeit in more measured tones, at the time of the competition for the Palace of the Soviets—although he never endorsed the shift toward "socialist realism" that came to mark Soviet art and architecture.

LE CORBUSIER, CONSTRUCTIVISM, AND ITS DETRACTORS

El Lissitzky, the caustic quality of whose comments has been noted, was far from being the only Soviet critic to express reservations about Le Corbusier's aesthetic theories, since his closest allies, the constructivists, also came to mark their skepticism concerning a number of his statements. The first instance of these divergences dates from the first OSA conference in 1928 when, in the course of an ambitious report on "constructivism in architecture," Moisei Ginzburg presented a critical appraisal of the work of a man he did not as yet know personally:

Le Corbusier is free from all the influences that weigh so heavily on the German architects (with their penchant for romanticism, symbolism and monumentalism). He has proposed a number of novel solutions, unlike the Germans, who always react emotively to technological progress. . . . Le Corbusier's outstanding merit is that of having clearly formulated the role of technology in the elaboration of a new model for architecture. Although he considers technology to be of paramount importance, he nonetheless considers its role subordinate to the fundamental task of architectural composition. Moreover, Le Corbusier is an architect capable of clear, global thinking—and this is his second great merit. Whereas the Germans are still prisoners of pure philosophy and theory, Le Corbusier never loses track of the lucidity that should be the hallmark of all architecture.

[16] Karel Teige, "Odpověd Le Corbusierovi," *Musaion*, no. 2 (1931): 52–53. In the previous year, Teige had already pointed out the "distance" between Le Corbusier and the new generation, and claimed that the latter had "begun the movement toward a new architecture." See Karel Teige, "Le Corbusier a nová architektura," *Index*, no. 11–12 (17 December 1930): 83–86. In the dossier that George Baird published in 1974 on the debate between Teige and Le Corbusier, the Czech's reply was omitted. See George Baird, introduction to "Karel Teige's Mundaneum, 1929, and Le Corbusier's *In Defence of Architecture*, 1933," *Oppositions* 4 (October 1974): 79–82.

[17] Teige, "Odpověd," pp. 52–53.

Although, Ginzburg lists the difficulties Le Corbusier had encountered in a manner not unsympathetic, he does not hesitate to blame him, from an essentially political viewpoint, for some of his "failures":

But when speaking of Le Corbusier and of his merits, it is impossible not to mention some negative aspects of the positions he adopts and the divergences that separate us from him and his disciples. Above all it is essential to emphasize that, despite the importance he attributes to the plan in architectural design, Le Corbusier is today caught in an impasse. His ideas on the virtues of the plan, and on the necessary transformation of life-styles, find no echo in his own social milieu. In fact, such ideas are mere fantasies. Armed with a sort of aesthetic puritanism, Le Corbusier finds himself banging his head against the wall of the new aestheticism. He is caught in a cul-de-sac, from which only the October Revolution has found a way out. . . . Confronted with quite different social conditions, Le Corbusier is looking to find his way through solutions that are often poorly defined and purely aesthetic in character. For example, he writes, "Curved lines constitute paralysis, and the winding path is the path of donkeys." Here we are clearly in the presence of an emotional reaction to the world of technology and the principle of the curve as professed by artists who view it as the expression of graphic purity and clarity. And this reflex is quite devoid of all other significance.[18]

This criticism of Le Corbusier's "purely aesthetic solutions" dates from a time when the "scientific principles" of constructivism were being explored with greater precision, especially in the sphere of housing distribution, on the subject of which research carried out by Frederick Taylor and Frank Gilbreth had been widely read in the USSR during the twenties. Yet the situation was in fact rather more complex in Moscow, where the debate revolved around the question of the aesthetics of the machine, a topic Ginzburg had taken up in *Stil i Epokha*. Despite Ginzburg's criticism of Le Corbusier's aestheticism, several other critics were in favor of his plastic approach, although for reasons that were quite contradictory. In his *Tekhnichesky byt i sovremennoe iskusstvo (Technical Life and Contemporary Art)*, A. Toropkov, who predictably attacks the chapter "Architecture or Revolution" from *Vers une architecture*, nonetheless finds merit in Ozenfant's studio:

It must be said to Le Corbusier's credit that he has done his best, against all odds, to introduce industrial norms into housing construction. His attempt to do so is in all aspects remarkable. His own villa is especially interesting, and has enabled him at last to achieve clear expression. The building in question is first and foremost a painter's studio. It is aesthetic and rather dry. It is full of clarity and light. In its construction only what was strictly necessary was retained—the rooms are practically empty.

His housing schemes are less satisfactory. They represent the attempt to create a contemporary housing type under present-day conditions; but there is, for the moment at least, no fundamental solution to this problem.[19]

Although the "dryness" of his solutions seduced proponents of machine aesthetics such as Toropkov, Le Corbusier's insistence on plasticity induced the playwright Vladimir Volkenshtein to consider him in opposition to Ginzburg. In an article that he wrote in 1929, Volkenshtein insists on the distinction between Ginzburg's "utilitarianism" and Le Corbusier's own approach, as exemplified in a number of aesthetic formulas that he quotes from *Vers une architecture*:[20]

The new architecture is hostile to all decoration. It is utilitarian, and thus it represents the triumph of geometry and constructivism. Le Corbusier writes that "decoration is offensive"; but there is a fundamental difference between Le Corbusier's position and

[18] Moisei Ginzburg, "Konstruktivizm v arkhitekture," *Sovremennaia Arkhitektura* 3, no. 5 (1928) 143–45.

[19] A. Toropkov, *Tekhnichesky byt i sovremennoe iskusstvo* (Moscow: Gosudarstvennoe Izdatelstvo, 1928), pp. 185–86.

[20] V(ladimir) Volkenshtein, "Estetika mashin i konstruktivnoi arkhitektury," *Iskusstvo*, no. 3–4 (1929): 141–49.

164. "Technology is the very basis of lyricism," sketch for a lecture held in Buenos Aires; published in *Précisions* (Paris, 1930).

that of the theorists of the new Russian architecture. For Le Corbusier, "beyond questions of construction, architecture is a fact of art, a phenomenon of the emotions." We must interpret this as saying: outside the field of pure construction, Le Corbusier is an enemy of decorative architecture; but the artistic dimension does not for him coincide with the utilitarian dimension.[21]

In his preface to Volkenshtein's book, Anatoli Lunacharsky supports the attack on the constructivists, whom he confines to the universe of the factory:

When we build a factory, we do not hesitate to think of ways to heighten its aesthetic "use value," that is, its visual qualities, its value as a contribution to the pleasure of all. This is a necessity. It is, therefore, right that a well-built factory should reflect a powerful, functional beauty. . . . But if, for instance, we are to build a town near that factory, then we must admit that our constructivist friends are in error. It is obvious that in the organization of its interiors, and in the outer aspect of the buildings, streets and squares, a housing scheme must also integrate beauty into its functional organization.[22]

Thus, while Le Corbusier was at odds with the OSA at a theoretical level, he had also been taken hostage by "rationalists" of the ASNOVA. Nikolai Dokuchaev also made attempts to drive a wedge between Le Corbusier and the constructivists who had helped him to victory in the 1928 Centrosoyuz competition, asking why "Le Corbusier's Russian followers [were] incapable of seeing the difference between "'aesthetic purism' and the utilitarian character of 'constructivism'."[23] Yet although he was drawn, against his will, into a debate that was not altogether clear, Le Corbusier did not hesitate to use his Moscow contacts in the wider European game.

LE CORBUSIER AND CONSTRUCTIVISM'S "LYRICAL INTENTIONS"

It was in Moscow that Le Corbusier finally discovered an architectural trend that had been summarily dismissed in 1924–1925, and which he had considered similar to the productions of his intimate enemies within the CIAM. Since relatively few constructivist designs had been built to date, Le Corbusier's assessment of constructivism continued to be influenced by the human warmth of its spokesmen and by projects that he studied at the school. Nonetheless, he did not hide his emotion:

I thought I would encounter my typical adversaries in Moscow—the creators of "constructivism." This opinion was grounded in the recent attitudes of German architects who, for some time now, have been proclaiming the eminently utilitarian principles of the *neue Sachlichkeit*. . . . Yet in Moscow I found, not spiritual antagonists, but fervent adherents to what I consider fundamental to all human works: the lofty intentions that raise these works above their utilitarian function, and which confer on them the lyricism that brings us joy.

Le Corbusier was surprised to discover in Moscow the "lyricism" born of technique that had been at the core of his theory in the mid-1920s:

Russia has created the architectural movement known as "constructivism." The idea was to express the fact that a new age (that of the machine), new materials (reinforced concrete and iron) and the existence of entirely new problems (offices, workshops, factories, dams, etc.) implied totally new forms of architectural expression, expressive of organisms that had never before existed.

. . . I say that constructivism, which denotes a revolutionary intention, is in reality

[21] Vladimir Volkenshtein, *Opyt sovremennoi estetiki* (Moscow: Academia, 1931), pp. 62–63.

[22] Anatoli Lunacharsky, preface to Volkenshtein, *Opyt*, p. 13.

[23] Nikolai Dokuchaev, "Le Corbusier–Saugnier," *Iskusstvo*, no. 3–4 (1929): 140. Since 1925, when Dokuchaev published a specific attack on Le Corbusier in Paris, his judgment on Western architects in general, and Le Corbusier in particular, had become much more favorable. See Nikolai Dokuchaev, "Sovremennaia russkaia arkhitektura i zapadnye paralleli," *Sovetskoe Iskusstvo*, no. 1 (1927): 5–12, and no. 2 (1928) 48–58.

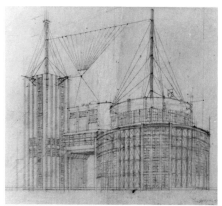

167. Alexander, Leonid, and Victor Vesnin, competition project for the Palace of Labor, Moscow, 1923, perspective.

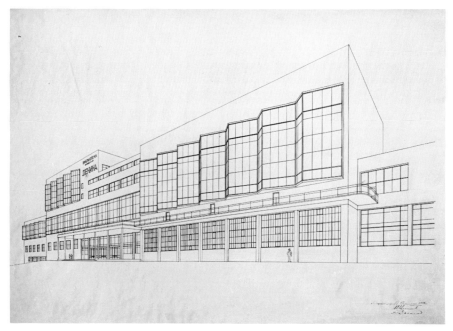

165. Victor Vesnin, Leonid Vesnin, Le Corbusier, Alexander Vesnin, and Andrei Burov (left to right) in Alexander Vesnin's studio, Moscow, October 1928.

166. Alexander, Leonid, and Victor Vesnin, competition project for the Lenin Library, Moscow, 1928–1929, perspective of first scheme.

the vehicle of an intensely lyrical intent, one that is even potentially transcendent. It reveals with fervor the exhilarating prospect of a future. My feeling is that what interests all these Russians is in fact a poetic idea.[24]

In his dispute with Karel Teige, Le Corbusier had discovered affinities between his own approach and that of the constructivists. In his *Defense of Architecture,* he used them as a kind of shield in response to Hannes Meyer, who seemed to personify the narrow-mindedness of functionalism, and by whom he felt personally attacked:

[24] Le Corbusier, "L'architecture à Moscou," p. 1.

168. Alexander, Leonid, and Victor Vesnin, culture palace for the ZIL automobile factory, 1931–1936; photograph taken in 1937.

I have just returned from Moscow, where I saw Alexander Vesnin, the creator of Russian constructivism (and a great artist) attacked with the same vehemence. Moscow is torn between constructivism and functionalism. There, too, intolerance reigns. If Leonidov, the poet who incarnates all the hopes of the Russian architectural "constructivists," claims he is a functionalist and rails against constructivism, I am ready to explain to him why he does so. It is because the Russian architectural movement represents a moral earthquake, a manifestation of the soul, a surge of lyricism, an aesthetic creation, an act of faith in modern life; a purely lyrical phenomenon, an unambiguous, decisive gesture; a decision.

Ten years later, the young spirits who based the graceful, charming but fragile edifice of their own lyricism on the productions of their elders (Vesnin), have suddenly been seized by the irrepressible desire to return to their classrooms and study calculus, chemistry and physics, new materials, new machines, Taylorism, etc. Absorbed in these necessary tasks, they anathematize those who, having already absorbed this curriculum, are busy making architecture, that is to say, studying how these different elements are to be assembled.[25]

In reality, the heady illusions of the first Moscow encounters were already a pale memory. As Le Corbusier discovered the conflict between "founders" such as Vesnin and the younger generation, he also raged against the excesses of the "disurbanizing" projects when consulted on the subject of the "Green City"; the debate on this theme reached its apogee in his correspondence with Ginzburg.

In Le Corbusier's intense personal relations with a number of his new friends, Alexander Vesnin, who was only four years older than he, occupies a special place. Already in the early 1920s, Leonid Vesnin had confided to his brother that he was reading *Vers une architecture* "attentively," that the Russians had already gone "further," and that Le Corbusier's vision was "less profound" than theirs.[26] Le Corbusier exchanged several drawings with Alexander[27] and never wasted an opportunity to call on him to witness his misadventures in Moscow, while Vesnin himself, as we have already seen, was to remain faithful in his support for the architecture of Centrosoyuz.

Thus Le Corbusier used a "postponed" understanding of constructivist theories in order to transcend both his machine aesthetics of the early twenties and his simplistic rationalism of the first years of Taylorism. But he also saw

[25] Le Corbusier, "Défense de l'architecture," pp. 58–60.

[26] Leonid Vesnin, letter to Alexander Vesnin (undated); quoted in Alexei Chiniakov, *Bratia Vesniny* (Moscow: Izdat. Literatury po Stroitelstvu, 1970), p. 99.

[27] Alexander Vesnin gave Le Corbusier at least two of his abstract compositions; Le Corbusier himself made a gift of a number of his drawings from the period 1923–1929. See Alexei Chiniakov, "Le Corbusier i Vesniny," in *Sovetskaia Arkhitektura*, no. 18 (Moscow: Izdat. Literatury po Stroitelstvu, 1969), pp. 133–42. It was Le Corbusier who advised Chiniakov, on graduating from MIT, to ask Vesnin for employment.

170. Postpurist composition given by Le Corbusier to Alexander Vesnin.

169. Postpurist composition given by Le Corbusier to Alexander Vesnin.

the "surge of lyricism" that he ascribed to Alexander Vesnin, especially after his 1929 visit, in fields other than architecture.

EISENSTEIN'S "PATHOS OF THE CENTRIFUGE"

It is difficult not to see convergences in opinion between the more measured position that Le Corbusier adopted toward constructivism in 1929, and Sergei Eisenstein's remarks on his own film *The General Line*, which Le Corbusier had seen during he first visit to Moscow. Moreover, Le Corbusier became so fond of the title that he used it on several occasions to conjure up the atmosphere of discipline and productive tension as he perceived it in the USSR—for instance, in the first issue of the review *Plans* he helped create in 1931.[28]

Le Corbusier did not merely see a "new clientele" in the cows and pigs of the model sovkhoz by Burov but rather a vision of the machine age, one diametrically opposed to functionalist "utilitarianism." In Eisenstein's film, a hymn to

[28] "La Ligne générale," *Plans*, no. 1 (1931): 7–9.

171. Ivan Leonidov, projection for a culture palace proposed on the site of the former Simonovsky monastery, Moscow, 1930, elevation.

the modernization and collectivization of architecture, the farmer Martha Lapkina is carried away with enthusiasm at the sight of the centrifuge creamer, and combats superstition and the bureaucracy in order to obtain a tractor. After its completion, the film was reedited under pressure from Stalin and released under the title *Old and New*. In his comments, Eisenstein made no attempt to hide his wish to celebrate, among other themes, the epic of machine culture:[29]

It is the first monumental film to have had agricultural machinery and peasants as its materials. It is an attempt to *highlight and make interesting the dullest and most down-to-earth problems of the peasants*, which are of colossal social and political significance.

. . . Danish troughs. Egg-laying competitions. Heated barns. Ploughing in spring snows. A thick layer of greasy manure on fields ploughed collectively. Communal labor in the cooperatives.

. . . And in the future, a few large-scale farm collectives in Siberia will be in a position to supply almost all the Union's wheat. But what is that when compared with the epic inspiration of the very first creamer in the newly formed cooperative?

From the creamer to the pedigree bull, from the bull to the tractor. Two, ten, a hundred tractors!!

What are all the Songs of Roland compared with this epic inspiration?

May our spectators' eyes become inflamed at the sight of the metal creamer of the kolkhoze![30]

As for *Potemkin*, Eisenstein elaborates a theory of composition based on "constructions of pathos":

[29] On the transformation on the film, see the remarks made by François Albéra, in the context of a broader discussion of Eisenstein's relationship to constructivism: François Albéra, *S.M. Eisenstein et le constructivisme russe; "Stuttgart": dramaturgie de la forme* Lausanne: L'Age d'Homme, 1990), pp. 149–68; Albéra has also discussed some aspects of Eisenstein's interest in modern architecture, including the "Glashaus" project, where the influence of Le Corbusier's Centrosoyuz can be felt: François Albéra, *S. M. Eisenstein, cinématisme peinture et cinéma* (Brussels: Ed. Complexe, 1980).

[30] Sergei Eisenstein, "Journées d'exaltation pour la sortie du film *La Ligne Générale*," in *Au-delà des étoiles*, ed. Jacques Aumont (Paris: UGE, 1974), pp. 51–54.

172. Sergei Eisenstein, *The General Line*, 1927–1929, the centrifuge.

173. Sergei Eisenstein, *The General Line*, 1927–1929, the tractors' carousel.

The principal hallmark of pathetic composition is a constant "frenzy," a constant movement "outside oneself"—a qualitative shift from one isolated element or one symptomatic sign to the next; and quantitatively, an intense emotional content within a given sequence, episode or scene, which never ceases to accumulate.[31]

According to Eisenstein, it is the "pathos of the machine"—and not the problem of understanding the "profound inner processes" related to collectiv-

[31] Sergei Eisenstein, "La centrifugeuse et le Graal" in *La non-indifférente nature/2*, ed. Jacques Aumont (Paris: UGE, 1976), p. 103.

174. Moisei Ginzburg and Ignati Milinis, communal house of the Narkomfin, Moscow, 1928–1929, view of facade with *pilotis*.

175. Moisei Ginzburg and Ignati Milinis, communal house of the Narkomfin, Moscow, 1928–1929, view of end facade.

ization—that takes "pride of place" in *The General Line*. The approach here differs radically from both Dziga Vertov's montage strategy, and the continuous narrative flow of the filmed theatrical epic: just as Le Corbusier achieves his "lyricism" through the juxtaposition of "prisms" conditioned by technical criteria, and accumulates spatial intensity by means of precisely controlled itineraries, so Eisenstein conditions narrative flow and transcends the material of his film through "patheticization." In his own elaboration of montage strategies, Eisenstein later borrowed from one of the major sources of Le Corbusier's theory, Auguste Choisy's *Histoire de l'architecture*, on which the architect had relied in his elaboration of the *promenade architecturale*.[32]

THE ISSUE OF "COMMUNAL DWELLING"

Whereas the discovery of Eisenstein's films strengthened Le Corbusier's resolve to transcend simplistic functionalism and the aesthetics of the machine, his study of collective housing briefs inspired a renewed interest in typologies. Le Corbusier's relations with constructivism came to be situated on two distinct levels: an initial aesthetic debate marked by theoretical discussions and personal contacts in 1928, and Le Corbusier's subsequent discovery of the first effective productions of the new Soviet architecture, in the field of collective housing.

Till the end of the twenties, housing schemes built by the new regime were little different from those inspired by public-sector housing policies of the reformist municipalities in western Europe—they, too, oscillated between the garden-city and low-rent housing in France and the German *Siedlung*: the Sokol estate in Moscow, and housing developments in Traktornaia Street in Leningrad or Usacheva Street in Moscow, are cases in point. Yet with the extension of the "cultural revolution" to the sphere of *byt*, or "daily life," and the increasing availability of funds for construction, there emerged two briefs that were to inspire the most radical of architectural treatment: the workers' club, whose ubiquity Le Corbusier had discovered in October 1928, and the communal dwelling.[33]

In the interval between his 1928 and 1930 visits, the problem of communal housing, in which apartments of reduced size were combined with a whole battery of collective services, was consolidated both in the field, with Ginzburg and Ignati Milinis's Narkomfin development and the construction of Ivan Nikolaev's university dormitories project, and with respect to methodologies, with the publication of research by the Stroikom and the RSFSR. Le Corbusier was familiar with both aspects of the problem, and took the best documents on that question back with him from Moscow. He found, among

[32] Eisenstein owned a copy of Choisy's *Histoire* in the Russian edition, which is still kept in the apartment-museum managed by Naum Kleiman in Moscow. On Eisenstein's use of Choisy's concepts, see his text on "Montage and Architecture" and the expert commentaries of Yve-Alain Bois: Sergei M. Eisenstein (introduction by Yve-Alain Bois), "Montage and Architecture," *Assemblage*, no. 10 (1989): 111–31. On the relationship between Le Corbusier's "promenade architecturale" and Choisy, see Jacques Lucan, "Acropole, tout a commencé là," *Le Corbusier (1887–1965): Une encyclopédie*, pp. 20–25; Richard A. Etlin, "Le Corbusier, Choisy and French Hellenism: The search for a new architecture," *Art Bulletin* 69, no. 2 (1987): 264–78.

[33] On communal housing, see N. Markovnikov, "Dom-kommuna v proshlom, nastoiashchem i budushchem," *Stroitelnaia Promyshlennost* 8, no. 1 (1930): 2–6; Moisei Ginzburg, *Zhilishche* (Moscow: Gosstroiizdat, 1934); Ernesto Pasini, *La "casa-comune" e il Narkomfin di Ginzburg* (Rome: Officina Edizioni, 1980).

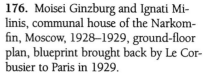
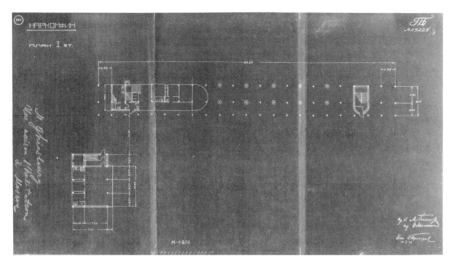

176. Moisei Ginzburg and Ignati Milinis, communal house of the Narkomfin, Moscow, 1928–1929, ground-floor plan, blueprint brought back by Le Corbusier to Paris in 1929.

177. Moisei Ginzburg and Ignati Milinis, communal house of the Narkomfin, Moscow, 1928–1929, fifth-and sixth-floor plans, blueprint brought back by Le Corbusier to Paris in 1929.

178. Moisei Ginzburg and Ignati Milinis, communal house of the Narkomfin, Moscow, 1928–1929, cross sections, blueprint brought back by Le Corbusier to Paris in 1929.

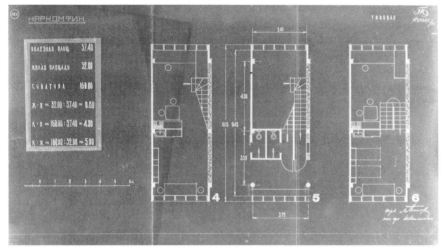

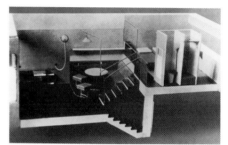

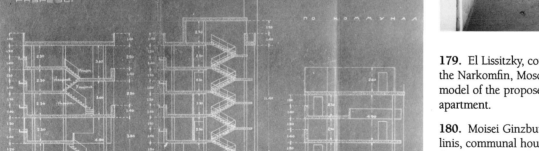

179. El Lissitzky, communal house of the Narkomfin, Moscow, 1928–1929, model of the proposed layout of an apartment.

180. Moisei Ginzburg and Ignati Milinis, communal house of the Narkomfin, Moscow, 1928–1929, view of a corridor, 1979.

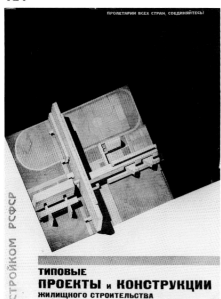

181. Stroikom (Construction Committee) of the RSFSR (Mikhail Barshch, Viacheslav Vladimirov), typical projects and structures for residential buildings, Moscow, 1929.

[34] *Sovremennaia Arkhitektura* 4, no. 1 (1929). This issue contains a story on "Sovremennoe Zhile" ("Contemporary Housing"). Le Corbusier also returned to Paris with an important article by Pasternak in his briefcase: Alexander Pasternak, "Novye sotsialnye tipy zhilishcha," *Stroitelstvo Moskvy* 6, no. 5 (1929): 9–16. Researches carried out by the Stroikom are published in V. I. Velman, ed., *Tipovye proekty i konstruktsii zhilishchnogo stroitelstva* (Moscow: Gosudarstvennoe Tekhnicheskoe Izdatelstvo, 1929).

[35] These plans, drawn to a scale of 1:100, are dated 15 May 1929.

[36] Le Corbusier, "Commentaires relatifs à Moscou et à la 'Ville Verte,'" Moscow, 12 March 1930, typewritten, p. 14, FLC.

[37] The second CIAM, on the subject of minimal housing, is discussed in L. Vygodsky, "Mezhdunarodnaia vystavka proektov zhilishcha, sootvetstvuiushchego prozhitochnomu minimumu," *Stroitelnaia Promyshlennost* 8, no. 4 (1930): 323–28.

[38] Velman, *Tipovye proekty*, pp. 17–21.

[39] See the lecture by Le Corbusier, "Une cellule à l'échelle humaine," *Précisions*, pp. 85–104.

[40] Le Corbusier, note on the back of an envelope, drawing no. 5537, FLC.

[41] Le Corbusier, letter to the editor of *The Studio*, quoted in Geoffrey Holmes and Shirley Wainwright, eds., *Decorative Art 1929* (London: The Studio, 1929), p. 4.

[42] El Lissitzky, letter to Sigfried Giedion, St. Johann in Pongau, 10 July 1928, Giedion archives, gta/ETH, Zurich.

other things, an issue of *Sovremennaia Arkhitektura* that contained the results of Stroikom research on the various rooms and housing types suitable for use in "communal dwellings."[34] But most important, Le Corbusier managed to lay his hands on a certain number of blueprints of the housing scheme built by Ginzburg for the employees of the Narkomfin (People's Commissariat for Finance).[35] Le Corbusier did not conceal his reservations concerning some of the more austere examples of communal housing which, on occasion, were built with extremely limited means:

I have had the opportunity to visit a Muscovite communal house: the construction is solid and well executed, but the internal organization and architectural concept are so cold, so impassive—in short, so totally lacking in all subtle or artistic intention that might have given life to the building—that one is struck with melancholy, not merely at the idea of living there oneself, but at the thought that several hundred individuals have been purely and simply deprived of the joys of architecture.[36]

Although the Narkomfin building made use of recurrent Corbusian themes such as *pilotis*, ribbon windows, and roof gardens, it nonetheless constituted a radical typological break, the fruit of Soviet experimentation with compact apartments built on lines similar to those followed by Ernst May's team in Frankfurt. The term *Minimalwohnung* was not used, but European accomplishments in the domain were well known to Moscow circles.[37] In any case, the Stroikom's studies of kitchens were based on flow diagrams used in German research, whereas the proposed amenities were taken from U.S. manufacturers' catalogues.[38] Le Corbusier was seduced by two aspects of Ginzburg and Milinis's communal scheme. The first was the notion of "residential" or "hotel" services grouped in a glass annex to the apartment building proper; the second was the organization of the apartments, with horizontal distributions based on the use of corridors on two of the five floors, lit by a long ribbon window that ran the whole length of the building, and which appeared to him in a vision as the element he had sought for so long for the organization of his future housing projects—his "street in the air."

The Narkomfin project was thus held up to Le Corbusier as a mirror, in that it demonstrated the validity of some of his most cherished ideas, and made it clear that he would have to reorganize and reduce the scale of his earlier schemes in order to see them realized at last. He was to devote his time to this task of reforming his earlier ideas during the trip to Latin America in the autumn of 1929.[39] Before his arrival in Moscow in 1928, Le Corbusier had noted the following on the back of an envelope postmarked in Prague, on the subject of one of his lectures:

Technology is the very basis of lyricism; therefore, I shall talk to you, not of lyricism, but of bases.[40]

The "enthusiastic declaration of faith in the architectural poem of the modern age," which he discovered in Moscow,[41] permitted him at last to collect some of these bases, but it also provided him with a potential source of aid in the CIAM's internal debates, which were already particularly tense.

LC, OSA, AND CIAM

For the inaugural meeting of the CIAM at La Sarraz in June 1928, a place had been reserved for El Lissitzky, but his Swiss visa arrived too late for him to attend.[42] Le Corbusier's firsthand discovery of the constructivists in June 1928, together with his Moscow conversations, led him to think that he might

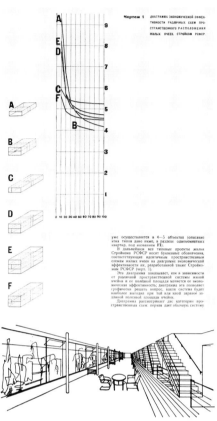

call on their support in conflicts within the organization. As the second (1929) congress at Frankfurt approached, Le Corbusier tried to persuade the CIAM president, Karl Moser, to adopt a precise strategy for the creation of an affiliated organization in the USSR:

The Russians have an extremely influential and active organization, the OSA, which publishes an important review; the board, 100 or so strong, includes Vesnin, Ginzburg and Leonidov (excellent).

For reasons of numerical balance, surely it is impossible for 100 Russians to be members of the Congress?

We must therefore *ask them to constitute a union*, composed to begin with of Vesnin (president), Ginzburg (CIRPAC delegate), Leonidov, Kolli, Nikolaev and Fisenko, Burov, Kozhin + Pasternak and Vladimirov and Lissitzky, who can stay if he likes, but he has not produced any architecture in Russia to date.

Also ask Moscow to obtain the membership of architects from Leningrad (Nikolsky among others, etc.) and from Kharkov (capital of the Ukraine, and a very alert city).[43]

Moser, who carried out these directives more or less to the letter, nonetheless passed on Le Corbusier's letter to Giedion with the recommendation that he exclude Lissitzky, "who has done nothing at all"—but not before the next congress—and appoint Ginzburg and Vesnin delegates, with the specific task of "training the group."[44] For the approaching Frankfurt congress on minimal housing, Le Corbusier suggested asking Kolli for a report on "the experience and consequences of the minimum dwelling imposed on Moscow by circumstances = a laboratory of domestic production."[45] But neither Kolli nor Ginzburg, who had both been co-opted onto the organization in Frankfurt, were in a position to participate in its future proceedings.[46] At a time when his hegemony over the French CIAM group was being contested by André Lurçat,[47] and when his visit to South America forced him out of the running at Frankfurt (where Pierre Jeanneret read his report), Le Corbusier thus attempted to infiltrate both the constructivists en bloc, as a counterweight to the Germans, and others such as Kolli and Ginzburg, in whom he had confidence.

With this maneuver, the theoretical reflections that Le Corbusier had nurtured during his two visits to Moscow found a direct outlet in institutional strategy. His third visit was to furnish the occasion for a more direct intervention, this time in the role of arbiter, in a domain that he had hardly touched on before in Russia: that of town planning.

182. Stroikom (Construction Committee) of the RSFSR (Mikhail Barshch, Viacheslav Vladimirov), communal house, Moscow, 1929, perspective on the refectory.

183. Stroikom (Construction Committee) of the RSFSR (Mikhail Barshch, Viacheslav Vladimirov), project for a collective housing unit, Moscow, 1929, efficiency study of different assemblages of cells.

184. Stroikom (Construction Committee) of the RSFSR (Mikhail Barshch, Viacheslav Vladimirov), project for a collective housing unit, Moscow, 1929, perspective of common corridor.

[43] Le Corbusier, letter to Karl Moser, Paris, 4 September 1929, FLC.

[44] Karl Moser, note to Sigfried Giedion written in the margin of the previous letter.

[45] Le Corbusier, handwritten note, undated, FLC.

[46] Martin Steinmann, ed., *CIAM Dokumente 1928–1939* (Basle: Birkhäuser Verlag, 1979).

[47] Cohen, "*L'architecture d'André Lurçat (1894–1970)*," pp. 286–95.

CHAPTER

6

"Response to Moscow"
and the Origins of
the "Ville Radieuse"

WHILE he was engaged in constructing the then largest block of offices in Moscow, Le Corbusier became involved in heated debate over the capital's future, which he had mentioned in passing during the lecture held at the outset of the 1920s, "L'Esprit Nouveau en Architecture," in the course of which he had defined the potential role of city planning in Europe:

Urban planning will tackle the large city and will not build new cities in new, unknown countries: its task is to deal with the current state of today's cities. Be it Paris, London, Berlin, Moscow or Rome, the environment of capital cities has to be completely transformed, whatever the cost, however radical the changes involved.[1]

At the time, however, Le Corbusier was not especially interested in Moscow. For him, it was the plan of Beijing that furnished evidence of the "spirit of geometry" that he intended to implement elsewhere. Yet he must have known of the importance of Moscow in Eugène Hénard's approach to the problem in *Etudes sur les transformations de Paris*, where he compared the French capital's traffic plan with that of other European cities.[2] During his 1928 visit, although he observed primarily the buildings and the people, Le Corbusier took the opportunity to sketch some broad outlines of the city's structure and noted that its plan was "that of the age of the horse."[3] During his conference at the Polytechnic Museum, he emphasized the urgency of "removing the business center to another part of the city." Moreover, one of the drawings executed in the course of the finalization of Centrosoyuz positioned the projected building within the district as a whole—a contextual approach that had become a habit of his.

While studying the plans for the new boulevard, I was struck by the idea that it would be useful to make some changes and to plan for the way in which the district might be built up on sounder urban principles. These modifications would have most happy repercussions on the general appearance of the new Centrosoyuz building.[4]

The drawing in question, in which the theme of the *redent*—an angular, tooth-shaped configuration invented by Hénard—was adapted to Moscow for the first time, the building's unusual appearance merged into a vaster structure with unlimited potential for growth. This theme, however, was not to be extended to the global problems of the city until later.

TOWARD THE "GREEN CITY"

One of the more original aspects of Muscovite life as Le Corbusier found it in 1928 was the existence of workers' clubs in all districts of the city. But the flattering impression of widespread community leisure activities was in fact only partially correct, in that the years of the New Economic Policy saw the gradual appearance around Moscow of weekend *dachas* for the privileged. The journalist Mikhail Koltsov denounced these individualistic tendencies in the pages of *Pravda*, considering that the warm, dry climate of the Northeast should be made accessible to all, thanks in particular to the electrification of the railway line between Moscow and Pushkino, and that an "immense proletarian sanatorium" should be built there.

The idea was not of a park, which could only be used during breaks or at the end of the working day, but rather of a *Kurort* in the forest, a place for short holidays, access to which would be facilitated by the construction of the first Soviet *avtostrada*.[5] Koltsov called on Soviet institutions, and especially the housing cooperatives, to build this "kind of cultural complement or socialist amendment of Moscow, with its stuffy bystreets and crowded and chaotic

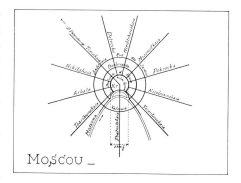

185. Eugène Hénard, "theoretical circulation diagram" of Moscow, 1905.

[1] Le Corbusier, "L'Esprit Nouveau en Architecture," lecture held at the Sorbonne on 12 June 1924, published in *Almanach d'architecture moderne* (Paris: G. Crès et Cie, 1925), p. 40.

[2] Eugène Hénard, "Plans comparatifs des voies principales de circulation dans les grandes capitales," in *Etudes sur les transformations de Paris* (1905), new edition with an introduction by Jean-Louis Cohen (Paris: L'Equerre, 1982), pp. 200–201. In 1925 Shchusev reproduced this plan and took up a number of Hénard's theoretical considerations: "Problemy novoi Moskvy," *Stroitelnaia Promyshlennost* 3, no. 3 (1925): 193–200.

[3] Le Corbusier, *Diary VII*, p. 32.

[4] Le Corbusier, note to Isidor Liubimov, October 1928, p. 1.

[5] Mikhail Koltsov, "Dacha—tak dacha," *Pravda* (30 January 1929). In Russian the term *Kurort* denotes a holiday resort in general, even if its functions are not exclusively therapeutic. Koltsov was to play an essential role in Soviet aid to Republican Spain before he was liquidated at the end of the thirties. See "Koltsov, Mikhail Efimovich," in *Bolshaia Sovetskaia Entsiklopediia*, vol. 33 (Moscow: IZOGIZ, 1938), pp. 537–38.

186. Konstantin Melnikov, "Green City" near Moscow, 1930, overall plan.

thoroughfares."[6] Once completed, and once the region had been cleared of "hooligans" who invaded the bathing resorts, this "Green City" would offer Muscovite workers cultural and sporting amenities that they could use on a rotating basis, one day per week, one day in five, or even for longer holidays. As N. Popov-Sibiriak remarked, "the only resemblance to the city will be its infrastructure; for the rest, it will be simply a place of rest and recovery."[7]

A 15,000-hectare site—including 11,500 hectares of forest—was selected near Bratovshchina, thirty-seven kilometers northeast of the center, where in 1930 the State, the Moscow Soviet, the Trade Unions, and a large number of governmental institutions grouped together in a joint stock company decided to build a broad range of public facilities and housing estates that would "carry out the utmost development of the collectivization of life possible in the present stage."[8] Architects were mobilized in response to Koltsov's call, and in the first weeks of 1930 a closed competition was organized with a view to elaborating a general plan for this "socialist garden city" for 100,000 inhabitants, with the participation of D. F. Fridman, N. A. Ladovsky, K. S. Melnikov, and a "brigade" from the OSA under the direction of M. O. Barshch and M. Ia. Ginzburg.

Present in Moscow for the third time at the beginning of March 1930 and busy finishing the working drawings of the Centrosoyuz,[9] Le Corbusier was invited to give his opinion on the competition entries. In order to enable him to understand the unusual brief, a summary in French was drawn up.[10] The architectural demands of the program were, ostensibly at least, of the most attractive kind:

The newest and most perfect advances of architecture require, most important of all, new forms of edification, with the widespread use of glass, open terraces, and movable partitions; they also require a minimum of clutter in the dwellings, the introduction of a new technique of objects and furnishings that are simple and rational in construction.[11]

The "Green City" was explicitly intended as a sort of test bed for urban solutions potentially applicable within the capital, and which were described in terms designed to justify Le Corbusier's intervention:

The problem to be solved by the "Green City," in particular as the experimental demonstration of new housing designs for Moscow, whose outmoded urban organism is chaotic and extremely complicated, requires two distinct solutions: first of all, it is necessary to embrace all aspects of the workers' life, so as to satisfy the widest possible variety of forms of communal living; second, it is necessary to implement, as exactly and coherently as possible, a union between the best results obtained by means of Western technique and socialist principles. This signifies that it is not enough to attain the levels of current Western urban economies (highly developed transportation, mechanization, electrification, comfortable housing) in the "Green City" project, but that these should be exploited from the point of view of socialist forms of living, with public services, maximum guarantees for workers' health, a rational organization of leisure, sporting activities and cures, child education, etc. The "Green City" must become a model proletarian health clinic where workers from Moscow and, to a certain extent, those of the outlying region, can either stay for protracted periods of time or spend their rest days.[12]

LE CORBUSIER'S "COMMENTARIES"

Over and above these considerations, and the essentially collectivist spirit of a venture grounded in unified systems of supply, the concept of the "Green

[6] Mikhail Koltsov, "Zeleny gorod," *Revoliutsiia i Kultura*, no. 2 (1930): 40; and in English, Mikhail Koltsov, "A Soviet Garden-City," *VOKS*, no. 8–10 (1930): 45.

[7] N. Popov-Sibiriak, "Zelenomu gorodu obshchestvennoe vnimanie," *Stroitelstvo Moskvy* 6, no. 8 (1929): 21.

[8] Koltsov, "A Soviet Garden-City," p. 47.

[9] He uses the excuse of the Russian frenzy to build to justify his failure to deliver other projects: Le Corbusier, letter to Paulo Prado, Moscow, 5 March 1930, Prado Archive, Rio de Janeiro.

[10] "La Ville Verte (résumé des matériaux)," Moscow, 1930, 11 pp., handwritten, FLC. This text is in fact a more or less literal, and even rustic, translation of an article published in May, presenting the results of the competition: Redaktsia, "Voprosy planirovki, opyt sotsialisticheskogo goroda-sada," *Stroitelnaia Promyshlennost* 8, no. 5 (1930): 450.

[11] "La Ville Verte," pp. 5–6.

[12] Ibid., pp. 2–3.

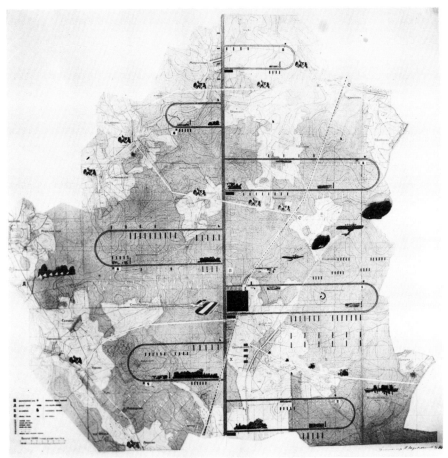

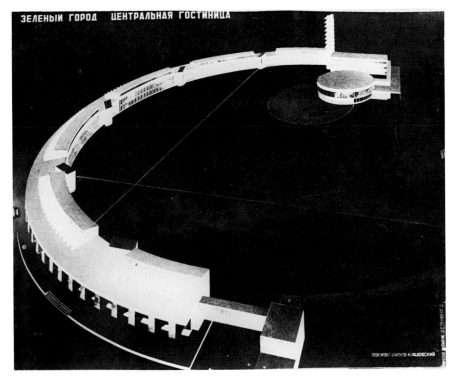

187. Nikolai Ladovsky, "Green City" near Moscow, 1930, overall plan.

188. Nikolai Ladovsky, "Green City" near Moscow, 1930, central hotel.

189. Nikolai Ladovsky, "Green City" near Moscow, 1930, "residential wigwam."

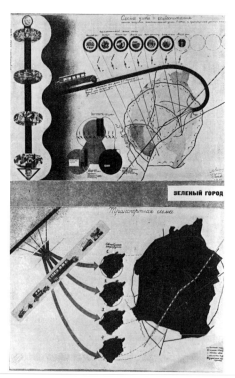

190. Mikhail Barshch and Moisei Ginzburg, "Green City" near Moscow, 1930, educational and transportation systems.

City" instantly seduced Le Corbusier. In particular, he became an enthusiastic advocate of the idea of "resting on the fifth day." In a letter to Ginzburg, he even outbid the Soviets when he compared the potential "clients" of the "Green City" to a kind of "automobile":

The Green City will be a garage where the automobile is serviced (oiling and greasing, inspection of the organs, repairs and maintenance).[13]

Among the projects submitted to Le Corbusier's better judgment, the strangest was certainly Konstantin Melnikov's "sleep laboratory," an idea as fantastic as it was subversive. Melnikov had openly derided the requirements of the brief by claiming to base his project on "hypnopaedia"—that is, the acquisition of knowledge during sleep by means of phonographs, "until the cure induces a change of character."[14] His "city of rationalized rest" was circular in plan and divided up into sectors with lightweight wooden constructions open to the beneficial effects of sun and wind.[15]

In a sober composition based on industrial building prototypes, Ladovsky retained the agricultural vocation of the site: the territory was cut in two by the *avtostrada*, and a series of looping service roads furnished access to the resort and the sanatorium. For the first phase he proposed using factory-assembled "shack cabins" for the housing.[16] Daniil Fridman's proposal, on the other hand, was based on a strictly functional layout, with zones of varying density and collective "rest houses" in tiers.[17]

The most radical entry was certainly the study carried out by Barshch and Ginzburg for OSA. At a time when the debate over the socialist city was entering a decisive phase, they treated the "Green City" as a pretext for tackling the problem of Moscow, which they proposed to raze except for its historical center and one or two zones of production, with housing scattered throughout the countryside. This fundamentally antiurban project for the "Green City" was merely "the first step toward the new Moscow"—a blueprint for national planning designed to "guarantee maximum harmony between man and nature," involving a whole series of linear devices, with housing units and public amenities located along service roads:[18]

The principle we have adopted involves placing the population along links with the centers, or interurban links. This simplifies not only the exploitation of the road network, but also that of all the other networks: sanitary systems, technical infrastructure, etc.

. . . In the cities, the inhabitants are deprived of fresh air and light; they lack open horizons and free spaces. Our development plan eliminates all these defects. The positioning of housing along the traffic links makes it necessary to plan for the means of protecting the inhabitants from dust and noise. Our final scheme is thus as follows: the housing zone is organized in a linear band 200–250 meters from the road, and is sheltered behind a densely planted park zone. In this way each housing unit will front the park on the one hand and face vast expanses of forest, fields and zoological gardens, on the other. It is not difficult to appreciate the sanitary advantages of this planning principle.[19]

In the "Commentaries relative to Moscow and the Green City," which he submitted to the Soviets before returning to Paris, Le Corbusier, who had doubtless fallen under the spell of the various projects' hygienist connotations, joined the advocates of disurbanization in his criticism of the existing city and emphasized his concern for the "decentralization of modern cities." In his view, Moscow's street plan had made the city, in terms borrowed from Hénard, "a traffic circle":

[13] Le Corbusier, letter to Moisei Ginzburg, 17 March 1930, published in *Précisions*, p. 268.

[14] Aldous Huxley would make use of this idea in *Brave New World*, published in 1932.

[15] Konstantin Melnikov, "Gorod ratsionalizirovannogo otdykha (proekt)," *Iskusstvo v Massy*, no. 6 (1930): 20–21, and *Stroitelstvo Moskvy* 7, no. 3 (1930): 20–25. See the analysis by S. Frederick Starr, *Melnikov, Solo Architect in a Mass Society* (Princeton: Princeton University Press, 1978), pp. 169–83.

[16] Nikolai Ladovsky, "Gorod otdykha i Sotsialisticheskogo byta," *Stroitelstvo Moskvy* 7, no. 3 (1930): 9–13.

[17] Daniil Fridman, "Sotsialistichesky lesnoi kurort," *Stroitelstvo Moskvy* 7, no. 3 (1930): 25.

[18] Mikhail Barshch and Moisei Ginzburg, "Zeleny Gorod, sotsialisticheskaia rekonstruktsiia Moskvy," *Sovremennaia Arkhitektura* 5, nos. 1–2 (1930): 17–37.

[19] Ibid.

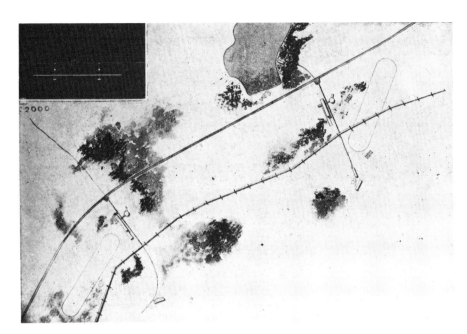

191. Mikhail Barshch and Moisei Ginzburg, "Green City" near Moscow, 1930, freeway, hotel accommodations, and sports facilities.

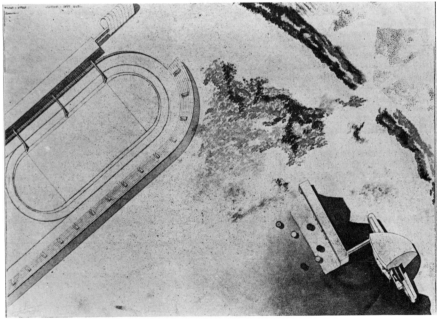

192. Mikhail Barshch and Moisei Ginzburg, "Green City" near Moscow, 1930, sports facilities.

When one speaks of decentralizing the great cities, one discards all notions of a "donkey path"; one empties the center, one introduces means of transport (trams, buses, cars, etc.) and one transforms the city center into a green zone containing some vestiges of the past—in Moscow, for instance, the Kremlin, the Museums, etc.

. . . When drawing up systems of urbanization, one should always remember that superseding these *systems* is one peremptory, incorruptible, indeformable value: the heart of the man who is free of all shackles and constraints, and who *must not feel shackled or constrained*, or he will consider himself a slave and, if sincere, will feel at the very least ill at ease. This atmosphere of malaise alone signifies the *failure* of the design.

All in all, one must appreciate the following: if one lives alongside the "donkey path," can one satisfy the present-day conditions of Russian labor?[20]

[20] Le Corbusier, "Commentaires relatifs à Moscou et la Ville Verte," pp. 1–2, FLC. The full original text of the "Commentaires" has been published in an appendix to the French edition of the present book. Le Corbusier had reproduced Hénard's "traffic circles" in *Urbanisme* (Paris: G. Crès et Cie, 1925), p. 110.

Le Corbusier's response to this fairly rhetorical question was of course a negative one. In his thinking about "labor," he considered of first importance facilitating "contacts between men," which should be "rapid, multifarious," and providing a "place for meetings, discusion, a GHQ [General Headquarters]." Concerning the "decision-making center," he therefore recommended the creation of a "business city"—an idea that had been an integral part of his 1922 "contemporary city." Apart from these considerations, he endorsed the analysis that formed the basis of the competition brief with fairly good grace, and generously appended the analogy of the machine:

But the USSR has seen an innovation of great import—the idea of *resting on the fifth day*—and a novel idea that seems to me quite remarkable, that of the *Green City* of repose.

How is this to be explained? In the terms of modern medical thinking: one does not cure the sick, one builds *healthy men*.

This is the spirit of the good mechanic; the machine is kept in good repair. Mechanical activity presents us with striking images: witness an engine turning at 3,000 revolutions for ten days or six months without a break. It's fantastic, one has simply ordered the operations, proportioned the effort required, harmonized the organs, prevented wear and tear.

The machine age ceased to be concerned with *wear* a century ago. The human body—and with it, by irrevocable extension, the human spirit—has been worn down, overworked, enfeebled and deformed. There is a veritable neurasthenia of the machine. An animal placed in conditions that are contrary to its normal existence becomes neurasthenic, defective.

The Soviet idea of resting on the fifth day is designed to combat wear. The Green City of repose offers physical, nervous and moral recuperation. This is so remarkable that a law of rest ought to exist along with the law of work, and one ought to have to "clock in" for one's day of rest just as one does at the factory. And one might add a suitable amount of sport individually prescribed by the physicians of the Green City.[21]

Le Corbusier's position resembled that of Ginzburg and Barshch in that he used the "Green City" as a pretext for the overall replanning of Moscow. But the shift toward a complete reconstruction of the capital was inspired by principles opposed to those of the antiurban planners, to the extent that he was not in favor of its complete dissolution. Although he agreed with the idea that the factories be "ordered and scattered throughout the Soviet territory," he nonetheless emphasized the need to "preserve the city" of "Soviet leadership" and to create a "city of offices," which already existed "in rudimentary form in the Gostorg, in the Centrosoyuz building currently under construction, etc." At the same time he insisted on the need to look for new housing solutions:

Housing must be completely reorganized, and we must cease to cherish the contradictory dream of working in the city and at the same time remaining a man of the woods (one must in fact choose between the life of the man of the woods or the shepherd, and that of the city dweller with his essentially urban activities—organization, planning, leadership).

He therefore proposed a tripartite structure, with a "central agglomeration" given over to "work," an "admirably designed inner ring" for housing, and a "city of recuperation" located "in any favorably situated place," whose functioning should be "as precisely regulated as labor."[22] Le Corbusier justified the essential features of his proposal by invoking military considerations, and especially aerial warfare. He considered the "Green City's useful bases" in detail, and above all examined the problem of access, which, "despite the hilly site," was based on the idea of "a straight, penetrating road" and the strict

[21] Le Corbusier, "Commentaires," pp. 3–4.
[22] Ibid., p. 8.

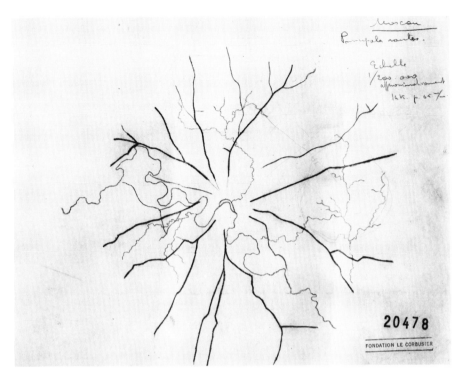

193. Le Corbusier, radial roads leading to Moscow, sketch opening his "Commentaries Relative to Moscow and the Green City," 1930, FLC 20478.

segregation of traffic—a foretaste of his "7 V" of the post–World War II period:

Access to the Green City should be provided by a straight, axial road for cars (and perhaps buses) only. No level crossings. Differences in level should not be taken into account, and engineering works will be used where necessary (bridges, trenches, embankments). There is no reason for the road to be close to the railway line. Tramway circuits should be independent; since they are highly sensitive to the contours of the ground, the tracks must be placed in the grass like railway lines.

Rural roads may, on occasion, be drawn parallel to the freeway. They will link staging posts at modest distances from each other—it is a network of dispersal. They will never cross the autostrada at the same level.[23]

With this differential network, Le Corbusier quickly solved the problem of zoning and concentrated his attention on "the creation of a type of housing cell" and "special buildings," expressing his confidence in his Soviet colleagues as long as their "architectural concept" was less "cold" than those that he had so far encountered. Far from assessing the various projects, Le Corbusier was in fact looking for a new approach to the "Green City," one as yet somewhat vague, in which the lineaments of a global plan for Moscow could be clearly perceived. But the president of the jury, O. Iu. Shmidt, considered for his part that although the entries did not lack originality, "none of the projects corresponded to the scale of the problem." In particular, he attacked the "fantastic visions" of Melnikov (which the jury as a whole also criticized in detail), the "unfinished quality" of Fridman's project, and the fact that Ginzburg had "shifted the problem elsewhere."

Ladovsky's project was duly selected as a "basis for the construction of the Green City," provided that considerable improvements were carried out.[24] Several young architects were called on to work under Ladovsky's direction on more detailed projects and even, if S. O. Khan-Magomedov is to be believed,

[23] Ibid., p. 13. Cf. the analysis of this aspect of Le Corbusier's proposals by Pier Giorgio Gerosa, *Le Corbusier, urbanisme et mobilité* (Basle: Birkhäuser Verlag, 1978).

[24] O. Iu. Shmidt, "Chto reshila rabochaia obshchestvennost o planakh 'zelenogo goroda,'" *Stroitelnaia Promyshlennost* 8, no. 5 (1930): 459–60. See also the editorial of *Stroitelstvo Moskvy* 7, no. 3 (1930): 30–31, together with V. N. Simbirtsev's postscript. Koltsov came to similar conclusions in *Pravda* (1 May 1930).

on the construction of a mock-up of the proposed buildings.[25] But subsequent discussion concerning the plan for Moscow spelled doom for the project, which at the end of 1930 was still considered "experimental" by the physician S. A. Gurevich, who was in charge of the project,[26] although the railway station was renamed "Pravda" and, in 1932, eight thousand inhabitants were resettled in the area following the adoption of a definitive plan.[27]

A DISPUTE WITH GINZBURG

The debate over the "Green City" nonetheless gave Le Corbusier a pretext for criticizing the options and bucolic tone of the "disurbanists," as reflected in the OSA project. Some days after writing down his views on the competition, he remarked in a letter to Ginzburg that only city dwellers were in a position to appreciate the resources of the countryside:

Disurbanization: this term is misleading; it is *fundamentally self-contradictory*, and has led any number of Western ideologists astray, a fact that has wasted a great deal of our industrialists' time—it is a contradiction in terms that is belied and disconfirmed by all the facts.

To lead industry away from the city, that is, to begin industrializing the countryside, to equip places of demographic density with machines. The machine will make the *muzhik* think; nature has never made the *muzhik* think. Nature is beneficial to the city dweller, who has galvanized all his resources in the city, and who has set in motion the diligent mechanisms of the spirit. It is by grouping, through conflict and cooperation, through struggle and mutual help, in activity, that the spirit matures and bears fruit. One fails to see this, but the reality is there; the peasant does not study the blossoms on the trees or listen to the lark's song. It is the city dweller who does this.[28]

For Le Corbusier the great city, far from being abandoned, had to be reformed, "adjusted" to new demands:

In particular, consider how ten centuries of premachine civilization built cities that represent an appalling and dangerous threat at this time of machine expansion. Admit that the evil resides in this heritage; and our salvation with it: by adjusting the cities that will become more and more dense . . . , to adjust our cities to contemporary needs, that is, to reconstruct them (just as they have always been rebuilt since their birth).

Consider the following characteristic detail: one plan for the disurbanization of Moscow envisages, among other things, the construction of straw huts in the forest of the Green City. Bravo, superb! . . . As long as it's only for the weekend! But do not claim that once you have built the straw huts, Moscow can be razed.[29]

Ginzburg replied to this letter by publishing carefully selected extracts in *Sovremennaia Arkhitektura*, and added that he and his "friends" considered Le Corbusier, "the most excellent surgeon of the contemporary city" and also "the most refined master of architecture, a man who has invented radical and fundamental solutions to certain essential questions of organization." Yet he also indicated that he was not interested in "curing" the contemporary city, which he considered "mortally sick," and which neither *pilotis* nor roof gardens could now save:

You refer to Perret's unsuccessful attempts to take housing out of the city. But this too is quite understandable. He severed an isolated member from a complex organism. That member inevitably wasted away. We are removing from the city nothing less than the city itself, its entire system of supply and culture. In other words, we are

[25] Khan-Magomedov, *Pioneers*, p. 515.

[26] S. A. Gurevich, in *K probleme stroitelstva Sotsialisticheskogo goroda* (Moscow: Planovoe Khoziaistvo, 1930), pp. 97–103.

[27] "Zeleny gorod," in *Bolshaia Sovetskaia Entsiklopediia*, vol. 26 (Moscow: IZOGIZ, 1933), p. 558.

[28] Le Corbusier, letter to Moisei Ginzburg.

[29] Ibid.

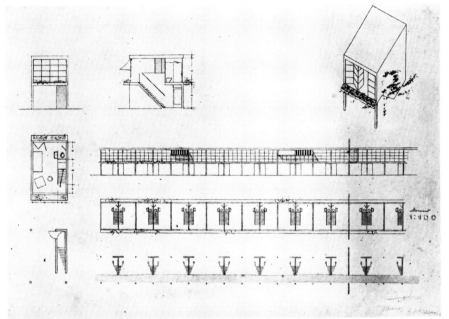

creating a whole new organism. This is quite different from what Perret was trying to do.

You write that the peasant does not love flowers and does not hear the song of the skylark. But of course he doesn't . . . when he is exhausted with backbreaking labor. But we want our peasant to listen to the skylark. And we know that for this it is only necessary to lighten his labor and bring more culture into his life. And all this will be possible not by smoothing out the contradictions with which the modern capitalist system is riddled, but by creating new forms of human settlement more worthy of the future.[30]

194. Mikhail Barshch and Moisei Ginzburg, "Green City" near Moscow, 1930, residential units.

195. Le Corbusier, caricature of the disurbanists, published in *La ville radieuse* (Paris, 1935).

RED PLANS FOR MOSCOW

In May 1930, some weeks after this exchange of views, Nikolai Kolli sent Le Corbusier a "formidable questionnaire" from Sergei Gorny, "administrative leader of the bureau for the preparation of the plan for the enlarging of the future, socialistic Moscow." Gorny invited him to answer "the various points of the life and development of Moscow" contained in the questionnaire, and to furnish "as many proposals" as he thought fit. The survey organized by Gorny for the MOKKh[31] came at a crucial time in the development of the capital.

The need for a new plan that would take into account both the considerable increase in population brought about by the NEP, and the consequences of the transfer of government functions to a city that even before 1914 had been the trade and cultural capital, was all the more pressing to the extent that no global plan had been drawn up before the revolution and none of the subsequent plans had ever been implemented: neither the plan for "New Moscow" elaborated for the municipal Soviet under A. V. Shchusev in 1923, nor S. S. Shestakov's plan for "Greater Moscow," which had been drawn up and discussed in the same period, had led to concrete public-works programs for the development of essential infrastructure.[32]

[30] Moisei Ginzburg to Le Corbusier, in *Sovremennaia Arkhitektura* 5, nos. 1–2 (1930): 61–62. English translation in appendix to Kopp, *Town and Revolution*, p. 254. In subsequent pages, Bruno Taut considers the problem of city planning in the USSR from a more general viewpoint and rejects the idea that Le Corbusier's *pilotis* "liberate" the ground: Bruno Taut, "Raspad goroda," *Sovremennaia Arkhitektura* 5, nos. 1–2 (1930): 63–64.

[31] Moskovsky Oblastnoi Otdel Kommunalnogo Khoziaistva (MOKKh), or Department of Municipal Economy for the Moscow Region.

[32] For the beginnings of city planning in Moscow after 1917, see V. L. Orleansky, "Iz istorii planirovki gor. Moskvy," *Stroitelstvo Moskvy* 12, nos. 7–8 (1935): 15–19; Manfredo Tafuri, "Les premières hypothèses de planification urbaine dans la Russie Soviétique 1918–1925," *Archithèse*, Zurich, no. 7 (1983): 34–41; Barbara Kreis, *Moskau 1917– 1935, Vom Wohnungsbau zum Städtebau* (Munich: Edition Marzona, 1985), pp. 11–31.

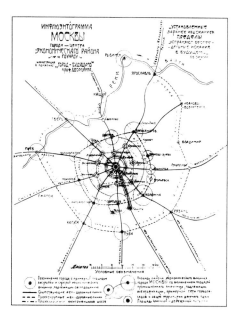

196. Boris Sakulin, "Influentogramme" of Moscow, 1918.

197. Alexei Shchusev and Ivan Zholtovsky, "Novaia Moskva" plan, 1923.

[33] T. Gelman, "The Planning of Moscow," *The Town Planning Review*, Liverpool, no. 1 (1924): 13–16; Cooke, "Le mouvement pour la cité-jardin," pp. 226–28.

[34] L. Vygodsky, "Podgotovitelnye raboty k planirovke 'Bolshoi Moskvy,'" *Stroitelstvo Moskvy* 4, no. 10 (1927): 25–28, and "Problema Bolshoi Moskvy,'" *Stroitelstvo Moskvy* 6, no. 2 (1929): 7–10.

[35] V. Lavrov, "Skhema novoi planirovki Moskvy," *Stroitelstvo Moskvy* 5, no. 6 (1928): 11–15; the stipulations contained in this document were subsequently applied to the Centrosoyuz project

Shchusev's plan left the city intact and created garden cities on the outskirts.[33] The engineer Shestakov's plan, also based on ideas of the garden-city movement but for the region as a whole, proposed the extension of the city's radioconcentric structure in order to reduce density, and the creation of two vast industrial areas on the outskirts. The orientations of this plan had been judged relevant in 1927, but subsequent intensification of rail traffic to and from Moscow increased ground occupation, and saturation of the existing networks seemed to indicate the need for a complete revision of the city's historical form.[34] In 1928, the Moscow Soviet's planning commission considered a "preliminary scheme" involving a general program for the widening of streets and overall zoning.[35]

With the launching of the first Five-Year Plan, Moscow's future was ruled by the policy of creating new industrial regions. At the outset of 1930, Sergei Gorny defined the objectives of the projected competition for the *pereplanirovka* or replanning of the city. These involved three distinct types of document: a general plan to be completed by 1933, an intermediate scheme running parallel with the Five-Year Plan, and a plan to regulate building. The objectives were demographic and aimed at attaining a population of ten million and extending the city to the southwest, but at the same time Gorny warned against the risks of "hypertrophy" in a "Leviathan" or "octopus" city growing at the expense of other towns in the Soviet Union.[36]

Gorny based his proposition on a remark made by a worker, according to whom it was important "to hear advice concerning what the city of the future should be like" before taking final decisions. To this end he launched a broadly based consultation among political leaders such as the Bulgarian V. Kolarov, from the Komintern praesidium; economists such as S. G. Strumilin, M. Liashchenko, and G. B. Puzis; hygienists such as Dr. S. Gurevich, who was in charge of the Green City project; as well as the principal architectural organizations such as ASNOVA, OSA, and MAO, the VOPRA, the ARU, and the cooperatives. Gorny also questioned Ernst May, who was still in Frankfurt, and Nikolai Kolli, who passed on the questionnaire to Le Corbusier.[37]

This questionnaire, apparently written in French in Gorny's own hand, contained thirty detailed questions concerning both the choice of development at the level of the USSR as a whole, and planning policies for Moscow's urban space. Some of the questions appeared to invite global reflection, since the very first raised the eventuality of transferring the capital from Moscow. Yet the document was in fact designed to elicit somewhat rudimentary territorial distributions. Moscow, for instance, was considered from the point of view of its agricultural or industrial productivity. Should the capital retain its importance as a farming region or should its agricultural role be diminished? Should industrial production aim to do more than supply the capital? In the transport domain, the question of a single railway station for the capital was raised. For the most part, however, the questionnaire concerned architectural, urban, and zoning solutions to the problems of housing, education, and public amenities, culminating in a number of questions specifically concerning the form of the city:

29. Which elements of the city and which architectural monuments of historic or revolutionary significance should be preserved on the future site of Moscow?
30. Should old Moscow:
    a. be the object of a new plan?
    b. be transformed into a closed center with satellite cities?
    c. be transformed in accordance with another plan?
    d. retain its radial and concentric plan?[38]

LE CORBUSIER'S "RESPONSE"

Le Corbusier's answers, which he prepared in less than six weeks and returned to Kolli on 5 July 1930 and which were certainly more complete and precise than any others received by Gorny, testify to the care and attention with which he examined the questions.

I am sending via the good offices of Mr. Popov:
    1 66-page report,
    1 portfolio containing 21 sheets of plans,
in response to the questionnaire concerning the reconstruction of Moscow.

I have given the subject considerable thought because it is is of the utmost interest to me.

I believe I have contributed some fundamental and just ideas.

Urban planning is neither a joke nor a game.

I hope your bosses appreciate this work.

[36] Sergei Gorny, "Planirovka Moskvy," *Kommunalnoe Khoziaistvo*, no. 6 (1930): 15–18.

[37] The results of the first set of responses were published before the summer. Sergei Gorny, "Kak rekonstruirovat staruiu i stroit novuiu Moskvu," *Kommunalnoe Khoziaistvo*, no. 6 (1930): 18–33.

[38] S. Gorny, "Moscou socialistique, centre politique et administratif," handwritten questionnaire, undated (first semester, 1930), FLC.

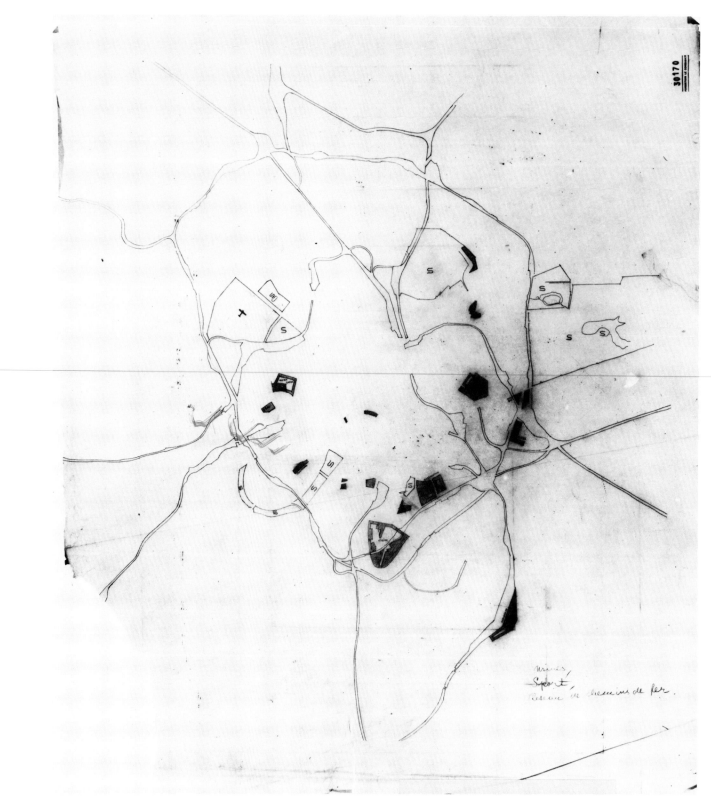

198. Le Corbusier, sketch of factories, sport facilities, and railroads in Moscow, 1930, FLC 30170.

One other thing: I am available for further studies. I should like to think that my ideas will be adopted for the great task at hand. Please communicate this to your bosses.[39]

Le Corbusier refused outright to answer questions that lay "outside [his] sphere of competence," concerning demographic projections and agriculture and specifically political choices. He was, however, extremely precise in his responses to the question of the reorganization of the city, which for him must remain the beating heart of a nation whose energies were concentrated there:

The concentration of a great population galvanizes the spirit, stimulates the energies, sharpens questions and creates intensity.

Extreme manifestations of vitality are to be found in places of great concentration. Politicians should be recruited from the higher echelons of the intelligentsia. They should feel the contemporary pulse; they should be sensitive to the breath of the present, which prefigures the future.

Why then deprive politics of an atmosphere so charged with tension?[40]

Le Corbusier believed that Moscow should remain the political center of the country and retain its productive capacity, and that one should avoid "imposing artificial destinies":

Energy is multiple, multiform. The elites, the constructive spirits are all "of the same nature": constructive powers (energetic qualities) acting in various milieux, indissociable, interdependent symphonic events of human activity.

In principle, the City is precisely, necessarily, the place of assembly, contact, competition and the struggle of diverse energies. It would be dangerous and artificial to separate and disperse [these energies]. It would be contrary to the instinctual forces of assembly that have given rise to the city. . . . To isolate would be to enfeeble.[41]

A single (in this case, geographical) consideration underlay Le Corbusier's views, which may usefully be compared with those of André Missenard:[42] given the "extremely harsh, extremely cold climate, which appears nonetheless to be excellent for an active population, and which maintains it in a state of stimulation," the capital must remain where it is. Le Corbusier's clearly formulated hypothesis of a great, densely populated city reflected his hostility to ideas of the garden city and disurbanization—a hostility reinforced since his earlier "Commentaries":

The principle of disproportionate urban extension is a sentimental heresy rooted in the devotion to garden cities, whose effect is to isolate the individual, and to force him to perform wearisome tasks and believe he is happy (I agree that this illusion can be useful).

Socially speaking, the garden city is a narcotic: it shatters the collective spirit, its initiatives, its galvanizations, and atomizes human energies into an amorphous, impalpable powder.

Last March, in the course of my previous visit to Moscow, I was asked to draw up a report on the early plans for a green city on the outskirts of the city. I thought it fit to adopt a categorical position relative to a utopia that appeared to be gaining some approval in Moscow.

"Disurbanization" amounts to the annihilation of human energy. If we wish to create a short-sighted people, let us disurbanize; if, on the other hand, we desire a people with strong, dynamic, modern ideas, let us urbanize, concentrate, build. History and its statistics show that the great periods are those of greatest concentration in the cities.[43]

[39] Le Corbusier, letter to Nikolai Kolli, Paris, 5 July 1930, FLC. The *Carnet noir* contains no record of the plans of the "response," which are separately numbered. Only some documents were attributed to Neidhardt in the spring of 1933—that is, some weeks before the fourth CIAM meeting on the "Functional City."

[40] Le Corbusier, "Réponse à un questionnaire de Moscou," handwritten, 8 June 1930, p. 2, FLC. The response was published in full in an appendix to the Russian edition of *Urbanisme*: Le Corbusier, *Planirovka Goroda*, preface by S. M. Gorny (Moscow: OGIZ-IZOGIZ, 1933), pp. 175–208. The full original text of the "Réponse" has been published in an appendix to the French edition of this book.

[41] Le Corbusier, "Réponse," p. 4.

[42] André Missenard, *A la recherche du temps et du rythme*, preface by Alexis Carrel (Paris: Librairie Plon, 1940).

[43] Le Corbusier, "Réponse," pp. 63–64.

199. Le Corbusier, "Response to Moscow," the proposed city on the site of Moscow in relationship to the "Green City," 1930, FLC 20471.

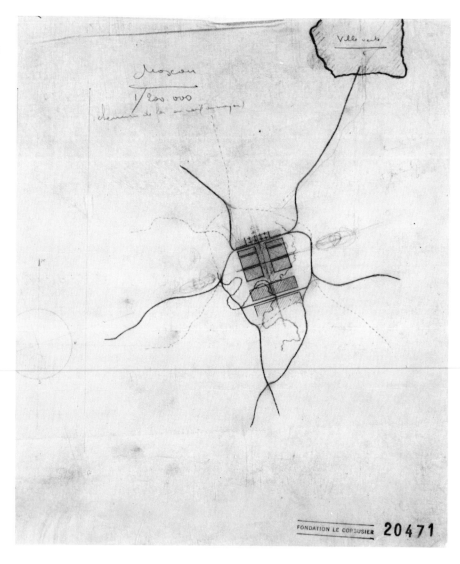

As evidenced in at least one analytical sketch, Le Corbusier studied the distribution of activities in the existing city with a view to implementing his ideas.[44] He then presented "an organic scheme for a great capital, equivalent to Moscow in size," that represents an "advantage over the urban plans of 1922 and 1925 in that it permits a completely flexible response to all future growth." A "living being," this plan does not in fact establish any clear limits, despite Le Corbusier's hostility to excessive territorial proliferation. On returning from his 1928 trip, Le Corbusier had already grasped that "Moscow, the embryo of a new world," continued to invest "the old carcass of an Asiatic village." This time he returned to the theme of the city's "precariousness" in order to justify both the obliteration of its existing structure, and the widespread—and even total—destruction of its very fabric:

The planner should direct his efforts toward avoiding the creation of a radial and concentric city. This is the great poverty [misère] of old cities, which have grown in piecemeal fashion over the centuries. It is also true of Moscow.

But, as we have already stated, Moscow is in reality a provisional city, in that it does not possess an indelible structure such as can be found in Paris, London, Berlin, etc. . . . In Moscow, therefore, the planner can break with the radioconcentric order.[45]

[44] See the trace drawing of the location of industries and sporting facilities, no. 30170, FLC, which has been mistakenly classified among the Palace of Soviets drawings.

[45] Le Corbusier, "Réponse," p. 30.

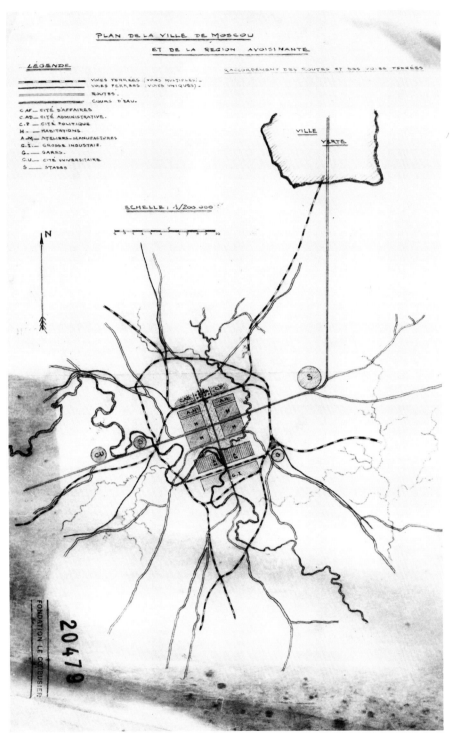

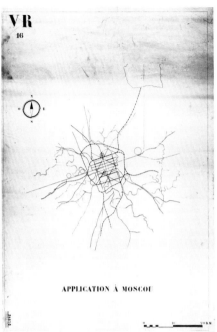

200. Le Corbusier, "Response to Moscow," Plan of Moscow and the surrounding region, 1930, FLC 20479.

201. Le Corbusier, the "Ville Radieuse," Application to Moscow, 1933, FLC 24910.

Le Corbusier's transformation of existing Moscow into "a great modern city" left standing only the Kremlin, the church of St. Basil, the Bolshoi theater, the Lenin Mausoleum, and occasional religious edifices, representative of a selective skyline that also provides a backdrop to his successive plans for Paris.[46] Elaborating on arguments that he had used in his "Commentaries," Le Corbusier stated that, although some industries were to be removed from Moscow

[46] Cf. Bruno Reichlin, "L'esprit de Paris," *Casabella*, no. 531–532 (January–February 1987): 52–63.

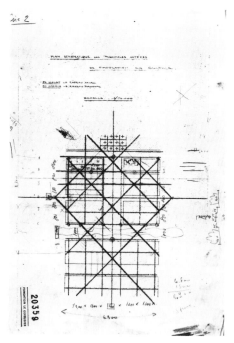

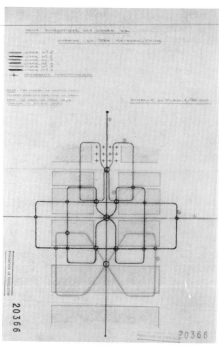

202. Le Corbusier, "Response to Moscow," 1930, Schematic plan of the main arteries, 20359.

203. Le Corbusier, "Response to Moscow," 1930, Schematic plan of the subways, FLC 20366.

so as to "give an impetus to industrialization in the countryside," his was nonetheless "an industrial city," "clean, joyous and alive," and one designed with a view to consolidating the "working-class elite."

As regards the problem of transport, Le Corbusier did not wholeheartedly endorse Gorny's idea of one central railway station, and considered that thirty minutes spent traveling from one station to another was little to pay in comparison with long days of journeying by train. Curiously, however, when it came to the problem of a landing strip for "airplane taxis" at the center of the new city, he placed it . . . on the station roof. Cars were to be reserved exclusively for trips to the Green City of repose. They would proliferate in the suburbs but be strictly prohibited for intercity travel. Their use in the city was to be regulated by means of a network of roads strictly dissociated from the subway system—that "suction and inversion pump for the masses," who thus "avoid the rigors of winter":

Rational planning precludes the idea of links between the subway and the existing street grid: the role of a subway is to pass through the city in a straight line.[47]

Although determined to a large extent by transport considerations, Le Corbusier's new city was nonetheless presented as "an organic scheme classifying various functions" in a "concerted order," with priority given to housing:

The proposed sketch contains the various sectors that make up a large modern city, with zones for administration, business, political activity, hotels, sports, the university, etc.

Each of these organs, representing precise functions, may be compared to the root of a tree, thus allowing for future growth; but these different roots also converge, and make contact in conformity with the destinies of a large modern city.

In a large city, the central zone is devoted to housing, and is cut through from top to bottom (a random image, here useful for discussion) by a broad "axis" that, in its upper reaches, leads to the economic district, with ramifications leading off to the political and administrative centers

In its lower reaches, the "axis" runs between zones for manufacturing and heavy industry.[48]

The network of streets leading off from this "great axis" did not reflect "a rigorous east-west orientation." Le Corbusier referred explicitly to the "error" he had made in the "contemporary city," and which the "sun's blinding rays" at twilight in Buenos Aires had made clear to him. He now used a "linear diagram" to "determine rigorously the orientation of the residential city." To this end, he in fact made use of the notion, invented by the astronomer Justin Pidoux, of the heliothermic axis.[49]

THE QUESTION OF HOUSING

Globally, the plan was based on the idea of a dual network, with "streets on the one hand, houses on the other," since "they are two completely independent phenomena." The rectangular grid of principal thoroughfares was cut by a "diagonal network of connecting streets." The housing was based on Soviet experimentation with communal dwellings—even Le Corbusier had reacted violently to the aridity and lack of "spiritual invention" of the first prototypes

[47] Le Corbusier, "Réponse," p. 16.
[48] Ibid., p. 31.
[49] Cf. Adolphe-Augustin Rey, Charles

Barde, and Justin Pidoux, *La science des plans de villes* (Lausanne: Payot; Paris: Dunod, [1928]).

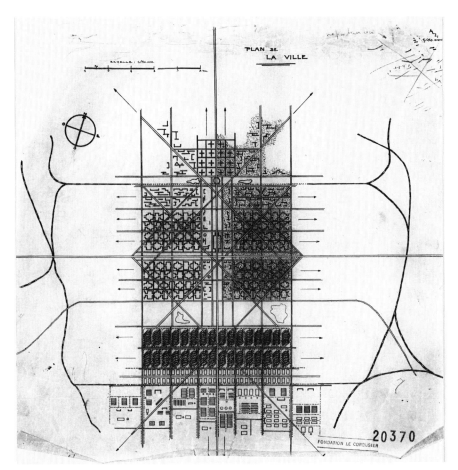

204. Le Corbusier, "Response to Moscow," 1930, Plan of the city, FLC 20370.

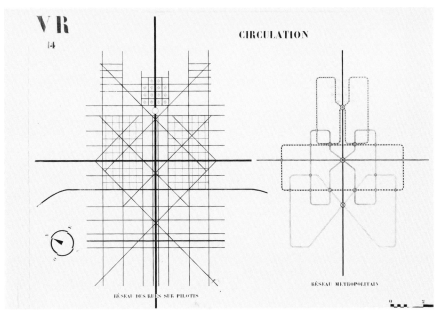

205. Le Corbusier, the "Ville Radieuse," Circulation, 1933, FLC 24894.

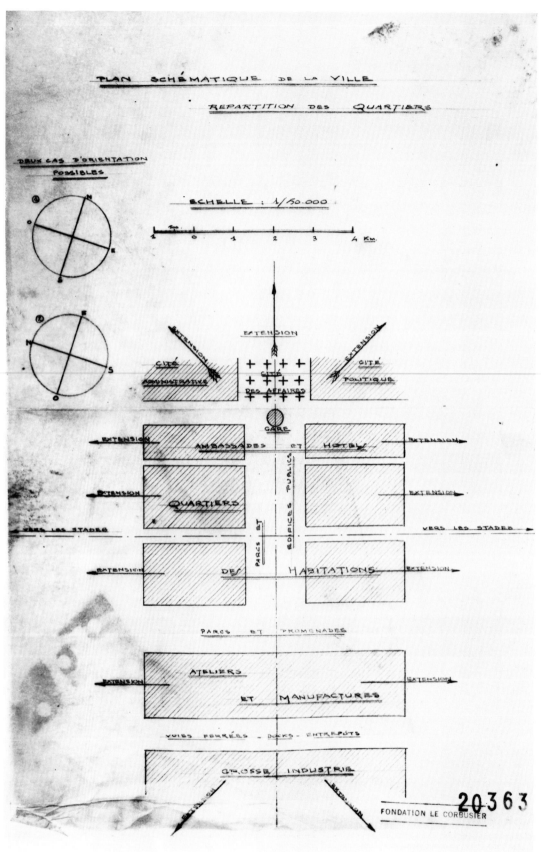

206. Le Corbusier, "Response to Moscow," 1930, Schematic plan of the city, distribution of neighborhoods, FLC 20363.

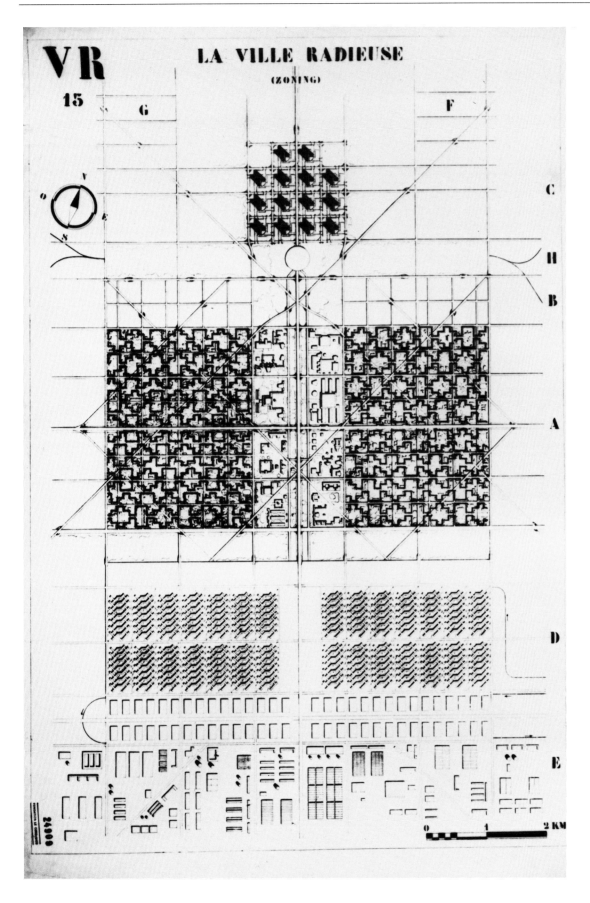

207. Le Corbusier, the "Ville Radieuse," Zoning, 1933, FLC 24909.

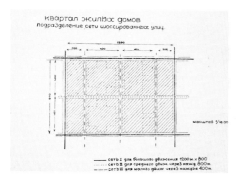

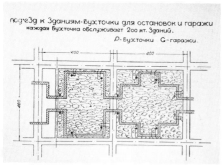

208. Le Corbusier, "Response to Moscow," 1930, Residential neighborhood, version published as an appendix to *Planirovka goroda* (Moscow, 1933).

209. Le Corbusier, "Response to Moscow," 1930, Access to *auto-ports*, version published as an appendix to *Planirovka goroda* (Moscow, 1933).

that he had seen in Moscow. In this context he emphasized the "independent, closed-off, private, sacred" character of each apartment, "away from all collective pressures," although he spoke out in favor of the collectivization of domestic service and supply:

A striking instance of waste and enslavement on both sides of the fence is the current universal practice of private service. A servant should no longer be bound to the family and forced to work all hours of the day. A servant performs specialized labor (cleaning: parquet floors, glass surfaces, furniture, etc.; in the kitchen: preparing and cooking food; service: restaurant service, room service; care for the children: cleanliness, hygiene, health care, education, instruction, etc.).

This list makes it clear that to entrust a single person with all of these tasks is first of all to make an exhausted and resentful servant, and second, to force the person to perform laborious tasks that, in many cases, are foreign to him or her. In consequence, it is to cause waste.[50]

All existing housing was to be destroyed and replaced by a network of *redents*. On this occasion, Le Corbusier recycled the theme of the Green City, for which he later claimed credit retrospectively. The whole city was to be green, achieving a high enough density to allow for further extension "without disturbing its biological state" and resolving, among other things, "the problem of residential sport," since this would henceforth be possible "at the foot of the buildings":

Taking the average for Moscow as 15 square meters of real living space per inhabitant, it is possible to achieve a density of 1,000 inhabitants per hectare in the "green city."

The consequence of this prodigious increase in density is that it solves the public transport crisis, repudiates the mistaken, reactionary and slovenly principle of garden cities on the outskirts of the city and, by building high-density green cities, eliminates the problem of suburban transport.[51]

Le Corbusier proposed a threefold network of amenities, integrated into the *redents* with direct access via "streets in the air." The first was that of educational institutions, from day nurseries to primary schools, with "complementary schools" for adolescents. The second was based on the idea of the club, "a place where people meet by affinity, which is not the case in the housing blocks." Thus the location of the clubs relative to housing was unimportant. Third, the "safeguarding of the race" was to be carried out in the sporting facilities, which were to be located in spaces between the *redents*. Here Le Corbusier again condemned the "myth of gardening . . . selfish and unsporting, which induces sterile fatigue and tendencies contrary to those of sound physical culture."

The housing units generalized the principles of communal dwellings: each "group" would contain a ground-floor "hotel unit" for collective services and a "harbor for automobiles"; from this "hall," a "vertical artery" gave access to the "streets in the air," which in turn led to the apartments. More generally, the threefold principle of "air, sound and light" was proposed as an absolute weapon in response to the questionnaire's hygienist preoccupations: *respiration exacte* was to provide a "revolutionary solution" to the problem of air, Gustave Lyon's researches in the "science of sound" would "make the housing units completely sound-proof," and the "hermetically sealed plate glass composed of existing or future vitrified materials" would let in generous amounts of sunlight.

Reconsidering his "Plan Voisin" project, Le Corbusier now claimed that it was "impossible to dream of harmonizing the city of the past with the present and future." He subsequently defended this contradiction between his atti-

[50] Le Corbusier, "Réponse," p. 23.
[51] Ibid., pp. 38–39.

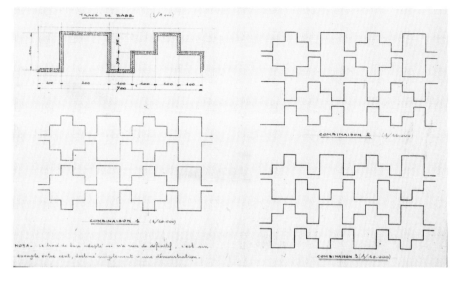

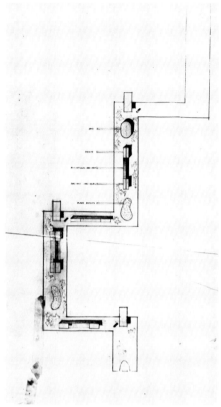

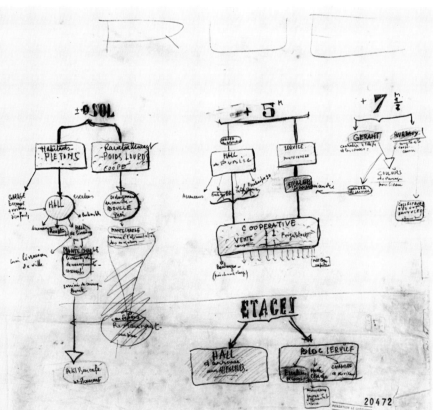

210. Le Corbusier, "Response to Moscow," 1930, Outline of the *redents*.

211. Le Corbusier, the "Ville Radieuse," study of communal facilities, the roof terraces, 1930, FLC 20398.

212. Le Corbusier, the "Ville Radieuse," study of communal facilities, 1930, FLC 20472.

tudes in Paris, where he fought "escape from the center by planners from Saint-Germain-en-Laye" and Moscow, where the business district was to be outside the center, "the heart of the city being the housing district":

Paris is not Moscow. Here capitalists, there communists; here firm, Western, there soft, Oriental; here old, entrenched, determined, there nomadic, recent, malleable. Here one "valorizes"; there the notion is deemed meaningless (indeed!).

The solution for Moscow (*Réponse à Moscou*) follows on from the solution for Paris

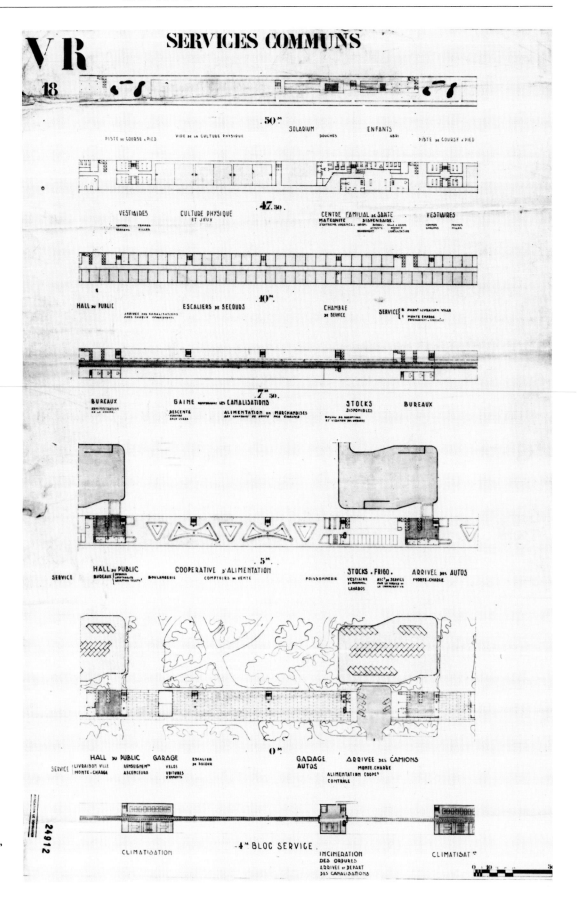

213. Le Corbusier, the "Ville Radieuse," "communal facilities," 1933, floor plans, FLC 24912.

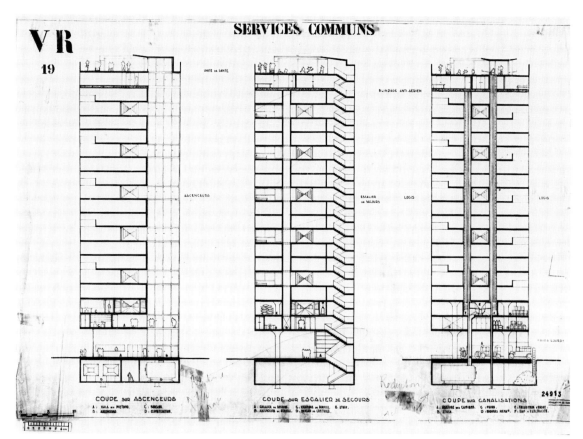

214. Le Corbusier, the "Ville Radieuse," "communal facilities," 1933, cross sections, FLC 24913.

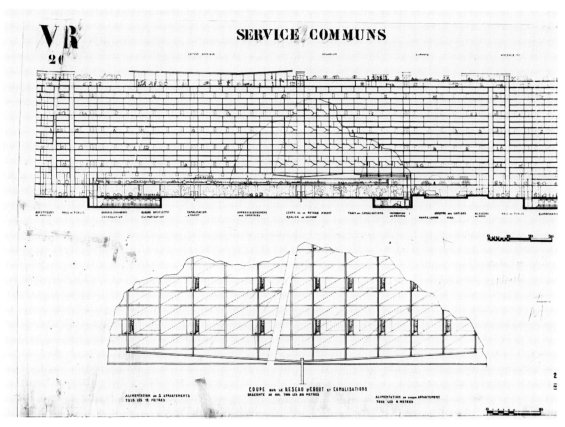

215. Le Corbusier, the "Ville Radieuse," "communal facilities," 1933, section and detail, FLC 24914.

216. Le Corbusier, fragment of a "Ville Radieuse" residential district, 1935, view of the model.

(1922–1925, Voisin Plan). There may have been progress. The solution for Moscow proposes an entity, a whole large city. The 1922 plan (a city of three million) had the same pretensions, but not all the ideas were clear. 1925, the Voisin Plan was no more than a city of Business.[52]

One should, however, note that in the schematic plan for Buenos Aires, drawn up on the spot in 1929, Le Corbusier had first isolated the business center on the outskirts of the existing city, and that the "solution for Moscow" is reminiscent of this.[53] While he was revising his earlier urban proposals, he integrated some Soviet experiments with public amenities into his plan, but at the same time he insisted on the individual character of the choice of lifestyles. Unlike some Soviet plans for cities based on the simple addition of "communal housing units," Le Corbusier's clear dissociation between the club and the apartment amounted to perpetuating the complex forms of sociability common to all large cities. At the same time, his subway plans proposed a clear demarcation between the "business city" line and the one for the "workshops and factories": bureaucracy and workers were not supposed to cross paths.

THE SOVIET RECEPTION OF THE "RESPONSE"

Le Corbusier submitted the text and the plans of his "Response" early in the summer of 1930. There does not appear to have been any immediate reaction, and it was not until mid-November that Kolli explained that at the time he had been too ill to transmit the documents to Gorny, who had himself been ill. Kolli nonetheless indicated that Gorny was then in the process of writing a critical evaluation of the proposals sent in.[54] Gorny wrote to Le Corbusier expressing his gratitude for a contribution that was "both attentive and detailed," and bluntly announced that his "initial review" was to be published in the press without delay.[55]

It is clear that Le Corbusier's proposals were granted special status, in that they were put into circulation with a wealth of comment and criticism that no other contribution was accorded. Gorny's remarks were cordial, but they furnished a disagreeable foretaste of his article published in the December issue of *Stroitelstvo Moskvy*. In his opening remarks, Gorny criticized the "talented responses" of "the greatest exponent of the reconstruction of material culture," considering that he had "not deemed it necessary to inform himself of what had already been achieved in the USSR" in his response to "a series of difficult questions concerning social life and the forms of existence," and had not realized that he was face-to-face with a "new society."

At times his imagination carries him away to the new Moscow—and here he proposes eminently interesting solutions to the question of the collective organization of living. At others he looks back toward Paris; images of the nervous inhabitant of a present-day capitalist city, who must be saved from the noise and tumult, from the throng and the evil-smelling streets, swim before his eyes and he is led to plan for vain measures of the most radical kind.

Le Corbusier's "respiration exacte" reminded Gorny of Herbert G. Wells's schematic vision of the city of the future, mechanized and hermetically sealed:

I repeat, we felt that this sort of morbid fantasy could only have been engendered in the stuffy atmosphere of a solitary office, by an intellectual representative of bourgeois society who knows of no other way to escape the noise and smell of the city. It is,

[52] Le Corbusier, "Réponse à Moscou, avant-propos," 1931, handwritten, p. 2, FLC.

[53] For a general comparison between the urban projects of the period, see Xavier Monteys, "Barcelona, La Ville Radieuse i el mar," in Fernando Marzá, ed., *Le Corbusier i Barcelona* (Barcelona: Fundacio Caixa de Catalunya, 1988), pp. 33–45.

[54] Nikolai Kolli, letter to Le Corbusier, Moscow, 11 November 1930, FLC.

[55] Sergei Gorny, letter to Le Corbusier, Moscow, undated (November 1930), FLC.

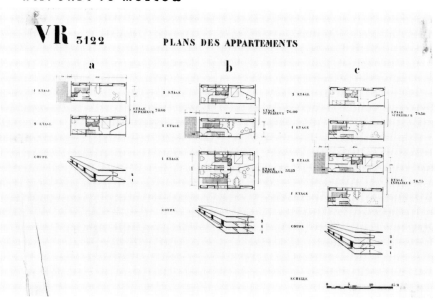

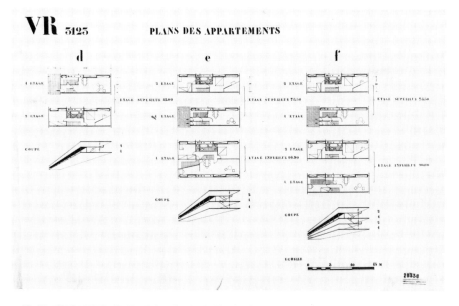

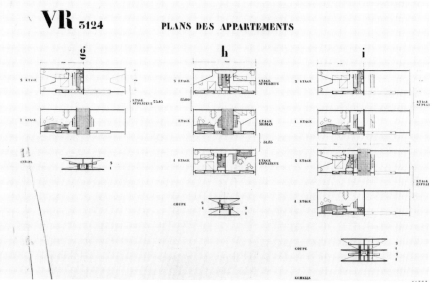

217. Le Corbusier, "Ville Radieuse," apartment plans, types a, b, and c, 1933, FLC 20337.

218. Le Corbusier, "Ville Radieuse," apartment plans, types d, e, and f, 1933, FLC 20338.

219. Le Corbusier, "Ville Radieuse," apartment plans, types g, h, and i, 1933, FLC 20339.

therefore, strange and unexpected to hear the same arguments from Le Corbusier, one of the most eminent practitioners in the field of the reconstruction of material life.[56]

More significant, Gorny lingered long over the question of Le Corbusier's ambivalent attitude to the collective dimension of city life. Far from discussing the structural content of the proposed plan, he directed his criticisms against the ideological premises underlying Le Corbusier's defense and made no mention of his spirited praise of the communal housing experiment:

When Le Corbusier considers society as a whole, he is inclined to recognize its right to impose some constraints on its members. He even expresses the view that sport should be compulsory in the interests of the physical purification of society. But no sooner does he abandon this stance and begin to deal with the sentiments of the individual viewed in isolation, than he sees a menacing, collectivist society with barracks, coercive discipline and a command mentality. At this point, he revolts.

. . . We consider the transformation of material culture less important than that of social organization as a whole. On occasion, Le Corbusier appears to share this vision of things, if only in part; when, for instance, he treats of the advantages of communal life and when he extends, develops and brings depth of focus to our points of view; but . . . he soon falls under the influence of the social and ideological conceptions of individualistic, bourgeois society, and then he strives to resolve specific problems outside the system as a whole—or rather, on the basis of the existing system.

Clearly, the panaceas proposed by Le Corbusier are merely a reaction to the present state of the great capitalist cities. Only these Leviathans, rumbling day and night in their ceaseless movement, could give rise to the idea of an "asylum" of steel, armor plated and hermetically sealed. Only this overcrowded octopus, with its poisoned air, could have given birth to the idea of "artificial respiration." Only the nervous system excited to an abnormal degree by the capitalist city could have inspired the pressing need to hermetically lock oneself away in a "sacred asylum."[57]

Despite these relatively caustic remarks, which are barely attenuated by Gorny's "sincere gratitude" (which was to be excised from the published version), Le Corbusier's own text was given in full, with eighteen accompanying plans and the comments of other "experts," in a book that Gorny devoted to the debate over the plan for Moscow. Despite Gorny's reservations (he took pains to restrict his remarks to questions of form), both the density and the relative weight of Le Corbusier's proposals made them the real subject of the book.[58] Faced with this "response *from* Moscow," Le Corbusier reaffirmed his "optimism" and the aims of his proposals:

If my response to Moscow had been clear enough, you would have understood that sun, air, light, comradeship and social cohesion are indeed the goals that I am seeking.[59]

In June 1931, a year after Le Corbusier had drawn up his "Response to Moscow," the Central Committee of the Party met to examine the question of the "socialist reconstruction of Moscow." Its decision was unequivocal: the relations of production were socialist, the city was necessarily so, and there could be no question of seeking at all costs to reconstruct it *ex nihilo*. In the "reconstruction of the urban economy," it was essential to use the skeleton and structure of the existing city as far as possible. In the elaboration and implementation of this decision, which was accompanied by a condemnation of theories "detached from real life,"[60] Le Corbusier's "Response" was singled out as an example by the press.[61] Henceforth, Gorny was no longer the only author to contest Le Corbusier's positions. The official review *Sovetskaia Arkhitektura* attacked the idea of unlimited growth and dismissed the notion

[56] Sergei Gorny, "Les vues de Le Corbusier sur la reconstruction de Moscou," handwritten in French, 25 October 1930, FLC. See also a later, revised version, Sergei Gorny, "New Soviet Cities," *VOKS*, no. 5–6 (1932): 147–54. The original Russian text was published in December as "Le Corbusier o rekonstruktsii Moskvy," *Stroitelstvo Moskvy* 7, no. 12 (1930): 16–17, followed by extracts from the "Réponse": Le Corbusier, "Kak rekonstruirovat plan Moskvy," ibid., pp. 17–20.

[57] Gorny, "Vues de Le Corbusier," pp. 7–8.

[58] S. M. Gorny, *Sotsialisticheskaia rekonstruktsiia Moskvy* (Moscow: Tekhnika Upravleniia, 1931), pp. 145–99.

[59] Le Corbusier, letter to S. M. Gorny, published in *Planirovka goroda*, pp. xi–xii.

[60] For the report presented on this occasion, see L. M. Kaganovitch, *L'urbanisme soviétique, la réorganisation socialiste de Moscou et des autres villes d'URSS* (Paris: Bureau d'Editions, 1932).

[61] N. Skvortsov, "Problema rasseleniia v svete markso-leninskogo ucheniia," *Za sotsialisticheskuiu rekonstruktsiiu gorodov*, no. 4 (1933): 17. On the general debate of the period, see Vigdariia Khazanova, *Sovetskaia arkhitektura pervoi piatiletki* (Moscow: Nauka, 1980), pp. 226–322.

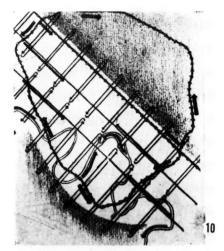

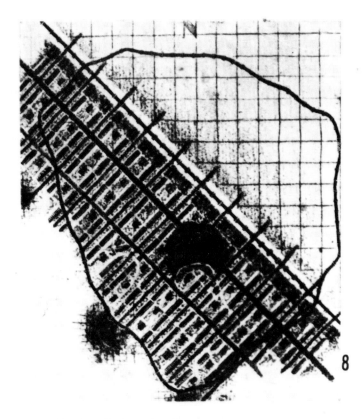

РАЗМЕЩЕНИЕ НАСЕЛЕНИЯ

На оси, параллельной оси промышленной зоны. Короткие поперечные пути к производству. Кратчайшее расстояние в среднем 2,0 км. Простейший транспорт. В отдельных случаях даже без транспорта
В жилкомплексах детские учреждения. Школы 1 ступени. Общественное питание. Диспансеры и физкультурные площадки. Распределение
Районные и общегородские базы физкультуры у реки, на горах, на стадионах

220. Sergei Gorny, scheme for the regional plan of Moscow, 1931, localization of housing.

ВНУТРИГОРОДСКОЙ ТРАНСПОРТ

Электрический поезд (пассажирский) по железной дороге осевой и по Окружной. По остальным направлениям—безрельссвый и водный. Внутри кольца «Б» трамвай заменен автобусом. Вводится единый тариф и пересадка для электропоезда, водного транспорта и автобуса.

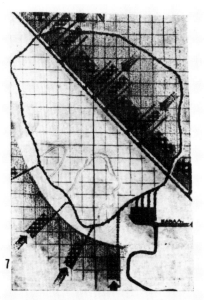

Транспортное обслуживание промышленности. Подвоз сырья и топлива. Увоз готовой продукции. Линия жел. дороги вдоль промышленной зоны с короткими ветвями к отдельным предприятиям. Порт на нижнем течении Москва-реки у дер. Кожухово

of a "third Rome" as a "leftist phrase"—although it did remark on the interest of the plan's military considerations.[62]

In this new context, other proposals began to be discussed, including Kurt Meyer's plan, based on a system of radial zoning reminiscent of some 1910 projects for Greater Berlin, and the plan proposed by German Krasin. Gorny himself submitted a plan for a city with two zones—housing and industry—rigorously separated by a rectilinear railway line that reflected the influence of Le Corbusier's ideas.[63] In comparison with these projects, all of which respected the existing plan in their own specific ways, the principles of the "Response to Moscow" were considered by Nikolai Miliutin, editor of the review and a theorist of linear planning, as a novel, abstract formulation of the

221. Sergei Gorny, scheme for the regional plan of Moscow, 1931, network of mass transportation.

222. Sergei Gorny, scheme for the regional plan of Moscow, 1931, accesses to industrial zones.

[62] "Zadachi planirovki Moskvy," *Sovetskaia Arkhitektura* 1, no. 4 (1931): 1–3.

[63] Sergei Gorny, "K voprosu o rekonstruktsii Moskvy," *Sovetskaia Arkhitektura* 1, no. 4 (1931): 17–23.

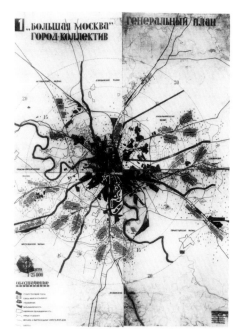

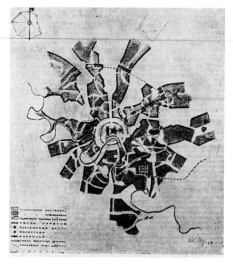

223. Ernst May, for Standartgorproekt, scheme for the regional plan of Moscow, 1932, overall plan. The graphical conventions are similar to those used for the Fourth CIAM.

224. Kurt Meyer, scheme for the regional plan of Moscow, 1931, overall plan.

ideas of the "Contemporary City." The forms of housing advanced by Le Corbusier were rejected as likely to lead to the creation of a sort of "hotel city." But in the final analysis, his contribution to the *Sotsgorod* (socialist city) was considered acceptable—even if, far from providing solutions, "it did not, in fact, succeed in formulating the right questions."[64]

In 1932 a new consultation was launched, and the best-known German architects then practicing in the USSR were invited to submit their ideas. Hannes Meyer proposed a dense, rationalized city, whereas Ernst May presented a Moscow decentralized into satellite cities by virtue of the *Trabantenprinzip*, which had already been tested in Frankfurt. In this last performance, the earlier plans of Ladovsky or Le Corbusier still played a minor role as foils to the new proposals.

This faltering progression of ideas gradually reinforced the position of Vladimir Semenov, a pioneer of urbanism in prerevolutionary Russia.[65] Whereas he had earlier been an arbiter of the various plans proposed, he quickly became director of the "General Plan" that was finally adopted in 1935, two years after the deadline initially fixed by Gorny. Semenov took inspiration from both Haussmann's Paris and the Vienna Ringstrasse.[66] Although he was certainly less severe than Gorny or Miliutin, Semenov, too, criticized Le Corbusier's "Response," considering that the "center of Moscow" was not fossilized and that, "as the principal nerve center, it will develop with the capital as a whole."[67] In presenting the broad lines of his plan, he insisted on the differences between his ideas and the earlier dreams:

What principles and real-life conditions are necessary for the implementation of the program? There can of course be no question of building a new city, but rather of its reconstruction. Given this, Le Corbusier's proposal to raze the whole city is quite unacceptable. Le Corbusier writes that he cannot recommend his system—the demolition of the city—for Paris, since Paris is a precious cultural center. Moscow would appear to be a city of the future, in which there is nothing of value except the Kremlin. Reconstruction demands radical measures. Surgery is necessary. But when one needs a surgeon, one does not seek out the executioner.[68]

Due to delays in publication, it was precisely at the moment when the ideas of the "Response" were definitively rejected that the plan itself was published in *Planirovka goroda*, the first—and last—Russian edition of one of Le Corbusier's major works, *Urbanisme*, the translation of which had been the object of negotiations before 1930.[69] Gorny translated and published the book himself, and added his own commentaries on the "Response," together with Le Corbusier's epistolary riposte.[70] The rejection of the "Response" did not consign Le Corbusier's earlier urban proposals to oblivion—on the contrary, they were

[64] Ot redaktsii, *Sovetskaia Arkhitektura* 1, no. 4 (1931): 24–25.

[65] Vladimir Semenov, *Blagoustroistvo gorodov* (Moscow: Tip I. I. Riabushchinskogo, 1912).

[66] A summary of the different stages of the debate is given in V.L. Orleansky, "Iz istorii planirovki gor. Moskvy," pp. 17–19.

[67] Vladimir Semenov, "Moskvu planirovat i zastraivat zanovo," *Stroitelstvo Moskvy* 9, no. 2 (1932): 2–6.

[68] Vladimir Semenov, "Kak planirovat i zastraivat Moskvu," *Stroitelstvo Moskvy* 10, no. 8–9 (1933): 8–11.

[69] In 1929 Ginzburg had even made detailed propositions for a translation; Le Corbusier agreed, but expressed reservations concerning the copyright: Le Corbusier, letter to Moisei Ginzburg, Paris, 22 January 1929, FLC.

[70] Le Corbusier, *Planirovka Goroda*. The choice of the title, which may be retranslated as "The Planning of Cities," is remarkable in that the term *Urbanizm* (from the French, with strong associations owing to its use by the ASNOVA) or *Gradostroitelstvo* (from the German *Städtebau*) was more common.

225. Vladimir Semenov, general plan of Moscow, 1935.

226. Comparisons of the major schemes submitted for the regional plan of Moscow, 1929–1931. (1) Nikolai Ladovsky (1929). (2) Le Corbusier (1930). (3) Ernst May (1931). (4) Hannes Meyer (1931). (5) Vladimir Kratiuk (1931).

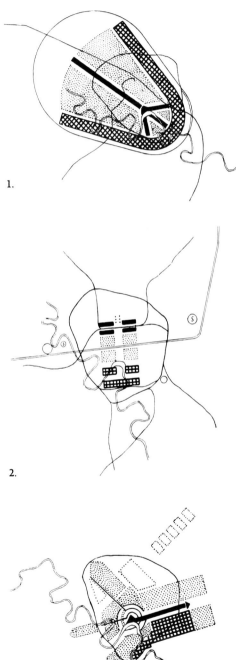

1.

2.

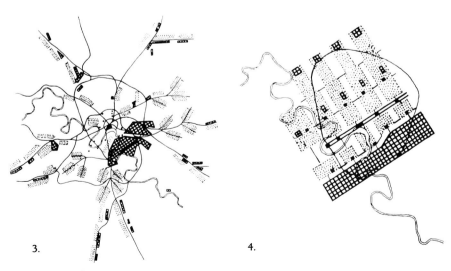

3.

4.

5.

227. Jacket of *Planirovka goroda* (Moscow, 1933), Russian translation of *Urbanisme.*

invariably integrated into all global planning studies, even if they were henceforth classified as the expression of an "ultraurbanist" and an exponent of the "individualistic bourgeois system."[71] The reactions to the publication of *Planirovka goroda* made no reference to earlier criticisms of the "Response," but were restricted to a condemnation of Le Corbusier's position, which "failed to choose between capitalism and socialism."[72]

FROM THE "RESPONSE" TO THE "VILLE RADIEUSE"

Despite the undoubted decline in his influence, Le Corbusier did not abandon all hope of persuading "the Moscow authorities," and he gloated openly over the final defeat of the "mystique" of the disurbanists, while emphasizing the points in common between them and American policies for industry and the automobile:

In Moscow in 1930 the fad of the moment was for "disurbanization."

"The murderous stone cannon of the city, the stifling, the crushing of the city dweller is a purely capitalistic manifestation."

Therefore the city must be smashed into ten thousand pieces and scattered across the countryside, in the woods, in the meadows, so that the houses will be in the heart of nature itself. Thus, man will have returned to the first wellspring of his inner harmony.

"All well and good," I replied. "But what about the work of the city (for the question of rural exploitation is in no way involved here), the work that must be be accomplished within the 24-hour daily solar cycle?"

. . . Plans were drawn up, propaganda films were screened for the benefit of committees. People were encouraged to entertain an idle dream: "The cities will be part of the country; I shall live 50 kilometers away from my office under a pine tree; my secretary will live 50 kilometers away from it too, in the other direction, under another pine tree. We shall both have our own car. We shall use up tires, wear out road surfaces and gears, consume oil and gasoline. All of which will necessitate a great deal of work; there will be a titanic demand for labor; enough for all; no threat of unemployment looming in the future, ever again."

Then, one fine day, authority, which is the door of reason against which all dreams, just and chimerical ones alike, must eventually knock, authority in the USSR said: "Enough! It's all over! And stop that laughing!"

The mystic belief in disurbanization had fallen flat on its face![73]

While he rejoiced in the common sense that had caused the disurbanists' downfall, Le Corbusier strove to give wider impact to the method he had employed in his "response" to Gorny:

The powers that be in Moscow once sent me a questionnaire asking me to give my solutions for the future of the Russian capital. It was possible to answer that questionnaire in everyday language: it was simply a matter of expressing one's ideas on the subject. So I did that. But as I was dictating my replies, there were images, rough plans, sketches beginning to take shape in my mind. For what am I, after all, but a technician trained in the techniques of architecture and city planning? "The simplest sketch in the world is worth more than a long report." Sketches could provide *the proof.*

And so it was that, after I had dictated my replies to the questionnaire, I undertook the execution of twenty or so sketch plans, without those plans having any direct connections with the questionnaire. The questionnaire was concerned wholly with

[71] A. V. Shchusev and L. E. Zagorsky, *Arkhitekturnaia organizatsiia goroda* (Moscow: Gosstroiizdat, 1934), p. 17.

[72] A. Kazarin, "Le Corbusier *Planirovka Goroda,*" *Sovetskaia Arkhitektura* 4, no. 1 (1934): 65–67.

[73] Le Corbusier, *The Radiant City,* p. 74.

Moscow; the plans dealt with the phenomenon of social organization in machine-age cities—in the cities of our times.

The "phenomenal, enormous, mad bravado" of asserting the need to "respect the sacred principle of individual liberty," which, according to Le Corbusier, provoked the Soviet reaction to the "Response," did not prevent him from consoling himself *a posteriori* by invoking visions of the "Slavonic soul" in 1935:

Why publish this "Response to Moscow"? My report and my twenty sketch plans have already been sent to the Russian authorities. I know that they will be welcomed there by minds anxious to discuss their implications. I also know that in Moscow they have, more or less—amid the cartoon crowd of gesticulating figures that tend to run the affairs of this world—established the reign of intelligence. Besides, the Russians are an artistic people—a fact that doesn't bring harm to a nation's affairs when it is a matter of choosing a line of conduct, a concept of life. My work will not remain—I trust—in some Soviet desk drawer until the next ice age.[74]

228. Jacket of *La ville radieuse* (Paris, 1935).

While he was waiting for this hypothetical thaw, Le Corbusier did not neglect to disseminate his project. The "Response to Moscow" was not restricted to the Russian public, and, even before he was sure that the documents had been safely received, he began to use it for his personal ends. He presented a more elaborate graphic version at the Brussels CIAM on the theme of "rational planning" on 27 and 28 November 1930.

Henceforth, having excised the initial reference to Moscow, his "organic scheme" was labelled "Ville Radieuse." Of the features of the original "Response," the new plans retained only the rail tracks, which are clearly perceptible in the general plan of the city.

While he was perfecting the graphics of the original drawings, Le Corbusier also envisaged publishing the "Response" in book form. This is clearly evidenced in a note giving details of the contents and some sketches of the layout, such as the title pages for the various chapters.[75] A later typewritten version of the text is accompanied by instructions to the publisher Crès, who intended to include the book in their *L'Esprit Nouveau* collection. The book would have been subtitled "Basic elements for the reconstruction of large cities" and would have contained the "Moscow letter," the "questionnaire" and the "Response," all the "analyses, calculations, drawings" and a recapitulation of the "doctrinal elements"—that is, the new ideas proposed in the text and identified by means of numbers in the margin. One of the most important articulations of the text was to have been the opposition between a chapter containing a highly critical evaluation of Manhattan entitled "Americanization?" and a somewhat more appreciative chapter entitled "Bolshevization?" with a "chart showing the Five-Year Plan." Another fundamental idea was that the city is not merely a series of streets but rather a combination of "organs"; this point was to have been illustrated by a reference to Roman circuses and aqueducts.[76] But in fact, the work of preparing the edition of the "Response" does not appear to have progressed very far before it was interrupted with the emergence of plans for a book on the theme of the "Ville Radieuse," elements of which first appeared in the review *Plans*:

But then, one fine day, the title *Response to Moscow* was submerged by something larger and deeper. It became a question of humanity as a whole. And then I chose the new title: *La ville radieuse*.[77]

Although, in the unpublished version, the Soviet example is cited in the context of wide-ranging, transnational comparisons or nostalgic reminis-

[74] Ibid., p. 90.

[75] "R à M," handwritten note, 2 September 1930, FLC. An addition to this text dated 4 January 1932 indicates that the idea was still in his mind at that moment.

[76] Ibid.

[77] Le Corbusier, *The Radiant City*, p. 91.

229. Le Corbusier, note for a publication based on the "Response to Moscow," 2 September 1930.

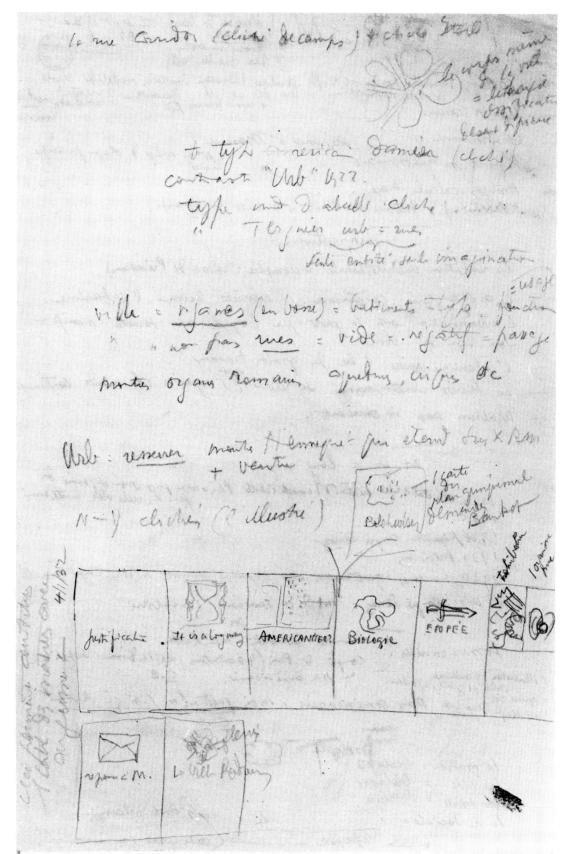

230. Le Corbusier, note for a publication based on the "Response to Moscow," 2 September 1930.

cences, it takes the rather modest form of the "application to Moscow" from more general rules. But one of the editorial principles envisaged and the highlighting of the book's most important concepts by numbering them in the margin were applied ten years later when Le Corbusier wrote his own version of the Athens Charter. The fact that discussions concerning the plan for Moscow culminated in failure was no doubt a lucky outcome for the city's historical fabric. But although Le Corbusier had not succeeded in having his ideas accepted, he nonetheless redeployed his urban theories and began formulating a scheme that was to inform much of his activity throughout the thirties. Some of its elements even survived the Second World War.

NIKOLAI MILIUTIN AND THE LINEAR CITY

In this context the influence of the "linear city"—an idea advanced by Nikolai Miliutin in his book *Sotsgorod* in 1930—on Le Corbusier's "linear industrial city," one of the *Trois établissements humains* that he was to propose following the Second World War, remains an open question.[78] Miliutin, who drew up territorial plans of the principal construction sites for heavy industry, based his ideas on the theories of Arturo Soria y Mata and Charles Gide, both of whom were well known in the USSR.[79] But he was also attentive to Le Corbusier's work in both its "positive" and "negative" aspects. Miliutin dismissed London and New York as "nightmares of the contemporary city," but he also denounced the Voisin Plan as a "nightmare of urban planning," while at the same time recommending "detailed study of the ideas of Le Corbusier, Gropius, Ginzburg, Vesnin, Leonidov."[80] And when it came to presenting his "choice" of acceptable components for the linear city, Miliutin cited the example of the *L'Esprit Nouveau* pavilion as an instance of "lightened structure," that of the "moving windows" at Corseaux and Garches, and, as examples of public buildings, the League of Nations and Centrosoyuz.[81]

On a more personal note, whereas Giedion saw fit to warn Le Corbusier of the attack on the Voisin Plan, Miliutin sent a signed copy of his book "to the creator of the new architecture";[82] Le Corbusier did not, however, acknowledge receipt until 1931 when, in an article published in *Plans*, he cited Miliutin but insisted that his own proposals for Moscow had been well founded:

The USSR is methodically pursuing its researches into the correct planning of housing and cities. The inquiry is of great importance: we all have to decide whether to go *this* way or *that*—"urbanization" or "disurbanization." Oversimplified definitions or even contradictory and paradoxical ones quite often can serve as valuable resting points during the ascent. In the USSR, they have decided to "disurbanize." This seems to me to be a grave error, or the result of confused thinking. . . . Miliutin, the people's commissar, has published a book on the subject of how the ideal housing unit and city should be organized, a book that is to be used as a working contribution to the Five-Year Plan, in which he denounces my Voisin Plan as being *capitalist*: a business center must be capitalist!!! Yet at this very moment we are building the vast Centrosoyuz building . . . in Moscow itself. This building is being constructed next door to the Gostorg, the Foreign Trade Center. And all around, the Russians are building, or are about to build, vast office buildings from which to administer their industries, business affairs, etc. In other words, they are building a business center. *In a very short time* the traffic situation in Moscow will be frightful. One look is enough to tell you that! If, instead of building this business center 7 or 10 stories high, they were to build it 50 or 60 stories high, then they could design a reasonable traffic system. In which case it would be nothing more or less than another Voisin Plan; a Soviet "Voisin" Plan.[83]

[78] Nikolai Miliutin, *Sotsgorod, problema stroitelstva sotsialisticheskikh gorodov* (Moscow: Gosudarstvennoe Izdatelstvo, 1930). English translation: Nikolai Miliutin, *Sotsgorod: The Problem of Building Socialist Cities*, ed. George R. Collins and William Alex (Cambridge, Mass.: MIT Press, 1974). A long-standing Bolshevik, Miliutin left memoirs of which only a fragment has been published: Nikolai Miliutin, *Po zadaniam Lenina* (Moscow: Gospolitizdat, 1975).

[79] Vitali Lavrov, "Gorod-Liniia," *Stroitelnaia Promyshlennost* 6, nos. 6–7 (1928): 472–74.

[80] Miliutin, *Sotsgorod*, pp. 7, 13–17.

[81] Ibid., illustrations on pp. 83–93.

[82] Sigfried Giedion, letter to Le Corbusier, Zurich, 2 July 1931, FLC; Miliutin, *Sotsgorod*, with a dedication to Le Corbusier, 25 October 1930, FLC.

[83] Le Corbusier, "L'élément biologique: La cellule de 14 m² par habitant," *Plans* no. 9 (November 1931): 51; in *The Radiant City*, p. 144.

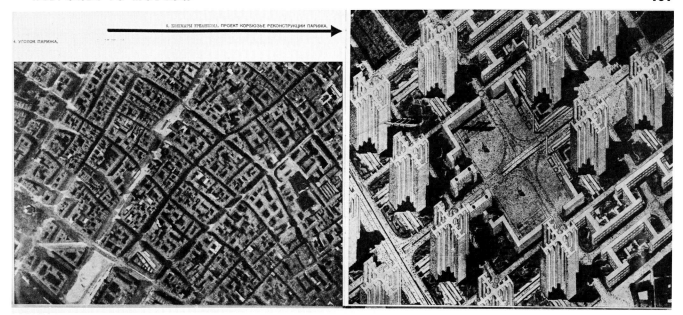

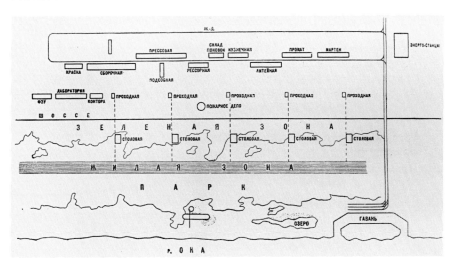

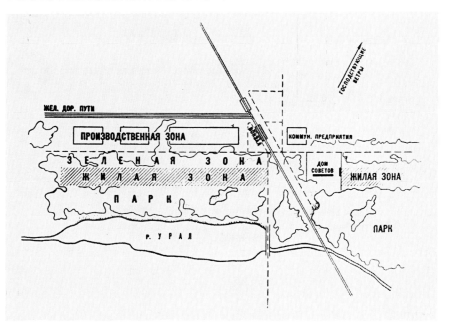

231. Nikolai Miliutin, Le Corbusier's "Voisin Plan" presented as one of the "nightmares of urbanism," in *Sotsgorod* (Moscow, 1930).

232. Nikolai Miliutin, linear city plan for the automobile factory in Nizhny Novgorod, 1930, in *Sotsgorod* (Moscow, 1930).

233. Nikolai Miliutin, linear city plan for Magnitogorsk, 1930, in *Sotsgorod* (Moscow, 1930).

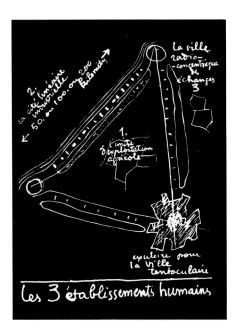

234. Le Corbusier, the three productive units of regional urbanism, 1945.

[84] Cf. Kenneth Frampton, "The Other Le Corbusier: Primitive Forms and the Linear City 1929–1952," in *Le Corbusier, Architect of the Century*, pp. 29–34.

[85] Cohen, "Nostro cliente è il nostro padrone," p. 53.

[86] Le Corbusier, *Les trois établissements humains* (Paris: Denoël, 1945): 169.

Although Le Corbusier was familiar with Miliutin's schemes, if not with his somewhat woolly economic and theoretical arguments, he did not make use of them at once, in that he was more anxious to disseminate the themes of the "Ville Radieuse." Only when this theoretical project ran out of steam did the linear city make its reappearance in the course of revisions, and in a rather peculiar context.[84] In 1935, Le Corbusier presented the shoe company Bat'a with a counterproject for the development of the Moravian valley where its factories were located; the parallel configurations of canal, road, and railway in the valley inspired Le Corbusier's designs for a linear industrial complex with housing running parallel to it.[85] The Bat'a project, together with ideas elaborated during the German occupation, led to renewed treatment of the urbanization-disurbanization debate in *Les trois établissements humains*, where Miliutin's linear city in fact played only a minor role in Le Corbusier's reformulation of the existing city, the land, and his new proposal:

The linear industrial city has a consequence of crucial significance, one that has the value of a principle: it creates *pure peasant reserves*, vast reserves, and yet it establishes the purest imaginable contiguity between land, industry, the peasant and the worker. A contiguity that signals the possibility of contact: a land that is clean, revivified and whole: an industry that is brilliant, optimistic, radiant with order, intensity and beauty. A reversal of industrial life. Finally, the linear industrial city has a role to play in the future of those predestined places that are the radioconcentric cities of exchange.[86]

Thus, while the question of the linear city continued its work in silence, the immediate effects of the Moscow experience in the city-planning context were in fact of quite another order: given Le Corbusier's recycling of the notion of the "Green City," restricted as it was to the sphere of housing, it is clear that its real impact is more to be seen in the development of collective or "hotel" services—which enabled him to progressively decompose the utopian *redents* into plausible "units of consonant size"—than in the global vision of the city as proposed in his "Response to Moscow."

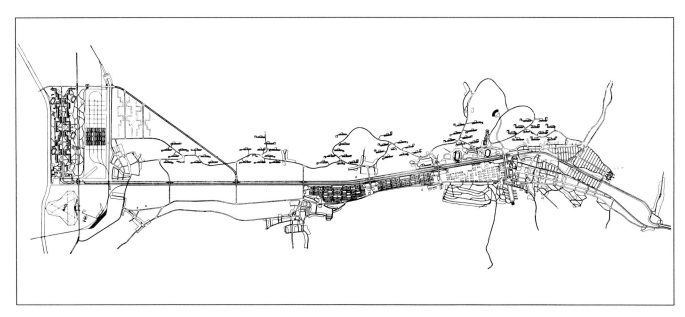

235. Le Corbusier, plan for the Zlín valley, 1935, in *Œuvre complète 1934–1935* (Zurich, 1938).

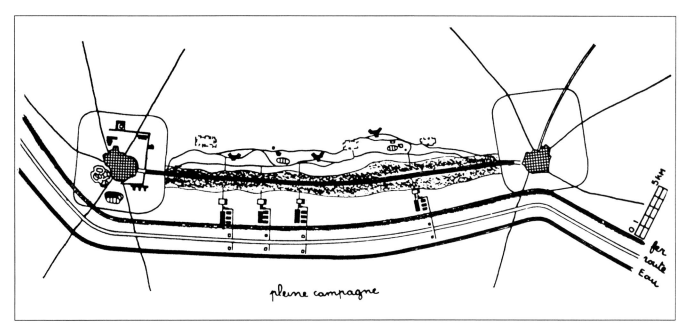

236. Le Corbusier, the "industrial linear city," 1945.

CHAPTER 7

The Palace of Soviets:
"Dramatic Betrayal"

THE PALACE OF SOVIETS competition, which in the eyes of the world marked a spectacular reversal in Soviet architectural policy, was both the final dream and the ultimate humiliation in Le Corbusier's Moscow adventure, of which it constitutes a brief but intense episode.[1]

A SPECTACULAR COMPETITION

The idea of "crowning" the capital of revolutionary Russia with a new "palace" was not merely pulled out of a hat at the outset of the thirties, for as early as 1923 the MAO had launched a competition for a Palace of Labor in Moscow. Although Noi Trotsky had taken the first prize, the Vesnins' "machine-age" project, which had come only third, created the greatest stir.[2] The brief for this competition had been "relatively" modest: an 8,000-seat auditorium with a tribune for 300, an assembly for the Moscow Soviet with a capacity of 2,500, other assembly rooms, a "social museum," and an office complex.[3] The site chosen was the Okhotny Riad below Red Square, where, in the thirties, Alexei Shchusev would build the Hotel Moskva.

But this idea of a major architectural symbol, which is to be perceived in the laying, in 1918, of the first stones of a "Palace of the People," and in Vladimir Tatlin's designs for a "Monument to the Third International," finds even more distant origins in nineteenth-century efforts to build a "Capitol of all the Russias."[4] Sergei Kirov reiterated the idea in a more official way in his proposals for the construction of a Soviet Congress, and in 1924 Leonid Krasin, writing in the pages of *Izvestia*, proposed the building of a monument to Lenin. In response to the latter suggestion, the young architect Victor Balikhin, who was then completing his studies at the Vkhutemas, suggested destroying the Church of the Savior as part of the development and zoning of the city center, in which the monument in honor of Lenin and the founding of the Soviet Union was to dominate the Moscow skyline.[5]

All possible means were deployed with a view to giving the new competition, which was launched as the first Five-Year Plan was drawing to an end, maximum publicity both within the Soviet Union and abroad. The method of consultation was somewhat complex, with three distinct procedures. The first of these was a "preliminary" assessment, several months before the deadline for the international competition, by various architectural organizations. The groups consulted were ASNOVA, ARU, VOPRA, SASS (an offshoot of OSA),

237. The unveiling of the Palace of Soviets' model, Paris, 1931.

[1] On this competition, see Peter Lizon, "The Palace of the Soviets: Change in Direction of Soviet Architecture," (Ph.D. thesis, University of Pennsylvania, 1971); Alberto Samonà, ed., *Il palazzo dei Soviet 1931–1933* (Rome: Officina Edizioni, 1976); Antonia Cunliffe, "The Competition for the Palace of Soviets in Moscow, 1931–1933," *Architectural Association Quarterly*, London, no. 2 (1979): 36–48; Christian Borngräber, "Der Sowjetpalast im Zentrum von Moskau," in Jürgen Harten, ed., *Die Axt hat geblüht* (Düsseldorf: Städtische Kunsthalle, 1987), pp. 417–25; Otto Máčel, "Tradition, Innovation and Politics," in Maarten Kloos, ed., *Soviet Architecture 1917–1987* (Amsterdam: Arts Unlimited Books, 1989), pp. 15–24.

[2] Le Corbusier must have known of this project, since it had been exhibited in Paris in 1925 and published in *L'Architecture Vivante* 4 (Spring 1926): pls. 1–3.

[3] "Programma konkursa na sostavlenie proekta dvortsa truda v Moskve," 1922, published in Kirill Afanasiev and Vigdariia Khazanova, ed., *Is istorii sovetskoi arkhitektury 1917–1925 gg., dokumenty i materialy* (Moscow: Izd. Akademii Nauk SSSR, 1963), pp. 146–47.

[4] On the very first intimations of architectural competition in the Soviet era, see Khan-Magomedov, *Pioneers*, p. 402.

[5] Selim O. Khan-Magomedov, "K istorii vybora mesta dlia Dvortsa Sovetov," *Arkhitektura i Stroitelstvo Moskvy* (January 1988): 21–23.

and the architects Bronshtein, Fidman, D. and B. Iofan, Krasin and Kutsaev, Ladovsky, Liudwig, Nikolsky, Rosenblum and Shchusev.[6] The second procedure involved twelve "commissioned" projects; the third was an open competition with "free" entries, some of which were designed by workers' collectives.[7] All in all, 272 projects, all judged in the same manner but reflecting a wide variety of origins, were submitted to the Council for the Construction of the Palace.[8]

The Council's brief defined both the building's general characteristics and its broad functional principles. It stipulated that the height of the palace was unlimited, but that the edifice should be monumental; and it was left to the entrants to regroup or clearly separate the two great auditoriums, which must be naturally lit. "Considerations of acoustics, wireless broadcasting and cinematography" were to be taken into account in the design of the halls. The financial and technical details of the brief were somewhat vague, and no advanced estimate was given, although the building systems envisaged were to allow for rapid completion. On the other hand, three architectural principles were clearly laid down:

From an architectural point of view, the design of the building must correspond:
a. to the character of the epoch and the workers' desire to construct socialism;
b. to the building's intended use;
c. to its significance as a monument of architectural art in the capital of the Soviet Union.[9]

The brief also stipulated a clear division of the building's functional components into three distinct "sections": the great, 15,000-capacity auditorium, together with a number of facilities for the public, the speakers, and the press, constituted section A, which was in fact a vast envelope capable of housing new types of activity:

The arrangement of this hall must satisfy the requirements of mass gatherings, and should be suitable for mass theatrical and cinematographic performances, the presentation of technical and industrial inventions, and various modes of participation from the audience, which must have direct access to the stage.

The design for the tribune will take into account the speakers's acoustic requirements, and will not only provide for modern methods of presentation, but will also furnish the speaker with the means of showing new discoveries, machines, methods of work. In addition, it should provide for the active participation of brigades, delegations and collectives.[10]

Besides this great hall inspired by "mass" theaters such as the one in Kharkov, for which there had also been an international competition in 1930, a second auditorium, with a seating capacity of 5,900, was to be designed above all with congresses in mind, but flexible enough for entertainment purposes. This was section B, to be positioned in immediate proximity to section C, containing two small theaters, one with 500 and the other with 200 seats, together with their service facilities. Section C was also to be adapted to everyday use. Finally, section D was to house permanent and temporary staff.[11]

This vast program was to be built on a highly sensitive site in the center of Moscow, further removed from the Kremlin than the 1922–1923 Palace of Labor but nonetheless in a direct visual relationship to it.[12] Located on the banks of the Moskva, the site was occupied by the neo-Russian Church of Christ the Saviour, which had been built to commemorate the victory over Napoleon's Grande Armée and designed by Konstantin Ton, architect of the Palace of Arms within the Kremlin.[13] Demolition of the church began without

[6] *Dvorets Sovetov*, no. 2–3 (1931): 3–4. This was the "Bulletin published by the council for the construction of the Palace of the Soviets for the Central Executive Committee of the USSR." See A. Mikhailov, "O vystavke proektov dvortsa Sovetov," *Za proletarskoe iskusstvo*, no. 9 (1931): 14–19.

[7] On the organization of the Palace of Soviets competition, and the results of the initial phases, see especially Soiuz Sovetskikh Arkhitektorov, *Dvorets Sovetov, vsesoiuzny konkurs 1932 g.* (Moscow: Izd. Vesekokhudozhnika, 1932).

[8] For the council's declarations, see Sovet stroitelstva Dvortsa sovetov, "O rezultatakh rabot po vsesoiuznomu okrytomu konkursu na sostavlenie proekta Dvortsa sovetov SSSR v gor. Moskve," 28 February 1932, in *Pravda* (29 February 1932).

[9] "Programma proektirovaniia Dvortsa Sovetov SSSR v Moskve," in *Dvorets Sovetov*, p. 123. This brief was also published in the press, together with impassioned appeals for participation: "Vse na konkurs" and "Programma proektirovaniia Dvortsa Sovetov SSSR v Moskve," *Stroitelstvo Moskvy* 8, no. 6 (1931): 8–10.

[10] "Programma proektirovaniia."

[11] I have here used the Latin alphabetical division which Le Corbusier received in translation, and not the Cyrillic letters used in the Russian brief.

[12] On the discussions leading up to the choice of this site, see Selim O. Khan-Magomedov, "K istorii vybora mesta dlia Dvortsa Sovetov," 21–23.

[13] On Ton's career, see Tatiana Slavina, *Konstantin Ton* (Moscou: Stroiizdat, 1989).

238. Konstantin Ton, Church of Christ the Saviour, Moscow, 1832, photograph, 1928.

239. Alexei Shchusev, "Novaia Moskva" plan, view of the Kremlin and its surroundings, 1924. In the foreground, the site of the 1923 "Palace of Labour" competition; in the background, Church of Christ the Saviour.

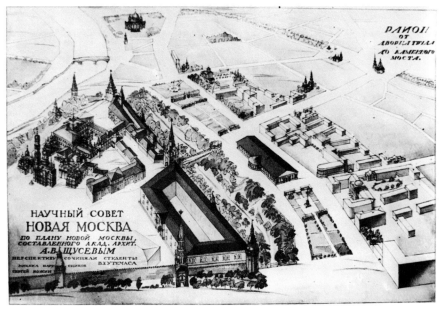

delay, since the deadline for its destruction was set for 15 December 1931.[14] The paintings and sculptures contained in the church were transferred to the Tretiakov Gallery.

[14] In a passage excised by the translator from his *Memoirs,* Alexander Pasternak evokes the demolition of the church, which was situated opposite his home. Khan-Magomedov insists on the fact that most architects of the 1930s did not value Ton's building very highly.

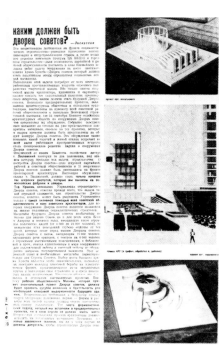

240. "How the Palace of Soviets Should Be," article with illustrations of the preliminary competition's projects"; in *Brigada Khudozhnikov* 1, no. 7 (1931).

THE INVITATION TO LE CORBUSIER

Apart from three Soviet teams (those of Ivan Zholtovsky, Boris Iofan, and German Krasin), nine foreign architects were invited to submit designs for the second phase of the competition. These included Erich Mendelsohn, Hans Poelzig, and Walter Gropius (Germany), William F. Lamb and Joseph Urban (United States), Armando Brasini (Italy), Auguste Perret and Le Corbusier (France), and Ragnar Östberg (Sweden). The fees requested by Östberg, however, were judged excessive, and his participation was not confirmed.[15]

On 2 September 1931 B. Breslov, a Soviet trade representative in France, wrote to ask Le Corbusier if he would agree to "design a project for this reconstruction," and if so, "to state his conditions."[16] After having seen Breslov's secretary, and in the knowledge that the competition was one "of ideas," Le Corbusier accepted at once but demanded a renegotiation of the fees (he asked for twice the amount proposed—four thousand dollars—half of which was to be paid on account) and the 1 December deadline:

I should be most happy to draw up studies for the Palace of Soviets, but on certain conditions, for the problem, which is extremely difficult from various technical viewpoints, is one that interests me greatly. I am sure that we can make an interesting response. But the Soviet authorities must understand that the project entails extremely delicate and costly engineering studies.[17]

Le Corbusier had learned his lesson from the bitter negotiations over Centrosoyuz and envisaged a new contract should his project be accepted:

In the event that our project is adopted—or at least, that the essential ideas contained in our design meet with approval in Moscow—a new agreement would be drawn up with a view to executing the final design and construction drawings, it being understood that our ideas remain our property until such a time as an agreement relative to the final designs and construction program is signed.

On 12 September, Le Corbusier succeeded in negotiating the sum of three thousand dollars (he cashed in a check for a third of this sum on 7 October); he also succeeded in extending the deadline for his designs till 15 December. Nothing now stood in the way of his participation. Although Eugène Freyssinet declined to assist, Gustave Lyon, who was to play a crucial role in the project, received a pressing request from Le Corbusier:

I should like to contribute answers to questions
  a. of acoustics
  b. of heating/*respiration.*
  This project, which should be executed without delay, is the object of a competition between the Russians, Perret, me, and possibly one or two Germans. The game is worth the candle. It is a magnificent problem to study.
  This is what, with all my heart, I desire: that you furnish the required consultations and sketches plus calculations concerning the two points above. This is no longer considered, as before, a generous gift of your expertise, but rather as a business contract, for which we should like to pay you well.[18]

THE CHANGING STAGES OF THE PROJECT

When Le Corbusier set to work, he was already familiar with the entries for the "preliminary" phase, which had been published in the council's official bulletin and he at once proceeded by literally "sticking" to the divisions indicated

[15] *Dvorets Sovetov*, no. 1 (1931), FLC. Two of the three Soviet teams had participated in the "preliminary" consultations.

[16] B. Breslov, letter to Le Corbusier, Paris, 2 September 1931, FLC.

[17] Le Corbusier, letter to Monsieur Breslov, Paris, 2 September 1931, FLC.

[18] Le Corbusier, letter to Gustave Lyon, Paris, 1 October 1931, FLC. On receipt of the first check from the Soviets, Le Corbusier in turn sent Lyon an advance payment of five hundred francs.

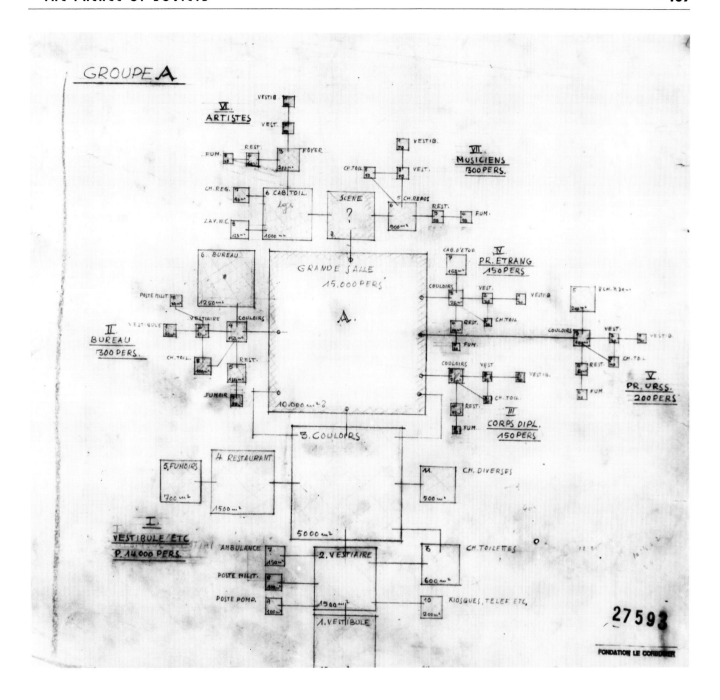

in the brief.[19] First he drew up a functional flow chart of the various components;[20] second, he pasted squares of Canson paper on to the surface of the different buildings required, so as to be able to analyze their assembly.

Luckily, Le Corbusier's initial interpretation of the brief was not called into question when a written response to entrants' queries reached Paris in the form of a clumsy French translation. This text gave details of the activities that were to be authorized within the palace, left entrants a degree of latitude as regards the relations between the different halls, and, most important, permitted a regrouping of the various foyers.[21] Le Corbusier's final project included a sheet that showed how he had arrived at his final decision. This assembly of eight variant sketches made at crucial moments in the design phase, drawn by Gyórgy Kepes on 22 November 1931, indicates the gradual emergence, from

241. Le Corbusier, Palace of Soviets, Moscow, 1931–1932, diagram of functional relationships in section A, FLC 27593.

[19] *Dvorets Sovetov*, nos. 1 and 2–3, FLC. Le Corbusier also had in his possession photographs of a number of models from the "preliminary" phase, together with the review by Mikhailov, "O vystavke."

[20] See drawings 2272ff. FLC.

[21] Document handwritten on the office's stationery, translated from *Dvorets Sovetov*, nos. 2–3, FLC.

6 October to 22 November, of a partial and highly localized symmetry linking the two small theaters of section C, a regional symmetry between the 5,900-seat hall and the two small theaters, and then the overall symmetries of the final composition.[22]

These variants also give evidence of a dissociation—during the first phase of the study at least—between the formal and structural treatment of the various halls and the mode of assembly of the different elements of the project. The overall composition only partially reflects the search for an optimal configuration occupying the whole of the site, as was the case with Centrosoyuz; rather, it is the result of decisions taken at the level of each of the brief's functional sections, which are then condensed by means of a specific additive process. This determines not only the shape of the halls, but also their orientation, which in each case was modified on several occasions. Le Corbusier's own sketches dated 12 and 13 October seem rather exceptional in the process: the various volumes are sheltered by a "grande muraille," a long and thick wall formed by contrasting box-like forms parallel to the Moscow River.[23]

Le Corbusier later claimed that "the independently determined organs can be seen to take up their respective positions little by little, thus achieving a synthetic solution."[24] The 15,000-capacity auditorium and the 5,900-seat hall were at first positioned on a tangential axis, and for a time the smaller theaters were grouped in an agglutinative manner along an axis perpendicular to the first. In the final variant, however, the covered spaces were all organized around a single point, an open-air meeting place or esplanade that the brief had not explicitly required.

In this way, 50,000 people could walk up ramps to a platform facing the tribune of the great auditorium. Moreover, this public could be "harangued by an orator whose position [was] particularly conducive to voice projection."[25] From the profile of the ceilings in the two main auditoriums, to the possibility of sound projection for open-air meetings, the acoustics and the layout that they justify thus determined the spatial organization of a palace that was also to allow for *respiration exacte*—a system that, as we have seen, had to be

[22] *Carnet noir*, p. 37, FLC.

[23] These original sketches are kept in the archive of Orestis Maltos (Athens), who worked for Le Corbusier in 1931, and were first published by Yorgos Simeoforidis, in *Architecture in Greece*, no. 21 (1987).

[24] Boesiger, *Œuvre complète 1929–1934*, p. 130.

[25] Le Corbusier and Pierre Jeanneret, "Projet pour la construction du Palais des Soviets à Moscou," competition report, handwritten, December 1931, p. 12, FLC.

242. Le Corbusier, Palace of Soviets, Moscow, 1931–1932, sketches for the articulation of buildings, FLC 27936.

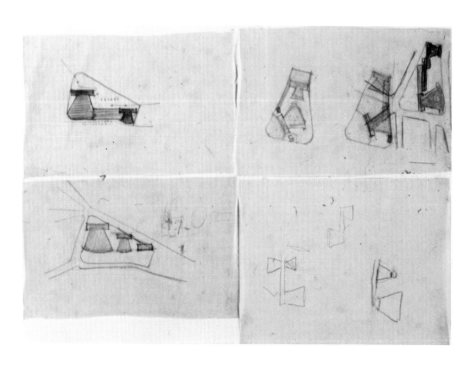

243. Le Corbusier, Palace of Soviets, Moscow, 1931–1932, sketch for the articulation of buildings, FLC 27558.

244. Le Corbusier, Palace of Soviets, Moscow, 1931–1932, sketch for the articulation of buildings, 9 October 1931, FLC 27542.

abandoned at Centrosoyuz. The written report accompanying the designs was, moreover, almost exclusively devoted to the project's technical and structural aspects, and not to the architectural choices, concerning which the tone remains defensive and almost snappish:

We are sending to Moscow a project that has been studied down to the last detail, one that meets the strictest professional requirements and those of the detailed brief we were given.

245. Le Corbusier, Palace of Soviets, Moscow, 1931–1932, sketch with the "great wall," 12 October 1931.

246. Le Corbusier, Palace of Soviets, Moscow, 1931–1932, sketch with the "acoustic wall," 13 October 1931.

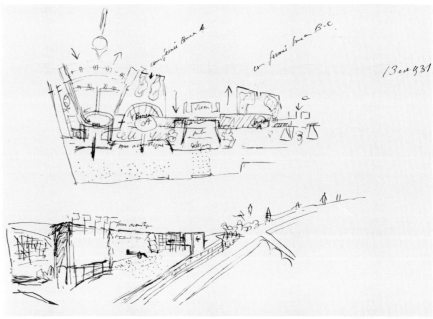

We have created organisms small or large. The synthesis of these fragmentary solutions in our project results in an overall expression of extreme simplicity.

It ought not to be thought that this simplicity is due to a lack of research; on the contrary, the project is the fruit of two and a half months of work on ten or so different solutions, beginning with complicated ones and culminating in the present synthesis.

It was not so much a unified series of architectural solutions as a gamut of local responses that was submitted for Soviet evaluation:

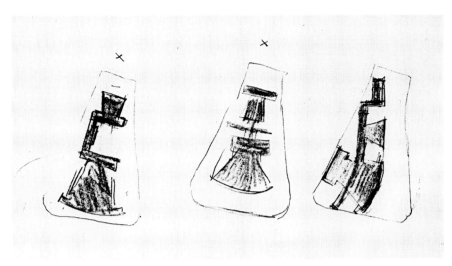

247. Le Corbusier, Palace of Soviets, Moscow, 1931–1932, sketches for the articulation of buildings, October 1931.

248. Le Corbusier, Palace of Soviets, Moscow, 1931–1932, overall view with Kremlin, October 1931.

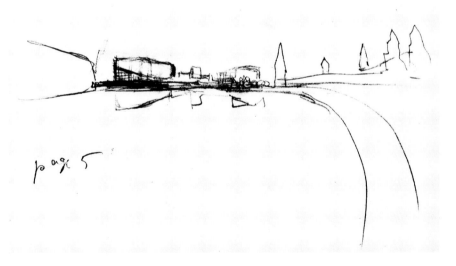

249. Le Corbusier, Palace of Soviets, Moscow, 1931–1932, overall view with Kremlin, October 1931.

Proceeding first by analysis, we have sought out the best possible solution for each of the different constituent elements of the problem:

a. *Pedestrian circulations (entrances, restaurants, cloakrooms, auditoriums, etc.)*. Links with outside traffic (trams, buses).

b. *Automobile traffic* (free, independent circuit for pedestrians, direct access to the various reserved entrances and garages). Pedestrians and motorists do not meet.

c. *Access to the auditoriums* for crowds of 6,000 or 15,000 people. Traditional stairs

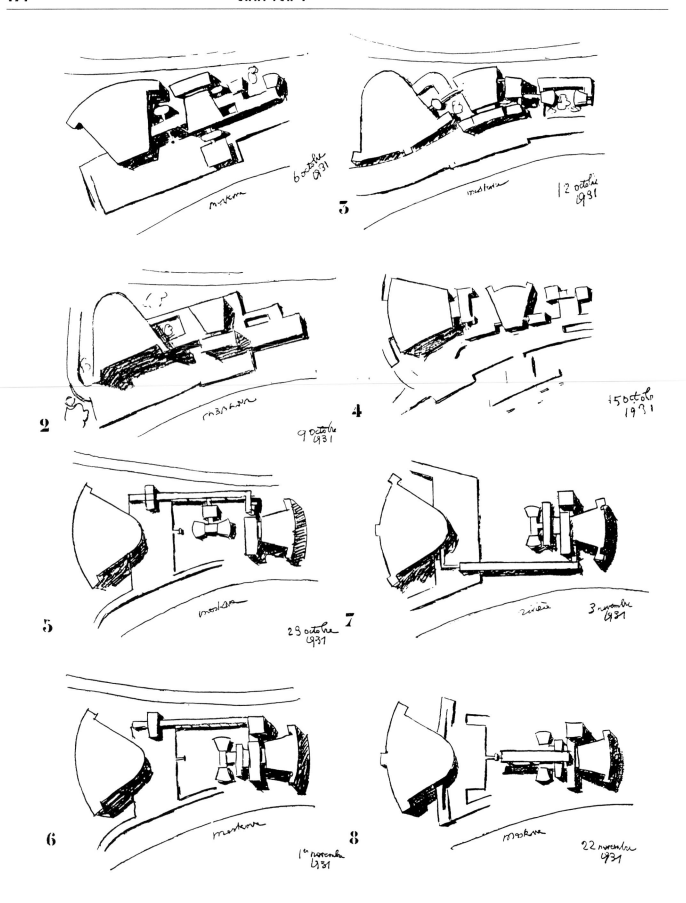

are replaced by inclined planes or ramps, the only methods that will allow for sufficient flow.

d. *Visibility*: We considered that all the seats in all the halls should benefit from
equal visibility.

e. *Acoustics*: since this problem is known to us, we have created suitable organisms.
But given the dimensions of the auditoriums, we have called on the assistance of the
world-famous physicist, Gustave Lyon. Thanks to his interventions, we are now in a
position to propose elements ensuring clear pronunciation and hearing.

f. *Heating-ventilation*: functions that we prefer to call *respiration exacte*.

. . . Since this crucial question is henceforth to be treated in an entirely novel manner
. . . the result will be an immense saving, an efficiency hitherto unknown, and a precious contribution to building techniques in the Soviet Union.

g. *Building systems* concerning the structures proposed for both the auditoriums
and the other elements.

h. *Urban planning*: the development of the palace surrounds. Here, let it be said in
all honesty that the solution can only be a piecemeal one as long as the City of Moscow
does not envisage an urban plan based on entirely new ideas—ideas that take into
account the new state of affairs ushered in by combinations of fast- and slow-moving
traffic in the modern city.[26]

In the progress toward symmetry, Le Corbusier thus abandoned all thought
of urban space—not without some bitterness in regard to his "Response to
Moscow." Whereas in the first sketches the esplanade constituted a direct link
between the palace and the river, and the palace was presenting its "grande
muraille" as an answer to the Kremlin's wall, in the final project it was posi-

[26] Ibid., pp. 1–5.

On Opposite Page:

250. Le Corbusier, Palace of Soviets,
Moscow, 1931–1932, comparative drawing of the successive solutions for the articulation of buildings, from 6 October
to 23 November, December 1931,
drawn by Gyorgy Kepes.

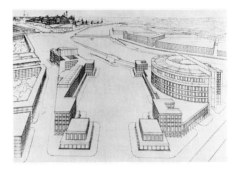

251. Auguste Perret, competition project for the Palace of Soviets, 1931.

252. Le Corbusier, Palace of Soviets,
Moscow, 1931–1932, general axonometric view sent to Moscow.

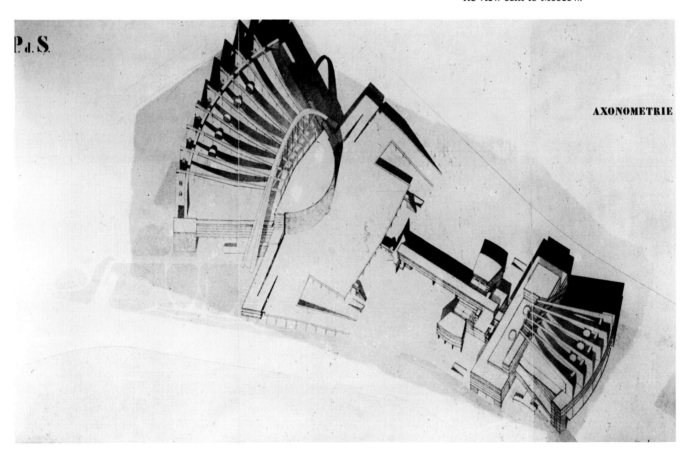

AXONOMETRIE

253. Le Corbusier, Palace of Soviets, Moscow, 1931–1932, site plan.

tioned on the symmetrical axis and raised above ground level, thus acquiring the status of fully fledged space—a fact that contrasts with Perret's designs, where the auditoriums are hemmed in between a great empty square and the streets surrounding the site.

This platform thus became, so to speak, the largest auditorium in the palace, which in turn lost all contact with the surrounding urban fabric. In its final form, the composition floats as freely and superbly as the churches of the Kremlin, whose contact with the ground is masked by the brick perimeter wall. Yet it is rather more rigid and assertive, and its austere appearance is only palliated by the elevation on the long axis, which prompted Le Corbusier to compare his project with the Piazza dei Miracoli at Pisa, which he visited in 1934. When Le Corbusier reflected "that the same architectural principle had presided over the Palace of Soviets design—of unity in detail (unity on a human scale); of lively tumult of the whole (as the Abbé Laugier remarked during Louis XIV's reign [sic])"—he was quite simply tipping his hat to a design strategy based on a collage of the various constituent parts.[27]

A "PURE, INTACT, ENTIRE ORGANISM"

Conceived of as an organism, or rather as a sum of "organisms small or large," Le Corbusier's project for the Palace of Soviets further developed his proposals for the League of Nations, Mundaneum, and Centrosoyuz. This time, however, the solid framework of office buildings, which constituted a sort of backdrop to the free treatment of the assembly halls or auditoriums, had disappeared. In fact, the project's administrative component was negligible, and the design was dominated by the two auditoriums:

[27] Boesiger, *Œuvre complète 1929–1934*, p. 132.

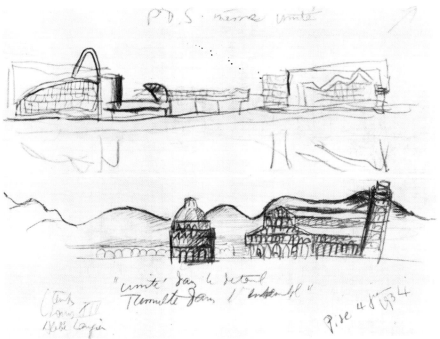

254. Le Corbusier, Palace of Soviets, Moscow, 1931–1932, perspective demonstrating the "fusion" of the palace and the Kremlin, drawing sent to Moscow.

255. Le Corbusier, comparison between the Palace of Soviets and the piazza dei Miracoli in Pisa, published in *Œuvre complète 1929–1934* (Zurich, 1934).

The hills of the Kremlin afford an uninterrupted view of architectural wonders (old churches and palaces). The hill overlooks the river and descends along the edge of the Kremlin, via gardens, toward the site allotted to the Palace.

Among a wide variety of considerations, we have chosen to position the Palace on the Kremlin's long axis, parallel to the river.

We feel that, in this way, we have achieved both a material and a spiritual unity.[28]

With the rejection of his "Response" still very much in mind, Le Corbusier

[28] Ibid., p. 35. The existence of an "axis" in the Kremlin's structure has, moreover, to be demonstrated; there is at most a "direction" echoing that of the Moskova.

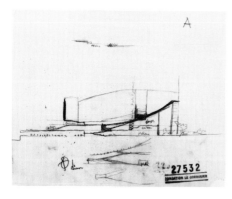

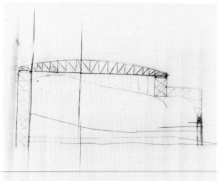

256. Le Corbusier, Palace of Soviets, Moscow, 1931–1932, cross-section of the steps of auditorium A, FLC 27532.

257. Le Corbusier, Palace of Soviets, Moscow, 1931–1932, cross-section of the roof of auditorium A, FLC 27489.

refused, as we have seen, to submit any plans for the development of the environs, although they were doubtless more familiar to him than to any of the other foreign architects "commissioned" by Moscow:

> We have placed this pure, intact, entire organism within the indicated area, without, however, concerning ourselves with the contours of the terrain.
>
> All that exists outside the Palace is merely the consequence of chance developments of the city through the centuries. Should these environs be urbanized? A highly interesting proposition! But as we have already stated, nothing can be seriously undertaken until a fundamental urban planning doctrine is agreed upon by the Moscow authorities.[29]

As a free though symmetrical figure standing against the backdrop of the city, the palace was in fact oriented relative to the Kremlin's long perimeter wall, and its integration of Moscow's urban culture was reflected not so much in its spatial structure, as in the way it controlled crowds, a problem raised by all those who visited Moscow at the time, from Georges Duhamel to Walter Benjamin, and which Le Corbusier had already grappled with in his Centrosoyuz designs. Deliberate control of the movements of crowds, whether motorized or on foot, is in fact what stimulated his ingenuity. Traffic was to be channeled by means of a double "automobile circuit" circumventing the palace—an element that Le Corbusier justified in a somewhat defensive manner:

> Traffic is one way.
>
> These two sole thoroughfares are linked to the four arteries that line the Palace by means of a series of crossroads which have been drawn up as the solution best adapted to current circumstances.
>
> Let us not forget what we have said from the start, that Moscow has not yet accepted the basic principles of urban planning that make it possible to eliminate, once and for all, the conflict between the pedestrian and the motorist.
>
> Until such a doctrine brings with it the benefits of revolutionary initiatives, all urban planning solutions, whatever they are—whether in Moscow or elsewhere—will be piecemeal ones.
>
> Following exhaustive study, we claim to be in a position to reserve almost 100% of the site for pedestrians, prevent all encounters between motorists and pedestrians, give the network of trams and buses their true role, and build modern cities in the form of "green cities," while at the same time considerably reducing distances.
>
> The sole aim of this digression is to emphasize the fact that the traffic links around the Palace represent solutions less pure than those adopted for the Palace itself.[30]

The festive or solemn "processional" aspect of the pedestrian flow, and its more macabre "disaster" implications, make the palace a gigantic crowd-sorting machine, in the definition of which Le Corbusier did not hesitate to use a biological metaphor:

> Having left the cloakroom area, 14,000 people proceed to an *inclined plane* leading up, *without stairs, in a perfectly smooth and continuous slope,* either to the *Hall,* or to the *Great Forum* beneath the Hall, which contains all the services.
>
> The inclined plane continues upward without a break and forms the very *amphitheater* of the hall. Access to the amphitheater is provided by three arteries . . . which divide up into secondary horizontal and vertical routes.
>
> The hall's circulation plan is based on the principle of blood flow, with its arteries, veins and capillaries.[31]

The inclined plane was thus a means of sorting, distribution, and evacuation. The ramp constituted a sort of mass architectural promenade, and its vast sloping surfaces led up to the great auditorium or, better still, to that proletar-

[29] Le Corbusier and Jeanneret, "Projet pour la construction," p. 36.

[30] Ibid., pp. 20–21.

[31] Ibid., p. 8.

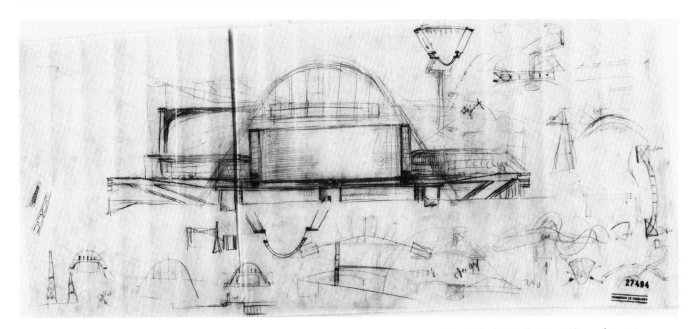

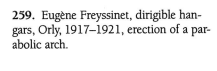

258. Le Corbusier, Palace of Soviets, Moscow, 1931–1932, study of the arch of auditorium A, FLC 27494.

259. Eugène Freyssinet, dirigible hangars, Orly, 1917–1921, erection of a parabolic arch.

260. Eugène Freyssinet, steel and concrete bridge over the Seine, Saint-Pierre du Vauvray, 1923, view of site and of finished bridge.

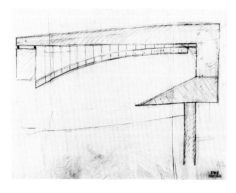

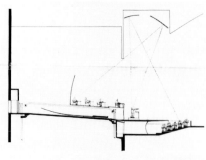

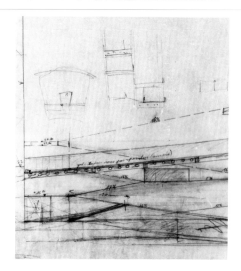

261. Le Corbusier, Palace of Soviets, Moscow, 1931–1932, cross-section of the "sickles" of auditorium B, FLC 27912.

262. Le Corbusier, Palace of Soviets, Moscow, 1931–1932, acoustic cross-section of auditorium B, FLC 27236.

263. Le Corbusier, Palace of Soviets, Moscow, 1931–1932, section across the steps of auditorium B, FLC 27280.

ian "variant" of the opera-house foyer, the "great forum" below. The generalized use of the ramp, which "afforded smooth, uninterrupted crowd flow," and which Le Corbusier sometimes compared with a "mountain path"—recalling the landscape imagery of the Centrosoyuz project, with its "cliff wall" and "basin"—coincided with the more or less complete disappearance of his earlier, "prismatic" forms.

The constructional and acoustic solutions, and in particular the arch from which the roof of the great auditorium was to be suspended, engendered whole families of curvilinear forms whose opposition to the overall rectilinear composition creates forceful plastic tension. The great concrete arch and sickle-shaped porticoes holding up the 6,500-capacity hall stand in counterpoint to the orthogonal plan. The arch, which may bear some relation to Auguste Perret's bridge solution for the roof of the Champs-Elysées Theater, is also clearly a reference to at least two of Eugène Freyssinet's celebrated structures. In the design of its supports, and in the principle of the tie beams holding up the roof, it may be compared with his bridge over the Seine at Saint-Pierre du Vauvray, built in 1923; but the curve of the arch evokes the dirigible hangars at Orly (the first arches of which were completed in 1921) as published in the eighteenth issue of *L'Esprit Nouveau*.[32] The hall designs were defined by a dual treatment of floor and roof. In relation to the overall distributions, they were "rigorously designed with the principle of theatrical and cinematographic visibility in mind" and were based "on the amphitheaters of Antiquity, which assembled immense crowds with the greatest of ease and afforded excellent visibility for all":

At the summit the three main arteries encounter a path encircling the great hall and leading to three large groups of escape stairs. The processions filing into the arena will use these arteries and stairs.

Having resolved the problem of circulation, it is useful to indicate that the design of this single inclined plane creates an impression of architectural grandeur and unity. Each of the 14,000 spectators passes in front of a series of volumes of varying dimensions; having penetrated the great hall via one of its three 25-meter-high entrances, he is faced with the immensity of the amphitheater with its acoustic cupola, and the effect is incontestably one of architectural grandeur.[33]

Le Corbusier, who made explicit reference to the fact that the Greeks had "perfectly resolved the question of acoustics in their theaters, since these were in the open air and had no roof," had delegated the ceiling designs to Gustave Lyon, who did not, however, send in his conclusions until after the plans intended for Moscow had been completed:[34]

The enclosed report and calculations by M. Gustave Lyon are the result of his preliminary studies. His sketches of the halls should be substituted for our sections and profiles. Moreover, the finalization of this question will require a vast quantity of work by specialist technicians under M. Gustave Lyon.

In fact, the ceilings' definitive curve was a compromise between Lyon's own graphic method and calculations "by MM. Morin, of the Ecole Polytechnique, and Marty, Doctor of Science, of the Ecole Normale":

[32] Jose A. Fernandez Ordoñez, *Eugène Freyssinet* (Barcelona: 2c Ediciones, 1978), pp. 306–24.
[33] Le Corbusier and Jeanneret, "Projet pour la construction," p. 9.
[34] See Gustave Lyon, *L'acoustique architectu-* rale, avec l'annexe: l'aération moderne des salles (Paris: Editions Film et Technique, 1932). For an assessment of Lyon's Salle Pleyel designs, see Michael Forsyth, *Buildings for Music* (Cambridge: Cambridge University Press, 1985), pp. 262–63.

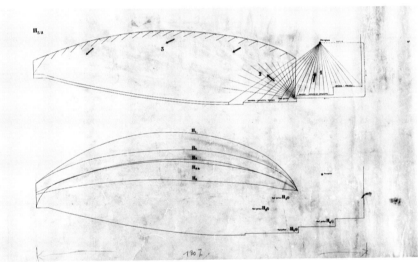

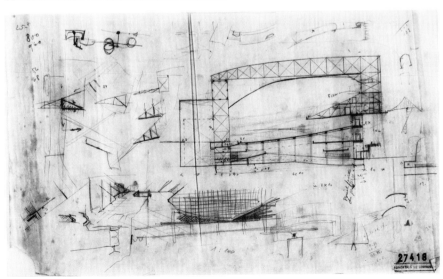

264. Le Corbusier, Palace of Soviets, Moscow, 1931–1932, study for the roof of auditorium A, FLC 27381.

265. Le Corbusier, Palace of Soviets, Moscow, 1931–1932, acoustic cross-sections of auditorium A, drawing sent to Moscow on 1 February 1932, FLC 27239.

266. Le Corbusier, Palace of Soviets, Moscow, 1931–1932 cross-section of the structure of auditorium B, FLC 27418.

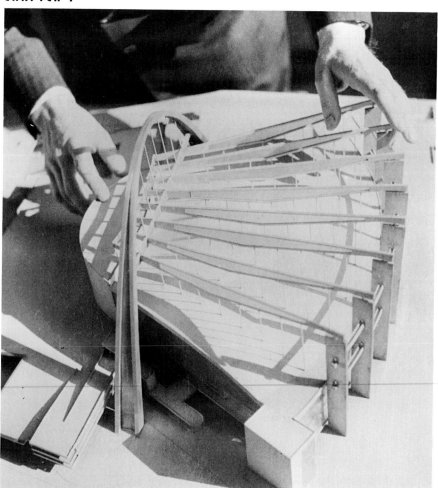

267. Le Corbusier manipulates the roof of auditorium A of the Palace of Soviets, 1934.

268. Le Corbusier, Palace of Soviets, Moscow, 1931–1932, general plan at the level of the auditoria, FLC 27252.

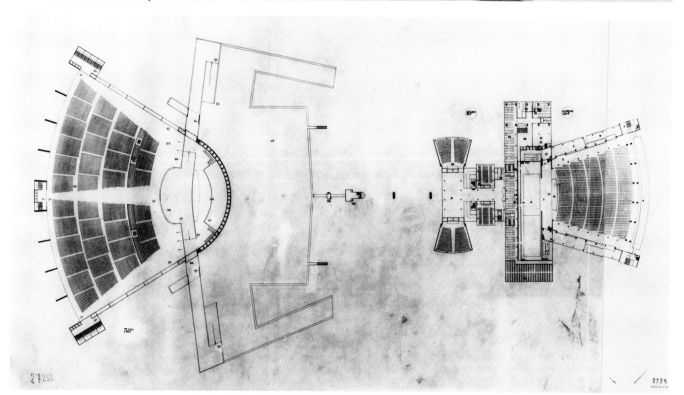

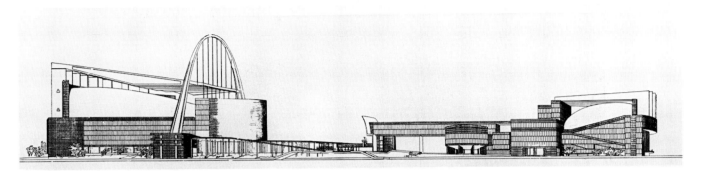

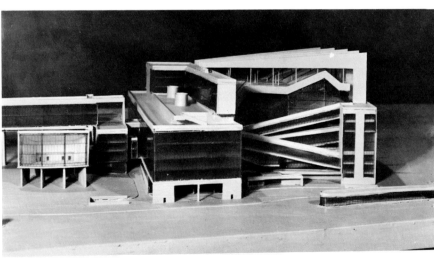

269. Le Corbusier, Palace of Soviets, Moscow, 1931–1932, elevation on the riverside.

270. Le Corbusier, Palace of Soviets, Moscow, 1931–1932, model, longitudinal view.

271. Le Corbusier, Palace of Soviets, Moscow, 1931–1932, model, view of auditorium A from the riverside.

272. Le Corbusier, Palace of Soviets, Moscow, 1931–1932, model, view of auditorium B from the riverside.

273. Le Corbusier, Palace of Soviets, Moscow, 1931–1932, model, view of auditorium A from the riverside with floors and roofs unmounted.

274. Le Corbusier, Palace of Soviets, Moscow, 1931–1932, model, view of auditorium A, *pilotis.*

275. Le Corbusier, Palace of Soviets, Moscow, 1931–1932, model, view of the floor of auditorium A.

The voices of the actors on stage are separated from the audience by an 11-meter "abyss." All sound from the stage is collected by a microphone positioned at a height of 30 meters, and transmitted through a loudspeaker placed at a strictly mathematical point at the front of the stage. This transmitter projects the sound waves up to the acoustic conch of the ceiling, which in turn distributes them equally to all the spectators.[35]

Absorbed as he was in these problems of acoustics, Lyon delegated the problem of heating and ventilation to a mining engineer, Rougnon, who recommended two distinct systems: "neutralizing walls" were to be used for the buildings in continual use, and *ventilation ponctuelle* for the halls and their annexes. These "neutralizing walls," which had been rejected for Centrosoyuz, were justified on the basis of experience accumulated in a competition sponsored by the the Saint-Gobain glass company. The *ventilation ponctuelle* involved the installation of "fresh-air lozenges" under the seats:

Using traditional methods, the 25 million cubic meters of air would have had to be heated. With *ventilation ponctuelle,* on the other hand, the air will be channeled in a closed circuit, and will have to be cooled. This will be achieved by a natural method of great simplicity, whereby the collecting ducts will come into contact with the cold air outside. Obviously, our plans for the Palace of Soviets do not necessarily imply the use of these heating and ventilation systems, and any other method may be used, but those will be less efficient and more wasteful. And we repeat: the principle of *respiration exacte* seems to us to be of decisive importance for the Soviet Union.[36]

Le Corbusier seems to have accepted the idea of monumental scale, and a twofold determination inspired by the building's institutional character and by the symmetry inherent in vertebrate organisms doubtless accounts for the project's strict overall axiality, compromised only by a slight, if deliberate, "imbalance." Work on the project in the rue de Sèvres appears to have been particularly exhausting, and discipline was sometimes difficult to maintain, as Le Corbusier later admitted:

The fatigue is intense, but we progress together, as a team. Each at his drawing board keeps a watchful eye open for errors and is quick to denounce them, from the smallest detail to the project as a whole. There are no errors, no omissions, no lies; all our work advances with astonishing unity. I remember one day (while we were drawing up the plans for the Palace of Soviets). Fifteen of us had been working on the project for three months. Time was short, and the working day continued long past midnight, and sometimes till daybreak. Someone proposed further modifications, someone else proposed still others. I intervened vigorously and said, "If anyone else proposes one more modification, he'll be out on his ear! We have to finish now." This shows the degree of our beautiful collaboration.[37]

The plans "drawn up in three months by a team of 15 architects from all nations who have brought to the task a moving spirit of enthusiasm" were completed by 15 December 1931. The team included Wanner, Sammer, Gruson, David, and Sakakura. The plans were delivered to the Soviet Embassy in Paris on 22 December, and forwarded to Moscow by diplomatic bag.[38] A number of decisive elements for a comprehension of the formal project were

[35] *L'Architecture Vivante* 10 (Fall–Winter 1932): pl. 10.

[36] Le Corbusier and Jeanneret, "Projet pour la construction," p. 31.

[37] Le Corbusier, introduction to Boesiger, *Œuvre complète 1929–1934,* p. 11.

[38] *Carnet noir,* p. 37, FLC. "The consignment includes sheets of plans, a general report, a heating report, a ventilation report"; Le Corbusier, letter to the chairman of the Council for the Construction of the Palace of Soviets, 24 December 1931, FLC.

276. Le Corbusier and Pierre Jeanneret review the model of the Palace of Soviets in the 35, rue de Sèvres studio, 1934.

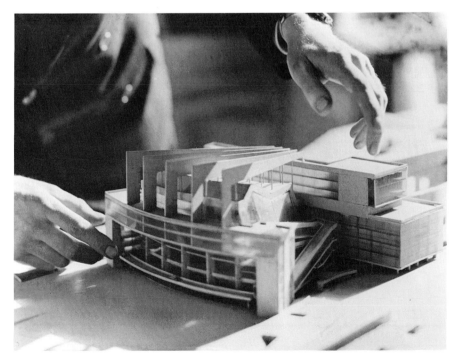

277. Le Corbusier manipulates the roof of auditorium B, 1934.

278. Le Corbusier, Palace of Soviets, Moscow, 1931–1932, model, frontal view of auditorium A *pilotis*.

279. Le Corbusier, Palace of Soviets, Moscow, 1931–1932, model, view of auditorium A floor.

still lacking, however: Gustave Lyon's report on the acoustics of the great hall was not sent in until 20 January, and the modified sections were not despatched until 1 February, when Le Corbusier apologized for the delays. A hundred-meter film of the model was sent even later. Apart from a few isolated frames, the only trace of this film to survive is a leader showing three essential types of view: lengthwise and lateral tracking or "dolly" shots; "aerial views"—that is, overhead shots, although the camera appears to have been positioned against a wall; and back projections, made possible by the fact that the sides of the model were transparent.[39]

Unfortunately, the film did not arrive in Moscow until mid-February, when the competition was to all intents and purposes over. More generally, the perfectionism that incited Le Corbusier to send off one document after another may well have played against him, for the Soviets received notification of every single modification and every single test carried out on the model with a view to simulating visually the acoustic phenomena:

The architectural treatment of hall A has been thoroughly modified for the better. The side view of the hall is now more monumental, forceful and simple. The cupola has assumed a categorical appearance quite different from that in the December designs.

Using the model currently in preparation, we have verified the distribution of sound on the basis of the comparable refraction of light waves.

This experiment has proved conclusive.

We installed a lamp inside the model, at the point where the loudspeaker is to be placed. When we turned the lamp toward the cupola, its rays broke up in accordance with laws of incidence identical to those of sound, and the amphitheater was uniformly lit from the first row to the last.[40]

Apart from the acoustic problem, Le Corbusier mentioned a number of other issues that were unresolved in the December dossier. He indicated that lighting would be provided by neon tubes installed "between the double layer of glass that constitutes the side walls of the two auditoriums," thus producing an "effect" at once "opulent, simple and extremely powerful." But above all, he discussed the problem of snow, both on the curved roofs of the auditoriums and on the terraces, invoking his long experience in a mountain environment in the latter case:

I lived for more than 25 years at an altitude of 1,000 meters, and had the occasion to study in particular the effects of heating on the behavior of snow.

. . . Flat terraces constitute the best possible receptacle for snow, on condition that the water pipes are installed in the warmth of the building and not on the outside. The snow can collect there without causing any inconvenience. When the building is heated, the snow will gradually melt on contact with the terrace, and be efficiently drained away to the interior of the building; when the building is unheated, the snow will be unaffected by heat and remain stable. This method, first tested by us in 1913, has always given excellent results (at an altitude of 1,000 meters).[41]

AN AESTHETIC AND TECHNICAL CHALLENGE

Le Corbusier's competition entry was certainly original. This originality can be perceived in a number of decisions, particularly in the refusal to consider the building as a central or hierarchic plan revolving around the great hall. In fact, he refused both to subordinate the rest of the composition to the great hall and to highlight the entrance to the building. Clearly, the attention paid to the circulation of people and their differentiation is nothing new. In the Paris

[39] Manuscript note in the FLC.
[40] Le Corbusier, letter to the chairman of the council, Paris, 1 February 1932, p. 2, FLC.
[41] Ibid., p. 4.

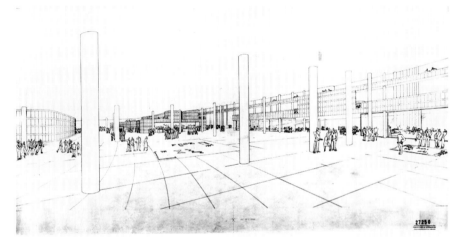

280. Le Corbusier, Palace of Soviets, Moscow, 1931–1932, perspective of the foyer of auditorium A, FLC 27250.

281. Le Corbusier, Palace of Soviets, Moscow, 1931–1932, perspective of auditorium A cloakrooms, FLC 27251.

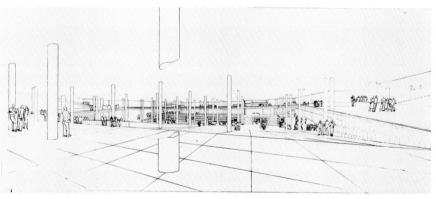

282. Le Corbusier, Palace of Soviets, Moscow, 1931–1932, perspective of auditorium B entrance, FLC 27244.

opera house, for instance, Charles Garnier had also based his treatment of the exterior on a clear distinction between the grand public entrance on the square and the side entrance for officials, which was prolonged by means of a series of passages within the building; inside, he also focused on the relationship between the grand staircase and the foyer, the treatment of which was, however, both delicate and monumental. Le Corbusier's approach is in many respects a comparable one, but the references to civil engineering works introduced a new type of register governing the relations between the building's inside and outside: landscape.

Coming only a few months after his *Obus* Plan for Algiers, this project allies plastic forms and technical objectivity on a quite different scale.[42] The use of curves on both horizontal and vertical planes to define the external appearance of the halls, and of contrasting lighting effects in the building's great public spaces, transformed the vocabularies that he had applied to his earlier studies of large buildings. This development toward greater plasticity may reflect Le Corbusier's return, at this time, to figurative painting. It is as if somewhere between the initial sketches—in which the palace's various volumes were still trapezoidal boxes—and the final designs, Le Corbusier had somehow geared his architecture to his painting. This evolution is no doubt less clearly visible in the Palace of Soviets than in the *Obus* Plan; but in the latter case, he had based his plan on a series of landscape sketches and an "impression" of Algiers women that he could not obtain in the case of Moscow.[43]

This interplay of forms intervenes in a context of astonishingly dense functional and technical systems. Some of these were conditioned by the laws of statics, others by acoustic considerations, and others still by the question of pedestrian "traffic" flow. The supple forms of the *Obus* Plan were linked to impressions of the city obtained from the air and in the automobile. If, on the other hand, the Palace of Soviets was "seen" from the air, this was due exclusively to the artifice of photography, and although the architectural promenade was treated on an urban scale, it was nonetheless inspired by the measured steps of the pedestrian.

FEBRUARY 1932: THE VERDICT OR "INSULT"

Le Corbusier later amused himself on occasion by rewriting the chronicle of events as a battle between himself and "Moscow"; but in so doing he concealed the fact that there had been three successive competitions from 1931 to 1933, and instead gave the impression that he had been engaged in single, hand-to-hand combat with an elusive institutional client. This is the impression that emerges from the letter he wrote to Alexis Léger in 1935:

Satisfaction with the plans we had drawn up was so acute that in 1929 the Soviet government commissioned further plans for a Palace of Soviets, which was to be the Five-Year Plan's crowning achievement. My project was favorably received in all active circles in Moscow; it was actually declared suitable for construction (although the scale of the project was formidable). And I was even informed that decisions had been taken to this effect.[44]

The process of reaching a verdict without appeal—not by jury, but by the council itself, chaired by Viacheslav Molotov and composed of high-ranking Soviet leaders including Lazar Kaganovich, Klim Voroshilov, Konstantin Ukhanov, and Avel Enukidze—appears to have been a laborious one, especially for the "commission of technical experts," which numbered the faithful Kolli in its midst:

There are still eyes which do not see. . . . No attempt was made to understand your project; instead, they vainly sought out a new monumentality, one worthy of the time, and failed to perceive it in the very essence of your designs. You were accused of

[42] For a chronicle of events in Algiers, see Mary McLeod, "Le Corbusier and Algiers," *Oppositions* 19–20 (Winter–Spring 1980): 55–85; McLeod, *Le Corbusier, from Regional Syndicalism to Vichy*, pp. 333–76; Jean-Pierre Giordani, "Le Corbusier et les projets pour la ville d'Alger," (Ph.D. thesis, Saint-Denis, Université Paris VIII, 1987).

[43] Stanislaus von Moos, "Les femmes d'Alger," in *Le Corbusier et la Méditerranée*, pp. 191–200.

[44] Le Corbusier, letter to Alexis Léger.

283. Le Corbusier, Palace of Soviets, Moscow, 1931–1932, model, overall view from the riverside.

284. Le Corbusier, "Plan Obus," Algiers, 1931–1935, version A, 1932, view of model.

having furnished a mere skeleton devoid of flesh and muscle rather than monumental architecture. Victor Vesnin and I tried hard to explain the broad lines of what you had achieved, and there was shouting![45]

Before the deadline for the competition entries, an unprecedented "workers' assessment" of the preliminary designs furnished a clear indication of what was to follow. On 18 November 1931, Arkadi Mordvinov presented these "preliminary designs" at the Stalin Factory (formerly the AMO) in

[45] Nikolai Kolli, letter to Le Corbusier and Pierre Jeanneret, Moscow, 25 April 1932, FLC.

Moscow, apparently before an unenthusiastic public whose own desires were themselves contradictory: the worker Fokin considered that "none of the projects leads anywhere. Here we see an old monastery, whereas what we need is something new, something that really expresses the dictatorship of the proletariat"; and for his part, the worker Filkov dismissed Iofan's project out of hand:

What is this? Is there anything solid about it? No, it is a mixture of styles.[46]

Other observers had already noted that "the first projects were not up to standard," or that they looked like "poor-quality designs for American schools."[47] In fact, however, these comments were part and parcel of a campaign organized by "proletarian" cultural organizations with a view to sabotaging the competition. In a poem to the greater glory of the future palace, the working-class bard Demian Bedny even challenged the "creative genius, the artist, the skilled architect" to ensure that

In Moscow no longer of white stone
But the red of her flag
In the heart of the city
Be raised the rostrum of the world
The tribune of tribunes.[48]

An early review of entries published in *Pravda* in January 1932 considered that the "heritage of the past" was all too present in the competition, and singled out Le Corbusier's designs for critical though deferential treatment:

Among the foreign entries, widespread attention has been given to the project by Le Corbusier, that eminent theorist and practitioner of the new architecture of the West. His auditorium designs constitute bold solutions. But his sparse "industrialist" approach is certainly questionable in its formal aspects, in that the building is treated as a sort of great congress hangar.[49]

Little evidence remains of the commission's working methods unless it be an article by N. Zapletin that makes passing mention of a classification based on the different modes of articulation of the two halls (back to back with the possibility of combination, whether superimposed, juxtaposed, or separate). But to the extent that the Palace of Soviets was "not a machine," Le Corbusier's project was clearly no longer in the running:

Le Corbusier's commissioned designs cultivate the aesthetics of a complex machine—a "melting pot" for large crowds of people—but their artistic and ideological significance disqualify them. It ought however to be noted that Le Corbusier's project contains a series of valuable and original proposals.[50]

On 28 February, the Council for the Construction of the Palace of Soviets awarded three first prizes to Ivan Zholtovsky, the veteran neo-Palladian; Boris Iofan, a young representative of the "proletarian" movement; and Hector Hamilton, an unknown British architect practising in the United States. Although the council, which considered the problem as one of "adapting the best methods of classical architecture to the achievements of modern building technique," mentioned in passing the "precious materials" (supplied by the foreign entrants) "which will be studied with the utmost care and attention in all future work," neither Le Corbusier nor any other foreign competitor was singled out for comment.[51]

Le Corbusier's project in fact came in for two quite distinct types of appraisal. Although it was attacked with some violence in the dailies, it received closer and more sympathetic attention from the architects. An exhibition of

[46] "Arkhitekturu v rabochie massy, osuzhdenie predvaritelnykh proektov D. Sovetov na zavode im. Stalina (b. AMO)," *Stroitelstvo Moskvy* 8, no. 10 (1931): 4–5.

[47] "Pervye proekty Dvortsa Sovetov," *Stroitelstvo Moskvy* 8, no. 8 (1931): 2–7.

[48] Demian Bedny, "Na vysshuiu stupen," in *Stroitelstvo Moskvy* 8, no. 8 (1931): 2.

[49] Gr. Roze, "Dvorets Sovetov (vystavka konkursnykh proektov)," *Pravda* (20 January 1932). A French translation of this article that Le Corbusier received is to be found in FLC.

[50] N. Zapletin, "Perelomny etap proletarskoi arkhitektury (po materialam komissii tekhnicheskoi espertizy)," *Stroitelstvo Moskvy* 9, no. 3 (1932): 28.

[51] Sovet stroitelstva Dvortsa sovetov, "O resultatakh rabot."

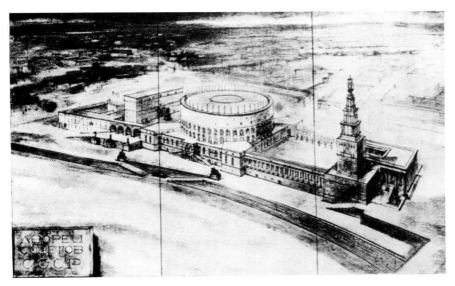

285. Ivan Zholtovsky, Palace of Soviets, Moscow, 1931, first prize (divided) at the international competition, perspective, in *Dvorets Sovetov* (Moscow: Izd. Vsekokhudozhnika, 1932).

286. Boris Iofan, Palace of Soviets, Moscow, 1931, first prize (divided) at the international competition, perspective, in *Dvorets Sovetov* (Moscow: Izd. Vsekokhudozhnika, 1932).

287. Hector Hamilton, Palace of Soviets, Moscow, 1931, first prize (divided) at the international competition, perspective, in *Dvorets Sovetov* (Moscow: Izd. Vsekokhudozhnika, 1932).

the projects at the Museum of Fine Arts, which overlooked the site, provided Alexei Tolstoy with the opportunity of publishing an article in *Izvestia* only a day before the verdict was announced. In this text entitled "The Roads to Monumentality," Tolstoy, having outlined the history of monumental architecture at great length, gave the new palace the modest aim of becoming the "eighth" wonder of the world while at the same time being the expression of the new society, for which the quintessentially imperialistic architecture of Le Corbusier and the Americans was quite unacceptable:

Americanism and Corbusianry have hitherto found a good number of partisans in this country, despite the fact that these two styles are hostile (and useless) to us. Corbusianry is quality of materials combined with the aesthetics of the High Bourgeoisie, whose sensory perceptions are restricted to the pleasures of the moment. Again, it is a geometrical form—that of a strongbox—in which the personality is free to evolve unencumbered by the world and spaces "devoured" by the eyes of the automobile. It is a latter-day feudal fortress—the home of a bandit protected by impregnable walls of gold. This is the ultimate devastation, a refusal of reality, a submission to materials, the cult of materials, fetishism; it is only one step away from the primitive condition of the psychological troglodyte.[52]

Tolstoy who, it must be said, also criticized the "primitive symbolism" of proposals submitted by the workers' collectives, found little in the exhibition that corresponded to the scope of the problem:

How can one resolve the extremely difficult question of how industrialization is to be expressed? Industrialization of the socialist state means the creation of an army of machines on which the physical labor of man can repose. Whence the liberation from servitude and the development of intellectual work, and the transition to a higher form of culture. In architecture, this is expressed by the control of mind over matter (the contrary of Corbusianry, in which matter predominates, reigns supreme and commands).

Given this preamble, Le Corbusier's project could now be rapidly brushed aside—but not without paying him discreet homage after all:

Le Corbusier's project is extremely "leftist" and amusing, being based on the aesthetics of the supercontemporary factory; it is a poem written in glass and steel. But where is the poem to the builders? Le Corbusier builds magnificent monuments to a refined form of exploitation.

The Soviet architects on the "commission of experts" were more measured in their judgment and—like Grigori Barkhin, who had designed the Moscow offices of *Izvestia*—took pains to furnish a precise account and assessment of the designs:

The sketched variants of the general plan, from the first (dated 6 October) to the last (22 November), indicate a gradual progression from complex combinations of isolated elements to the final, simplified version. Given this, the major elements of the project—two halls, annexes and administrative buildings—are not studied in any depth. This is indicative of Le Corbusier's creative process: he moves from the particular to the general, or, as he himself states in a lengthy explanatory text, "from the complicated to the synthetic." That such an approach makes it impossible to achieve sufficient overall coherence and integrity is clear not only here, but also in Le Corbusier's earlier designs for the Centrosoyuz and the League of Nations.[53]

Although Barkhin appreciated the "originality of the general composition of the great hall," he considered that its "vertical profile" had not been studied in sufficient detail. Above all, he criticized the fact that spectators must turn their backs on the stage in order to reach their seats. At the same time, while emphasizing its "utilitarianism," he admitted that the project was "of considerable interest." Shchusev thought "extremely valuable" the contribution of an "innovator whose ideas are always exceptionally intelligent and original," and thanked Le Corbusier for his "interpretation" of the brief. All in all, however,

[52] Alexei Tolstoy, "Poiski Monumental-nosti," *Izvestia* (27 February 1932). The term *korbiuzianstvo* is translated as "Corbusianry" rather than the more common "Corbusian-izm" because it rhymes in Tolstoy's discourse with *krestianstvo* ("peasantry").

[53] Arh. G. B. Barkhin, "Inostrannye arkhitektory na konkurse Dvortsa Sovetov," in Soiuz Sovetskikh Arkhitektorov, *Dvorets Sovetov*, pp. 83–84.

although Shchusev's criticisms of the internal organization of the auditoriums were mild, his rejection of the project as a whole was firm:

The author has devoted care and attention to problems of the building's structure and external appearance. So as to minimize its thickness, he has suspended the roof of the great hall from an enormous concrete parabola, which dominates the building's exterior and determines its overall character. The use of suspended tie beams exposed to atmospheric conditions cannot be considered a judicious solution for Moscow. And the parabolic arch, which makes the building as a whole look rather like a bridge or hangar, in no way corresponds to the idea of a Palace of Soviets.

Le Corbusier's proposal to introduce the industrial frame into the very heart of Moscow lends an incongruous tone to the form of the building. This error is aggravated even further by its position on the site, which is reminiscent of the disorder of an industrial zone.

All in all, despite controlled treatment of the different parts and of the interiors, Le Corbusier's project does not constitute a solution to the problem set in the competition and reveals itself to be a production of a somewhat academic character.[54]

LE CORBUSIER'S FURY

Before the winning entries were finally published in the twelfth issue of *Bauwelt*,[55] Le Corbusier was partially informed of the result by the former people's commissar, Anatoli Lunacharsky, and hastened to disseminate the news in a provocative fashion, while at the same time hedging his bets with an emphatic homage to Zholtovsky:

Message:
We have learned from M. Lunacharsky, People's Commissar of the Soviet Union, that the Palace of Soviets is to be executed in the Italian Renaissance style by M. Zholtovsky of Moscow.
M. Zholtovsky is a truly talented architect.[56]

Faced with what he later judged to have been a "blind force, a latent urge, nature, something primitive out of the Steppes, which put the clock back,"[57] Le Corbusier appealed to Lunacharsky on two separate occasions, first at a meeting in Geneva, and then in a letter:

The Palace of Soviets, just like the League of Nations, will be built in the style of the Italian Renaissance!

The Italian of the Renaissance—like the Romans and Greeks—built in *stone*. However great the conception, the boundaries of the Renaissance's actual achievement, and its subordination to the laws of gravity, were determined by stone construction.

In the age of the Renaissance there were enlightened princes who ruled over the masses. A gulf separated the rich from the masses. A gulf separated the palace where the prince lived from the masses of people.

The USSR, a Union of Soviet proletarian republics, will erect its palace, which will be superior and beyond the people.

Let us not delude ourselves with rhetoric: I know perfectly well that the people—and the *muzhik* too—greatly admire the palaces of kings and that they eagerly ornament their wooden beds with pediments as on a church.

But what should the thinking leaders of the Soviet republic do: move forward, or patronize and cultivate tastes that only attest to human frailty?

We were expecting from the USSR an example of authority, edification and leadership, since such an example expresses the noblest and purest judgment.

[54] Akademik A. V. Shchusev, "Mezhdunarodny konkurs Dvortsa Sovetov," *Dvorets Sovetov*, pp. 77–78.

[55] Max Meyer, "Ergebnis des Wettbewerbs um den Palast der Sowjets in Moskau," *Bauwelt*, Berlin, no. 12 (1932): 6–8; Max Meyer and Max Höchster, "Die Vorentwürfe für den Räte-Palast in Moskau," ibid., pp. 77–78.

[56] Le Corbusier, handwritten note, 10 March 1932, FLC.

[57] Le Corbusier, *Sur les quatre routes* (Paris: Gallimard, 1941), p. 140; English translation: *The 4 Routes* (London: Dennis Dobson, 1947), p. 125.

288. Anatoli Lunacharsky, 1931.

[58] Le Corbusier, letter to Anatoli Lunacharsky, Paris, 13 March 1932, FLC. English translation see Starr, "Le Corbusier and the USSR: New Documentation," p. 128.

[59] Anatoli Lunacharsky, letter to Le Corbusier, Geneva, 20 April 1932, FLC.

[60] Le Corbusier, letter to Anatoli Lunacharsky, Paris, 10 April 1932, FLC.

[61] Le Corbusier, letter to Anatoli Lunacharsky, Paris, 25 April 1932, FLC.

[62] Anatoli Lunacharsky, "Socialistichesky arkhitekturny monument," *Stroitelstvo Moskvy* 10, nos. 5–6 (1933): 6.

[63] Sheila Fitzpatrick, *The Commissariat of Enlightenment: Soviet Organization of Education and the Arts under Lunacharsky, Oct. 1917–1921* (Cambridge: Cambridge University Press, 1971), p. 13.

[64] Ibid., pp. 89–109.

[65] Anatoli Lunacharsky, cited in M. Kut, "Dvorets Sovetov," *Sovetskoe Iskusstvo* (26 January 1932).

And if this is not to be? Then there is no more USSR, no doctrine, no mystique, or anything else!!!

The very thought that I should have to pose such questions in our days is *awful*.[58]

But Lunacharsky carried little weight in the new balance of power within the USSR. Although he declared himself Le Corbusier's "sincere admirer," all he could do was promise to pass on the "beautiful Russian translation of [his] long letter" to Mikhailov, the council's secretary, and undertake to support him in his attempts to visit Moscow.[59] In the meantime, Le Corbusier had intervened a second time "to evoke the position of [his] colleagues at the CIAM," who were "a good deal more affected than [he was] by the Moscow verdict."[60]

Direct relations between the two men came to a close with a letter of thanks from Le Corbusier; henceforth Giedion acted as intermediary. In this final letter, Le Corbusier pleaded that "danger walks at the hero's side, and for those who risk everything for a beautiful adventure (the plans for Moscow) the path is full of pitfalls."[61] Lunacharsky later paid homage, in terms relatively out of phase with the new climate in Moscow, to the "talented French architect Le Corbusier, [who] has sent what is, in its own way, a masterpiece of the functionalist style."[62] He had always been relatively prudent in his reactions to the nihilistic excesses of the avant-garde; in particular, he had resigned immediately after his appointment as people's commissar on hearing (false) news of the destruction of the church of Saint Basil during the 1917 Bolshevik uprising.[63] This episode bears further witness to the fact that he steadfastly refused to turn his back on history, although he subscribed to many of the Proletkult's ideas for the creation of a new working-class culture.[64] Henceforth, he would be a moderately sincere supporter of a "critical assimilation" of the art of the past:

The new construction must be grounded more in classical than bourgeois architecture—in other words, in the architecture of the Greeks, for Marx held different positions on Greece and Rome.

This does not mean that those who say, "We shall build like the Athenians" are necessarily right, nor that those who say, "We shall build like the Americans"—or those strongly influenced by engineering techniques, whose sole aim is to meet utilitarian requirements—are wrong.

What is needed is a new type of construction. The attempt to combine two completely different principles, such as the ancient and the modern, can only lead to flagrant contradictions; but it is absolutely essential to take into account such possibilities to the extent that proletarian building initiatives should be based on neither. One ought rather to master both approaches, thus enabling a third to emerge in their wake. Synthesis is not eclecticism.[65]

Lunacharsky also took pains to dissociate Le Corbusier's method from that of the "functionalists," as witness another extract from this speech delivered before the "proletarian architects" on 14 January 1932:

A word or two in the ear of those artists who, like Le Corbusier, are exposed to the strong influence of engineering technique and proclaim this from the rooftops. Le Corbusier's teaching is based on the idea that beauty is no longer in question—or rather, that there is today a new kind of beauty. In the pursuit of his goals, man has created objects such as the new transatlantic liners, which far transcend what artistic thought has achieved; and architecture must draw its object lessons from this. But Le Corbusier is no mere functionalist. Pure functionalism states that architectural production resides in the best possible response to the building's intended use. This is far from being the case with Le Corbusier, who declares that poetry can only emerge if you take and combine engineering features so as to obtain an artistic effect.[66]

In one of his letters to Lunacharsky, Le Corbusier offered to meet Zholtovsky, "a true, serious architect, with much talent," and added:

With him I shall talk about architecture more satisfactorily than with most of my Western colleagues who call themselves "modern architects."[67]

Yet such offers continued to fall on deaf ears.

THE CIAM ENTERS THE FRAY

Despite the compromise toward which Le Corbusier appeared to be heading, he was in fact launching a new League of Nations campaign—with the assistance of the very organization that had been born in reaction to the failure of modern architecture in Geneva: the CIAM. Subsequent to a meeting of the CIAM's executive body, CIRPAC, in Barcelona from 29 to 31 March, a telegram was despatched to "Monsieur Stalin, President of the Council of the People's Commissars." The text of the telegram included Le Corbusier's less virulent draft reproaches but omitted passages stigmatizing a result that appeared "to have doomed the objectives of the USSR to a miserably mediocre, retrograde and decadent end," and which constituted "an insult to world Revolution." By their decision to construct, "in the very heart of the Soviet Union, the resurrected cadaver of secular autocracies, the Committee has betrayed the grandiose venture of the Five-Year Plan with criminal thoughtlessness."[68]

The final text countersigned by Le Corbusier's friends was more measured in its political connotations, yet equally clear in its indignation at this "dramatic betrayal." The letter begins with a reminder of the declared aims of the competition; this was intended to place the Soviets in an untenable position relative to their own declarations:

In 1931 the government of the USSR, through the intermediary of a Committee for the Construction of the Palace of Soviets, called for worldwide cooperation when it launched an international competition with a view to procuring plans for the Palace. No jury was designated, yet it seemed obvious that the verdict would take its inspiration from the broad lines of the Five-Year Plan and constitute the most resounding manifestation of contemporary thought. Through the unfalsifiable language of architecture, the Palace of Soviets was to express the Revolution accomplished by the new civilization of modern times.[69]

In the CIRPAC's view, the Russians had therefore betrayed their own policies:

The verdict of the committee is a direct affront to the spirit of the revolution and the fulfillment of the Five-Year Plan, turns its back on the inspirations of modern society which found its first expression in Soviet Russia, and sanctions the ceremonial architecture of the old monarchies. The Palace of Soviets, which is offered to the world as the crowning achievement of the Five-Year Plan, will reveal the utter subservience of modern techniques to the spiritual reaction. In the form that the committee intends to give it, therefore, the Palace of Soviets will embody the old regimes and manifest complete disdain for the enormous cultural effort of Modern Times. Dramatic betrayal!

In a frontal attack on the man who had yet to become the "Great Guide of Arts and Letters," the CIRPAC also exercised a relatively precise form of blackmail concerning the fourth CIAM, which, for a whole variety of reasons relat-

[66] Anatoli Lunacharsky, "Rech o proletarskoi arkhitekture," *Arkhitektura SSSR* 2, no. 8 (1934): 3–7. This is a (posthumous) transcription of the address; an earlier version is to be found in M. Kut, "Dvorets Sovetov."

[67] Le Corbusier, letter to Anatoli Lunacharsky, Paris, 13 March 1932, FLC. English translation in Starr, "Le Corbusier and the USSR: New Documentation," p. 129.

[68] Le Corbusier, draft of a letter to "Monsieur Staline," handwritten, undated (April 1932), FLC.

[69] Le Corbusier, "Manifeste des CIAM à Monsieur Staline," handwritten, 19 April 1932, FLC.

ing to the German members' positions and Le Corbusier's firm intention to defend his "Response to Moscow," was scheduled to be held in the Russian capital:

The CIRPAC has decided to address itself to the supreme authority of the USSR in order to warn him of the gravity of the above-mentioned events, and considers that the spirit of the committee's decision constitutes an error that must not be allowed to stand. It therefore asks him, by an opportune intervention, to have the committee's verdict modified in accordance with the desires of the elites. For, were the committee's choice for the construction of the Palace of Soviets to be maintained, it is to be doubted whether the CIRPAC, which is committed in the public eye both to its previous work and to its future destiny, would be able to consider the USSR as a suitable setting for a fruitful congress on a subject that will suffer no compromise: the functional city.[70]

Several days later, Cor. van Eesteren and Sigfried Giedion signed a second message, one as confidential as the first, inviting Stalin and the people's commissars to make "an essential gesture in order to avoid this catastrophe."[71] This message was sent by registered mail, together with a photomontage by Giedion in which Hamilton's project is seen to resemble the religious architecture of the expressionist Fritz Höger and the commercial buildings of Berlin.[72] Thus the competition, which put an end to Le Corbusier's illusions regarding the "Promised Land"—the first nation to take him seriously as an expert of international stature—also marked the beginnings of the break between the CIAM and the Soviet Union. The preparations for the fourth congress were, however, too far advanced to be abandoned because of the misfortunes of one of its members, as Ernst May, Fred Forbat, and Hans Schmidt explained in a letter to the CIAM executive, adding that "by a stroke of luck, the existence of the protest letter to Stalin is practically unknown here, as it is to Stalin himself" and criticizing the "frenzied accents" of the telegram's "threat concerning the Moscow congress."[73]

In December 1932 Giedion was in Moscow finalizing details for the congress, and chaired what was doubtless the only CIAM meeting ever to be held on Soviet ground. On Giedion's request, Le Corbusier sent him a letter containing, in the margin, a suggested title for a "conference outside the conference, to be held before a large public": "The Spirit [of] Great Public Works." But Giedion was aware of the conflicts at work in Moscow; in his reply he indicated that "the Congress will be of great importance as an opposition group," and added, "You are much talked about in Russia, but for the moment in the same way as one speaks of Picasso and Braque."[74] Further preparations, which were pursued until late in 1933, reveal that the sudden decision to postpone the congress and, finally, to hold it on the shores of the Mediterranean, was precipitated not so much by the fate of the Palace of Soviets competition, as by subsequent changes in Soviet attitudes to the CIAM.[75] The shadow of the Soviet controversy would, however, follow the CIAM to Athens, where Le Corbusier indulged in violent attacks on Zholtovsky—attacks that were duly reported back to Moscow.[76]

INTERNATIONAL CRITICAL ASSESSMENT

The CIAM was not the only foreign observer to view the competition as evidence of a spectacular about-face in Soviet architectural policy. Numerous

[70] Ibid.

[71] CIAM, "Message to Stalin," 28 April 1932, FLC.

[72] The acknowledgment of receipt of this letter is to be found in the van Eesteren archives. See Jos Bosman, "CIAM 1928–1959: Inwieweit ist die *communis opinio* der modernen Bewegung eine Schöpfung Giedions?" in *Sigfried Giedion 1888–1968: Der Entwurf einer modernen Tradition*, ed. Werner Oechslin (Zurich: Amman Verlag, 1989), pp. 127–45.

[73] Fred Forbat, Ernst May, and Hans Schmidt, letter to the CIAM, Moscow, 24 July 1932, gta/ETH Zurich.

[74] Sigfried Giedion, letter to Le Corbusier, Zurich, 27 December 1932, gta/ETH Zurich.

[75] The French CIAM group held another preparatory meeting on 27 February 1933 (see the minutes by Karl Moser, gta/ETH Zurich); the telegram postponing the congress was not sent to Moscow until 22 March. See Borngräber, "Le Corbusier a Mosca," p. 85; Marco de Michelis, "Ville fonctionnelle, ville soviétique: Une impossible rencontre," in Cohen, de Michelis, and Tafuri, *URSS 1917–1978*, pp. 106–8.

[76] During the congress, a protest note was sent to the Soviet embassy in Athens. Today it can be found in the VOKS archives (information communicated by Irina Kokkinaki).

289. Sigfried Giedion, protest photo-montage sent to Stalin in the name of CIAM.

commentaries and analyses of the results, which were published on the front pages, emanated from representatives of all the major currents of world opinion, thus bringing the Soviets' verdict into the limelight.[77] These critical analyses fired the pages of the press for nigh on two years—that is, throughout the period of the last two phases of the competition, which saw the final victory of Boris Iofan, with whom Vladimir Gelfreikh and Vladimir Shchuko had joined forces in decorating a monument that was now a giant pedestal for a colossal statue of Lenin.

In *Casabella*, Edoardo Persico drew parallels between the Palace of Soviets and the League of Nations and remarked that "this competition could serve, in architecture at least, as a declaration of the failure of an aesthetics of con-

[77] Hamilton's designs, for instance, were published in *Comœdia*: "Moscou aura un Palais des Soviets," *Comœdia* (9 March 1932).

290. Alexander, Leonid, and Victor Vesnin, Palace of Soviets, Moscow, third phase, 1933.

tent."[78] In the United States, where the architectural press discovered the hitherto unknown and henceforth illustrious Hector Hamilton,[79] Talbot Faulkner Hamlin, writing in the *New Republic,* pondered over the "official death of the international style" in Russia:

The picture of a new Renaissance under Soviet auspices is surprising; the romantic basis of it, so similar to that of the classic revivals a hundred years ago, more surprising still. Yet stranger things have happened, and where a central body is so all-powerful in creating taste as in Russia almost anything is possible. And it must not be forgotten that without doubt the best secular work in Russia is the classic revival work of the early nineteenth century. That tradition is evidently still alive.

This whole right-about face in Russian architecture has more than a historical importance. Perhaps it may be true that the International Style symbolizes a brutal subjugation of mankind, of life, to machinery. So Frank Lloyd Wright has claimed; so it has seemed to many others. Perhaps our skyscraper modernism is expressive of exactly as material, as brutal, a profit-hunting at any cost. What, then, is the future—our future? Shall we, too, be forced to turn back to reexamine and rework the past? Or is there another, more creative, way?[80]

In a letter to Le Corbusier, Oscar Storonov, coeditor of the first volume of the *Œuvre complète,* who had emigrated to the United States and who, along with Alfred Kastner, had received one of the second prizes, attributed Hamilton's success to the intrigues of Albert Kahn, "God-engineer and pig-architect to the Soviets."[81] Le Corbusier's Paris friends, past and present, joined in the controversy. Amédée Ozenfant published, in the pages of *L'Intransigeant,* an open letter in response to Camille Mauclair's attack on Le Corbusier as a

[78] Edoardo Persico, "Due Palazzi a Ginevra ed a Mosca," *Casabella* 82 (October 1934): 44–48. The eclectic traditionalist Piacentini took pains to avoid criticizing the Soviets: "Il Palazzo dei Soviet a Mosca," *Architettura,* Rome, 13 (March 1934): 129–40.

[79] "Prize-winning Designs for the Palace of the Soviets in Moscow," *The Architectural Record* 71 (April 1932); "Soviet Palace Competition," *The Architectural Forum* 41 (March 1932); Knud Lönberg-Holm, "Monuments and Instruments," *Shelter* 2 (May 1932): 5–8.

[80] Talbot Faulkner Hamlin, "Greece in the Kremlin," in *The New Republic* New York, (28 December 1932): 187.

[81] Oscar Storonov, letter to Le Corbusier, New York, 22 March 1932, FLC.

"Bolshevik." As evidence of the virtues of modern architecture in the "influence of France on peoples that are looking to find a way," Ozenfant cited the fact that "the simple mores we have advocated should have been understood in Russia," and commented with irony that Mauclair was henceforth to be compared with Alexei Tolstoy.[82] For Jean Badovici, the competition verdict marked the end of "the heroic phase of modern architecture in the Soviet Union":

We well understand that various considerations have led the jury to dismiss Le Corbusier's design, which, they claim, would have destroyed the overall harmony of the Kremlin and which was not without its faults from certain points of view. Le Corbusier ought to have maintained both the city of the Kremlin and architectural principles. But in its insidious recommendations for a return to the Greek, and above all the Roman, tradition, the Committee's report has been harmful. With support from Count Tolstoy in the Soviet press, the ex-academicians are against all instances of modern architecture. Le Corbusier and May have built little, and always with difficulty. Little of theirs gets beyond the design phase, on the pretext that money is lacking for modern architectural productions.[83]

291. Boris Iofan, Vladimir Gelfreikh, Vladimir Shchuko, Palace of Soviets, Moscow, final project, 1934.

[82] Amédée Ozenfant, "Lettre ouverte à Camille Mauclair," *L'Intransigeant* (20 March 1933), quoted in Ozenfant, *Mémoires*, p. 258.

[83] Jean Badovici, "Le moment héroïque de l'architecture moderne en URSS," *L'Architecture Vivante* 11 (Spring–Summer 1933): 22. This was to be the last issue of the magazine founded in 1923.

[84] Karel Teige, "Vyvoj sovetské archi-tektury," Prague, 1936, reprinted in Karel Teige and Jiří Kroha, *Avantgardní architektura* (Prague: Československy Spisovatel, 1969), pp. 70–71. See also Karel Teige, "Dvorec Sovetov v Moskve," *Žijeme* 2 (1932): 20–23.

[85] Max Raphaël, "Das Sowjetpalais, eine marxistische Kritik an einer reaktionären Ar-chitektur," 1933, reprinted in *Für eine demo-kratische Architektur*, with an afterword by Jutta Held (Frankfurt: S. Fischer Verlag, 1976), pp. 129–30. Max Raphaël (1889–1951) was interested in art theory, but he also wrote a large number of texts on architecture. Some of these concern the work of Auguste Perret or André Lurçat; Raphaël gave a series of lectures in Lurçat's studio in 1934. See Cohen, "L'architecture d'André Lurçat (1894–1970)," pp. 589–606.

[86] Max Raphaël, letters to Le Corbusier, Paris, 22 October 1933 and 18 February 1934, FLC. Raphaël contributed critical stud-ies of Le Corbusier's work in two articles: "Das Werk von Le Corbusier," *Davoser Revue*, Davos (15 March 1930), and "Ist die moderne Architektur international?" 1933, reprinted in *Für eine demokratische Architektur*, pp. 27–32. The latter text compares Le Corbusier's work with that of Lurçat.

[87] Moshe Lewin, "L'État et les classes so-ciales en URSS 1929–1932," *Actes de la Re-cherche en Sciences Sociales*, no. 1 (February 1976): 2–31.

[88] Victor Nekrasov et al., letter to Le Cor-busier, Kiev, undated (1932), FLC. This cor-respondence is recalled by Nekrasov himself: Victor Nekrasov, *Pervoe znakomstvo* (Moscow: Sovetsky Pisatel, 1960), pp. 103–8; S. Freder-ick Starr has discussed it: "Deux lettres in-édites de Le Corbusier à Victor Nékrassov," *Cahiers du Monde Russe et Soviétique* 21 (April–June 1980): 201–7; English translation of this letter in Starr, "Le Corbusier and the USSR," p. 130.

At the same time, the competition furnished an occasion for most left-wing European critics to formulate often astonishing theories concerning the rela-tionship between architecture and politics. In a 1936 text, "The development of Soviet architecture," Karel Teige sharply criticized Iofan's project and the general tone of the competition. Far from harking on his long-standing differ-ences of opinion, Teige now considered Le Corbusier's analysis in the second volume of his *Œuvre complète* to be the "most considered judgment" on the whole affair.[84] This was also the case of the German philosopher Max Raphaël, who took refuge in Paris in 1932, and who wrote a lengthy document to Stalin, a "Marxist analysis of a reactionary architecture," in which he criticized both the competition brief and the taste for monumentality that had perme-ated the whole process. Raphaël claimed that "the bureaucracy had earmarked a considerable part of national revenues for a project that is of no immediate necessity and for which no Marxist solution can at present be found." Further, he viewed Iofan's winning designs as "the expression of an abstract, central-ized and dominant bureaucracy," and advocated a simultaneous reversion to true Marxist criticism and internationalist culture.[85]

In an unfinished passage, Raphaël wanted to study Le Corbusier's project, "since I am in disagreement with both the jury's and Zapletin's analysis of your work," and to compare it with Iofan's prizewinning project. He had, however, to send the article off without meeting Le Corbusier.[86] Yet Raphaël's analysis of the new Soviet bureaucracy furnished new insights into the political and sociological context of the competition.

The cultural shift, in the Soviet Union, toward realistic, narrative themes, as advocated by certain "proletarian" organizations, cannot be attributed merely to one of Stalin's authoritarian gestures, but must rather be seen as the culmi-nating point in the profound transformation of the ruling classes and, over and above the intelligentsia, as a direct consequence of collectivization. The growth in the number of intellectuals and "technicians" thus went hand in hand with changes in their social origins and education, which have been well described by Moshe Lewin,[87] a fact that would account for the provincialism of Soviet critical references and their quest for national forms and roots, in contrast to the first wave of revolutionary leaders, who had remained deeply attached to Western culture.

QUESTIONS FROM KIEV

Oddly enough, Le Corbusier was himself contacted by a number of outspoken and enlightened representatives of the emerging intelligentsia. In 1934, a group of students from Kiev wrote to him on the subject of the Palace of Soviets:

1. What do you think of the results of the international competition for the Palace of Soviets in Moscow?

2. Whom do you consider to be the most eminent among contemporary architects in western Europe and the Soviet Union?

3. Do you not find that in recent times architecture has shown a marked tendency to drift to the right, and how would you explain this?

4. How do you explain the fact that some of the most interesting and original works, in terms of modern architecture in western Europe, are churches?[88]

Le Corbusier sent the students, among whom was the future writer Victor Nekrasov, a serious reply denouncing the "bourgeois caricature . . . selected by the jury" and wondering how it could be "tolerated in Moscow":

The Soviet authorities asked me for a project. The brief was such that we had to use the whole range of modern techniques. For three months, fifteen draughtsmen busied themselves with an analytical study of the project; in the last month, we worked day and night in our office in an atmosphere of total enthusiasm. The tiniest, most sensitive details were analyzed with intense interest. With every discovery, every solution, one or another of the team cried out, "They'll be happy in Moscow." Indeed, we all believed *that the project would be examined technically*, in the context of building and architectural realities. The project focused on the following basic questions: *circulation, visibility, acoustics, aeration-ventilation, statics*. And the verdict? None of these points was taken into consideration! Not one. Prizes were awarded for sketches of facades and academic domes; in its report the jury *recognized that the winning designs had furnished no indication of how the ceilings of the halls were to be held up, their acoustics*, their heating and ventilation!!! The crowning achievement of the Five-Year Plan collapsed amid a "spirit of Geneva."

The disappointment of the fifteen draughtsmen is scarcely to be imagined, such was their anger and disheartenment.

Le Corbusier avoided answering the second (and most personal) question and was somewhat evasive in his answers to the fourth, but he interpreted the "drift to the right" cited by Nekrasov as "an instance of regression" in a nation that constituted "a new social order in a bourgeois world." In relation to the "academicians"—"an element of paralysis and regression"—and the "young" who were "at the outset of their journey," Le Corbusier reaffirmed his faith in paternal "authority":

What is crucial is that *authority is vigilant*, and *requires* you to *move forward*—to advance and not look back. They want you to practice *nationalism*. Is this not an astonishing item in the Soviet vocabulary? Modern sciences (the most efficient and advanced) are to be applied to regional, ethnic and climatic conditions. This is *a true and useful form of nationalism*.[89]

A further exchange of letters ensued, in which the discussion shifted, on Nekrasov's request, toward the question of the relation between painting and sculpture on the one hand, and architecture on the other. In his second letter, Le Corbusier referred to his "rights" to a joint project with the Vesnins, who appeared to have been on the ascendant at this stage of the competition, while at the same time giving vent to his "sorrow":

On several occasions I have been asked to draw up plans of cities for the Soviet Union; unfortunately, it was all hot air. I am extremely sorry about this, for I am currently in possession of truths that I should like to share with others. I have studied the basic social truths in such depth that I have been the first to create, in a natural way, *the great classless city*, harmonious and joyful. It sometimes pains me to think that in the USSR I am resisted for reasons that to me do not appear valid.[90]

While Iofan's project achieved its ultimate triumph, Le Corbusier's designs were exploited in an unexpected manner. In the fall of 1933, Sergei Eisenstein, Moisei Ginzburg, and one of the brothers Vesnin were chosen to assess various projects for a monumental center at Nalchik, in the Caucasus. Eisenstein thus became involved in the debate over the requisite "national character" of architecture in the city.

[89] Le Corbusier, letter to Victor Nekrasov, Paris, 13 October 1932, FLC.

[90] Le Corbusier, letter to Victor Nekrasov, Paris, 20 December 1932, FLC. Nekrasov's second letter has been lost. In a third letter, Nekrasov, who in the meantime had spoken to Ginzburg, asked for clarification on the question of decoration at Centrosoyuz, and concerning the 'Ville Radieuse' in relation to Soviet conditions": Victor Nekrasov et al., letter to Le Corbusier, Kiev, 28 February 1933, FLC.

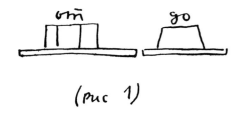

(рис 1)

рис. 2

292. Sergei Eisenstein, reflections on national architecture for the Kabardino-Balkarian Republic, 1934.
(1) The vernacular hat and its geometry.

293. Sergei Eisenstein, reflections on national architecture for the Kabardino-Balkarian Republic, 1934.
(2) The recycling of Le Corbusier's Palace of Soviets' forms.

[91] Sergei Eisenstein, "Rodin et Rilke," in Albéra, *Cinématisme*, p. 265.
[92] Sergei Eisenstein, "Prikliuchenie na kurorte," handwritten, TsGALI, Moscow; published and discussed in Oleg Khadyka, "'Prikliuchenie na kurorte' S. Eisensteina," *Tvorchestvo*, no. 11 (1971): 18–20. On the project criticized by Eisenstein, see Sergei Kozhin, "Dvorets Kultury v Nalchike," *Arkhitektura SSSR* 2, no. 8 (1934): 17; M. P. Parusnikov and I. N. Sobolev, "Dvorets Kultury Kabardino-Balkarii v Nalchike," ibid., pp. 18–19.

A PALACE—A HAT: EISENSTEIN'S USE OF LE CORBUSIER'S SCHEME

Eisenstein made fun of a project for a house of the Soviets by one of Zholtovsky's pupils—a cross between Piranesi and the Palazzo Pitti, which, for the sake of "interest," was "peopled with characters draped in robes, in poses characteristic of Ghirlandaio or Uccello." Eisenstein had already shown a marked interest in the theme of the glass wall:

The architecture of glass walls, an enlargement of the earliest openings envisaged—windows—permits unlimited lateral expansion of the dwelling as far as mountain chains and the horizon lines of the ocean; only the constraints of window panes, within which the inventiveness of Le Corbusier or Gropius places Man, could hamper the illusion created in this way.[91]

Eisenstein denounced the "show-offish," "do-it-yourself" character, and "profanation of Le Corbusier" and concluded that they "discredited the new architecture." In his description of the countryside and traditional housing, whose *genius loci* stood in marked contrast to imported solutions, Eisenstein—shifting from panoramic vistas of the valleys of the Caucasus to a close-up—made a surprising proposal for new buildings:

Where then are we to find an aesthetic criterion for constructions? Where a *specific*, Balkarian-Kabardian harmonics corresponding to the extremely fertile architectural ideas and forms that Le Corbusier has brought us?
Three fellows approached in a cloud of dust.
And on their heads they wore . . . that melody in embryo, plastic in form, which Beethoven discovered on his faltering course toward his symphony, or which Rimsky-Korsakov captured in the three notes of the bullfinch and in the crowing of the cock in *Snow White*.
On their heads, they wore snow-white felt hats.
Their simple yet very beautiful shape might form the basis of an infinite number of variations in any number of classic problems posed by volume and surface.
Let us therefore try to get straight to the point: the beauty of their forms should fulfil three conditions: capacity, enclosure and protection from the sun's rays. In other words, the envelope, the idea of the building and its cornice.
Let's turn the hat over,
make incisions at various levels,
transform the cornice into a balcony.
Place it on its side.
We can obtain variations on any number of themes!
The rest is a question of site, function, concrete, relief and so on.[92]

Unaware that his project was being exploited in this way in the Caucasus, Le Corbusier sent the model of the Palace of Soviets to New York, where it was exhibited at the Museum of Modern Art in 1935 before touring the country—without, however, being returned to Paris. Three years later, in a letter to Wallace Harrison, one of the architects of the Rockefeller Center, Le Corbusier, who was then short of money, proposed selling the model to the museum and emphasized "the value to America of these works":

The rare museums that possess Renaissance models are extremely proud of them.

Why should the Palace of Soviets not one day represent something like a Renaissance, too?[93]

Le Corbusier tried on several occasions to secure the help of Fernand Léger, then in New York. He confided to him, "Given the present crisis the dollar changed into French francs will do nicely."[94] But whether or not Le Corbusier received the dollars, the model stayed in New York, and fond memories were all that lived on in Paris. In time, moreover, he became more indulgent in his attitude to the Soviets. As early as 1934—at a time when his battle to recover the Centrosoyuz fees was starting—he had already considered their arguments "reasonable given the historical context" and judged that "an incipient civilization such as Russia's requires florid, appealing, substantial nourishment and everyday canons of beauty for its people."[95]

Although the organic forms of the palace, which Le Corbusier came to acknowledge as premature, persisted in his subsequent architectural achievements as the basis of a new definition of organic art, also inspired by his early education at La Chaux-de-Fonds, and some of its interior features finally materialized in the fifties in Chandigarh's Assembly, the strong ties of affection with Moscow had gradually disintegrated.

[93] Le Corbusier, letter to Wallace Harrison, Paris, 15 October 1938, FLC. At the same time, and for identical reasons, Le Corbusier succeeded in selling the original plans for the League of Nations to the Eidgenössische Technische Hochschule in Zurich. See Werner Oechslin, "Kleinliche Begebenheiten—und ein grosses Projekt," in Oechslin, *Le Corbusier und Pierre Jeanneret: Das Wettbewerbsprojekt für den Völkerbundspalast in Genf 1927*, pp. 8–19.

[94] Le Corbusier, letter to Fernand Léger, Paris, 15 October 1938, FLC.

[95] Le Corbusier, introduction to Boesiger, *Œuvre complète 1929–1934*, p. 13.

CHAPTER

8

Moscow Temperatures, Paris Atmosphere

DESPITE THE REJECTION of his theoretical positions concerning the reconstruction of Moscow, and the failure of his Palace of Soviets competition entry, Le Corbusier did not easily vanish from the Russian architectural scene.

In 1932, when the last two phases of the Palace of Soviets competition culminated in the definitive selection of the project submitted by Iofan, Gelfreikh, and Shchuko, the various competing organizations that had lent so much vitality to the Soviet architectural debate were fused into a single body, the Union of Soviet Architects. In the five years between its founding and its first congress in 1937 (which was postponed on several occasions) the Union was the focus of more or less polite controversy over the question of "the assimilation of the heritage of the past" and the "national" face of Soviet architecture. At the same time, Soviet design and production was beset with violent contradictions, as witness the subterranean pluralism of the stations of the Moscow subway inaugurated in 1935. In the housing sphere, Zholtovsky's neo-Palladian initiatives found an echo in the researches of many architects, including Andrei Burov, who, along with Boris Blokhin, used industrial components in their apartment buildings, where the excess of applied ornament made for a distinctly ironic emphasis.[1]

The tortuous route that led Soviet architecture to "socialist realism" was not, however, entirely cut off from world culture—not, that is, until the end of the decade, when Russian references began to predominate. The influence of Western production on the debate over architecture and urban forms remained strong, whether in terms of American technical innovations, or of the return to monumentalism that was then taking place in Mussolini's Italy, the architecture of which was the object of a detailed study in Russia.[2] In the chronicle of events concerning "architecture abroad" (a review devoted to Western architecture bore this simple title),[3] the French scene made regular appearances, and Le Corbusier himself was considered from a variety of different (and often contradictory) viewpoints. Given the controversy surrounding the completion and inauguration of Centrosoyuz, its ineluctable legacy formed the initial basis for continuing discussion. But the material heritage of Centrosoyuz—a building so embarrassing after 1936 that, despite its size, it simply disappeared from panoramas of Soviet architectural production since 1917—was caught up within a network of less tangible traces of Corbusian influence on the work of young Soviet architects.

294. Andrei Burov, Boris Blokhin, housing block on Leningrad Avenue, Moscow, 1939–1940.

THE CONDEMNATION OF "CORBUSIANIZM"

The existence, in the Soviet Union, of a whole gamut of buildings that exploited Le Corbusier's design paradigms was revealed to the French public by the Moscow correspondent of *L'Architecture d'Aujourd'hui*, Mikhail Ilin, who first spoke of "Corbusianizm" in an article published at the end of 1931—that is, at the outset of the Palace of Soviets competition. Ilin took pains to pinpoint certain formal borrowings and typological approaches exemplified in a number of edifices, and his analysis deserves to be quoted at length:

These various buildings reflect the same principles in the organization of forms and volumes as those that we find in the work of Le Corbusier.

. . . The Moscow planetarium by the architects Barchsch and Siniavsky is the first construction to have been designed on these novel lines: the entrance to Centrosoyuz and the staircase in the villa at Garches have been adopted, thus demonstrating that it is possible to use Corbusian forms in buildings of quite different significance. The

[1] On the new Soviet architectural scene, see Kopp, *L'architecture de la période stalinienne*, and Vladimir Paperny, *Kultura "dva"* (Ann Arbor, Mich.: Ardis, 1984).

[2] L. I. Rempel, *Arkhitektura poslevoennoi Italii* (Moscow: Izd. Vses. Akademii Arkhitektury, 1935). Rempel was imprisoned following the publication of this study, which had escaped the attention of the censors.

[3] The birth of this review was heralded with some interest by Ginzburg: "Arkhitektura za rubezhom," *Arkhitektura SSSR* 3, no. 1 (1935): 63.

second example is the housing scheme for the employees of the Commissariat of Finance by the architects Ginzburg and Milinis. This building merits detailed analysis in that its "Corbusianizm" is at once more real and more broadly based.

. . . The building combines elements of the large house at the Weissenhof (multiplied on several floors) and of the one in Ville-d'Avray. The communal dwelling is to the main building what the "living room" is to the massive forms of the house as a whole. The solarium is also taken from Ville-d'Avray and the Weissenhof. The organization of the interior is derived from the two corridors that run through the whole length of the block. . . . The communal building extends to the right and the office block to the left, thus affording optimal deployment of the architectural form. This layout was influenced by Le Corbusier's marvelous League of Nations' project which, unfortunately, has not been executed. This palace, which I consider to be the most beautiful expression of contemporary architecture, has already influenced large numbers of architects. Even Le Corbusier was unable to free himself entirely of its influence when he came to build Centrosoyuz in Moscow.

In the external treatment of the immense students' communal dormitories near the Donskoy cloister, "Corbusianizm" has triumphed once again. The windows extend in a 200-meter-long strip; the winding stairs on the terraces and the sheds reproduce, albeit on a larger scale, those of the Ozenfant house, one of Le Corbusier's earliest productions. The teaching block is derived from the garden front of the villa at Garches[4].

One of the more striking examples of "Corbusianizm" was the office building for the Electrotechnical Institute, designed in 1929 by L. Meilman, V. and G. Movchan, and R. Chuenko and built in 1933 on the outskirts of the city at Lefortevo. The constituent parts of Centrosoyuz were reproduced, on a reduced scale, in their entirety: two rectangular prisms reflecting the treatments of the office buildings—glass facades or ribbon windows—were articulated by means of a vertical cylinder whose section is a horseshoe and which houses a ramp. The meeting hall at the end of the building is treated in the same way as that of Centrosoyuz.[5] The introduction of Corbusian vocabularies was not, however, positively appraised by Ilin, who considered them ill-adapted to "social and economic conditions within the Soviet Union":

This brief overview has enabled us to establish some basic principles of this school of architecture. Volumes are broad and deep but enclosed (and not infinite as in the baroque period); inside, walls are eliminated, and ceilings are of varying height, allowing for the deployment of S-shaped facades; architectural forms are inspired by the automobile, the airplane or the railway carriage, yet the proportions lend no dynamic inspiration, but rather engender a static architecture closed in on itself, reflecting purist principles. Such architectural forms are unsuited to contemporary life-styles in the USSR, where social and economic conditions are quite different from those in France; yet the new Soviet architects have employed them as being more radical than any other foreign examples shown to us. In their search for a "style" that corresponds to the brand-new life of the Soviet Union, these architects' first realizations have been inspired by the work of Le Corbusier—the most radical artist of new forms—with a view to discovering the formal, volumetric and compositional principles of creative rationalism.[6]

Ilin's criticisms were mild in comparison with those launched by V. Lavrov and V. Popov who, some months earlier, had denounced "uncritical attitudes toward the researches of Western architects." Focusing their attack on the Narkomfin building, which again emerged as a pivot between the positions of the constructivists and those of Le Corbusier, Lavrov and Popov, whose own views were close to those of the ASNOVA "rationalists," strove in turn to

[4] Michel Ilyine, "Le Corbusianisme en URSS," *L'Architecture d'Aujourd'hui,* no. 6 (1931): 59–61.

[5] D. Aranovich, "Dom Vsesoiuznogo Elektrotekhnicheskogo Tresta," *Stroitelstvo Moskvy* 11, no. 8 (1934): 18–21. The building, which was in excellent repair at the end of the eighties, is situated at no. 13, Krasnokazarmennaia Street. On the buildings of the institute, including this one, see Galina Makarova, "Razmyshleniia vokrug VEI," in *Arkhitektura i Stroitelstvo Moskvy,* no. 11 (1988): 10–11.

[6] Ilyine, "Le Corbusianisme," p. 60.

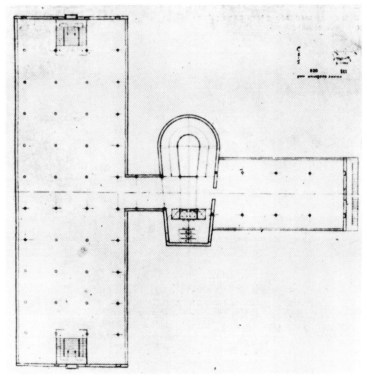

295. Lev Meilman, Gennadi and Vladimir Movchan, Rotislav Chuenko, Electrotechnical Union, Moscow, 1929–1933, photographed in 1989.

296. Lev Meilman, Gennadi and Vladimir Movchan, Rotislav Chuenko, Electrotechnical Union, Moscow, 1929–1933, floor plan.

297. Le Corbusier, "L'esprit nouveau en architecture," lecture given at the Sorbonne, 12 June 1924; published in David Arkin, *Arkhitektura Sovremennogo Zapada*, 1932, layout by El Lissitzky.

identify points of contact between Ginzburg and Milinis's building and Le Corbusier's ideas—but this time with negative emphasis:

The development of this type of housing design, based on the treatment of new architectural forms, can be perceived in the productions of a whole range of innovative Western architects whose recent work has been shown at housing exhibitions in Stuttgart and elsewhere.

All the examples executed in the West indicate the emergence of highly specific working methods whose social origins are quite obviously foreign to the Soviet Union. In the spheres of architecture and technology, such methods have been formulated in the most precise and concrete manner in the architect Le Corbusier's well-known "five points."

On the basis of these contemporary principles and technical methods, which have already been fully developed in the West, Le Corbusier exploits novel techniques so as to resolve the new aesthetic problems that he faces. He does this most consistently in his best-known work (the villa Savoye, the villa at Garches, the houses for the Stuttgart exhibition, etc.).

The creative system of such architects (Le Corbusier and others), on the basis of which they have resolved problems linked to the search for new forms and housing types, is designed to constitute an accurate expression of "social demand" in capitalist society, which has made its requirements known to the architect. When applied en bloc to living conditions within the Soviet Union, this system merely reiterates its formal devices, without considering the rank and file or modes of existence. The end result is that the functionalist methods applied to the Narkomfin building cannot claim to constitute a program for the construction of new housing types.[7]

This denunciation of the doctrinal "weakness" of certain Soviet architects in the face of Western production, which came at a time when Le Corbusier was still highly thought of in Moscow, was to be reiterated again and again through the thirties, even if the influence of Western architects as a whole remained strong. Thus the review *Arkhitektura SSSR*, founded in 1933 as the central organ of the newly formed Union, devoted its first issues to a vast overview of the design methods of Soviet and foreign architects, including Hannes Meyer and Hans Schmidt (both of whom practiced in the Soviet Union), but also Raymond Fischer, Josef Frank, Francis Jourdain, André Lurçat, Mallet-Stevens, J.J.P. Oud, Victor Bourgeois, and Frank Lloyd Wright.[8] But although Le Corbusier was excluded from this somewhat eclectic survey, his presence continued to be felt at the various levels of Soviet architectural culture until the end of the decade.

MOSCOW TEMPERATURES

Le Corbusier's architectural production in the thirties was presented to Soviet architects—and, presumably, to the public at large—from two basic viewpoints, that of the doctrinal struggle and that of his designs. His work was now considered from a new angle: there could no longer be any question of referring to his work as a qualitative or innovative model for Soviet production, as had been the case in the twenties. Henceforth, it was a question of seizing on every available opportunity to place the most celebrated of foreign architects at an ever greater distance, while continuing to inform a public increasingly cut off from Western events. This was achieved by confronting Le Corbusier's architectural production with Soviet requirements, and by "rediscovering" figures and buildings previous to or contemporary with Le Corbusier, yet eclipsed by him.

Accused of "Corbusianizm" by his detractors, Moisei Ginzburg was forced to publish a disavowal in *Zhilishche*, a work devoted to the problem of housing. In his contrast between Le Corbusier's own output and that of the German functionalists, Ginzburg assimilated the former to the Roman and French traditions:

It is interesting to note that the most brilliant representative of latter-day Roman architecture, Le Corbusier, has in essence remained faithful to his own national heritage. For all his plastic acuity and wealth of spatial ideas, and his correct assessment of the importance of industry as the sole means of housing production, Le Corbusier has failed to transcend the visual manipulation of rich spatial devices in his housing research. In the place of his predecessors' use of *trompe-l'oeil* and ornament, he has

[7] V. Lavrov and V. Popov, "Protiv nekriticheskogo otnosheniia k eksperimentam zapadnykh arkhitektorov," *Stroitelstvo Moskvy* 7, no. 9 (1930): 8–12.

[8] This series was entitled "Kak ia rabotaiu" ("How I work"). The presence of Fischer, who was less well known than the others, is to be attributed to the fact that he traveled to Russia with *L'Architecture d'Aujourd'hui* in 1932 (see subsequent discussion).

contributed a series of brilliantly illusionistic spatial concepts. In this the intelligence of his designs resides; and yet all these "exhibition spaces," with their fittings and their concrete or steel furniture, can in no way be considered the significant elements of a new housing culture.[9]

For his part, David Arkin considered the question of architectural "heritage" and its "assimilation"—a keystone of the theory of "socialist realism"—in what may be considered his position of reference vis-à-vis Le Corbusier for the coming years:

The most important and gifted of the ideologists and practitioners of the new Western architecture, Le Corbusier, considers that the technology of rationalized modern industry contains laws that are valid for all walks of life and culture, regardless of the extent to which that life is socially determined. Le Corbusier proposes not only to introduce elements of rationalization from the viewpoint of architectural technique, but also to "deduce," from contemporary technique itself, the laws of a new life-style, a new artistic content for architecture.

Whence the next step, the aestheticization of technique, apart from which the architect sees no basis for the determination of architectural form. In his celebrated "five points," he has attempted to ground all architectural creation in an absolute dependence on modern building techniques—in particular, on reinforced concrete—and to use its constructional potentialities as the basis for new formal canons.

This new "concrete" dogmatism, which, for a time at least, made it possible to envisage new architectural forms, has at the same time ushered in a new type of architectural formalism. Instead of proposing effective mastery of this new material—a mastery both technical and artistic—Le Corbusier's aesthetic positions have in fact resulted in total and unconditional surrender to the *idea* of new building techniques and materials.[10]

Yet despite these remarks, it was still possible for Le Corbusier to publish in the USSR. In March 1933 Nikolai Miliutin, now editor-in-chief of *Sovetskaia Arkhitektura*, was speaking in the name of his old "proletarian" colleagues when he called on Le Corbusier's "competent assistance" and "collaboration" in the form of one or several articles on topics of [his] own choice":

We feel obliged to draw your particular attention to questions of special importance to our review in the field of the latest forms of contemporary Western architecture, designs for social institutions such as kindergartens, schools, theaters, etc., and recent work on furniture, housing interiors, etc.[11]

The transformation of Le Corbusier into an architectural correspondent did not, however, take place. Instead, it was as an author that he continued to appear in the pages of the Moscow press. In December 1933, the Russian translation of *Urbanisme* was reviewed with skepticism by A. Karra, who nonetheless acknowledged that the book "filled an existing gap in the field of serious publications on urban planning," but who regretted that the author of the preface (Sergei Gorny) had omitted to indicate "Le Corbusier's failings on the subject of urban architecture":

The following essential points should be borne in mind: the "static character" of the schematic plan, based on the juxtaposition of three finite bands that, in their quadrilateral layout, preclude all possibility of further extension; the "closed" aspect of the thematic treatment; and the absence of any indication as to urban development and the transition from the city as it is now to its proposed future state. Apart from these errors and abstractions, and the fantastic notion of *respiration exacte*, Le Corbusier contributes a whole series of brilliant ideas and propositions.[12]

298. David Arkin, "Le Corbusier," article in *Sovetskaia Arkhitektura* 1, no. 3 (1931).

[9] Moisei Ginzburg, *Zhilische*, p. 22.
[10] David Arkin, "Tvorcheskie puti sovetskoi arkhitektury i problema arkhitekturnogo nasledstva," *Arkhitektura SSSR* 1, no. 3–4 (1933): 4–10.
[11] F. Miliutin and L. Cherniavsky, letter to Le Corbusier, Moscow, 23 March 1933, FLC. In the margin of this letter, Le Corbusier noted "Algiers, Antwerp, Stockholm."
[12] A. Karra, "Le Corbusier. Planirovka goroda," *Arkhitektura SSSR* 1, no. 6 (1933): 72.

Karra restricted his attention to the book's technical indications:

The need to assimilate critically all Western architectural and urban planning initiatives takes on all its significance for Soviet architecture.

Urbanisme contains a lucid enumeration of the various technical possibilities that have enabled contemporary architects and planners to shake off the excessive burden of secular tradition, and outlines with equal clarity the insoluble contradictions that have led this approach to a desperate impasse.[13]

In 1934, Le Corbusier's publishing activities were considered important enough for *Croisade*, a work whose "technical" interest may be considered zero, to be reviewed in both the specialist press and *Izvestia*. Once again, David Arkin was given the task of assessing the qualities of a book whose objectives he appeared to share—namely, a refutation of the theses of academicism. Arkin agreed with most of the positions expressed in this "pamphlet," and joined with Le Corbusier in condemning the "archaic" propositions of Gustave Umbdenstock, one of the work's main targets:

Le Corbusier's energetic attack on the retrograde archaism of his opponents is not, however, grounded in the social postulates of modern Western architects. The campaign against new building technologies and in favor of a return to "national styles" in architecture is merely an episode in the general "attack on the machine," against industrial technology and industrial progress—a movement characteristic of fascist bourgeois culture. Umbdenstock's diatribe is nothing less than a sort of architectural variant of Spengler's ideas.

When faced with this, Le Corbusier, the well-known theorist of the "machine age," assumes the role of "advocate of the machine," taking pains to demonstrate that the machine and technology are not as frightening as all that, and that there is a means of adapting them to contemporary needs without "reverting to crafts." The means in question is capitalist rationalization. As far as aesthetics is concerned, Le Corbusier reiterates the age-old adage concerning "technologies as the very basis of a new lyricism."

Le Corbusier can find nothing else to propose, in the guise of a positive program for his art, than the "lyricism of the machine." The whole social aspect of the architectural question is thus perceived and treated from the point of view of capitalist "machine civilization." Whence the simplistic "radicalism" of his positions, and the fact that his thought is caught up in the same vicious circle as that wearing out his adversaries of the academic camp.[14]

Yet Arkin's reservations are slight when compared with those of N. Liamin, who, in an article published in *Arkhitektura SSSR*, regarded Le Corbusier as being far closer to the fascist reaction than he would have one believe in his battle against the "academicians." In this context, Liamin cites Le Corbusier's bitter remarks concerning his Soviet experience, and his "conscious refusal" to grasp "the gigantic creative tasks" awaiting Soviet architecture.[15]

LA VILLE RADIEUSE AND TRAVELS IN THE UNITED STATES

Doubtless as a direct consequence of its numerous allusions to the Soviet scene, Le Corbusier's most important work of the thirties, *La ville radieuse*, was completely ignored by the Muscovite critics. At the same time, all his attempts to distribute copies of the book among his friends and to the bookshops were thwarted by the censors. In his episodic epistolary exchanges with Alexander Vesnin and Nikolai Kolli, Le Corbusier expressed his surprise at the fact that the copies his publishers dispatched to Moscow in 1935 were returned

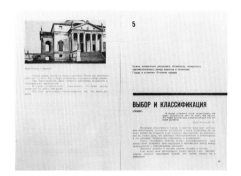

299. Le Corbusier, "Classification and Choice," chapter of *Urbanisme*, translated in *Planirovka Goroda* (Moscow, 1933).

[13] Ibid.

[14] D. Arkin, "Le Corbusier 'Krestovy pokhod ili sumerki akademizma," *Izvestia* (6 April 1934): 72.

[15] N. Liamin, "'Krestovy pokhod' G. Le Corbusier," *Arkhitektura SSSR* 1, no. 3 (1933): 70.

marked "of no interest here."[16] He also drew Liudvig's attention to this refusal to admit a work outlining his theoretical positions and the "applications" of his urban designs since 1930. Acting in the name of the Academy of Architecture, Liudvig duly asked Le Corbusier for information regarding "new materials and constructions, and their influence on the forms of contemporary architecture."[17] In his reply, Le Corbusier emphasized the opposition between "damp" reinforced concrete constructions and "dry" steel techniques:

In order to comprehend the problem of "dry" construction, one must first of all resolve that of the urbanization of residential districts, and here differences of opinion begin to emerge. I have analyzed the question in great detail and have come up with the "Ville Radieuse" housing type. These designs are discussed at length in my book *La ville radieuse* (Editions de *L'Architecture d'Aujourd'hui*, 1935), but my publisher informs me that it has had no success in Russia, and that the copy sent there was returned to Paris. This astonishes me greatly. I have attempted to make my own enquiries, but to no avail.

It is my belief that, given the current spirit of enquiry in the USSR, my theses are considered undesirable there. I am sorry for this but am pursuing my own researches, which have gone on uninterrupted and undistracted for more than fifteen years.[18]

Turning to the question of difficulties encountered during the Centrosoyuz project, Le Corbusier then cites recent American "discoveries" as evidence that his choices were justified:

As regards housing (the *logis*, or dwelling), I have concluded that one must incorporate common service areas, which for me represent considerable domestic savings, whether in the sphere of supply, cleaning, heating or refrigeration. But my specific ideas on the subject of *respiration* (see my chapter on this in *La ville radieuse*) were poorly received by Moscow in 1929 during the construction of Centrosoyuz. I deeply regret this fact, and am still convinced that such methods were the only ones adapted to the city's continental climate. . . . Since they were first proposed (1927–1928), enormous progress has been made in the USA, and ideas held to be revolutionary by Moscow in 1930 are currently in constant use in office blocks, tall apartment buildings, railways, tunnels, airplanes, etc., in the USA.

. . . Should you happen to read *La ville radieuse* you will notice that, on occasion, I show bad blood as regards decisions by Moscow which seem to me to have been inspired by pure and quite irrelevant sentimentality. This was my right, and I do not think it can be contested.

[16] Le Corbusier, letter to Alexander Vesnin, Paris, 28 January 1936, FLC.

[17] G. Liudvig, letter to Le Corbusier, Moscow, 31 March 1936, FLC.

[18] Le Corbusier, letter to G. Liudvig, Paris, 28 May 1936, FLC.

[19] F. Dvinsky, "Le Corbusier o budushchem Niu Iorka," *Izvestia* (27 June 1936).

[20] Le Corbusier, "Chto takoe amerikanskaia problema?" *Arkhitektura za rubezhom* 3, no. 5 (1936): 46–47. Published in English: Le Corbusier, "What is America's Problem?" *American Architect* 148 (March 1936): 17–22. Le Corbusier had sent it with a letter to G. Liudvig on 18 May 1936, FLC; see also Liudvig's acknowledgment, 7 June 1936, FLC.

[21] "Chetyre dokhodnykh doma," *Arkhitektura SSSR* 3, no. 1 (1935): 79.

[22] "Luchezarnaia derevnia po Le Corbusier," *Arkhitektura SSSR* 3, no. 5 (1935): 77.

While a dense cloud of silence hung over *La ville radieuse*, the long-awaited encounter between Le Corbusier and America did not go unnoticed in Moscow. Once again, it was *Izvestia* that recorded his reactions and quoted his provocative remarks as to the errors of town planning in Manhattan.[19] Le Corbusier's reflections on America were cited in a different form with the publication, in *Arkhitektura za rubezhom*, of a translation of his article "What is America's problem?" This was to be one of the last articles to be published in a review whose internationalist leanings were becoming an embarrassment with the rise of Stalinist cultural autarky, and the last article by Le Corbusier to be published in Moscow until the end of the fifties.[20]

Just as Le Corbusier's theories continued to be discussed beyond the controversial question of Centrosoyuz, his architectural production also continued to receive coverage by the Moscow critics. This took the form of a mass of brief references taken from the French press concerning both his building in the rue Nungesser-et-Coli[21] and his "Ferme radieuse,"[22] and although the publication of Willi Boesiger and Oscar Storonov's *Œuvre complète* was not announced, mention was made, in a brief article, of the edition published by

РИ Г МАНХЭТТЕНА С АЭРОПЛАНА

300. Le Corbusier, "What is America's problem?", article published in *Arkhitektura za rubezhom* 3 (1936).

Ле Корбюзье—
«ЧТО ТАКОЕ АМЕРИКАНСКАЯ ПРОБЛЕМА?»

(«AMERICAN ARCHITECT», март 1936 г.)

С острова Джерсей, сквозь дымку утреннего тумана, Нью-Йорк кажется райским городом обетованной земли—далеким, воздушным и матово-жемчужным.

Но, когда въезжаешь в город, иллюзия воздушности пропадает. Всюду небоскребы, скрывающие небо и солнце, грубые, однообразные, варварские небоскребы. И все же вид их никого - может оставить равнодушным. Они потрясают, волнуют, подавляют. Какая мощность в правильной громаде их призм! Какая захватывающая высота — 300 метров! Высота всегда прекрасна уже сама по себе. Небоскребы Нью-Йорка романтичны, но нецелесообразны. Это гордый жест, но не более, чем жест. Они только доказывают, что можно сооружать здания вышиной в 300 метров и населять их доверху. Но они убивают улицу и делают город похожим на дом умалишенных.

Нью-йоркский небоскреб дает в настоящее время только отрицательный эф-фект: он загромождает улицу, он тормозит движение. Это настоящий канни бал, обескровливающий целые кварталы вокруг себя, обезлюживающий и разоряющий их. Но спасение возможно: ключ к нему — урбанизация города. Современный небоскреб чересчур мал. Сделайте его большим и рациональным, и вы сэкономите огромную площадь: утраченные качества вернутся, и город будет иметь зеленое открытое пространство, а проблема движения будет разрешена. Участки земли, незанятые домами, станут парками для пешеходов, автомобили будут передвигаться в воздухе по надземным дорогам. Но такая задача под силу только коллективу, сплоченной группе. Рано или поздно, а придется перейти к организации строительных кооперативов и государственных синдикатов и к государственной инициативе, опекающей отечески, но властно.

Средняя высота здания в Нью-Йорке—4½ этажа. Если бы средняя высота их была хотя бы только 16 этажей, то поверхность, занятая в настоящее время домами, была бы на ¾ свободна. При каждом здании был бы свой сад, свои собственная площадка для игр, и новые здания строились бы в самом городе, а не в Коннектикуте.

И все города в Америке строятся по этому же образцу, так же беспорядочно, и придет день, когда они будут в том же положении, что Нью-Йорк и Чикаго.

Конечно, и в Чикаго и в Нью-Йорке есть прелестные дома и в центре, и в отдаленных предместьях, у воды, обрамленные парками. Но кто в них живет? Так называемые «влиятельные лица». Они и их семьи уверены, что на свете недурно живется. Но мне приходят на ум те миллионы несчастных, которые возвращаются по вечерам на далекие окраины в их безрадостные жилища, те, для кого

46

301. Le Corbusier, Clarté apartment block, Geneva, 1930–1932, published in *Arkhitektura za rubezhom* 2, no.1 (1935).

ДОХОДНЫЙ ДОМ „LA CLARTÉ" В ЖЕНЕВЕ

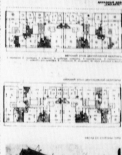

302. Le Corbusier, Swiss Pavilion at the Cité Universitaire, Paris, 1930–1932, published in *Arkhitektura SSSR* 2, no. 1 (1934).

[23] "Polnoe sobranie postroek i proektov Le Corbusier i P. Jeanneret za 1925–1934," *Arkhitektura SSSR* 2, no. 8 (1934): 77.

[24] "Poslednie raboty Le Corbusier, " *Arkhitektura SSSR* 3, no. 3 (1935): 51–53; "Dokhodny dom 'la klarte,'" *Arkhitektura za rubezhom* 2, no. 1 (1935): 18–20.

[25] I. L. Matsa, "Novaia arkhitektura," *Arkhitektura SSSR* 2, no. 1, (1934): 3–10.

[26] Olga Bubnova, "Za ili protiv ornamenta," *Arkhitektura SSSR* 1, no. 2 (1933): 35.

[27] L. Rempel and T. Viaznikovtseva, "Kolonialnaia Arkhitektura," *Arkhitektura SSSR* 1, no. 6 (1933): 48–60.

[28] H. Schmidt, "Arkhitektura ulitsy," *Arkhitektura SSSR* 4, no. 6 (1936): 37–45.

[29] David E. Arkin, *Arkhitektura sovremennogo Zapada* (Moscow: OGIZ-IZOGIZ, 1932), pp. 36–66. In terms of volume, this is the most exhaustive Soviet study of Le Corbusier's architecture to be published in the thirties, and includes, over and above Arkin's own analyses, extracts from *Vers une architecture*, *Urbanisme*, and his lecture, "L'esprit nouveau en architecture" as published in the *Almanach d'Architecture Moderne*.

[30] D. Arkin, "Risunok Arkhitektora (zametki)," *Arkhitektura SSSR* 1, no. 1 (1933): 32.

[31] A. V. Shchusev had already given Le Corbusier some coverage in his contribution "Arkhitektura, novaia," published in 1926.

Albert Morancé.[23] Few articles were devoted to serious discussion of the projects. Commentaries concerning the Cité de Refuge or the Swiss pavilion and analysis of the Clarté apartment block concentrated for the most part on building technique.[24] In fact, Le Corbusier's continuing presence in the Russian architectural debate was due neither to discussion of his theories nor to analysis of his architecture, but rather to the obsessive mention of him in all comprehensive critiques of contemporary architecture. Thus, his ideas and projects were presented in artificial clusters, so as to eliminate their threat to the rising trend of "socialist realism."

Le Corbusier was given a respectable role in accounts of the development of twentieth-century architecture[25] and in analysis of the problem of ornament.[26] His *Obus* Plan for Algiers was reviewed in the context of a whole series of French and Italian colonial projects,[27] whereas urban projects such as the plan for Antwerp were included without comment in Hans Schmidt's discussion of the "architecture of the street."[28] Once again it was David Arkin, now "assistant chief editor" of *Arkhitektura SSSR*, who was most attentive to Le Corbusier's work, which he reviewed in some detail in his 1932 book, *Architecture in the Contemporary West*, and continued to discuss in lively manner in published articles.[29] Thus, in his "Remarks on architectural drawing" (1933), he went to some lengths to define Le Corbusier's graphic techniques in contrast with those of Leonardo, Bramante, Michelangelo, Borromini, Piranesi, Frank Lloyd Wright, and Erich Mendelsohn:

Le Corbusier practices an astonishing variety of graphic techniques: one might say that his drawings are deliberately controversial to the extent that they give sharper definition to the formulation of an aesthetics, thus furnishing an occasion for discussion with adversaries and propaganda for "new architectural morals." Le Corbusier's drawings are more an extension of his writings than of his architecture. They seem to have been scratched out hastily in chalk on the blackboard in the course of a polemical lecture—or rather, architectural sermon. The very construction of his drawings reflects a polemical intent, with slogans, ironic comments, interplay of contrasting graphic techniques and caricature of architecture—such are the characteristic elements of Le Corbusier's graphics. Here are two versions of Paris, whose architectural "gems"—the Arc de Triomphe, Notre-Dame, the Sacré-Cœur—are seen to converse with the Eiffel Tower and . . . the high-rise blocks of the "Voisin Plan."

Yet however intelligent his graphic approach, even in the sketches of his own buildings, it amounts to no less than a misappropriation of the primary function of architectural drawing.[30]

The article devoted to Le Corbusier in the *Great Soviet Encyclopedia*, published in 1937 as part of volume 34 of a work begun in the twenties and whose perception of modern architecture depended very much on the alphabetical position of the respective articles, furnished a fairly eloquent summary of Soviet attitudes.[31] This article designated Le Corbusier as the "leader and ideologist of the new architecture, of architectural constructivism" and included a number of his slogans together with brief list of works; but the general tone was acutely hostile:

In his theoretical positions, as in his architectural practice, a purely utilitarian approach, incorporating the very latest techniques, goes hand in hand with pure formalism. This accounts for the aestheticization of reinforced-concrete surfaces, contrasting effects of concrete and glass, "fluid spaces," etc. Although they direct the architect's attention toward modern building techniques, criticize the outmoded methods of the "academic" school and thus fulfill an especially positive role, Le Corbusier's conceptions impose excessive restrictions on architecture's creative possibilities and lead to

Корбюзье   Corbusier

303. Le Corbusier, "The Academy says no!" sketch published in *Précisions*, reviewed by David Arkin in *Arkhitektura SSSR* 1, no. 1 (1933).

an impoverishment of its artistic means of expression. Such conceptions reveal the widespread decadence of today's artistic culture in the West. Le Corbusier's supporters in various countries, and notably in Germany, have transformed the negative aspects of his teaching into a simplified and extremely utilitarian vision of the tasks of architecture, leading to the appalling monotony of "box housing" (cf. the article on "Functionalism"). In the field of town planning, Le Corbusier has proposed a utopian scheme for the reconstruction of the contemporary city by dividing it up into three distinct zones for business (the City), housing and industry.[32]

LE CORBUSIER AND HIS SOVIET PARTNERS

Despite the attacks on Le Corbusier, he was continually invited to participate in the new institutions of Soviet architecture. While the journals kept in touch with him, at least until 1936, other strategies were set in motion with a view to establishing a novel type of relationship with a figure who was doubtless controversial, but whose role as a "friend of the Soviet Union" appears to have worried at least some of the leading members of the Union of Architects.

In 1935, Le Corbusier was invited to accept his nomination as a correspondent of the Soviet Academy of Architecture,[33] an honor he accepted with some reservations. He even included a proposal to change the name of the institution, although he insisted that he could not "for one moment confuse [this] society with what we call 'academic' in everyday speech."[34] The fact that Victor Vesnin played a leading role at the academy before becoming its president in 1939 doubtless explains why this Soviet body, which devoted its energies essentially to typological research and, in the theoretical sphere, to new editions of classical treatises, was so eager to solicit Le Corbusier's services at a time when his reputation was already doubtful (to say the least).

In the following year, while the Union of Architects was finally preparing to hold its first congress, Le Corbusier was invited to the Soviet Union, thus at last providing him with the opportunity that he had sought in vain since 1930 to visit Moscow again; and yet he refused this invitation on the ground that he

[32] "Le Corbusier," in *Bolshaia Sovetskaia Entsiklopedia*, vol. 34, (Moscow: OGIZ, 1937), p. 256. David Arkin was very probably the author of this unsigned article.

[33] Architectural Academy of the USSR, letter to Le Corbusier, Moscow, 31 August 1935, FLC.

[34] Le Corbusier, letter to the Architectural Academy of the USSR, Paris, 13 September 1936, FLC.

had not received the balance of his fees for Centrosoyuz—a subject that had preoccupied him since 1935.[35]

Soviet architects rarely had the opportunity of studying Le Corbusier's work at first hand. Such an opportunity presented itself in 1935 when Andrei Burov, Boris Iofan, Nikolai Kolli, Alexander Vlasov, and David Arkin visited Paris on their return from an international congress at Rome. This delegation took part in a round table organized by the Société des Architectes Diplômés par le Gouvernement (SADG),[36] but they did not meet Le Corbusier, who was in the United States at the time. Although Kolli, who was greatly disappointed at having missed this reunion with Le Corbusier (and all the more so since postal censorship made it practically impossible for them to correspond), was moderate in his comments, Andrei Burov manifested his reservations regarding Le Corbusier's buildings:

Concerning Le Corbusier. His most characteristic and most expressive work is the Cité Universitaire. This is a plastic combination of volumes (an "object in space"). It reminds one of still lifes, and a sort of tray held up by hands whose form he has retained. The hall is decorated with macrophotographs of marine life. One has to consider the works of Le Corbusier with a "cold eye": in the place of purism, snobbery.[37]

Burov's reservations were expressed even more radically in a letter to his wife, in which he wrote, "'Purism' rhymes, not with 'pure' but with 'pourri' [rotten]."[38] In fact, the delegation was interested in two types of building: on the one hand, they sketched and photographed monumental Paris, a key reference in the debate on urban composition in the USSR; on the other, they were fascinated by the latest developments in building prefabrication, as witness Nikolai Kolli's complimentary article on the cité de la Muette by Eugène Beaudouin and Marcel Lods, which may well have occasioned Lods's invitation to the Moscow congress in the following year.[39]

Various accounts of the trip to Paris provide clear evidence of a reversal of the way in which Le Corbusier had been perceived in 1932: for Soviet observers, he was no longer the cynosure of the international scene in general, nor of the French scene in particular; instead, he was now considered an important but questionable figure in a more complex, markedly pluralist environment whose antecedents were henceforth perceived in greater detail.

A NEW VIEW OF FRENCH ARCHITECTURE

This reversal of Soviet attitudes manifested itself first and foremost at the historical level, when David Arkin reviewed Emil Kauffmann's *Von Ledoux bis Le Corbusier* in the journal of the Academy of Architecture.[40] All the major episodes of the French rationalist tradition were subsequently brought to light: on the one hand, the academy's "cabinet of theory" decided to translate Viollet-le-Duc's *Entretiens sur l'architecture* and *L'art de bâtir chez les Romains* by Auguste Choisy, whose *Histoire de l'architecture*, first translated in 1906–1907, had already been republished.[41] The significance of this initiative was pointed out by Nikolai Miliutin, who contrasted Choisy's work with that of Le Corbusier in his search for an acceptable "building aesthetics":

The role of technology, and in particular that of structure, in the definition of architectural forms, cannot be underestimated. Structure significantly determines the very framework of architectural styles. Structure is a consequence of man's knowledge and capacity. But at the same time, one ought not to forget that the products of architecture furnish not only use value but also (and most often) instruments of labor. Seen

[35] Le Corbusier, letter to the Union of Architects of the USSR, Paris, 22 May 1937, FLC.

[36] "L'urbanisme et l'architecture en URSS," *Bulletin de la SADG*, no. 20 (November 1935). Also published in *L'Architecture* 48 (15 December 1935): 177–85.

[37] Andrei Burov, "Iz putevogo dnevnika arkhitektora," *Arkhitektura SSSR* 4, no. 9 (1936): 69–74.

[38] Andrei Burov, letter from Paris, 22 November 1935, published in O. I. Rzhekhina and R. G. Burova, *Andrei Konstantinovich Burov* (Moscow: Iskusstvo, 1980), p. 65. In his last work, published in 1960, Burov was still scathing in his comments on his former role model: Andrei Burov, *Ob Arkhitekture* (Moscow: Gos. Izd. Lit. po Stroitelstvu, Arkhitekture i Stroit. Mat., 1960).

[39] Nikolai Kolli, "Iz frantsuskogo opyta industrializatsii zhilishchnogo stroitelstva," *Arkhitektura SSSR* 4, no. 3 (1936): 20–23. An overall account of the visit to Paris is given in *Arkhitekturnye zapiski* (Moscow: Izd. vses. Akademii Arkhitektury, 1937).

[40] David Arkin, "Arkhitektura epokhi frantsuskoi revoliutsii," *Arkhitektura SSSR* 4, no. 3 (1936): 20–23.

[41] Viollet-le-Duc, *Besedy ob Arkhitekture* (Moscow: Izd. Vses. Akademii Arkhitektury, 1937); Auguste Choisy, *Stroitelnoe iskusstvo drevnykh remlian*, and *Istoriia Arkhitektury* (Moscow: Izd. Vses. Akademii Arkhitektury, 1935; and Moscow: Izd. Vses. Akademii Arkhitektury, 1938).

in this light, Choisy's history of architecture takes on considerable interest, for the author understood and explained the role of structure and materials in the development of architecture. The constructivists—and Le Corbusier in particular—must be given credit for having demonstrated that contemporary structures and materials, contemporary modes of production and science not only offer architecture with new possibilities—a fact that neither the formalists nor the eclectics would contest—but also have a direct influence on form. Even if we reject the "leftist" nihilism of the constructivists and notions of the absolute primacy of structure, we ought not to fall back into a rejection or ignorance of new technologies and new forms of architecture.[42]

But if Choisy furnished a point of historical reference, it was the contemporary work of Auguste Perret that inspired new approaches to the relationship between form and structure, one to which Sigfried Giedion's *Bauen in Frankreich* also made a significant contribution.[43] Perret's reputation grew in inverse proportion to that of Le Corbusier. A cover story was devoted to him in the review *Arkhitektura za rubezhom*, and his aphorisms on the theory of architecture were solemnly published in *Arkhitektura SSSR*.[44] For his part, Arkin made use of Perret (who, it must be remembered, had been invited to participate in the Palace of Soviets competition in 1931) as a "negative foil" to Le Corbusier, and did not hesitate to adopt the tone of traditionalist French criticism:

That remarkable master Auguste Perret, who is the first to have built a reinforced concrete housing block, continues to work intensely in this field. . . . A fan of reinforced concrete, Perret assures us that these constructions open endless vistas for the future, a fact of which today's architects are unaware. Either they lack courage and remain attached to old forms, or they are fond of the stripped architectural forms which Perret terms "nudism," with specific reference to Le Corbusier. In his own buildings, and especially the Mobilier National building in Paris, Perret is at pains to show that reinforced concrete can be used in such a way as to escape the harsh forms, coldness, and mechanical appearance that architects reject—in short, all that constitutes the Achilles' heel of the constructivists, who have been unable to avoid the stiff forms of angular boxes devoid of all warmth and humanity.[45]

The article on Perret that appeared in volume 47 of the *Great Soviet Encyclo-*

[42] N. A. Miliutin, "Konstruktivizm i funktsionalizm, k kharakteristike arkhitekturnykh techenii XX veka," *Arkhitektura SSSR* 3, no. 8 (1935): 5–10.

[43] Sigfried Giedion, *Arkhitektura zheleza i zhelezobetona vo Frantsii* (Moscow: Izd. Vses. Akademii Arkhitektury, 1937).

[44] P. Balter, "Auguste Perret," *Arkhitektura za rubezhom* 3, no. 1 (1936): 1–14; Auguste Perret, "Mysli ob Arkhitekture," *Arkhitektura SSSR* 4, no. 1 (1936): 10–14. This was a translation of the lecture "L'architecture" delivered on 31 May 1933 at the Institut d'Art et d'Archéologie and published in the *Revue d'Art et d'Esthétique* in June 1935.

[45] D. Arkin, "Zapadno-evropeiskaia arkhitektura, vpechatleniia ot poezdki," *Arkhitektura za rubezhom* 3, no. 2 (1936): 47.

304. "A. et G. Perret's theaters," article published in *Arkhitektura za rubezhom* 3, no.1 (1936).

pedia in 1940 highlighted the differences between him and his contemporaries (implying Le Corbusier):

Unlike many of today's French architects, Perret has not followed the path of formalism in his treatment of reinforced concrete; rather, he has demonstrated the plastic potential of this material and given his concrete constructions an expressive, architectural quality.[46]

In addition to the father figure Perret, other protagonists on the French architectural scene were henceforth given greater attention by the Soviets, be it Beaudouin and Lods, André Lurçat, or the editorial team of the review *L'Architecture d'Aujourd'hui.*

PIERRE VAGO AND *L'ARCHITECTURE D'AUJOURD'HUI*

With the implementation of the Five-Year Plan at the outset of the thirties, the number of Western visitors to the Soviet Union, including intellectuals and architects, increased sharply. In a sense, some of the French who visited Moscow at the time contributed unwittingly to the growing ostracism of Le Corbusier by official Soviet culture. But the 1932 trip to Russia organized by *L'Architecture d'Aujourd'hui,* which brought a significant group of French and Western architects to Moscow, was on a quite different scale. On 26 August the editor, Pierre Vago, and the advertising manager, Honoré Bloch, boarded the Paris–Berlin–Warsaw train with, among others, Armand Guillemot-Saint-Vinebault, chief editor of *La Construction Moderne,* Donat-Alfred Agache, Marius Boyer, Raymond Fischer, Georges-Henri Pingusson, Josef Vago, and the Italian critic Pietro Maria Bardi.[47]

In the course of this trip, which took in Leningrad, Moscow, Kharkov, and the Dnieper dam, the visitors saw evidence of the state of existing cities, the latest constructions and buildings in progress; two members of the group subsequently published books recording what they saw.[48] They were given two opportunities to gauge Le Corbusier's standing at this time, only a few months after the publication of the results of the Palace of Soviets competition. The first of these was a visit to the Centrosoyuz site, and the second, the "First International Meeting of Architects" organized by Vago in a bid to preempt both conservative professional bodies and the CIAM.[49] Georges-Henri Pingusson saw the construction sites that he visited as evidence of the continuing influence of Le Corbusier:

A reaction against constructional logic [*logique constructive*] has asserted itself under the influence of Le Corbusier. Clear decisions, readable plans and marked elevations, rigorous composition by means of a *canevas régulateur* that, through large, harmonized proportions and simple relations, create a beautiful architectural aspect and, on occasion, a certain austerity. This trend which, regardless of what has been said on the subject, is in no way repressed, owes its quick success to the virtues of the bold and rational application of reinforced-concrete techniques.[50]

The engineer Jean-Jacques Coulon recounts the effects of "socialist emulation" as practiced on the Centrosoyuz site, where he perceived a degree of concern for economy:

In order to activate production, piecework is occasionally employed. In other cases, an effort is made to stimulate pride in what the workers are doing. At the headquarters of the Moscow Cooperatives, for instance, building progress is shown on a large notice board. The work of each group or shift of workers is indicated and compared with

[46] "Perret Auguste," in *Bolshaia Sovetskaia Entsiklopediia* vol. 45 (Moscow: OGIZ, 1940), p. 130.

[47] In the absence of any explicit written evidence, a fairly exhaustive list of the participants can be renconstituted from the legends of photographs published in *L'Architecture d'Aujourd'hui* and the account published by Guillemot-Saint-Vinebault, "Un voyage d'architectes en URSS (août–septembre 1932)," *La Construction Moderne,* suppl. (23 October 1932).

[48] Marius Antide-Boyer, *Chez les "tovaritschi," notes de voyages en URSS* (Casablanca: Imprimeries Réunies, 1933). Boyer (1885–1947) was one of the most influential Casablanca architects of the interwar period, building stepped apartment buildings in the Sauvage vein; Pietro Maria Bardi, *Un fascista al paese dei Soviet* (Rome: Le Edizioni d'Italia, 1933). Bardi (1900–), an art critic, was one of the principal propagandists of rationalist architecture in Italy, and the author in 1931 of a "report on architecture (for Mussolini)."

[49] Pierre Vago, interview with Jean-Louis Cohen, Milly-la-Forêt, 11 April 1986.

[50] Georges-Henri Pingusson, "Un formidable champ d'expériences," from "Les problèmes techniques en Russie Soviétique" in "Architecture et urbanisme en URSS, à l'occasion du voyage d'étude et des réunions d'architectes organisées en URSS et en Pologne, septembre 1932," *L'Architecture d'Aujourd'hui,* no. 8 (1932): 77–78.

305. The participants of *L'Architecture d'Aujourd'hui*'s expedition in Moscow, August 1932.

planned objectives. The result is illustrated by means of suggestive color drawings at the head of the column reserved for each group.

On the day of our visit the carpenters, who had largely "overfulfilled" their objectives, were shown as a locomotive; a tortoise indicated the lamentable progress of the steelwork; and the cement pourers' achievements had been depicted as a magnificent camel, as much for the mediocrity of their work as for their exemplary sobriety—or so we thought.

We do not know what effect this procedure has on the progress of construction, but it clearly denotes a desire to limit costs, which must be the concern of any well-organized enterprise.[51]

Both in his book and in his contribution to the account published in *L'Architecture d'Aujourd'hui*, Bardi, who also visited the site, did not scruple to cite the criticisms that he had heard there:

Although the Palace of the Commercial Trust—designed by Le Corbusier with rare originality, subtle manipulation of volumes and rigorous functionalism—was chosen from a number of competition entries, it has ended up by appalling the authorities, who have called in the architect Kolli to reconcile its extremely cerebral art with a pronouncedly materialist taste.

Instead of the planned glass walls, a red-brick facade with small window-openings is now envisaged. A part of the building has already been faced in this way, thus masking the slender framework that confers such lightness of being on the architecture of this Swiss-born architect living in France.[52]

Bardi ascribes Le Corbusier's discredit in Moscow to the exceptionally advanced character of his architecture rather than to the influence of a generalized cultural regression:

In the course of a meeting at VOKS, I heard extremely sharp criticisms voiced against Le Corbusier and the whole system of the machine dwelling, which appears nonetheless to have been specially invented for socialist nations that aspire to communism.

Schizzo del palazzo del trust del commercio.

306. Pietro Maria Bardi, sketch of Centrosoyuz done during the trip of *L'Architecture d'Aujourd'hui* to Moscow, August 1932.

[51] Jean-Jacques Coulon, "Les problèmes techniques en Russie Soviétique," *L'Architecture d'Aujourd'hui*, no. 8 (1932): 68.

[52] Pietro Maria Bardi, "La soi-disante architecture russe," *L'Architecture d'Aujourd'hui*, no. 8 (1932): 73, published in fuller form in *Un fascista al paese dei Soviet*, p. 138. Kolli wrote to Le Corbusier to express his indignation at this "piece of filth," and asked him to "write to M. Bloc to explain the role of the Soviet architect": Nikolai Kolli, letter to Le Corbusier, Moscow, undated (handed to Le Corbusier by Giedion on 27 December 1932), FLC.

The Soviet authorities have created serious difficulties for the author of *Précisions*, and his project for the Palace of Soviets is considered a sort of joke here, whereas to me it seems to be a work of quite exceptional quality, and one designed for a people that has not yet appeared on this earth.[53]

The Moscow "meeting" furnished the occasion for various Soviet orators to dissociate themselves from Le Corbusier, including Vladimir Semenov, whose task it was to criticize his urban planning (to the great joy of Alfred Agache), and David Arkin, who attacked his architecture.[54] All in all, the "meeting" went off as Vago had envisaged: between the Moscow CIAM, which at the time was still a vague prospect, and which would subsequently be scratched, and the sending of an official delegation to the International Congress at Rome, it constituted a "third way" and an opportunity to "cut" Le Corbusier.

It is, therefore, hardly surprising that the Soviet press gave extensive coverage to the events organized by *L'Architecture d'Aujourd'hui*. VOKS published various declarations and illustrations in its official bulletin, and emphasized the evident convergence of views between Vago's attacks on the "new formalism" and Arkin and Khiger's anticonstructivist positions.[55] In addition, *Stroitelstvo Moskvy* published the discussions relating specifically to the state of the Soviet capital,[56] while Pierre Vago, who raged pugnaciously against Raymond Fischer's extreme antidecorativism and the celebration of Le Corbusier's *respiration exacte*, was given space in the pages of *Sovetskaia Arkhitektura*.[57]

After the return from Moscow, some members of the group felt the need to "defend the USSR"; this was the case of Agache, who soberly referred to its "considerable effort."[58] Yet one did not have to make the trip to contribute to this general movement: in a polemical "diptych" published in *Russie d'Aujourd'hui* Ozenfant, then allied to the Communist party, recounted the differences between the "Czar's empire" (which he had known at first hand) with its "prehistoric agriculture" and its "languid art of pleasure," and the USSR with "motorized agriculture." Ozenfant, who had commented ironically on the Palace of Soviets competition, now emphasized the provisional nature of the new artistic trend and cited the "revision of art until such a time as it should emanate naturally and Marxistically [sic] from the new society."[59]

A LECTURE BY ANDRÉ LURÇAT AND ITS EFFECTS WITHIN THE CIAM

At the outset of 1924, the presence in Moscow of André Lurçat, whose altercations with Le Corbusier within the CIAM-France group had reached an unprecedented pitch of virulence in 1929 and 1930, was the occasion for an unbridled conflict with significant consequences for the relations between the two men and the Soviet scene.[60]

At the end of 1933, Lurçat in turn received an invitation from VOKS to spend ten weeks in the USSR. Basking in the success of the school that he had built in Villejuif in that year, and given the fact that he was considered a pro-Soviet ideologist quite independent of all architectural trends, Lurçat found all the doors to Moscow's cultural and architectural life open to him. In a lecture delivered on 31 January on the theme of "Contemporary Architecture in the West," Lurçat spoke of the year 1932 as a turning point in the history of modern architecture marked by a divergence of views between Le Corbusier and himself:

At present, Le Corbusier and myself are in absolute opposition, given the difference between our respective ideologies. In his search for a modern solution to the problems

[53] Bardi, *Un fascista al paese dei Soviet*, p. 138.
[54] "Discours du prof. Semenov," "Réunions internationales," and "Discours du prof. Arkine," *L'Architecture d'Aujourd'hui*, no. 8 (1932). Semenov's discourse was later published under the title "Kak planirovat i zastraivat Moskvu."
[55] "Foreign Architects in the USSR," *Soviet Cultural Review*, nos. 10–12 (1932): 68–71.
[56] S. Kravchenko, "Frantsuskie Arkhitektory v SSSR," *Stroitelstvo Moskvy* 9, no. 10 (1932).
[57] Pierre Vago, "Segodniashny den evropeiskoi arkhitektury," *Sovetskaia Arkhitektura* 3, no. 6 (1933): 12–17. Fischer has since confirmed the violence of the discussions: Raymond Fischer, interview with Jean-Louis Cohen, Paris, 11 April 1986.
[58] Alfred Agache, "Une enquête auprès des intellectuels," *Russie d'Aujourd'hui* (15 May–15 June 1933): 4.
[59] Amédée Ozenfant, "Dyptique," *Russie d'Aujourd'hui* (15 May–15 June 1933): 4.
[60] For a detailed account of this, see Cohen, *L'architecture d'André Lurçat (1894–1970)*, pp. 629–43.

posed by the avant-garde and bourgeois society, he has joined battle with the architects of the Academy, but I view both sides as being against me, from both the æsthetic and the political point of view.

I speak of the abolition of class and its antagonisms, and of the confiscation of private property; in his discourse on the reorganization of cities, Le Corbusier talks of a "momentary mobilization of private property." He speaks of Authority, whereas I talk of the Dictatorship of the proletariat. Under such circumstances, you will understand how little our individual relations matter.[61]

Charlotte Perriand, who was in Moscow putting the final touches to the interiors of Centrosoyuz, received confidential word (in all probability from Kolli) of an even sharper attack made by Lurçat some days earlier, and which she duly communicated to Le Corbusier:

According to L., Le Corbusier refuses to take into account the society for which he builds, but with the "Ville Radieuse" he has shown himself to be reactionary and not revolutionary (by creating a city in which the problem of transport and the Business Center is treated as of first importance), whereas he (Lurçat) has studied for the last ten years and now fully understands that social questions are of the utmost importance in architecture.[62]

307. André Lurçat examines the projects for the Palace of Technique during his January 1934 trip to Moscow.

Charlotte Perriand then asked Le Corbusier to intervene with the CIAM, and to send the means of lauching a counterattack without delay:

Sammer and I (and also Kolli) are disgusted, and will do what we can so, Corbu, don't leave us in the lurch, as we are going to set about the task even without documents, and we have to win.

Naturally, Corbu, I'm only trying to keep you informed and asking you for documents that I don't have.

For the rest, it's our business to say what we think, and you are absolutely not involved.

Perriand was concerned about Lurçat's "skillful and dangerous campaign" and the risk of his getting "access to New Russia," which would be "a pity, for it's a serious organization."[63] On 6 February, armed with the two accounts diligently sent from Moscow, Le Corbusier wrote to the CIAM's president, van Eesteren, severely criticizing Lurçat and threatening to resign.[64] Van Eesteren, who was sick at the time, failed to reply to the letter. Giedion, who was called in to direct operations, wrote to Le Corbusier to confirm his firm intention to "wind up the affair in London," where the CIRPAC was scheduled to meet,[65] while at the same time writing to Lurçat to pass on the charges laid against him so that he could prepare his defense.[66]

The matter was discussed in Le Corbusier's absence on 20 and 21 May. Lurçat assured Victor Bourgeois, Sigfried Giedion, and Walter Gropius that his intentions had in no way been defamatory.[67] In the end, a commission composed of Bourgeois, Gropius, and Wells Coates was entrusted with the task of a further enquiry, and in particular that of sounding out what friends the CIAM was still presumed to have in Moscow. Bourgeois wrote to Kolli, who had attended the VOKS discussion, but who was obviously in no position to take sides publicly. Without explicitly corroborating Charlotte Perriand's version, he did not challenge it, but instead concentrated his attention on the public lecture of 31 January:

In a frank but polite address Mr. A. Lurçat, who spoke from a political viewpoint, explained the difference between the fundamental principles of his architecture and Le Corbusier's. The disagreement between these two men can in my view be ascribed

[61] André Lurçat, "L'architecture contemporaine en Occident," Moscow, 1934, handwritten, p. 1, Archives Nationales, Paris. This lecture was given extensive coverage in Moscow, e.g., "Dva Lageria, André Lurçat o frantsuskoi Arkhitekture," *Sovetskoe Isskustvo* (5 February 1934), and André Lurçat, "Segodniashny den frantsuskoi arkhitektury," *Arkhitektura SSSR* 2, no. 5 (1934): 48–50.

[62] Charlotte Perriand, "Extrait des paroles prononcées par André Lurçat, 1st VOKS meeting, 26 January 1934, evening," Moscow, handwritten, FLC. Charlotte Perriand has since confirmed these remarks word for word: Charlotte Perriand, interview with Jean-Louis Cohen, Paris, 29 September 1987.

[63] Charlotte Perriand, "Conférence Lurçat, le 31 février [sic] 1934," Paris, handwritten, pp. 2–3, FLC.

[64] Le Corbusier, letter to Cor. van Eesteren, Paris, 6 February 1934, FLC, gta/ETH Zurich.

[65] Sigfried Giedion, letter to Le Corbusier, Zurich, 12 May 1934, gta/ETH Zurich.

[66] Sigfried Giedion, letter to André Lurçat, Zurich, 10 May 1934, gta/ETH Zurich.

[67] André Lurçat, letters to Sigfried Giedion and Victor Bourgeois, gta/ETH Zurich, and to Walter Gropius, Bauhausarchiv, Berlin.

to a profound but purely political divergence of views regarding the social role of architecture.

As for other conferences held by Lurçat in the presence of extremely restricted groups of architects, in my view the private nature of these conferences precludes all publicity.[68]

For his part Hans Schmidt implicitly acknowledged that the accusations were well founded, but took pains to calm the situation:

A little before the start of Lurçat's lecture at the Union of Architects, Charlotte Perriand approached me on the subject of the evening at VOKS. I remember above all that Lurçat is supposed to have claimed that the young people were deserting Le Corbusier and following him. . . . I attended the lecture myself, but I did not pay much attention for it was uninteresting. Le Corbusier figured above all in a comparison that I considered doubtful—between his architecture and Monsieur Lurçat's. But Lurçat was rather vague, and had apparently received notification that an attack on Le Corbusier would not be understood.

. . . Personally speaking I do not really grasp the purpose of all this business. No Lurçat will be able to weaken Le Corbusier's prestige in the [Soviet] Union. The people here are not peasants. Lurçat has simply employed the same tactic that one of my compatriots also used at VOKS four years ago, with the intention of denigrating his foreign colleagues; but these acts invariably blow up in the face of their author.

I feel the matter could be ended with a reprimand for Lurçat and that this would also satisfy Le Corbusier. My view is that there's no other solution, for the exclusion of Lurçat would create a pointless split in the group. To my knowledge, nobody would profit by it.[69]

Although Le Corbusier insisted, calling again in November for "surgical measures," in the end Bourgeois, acting on behalf of the commission, dismissed the case, which left Le Corbusier dissatisfied[70] but which, in Gropius's view, was the best solution, especially since Lurçat had settled in Moscow and would stay there until 1937. This "cleared the air" and enabled Lurçat to "insist that Le Corbusier not hinder the formation of a new group" in Paris.[71] The Soviet press seized on this opportunity to emphasize the opposition between Lurçat and Le Corbusier, or rather, the latter's "fascist" positions:

The rise of unemployment is driving architects toward fascism and one of them, Le Corbusier, has become the editor of a review with conspicuous fascist orientations. This is in no way surprising when we recall how, in the last few years, Le Corbusier has disclaimed all connections with politics, declaring proudly that his only preoccupation is with "pure architecture."[72]

Thus it seems clear that Soviet attitudes to Le Corbusier in the mid-1930s were no longer conditioned solely by an assessment of his theories and projects, but also by more directly ideological considerations, a fact remarked on by travelers like Pierre Herbart, Gide's secretary who in 1937 published a corrosive travelogue in which he related the struggle "against formalism," a label attached to "the whole French school from Cézanne to Picasso":

There's Debussy, Milhaud, Auric, Stravinsky; there's Le Corbusier; there's Meyerhold.[73]

PARIS ATMOSPHERE

Although these Parisian polemics were played out before a growing audience in Moscow, thus leading Le Corbusier to imagine that a conspiracy was being

[68] Nikolai Kolli, letter to Victor Bourgeois, Moscow, 3 July 1934, gta/ETH Zurich.

[69] Hans Schmidt, letter to Walter Gropius, Moscow/Kharkov, 18 September 1934, gta/ETH Zurich. The "compatriote" to whom Schmidt refers is doubtless Hannes Meyer.

[70] Victor Bourgeois, letter to Le Corbusier, Brussels, 20 November 1934, gta/ETH Zurich, and letter to André Lurçat, Brussels, 20 November 1934, gta/ETH Zurich.

[71] Walter Gropius, letter to Sigfried Giedion, London, 28 December 1934, Bauhaus-archiv, Berlin.

[72] E. Delman, "Arkhitekturnye dekadniki: put André Lurçat," Literaturnaia Gazeta (5 February 1934).

[73] Pierre Herbart, En URSS 1936 (Paris: Gallimard, 1937), p. 39.

orchestrated there by his Parisian "rivals," his experiences within the Soviet Union certainly did not pass unnoticed in the French ideological debate. One of the first effects of this was to reinforce the characteristically anti-Soviet image of Le Corbusier as the "Trojan Horse of Bolshevism," at least during the years running up to the Palace of Soviets competition; and his failure to win clearly indicated that he had fallen into disfavor in Moscow.

The rejection of the "Response to Moscow" produced a significant change of attitudes among the "friends of the Soviet Union," on whose behalf Francis Jourdain had tried to persuade Le Corbusier to contribute to their journal. The task of condemning Le Corbusier's theses fell to Léon Moussinac who, writing in *L'Humanité*, outbid the reactions of Gorny and other Soviet officials. Moussinac's attack hinged on an idea later reiterated in *La ville radieuse*, according to which "Soviet free terrain will bring with it the free plan":

Le Corbusier refuses to face the fact that only the Socialist Revolution has created the conditions of such freedom. For capitalist nations he demands a sort of extension of the State's right to expropriate land in aid of *his* urban schemes, in the name of the defense of private property which forms the basis of his system. Le Corbusier turns a blind eye to political problems: for him it is enough to adopt a radical republican stand: "the mobilization of the soil for the cause of the public good." Le Corbusier does not believe in class struggle. Only one thing counts: the "plan."[74]

Following the arguments of L. M. Kaganovich's June 1931 report to the Central Committee, Moussinac went on to accuse Le Corbusier of basing his "Response to Moscow" on "man" and not on the working class:

The originality of his treatment of the planning and urban economy of Moscow lies in the fact that his proposals fail to account for a revolutionary fact: workers' control of the municipal economy, the socialization of the means of production, etc.

This is quite obviously absurd.

Such a fundamentally idealistic position has nothing to do with the true position of architects in the Soviet Union; and it makes a scheme like the Ville Radieuse essentially petit-bourgeois and counterrevolutionary, since it hallows the capitalist system of production.

Two years later, after the debacle of the Palace of Soviets, the architect Roger Ginsburger (who had been converted to communism by Moussinac) criticized not only Le Corbusier's theoretical stance, but also his attitude toward the Soviet situation, which he ascribes to the excesses of the twenties:[75]

At the outset, Soviet architecture was the work of young petit-bourgeois elements rallied to the cause of revolution, who, in order to mark their opposition to the architecture of the aristocracy and the bourgeoisie, designed much and built little in a purely formal cubist style. With the decision to implement the Five-Year Plan, the Soviet Union called in the best European architects, Le Corbusier and May, etc., and also American architects. The results of the experiment were far from marvelous—on the contrary. As an explanation of this, in-depth analysis of the differences between bourgeois architecture and bourgeois technology would be required to show that the most advanced bourgeois technologies can be placed at the service of the proletariat, whereas the most advanced bourgeois architecture cannot as such serve the needs of the proletariat, since it contains a whole series of elements that are in no way conditioned by the technical problems in hand, but rather, by the need to show off and the desire to display the power of credit and the domination of the bourgeois as individuals, the bourgeoisie as an organized class, and the imperialist State.[76]

Ginsburger who, following Giedion, had adopted the role of spokesman for

[74] Jean Peyralbe (the pseudonym of Léon Moussinac), "Deux conceptions de l'urbanisme," *L'Humanité* (31 March 1932).

[75] In 1924 Ginsburger, then in Germany, had tried to have a translation of *Vers une architecture* published there. His architectural career was brief, for in 1933 he entered politics; after 1945, he became a member of Parliament as Pierre Villon. For further details, see Jean-Louis Cohen, "Roger Ginsburger—von der Architektur zur Revolution," *Wissenschaftliche Zeitschrift der Hochschule für Architektur und Bauwesen*, Weimar, no. 5–6 (1983): 408–10; Cohen, "Roger Ginsburger and the Construction of Modernity."

[76] Roger Ginsburger, "L'architecture dans l'Union Soviétique," *Commune*, no. 5–6 (January 1934): 639–40.

the new techniques in his 1930 publication *Frankreich*,[77] now disavowed the emphasis that the early twenties had placed on building technology:

The search to integrate new means of production in architecture, which for long has been applied to the construction of factories, has on several occasions led these "best bourgeois architects"—because they were merely bourgeois architects—to adopt solutions of a technical, pseudoscientific and falsely functionalist sort—elements of ostentation in the same way as the decorative forms of the academics. To demonstrate this, it is enough to cite Le Corbusier's *air exact* and his "heat curtain"![78]

In his condemnation of the "sectarian utopianism of certain groups of modernist Soviet architects," Ginsburger was of the view that "only those have remained or will continue to remain who, even before their departure, had grasped the contradictions of bourgeois society as reflected in modern architecture—men such as [Mart] Stam, Hans Schmidt, Hannes Meyer and a few others." Turning to ridicule the the attacks "from the left" on the result of the Palace of Soviets competition, Ginsburger viewed the selection of Iofan as the very proof of the involvement of the "masses" in Soviet architectural choices:

Far from viewing the columns of the Palace of Soviets as a regression, we see in the absolute harmony of the masses with architectural production a positive indication of the future development of Soviet architecture. The very fact that, in the teeth of the capitalist world and what remains of the Soviet bourgeoisie, the masses have chosen the most monumental architecture that they know to symbolize the Soviet regime, is clear evidence of their attachment to and affection for it.

Those who have nothing else to do will have to decide whether the Soviet Union would do better to talk of bourgeois architecture in the manner of Le Corbusier or of Nénot, or whether it ought rather to prove which of the two is more bourgeois![79]

These attacks from the left-wing communist press were nothing new, since they had been inaugurated by Jacques Mesnil in 1922. But this time the reticence concerning Le Corbusier's explicit positions was fostered both by his public commitment to publishing the reviews *Plans* and *Prélude* and by the rejection of his theses at the very center of the world communist movement.

MOSCOW AND THE POPULAR FRONT

With the rise of antifascist unity, worried at the prospect of German rearmament and under friendly pressure from many at the office in the rue de Sèvres, Le Corbusier decided to adopt a more active commitment to the Popular Front, based on a coalition between the three principal parties of the left. In particular, he began to play an active role in the activities of a "union of architects" founded under the auspices of the Maison de la Culture, which had been created by Louis Aragon and André Malraux as an extension of the Association of Revolutionary Artists and Writers. In the letters that he sent to the leaders of the Popular Front to underpin his project for the reconstruction of the "insalubrious block no. 6," Le Corbusier claimed to be "president" of the union of architects.[80] Be that as it may, he joined in the discussion on "realism"

308. Le Corbusier, 100,000-seat stadium for popular events, Paris, 1936, model.

[77] Roger Ginsburger, *Frankreich*.

[78] Ginsburger, "L'architecture dans l'Union Soviétique," p. 641.

[79] Ibid., p. 643. Paul-Henri Nénot was the architect of large numbers of housing blocks and the New Sorbonne in Paris, and he was one of the prizewinners in the League of Nations competition.

[80] Le Corbusier, letter to Léon Blum, Paris, 30 December 1937, FLC.

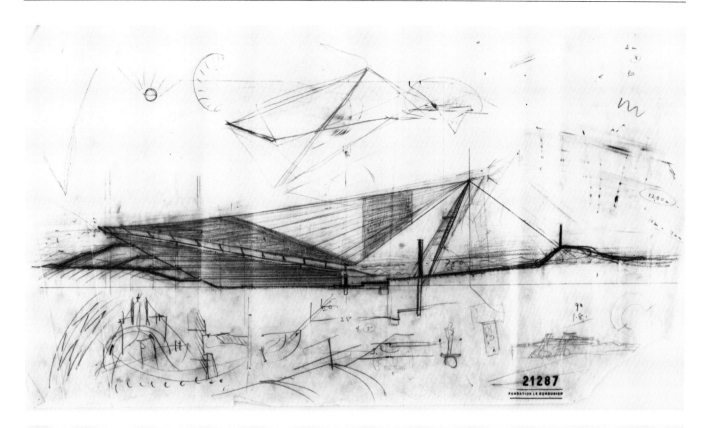

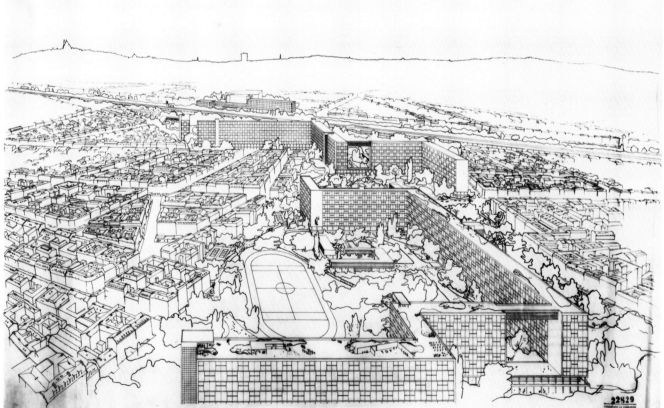

309. Le Corbusier, 100,000-seat stadium for popular events, Paris, 1936, section across the steps, FLC 21287.

310. Le Corbusier, Insalubrious block no. 6, Paris, 1936–1937, perspective from the air in Paris cityscape, FLC 22829.

organized by the Maison de la Culture and actively opposed Fernand Léger and the painter Jean Lurçat, for whom "the new age demanded imitative arts, that the popular masses be satisfied":

> I choke and my blood boils when I hear obsequious statements addressed to the laboring masses whom one ought instead to inspire.
>   . . . French art, called abstract, is concrete. It is essentially concrete. There is realism in it.[81]

Apart from his active participation in theoretical discussions in the institutions and reviews of the Popular Front,[82] Le Corbusier devoted his energies to three distinct projects: the "insalubrious" block no. 6; the 100,000-seat stadium "for popular events," for which Pierre Jeanneret's contribution proved essential, and in which the visual, acoustic, and crowd-management problems initially tackled in the Palace of Soviets project were finally resolved; and the pavilion of the *Temps Nouveaux* for the 1937 International Exposition. He also badgered the socialist mayor of Boulogne-Billancourt, André Morizet, with a project for the town-hall square and the Saint-Cloud bridge. Both in his contacts with the Blum cabinet and his correspondence with Paul Vaillant-Couturier and Maurice Thorez, Le Corbusier now assumed the role of a left-winger concerned for the success of the Popular Front. Vaillant-Couturier claimed to regret the attacks of Mesnil and Moussinac, while Le Corbusier assured him that the project for the "insalubrious" block no. 6 was politically well timed:

> For the Popular Front, there is only one way to show that something new has been done in the sphere of social justice—by building at once, in Paris, the elements of housing that will reflect both the latest technical developments and your firm intention to make them serve the interests of mankind.[83]

Le Corbusier's "drift to the left" does not quite tie up with his positions vis-à-vis the Soviet Union, even if, in 1931–1932, the pages of *Plans* were still full of praises for the Five-Year Plan and the great Soviet initiatives.[84] In fact, it reflected both the ambivalence of his earlier commitments to the technocrats and the pressure of circumstances that led him to "revise" his version of the events in Moscow. Thus, in his 1937 account of his trip to the United States, *Quand les cathédrales étaient blanches*, he continued to consider himself a "sympathizer" with the Russian experiment while at the same time citing the failings of an "ill-informed authority":

> The USSR had created an admirable term, "the general line"—"That's in the general line!" "That's not in the general line"—but men failed to measure up to the ideal; they fell far short of it in some circumstances. In architecture and planning, for instance, they were caught and choked in the most perfidious of quicksands. Disaster, betrayal—a slap in the face for the sympathizing, universal elite. We consoled ourselves by saying, "Growing pains, insignificant—a passing phase!"; but in the meantime, how acute the pains were![85]

With the project for a monument to the memory of Paul Vaillant-Couturier at Villejuif (of which he had been the mayor), Le Corbusier took a further step in the direction of the communist left. The jury for this competition organized by the Maison de la Culture (Jean Renoir, Francis Jourdain, and Léon Moussinac) ruled out Le Corbusier's project under pressure from Moussinac. In its location, the monument evoked the age of the automobile, but its "three symbolic motifs"—"the head of the orator, the hand of the orator, the book"—played a more rhetorical role:

> The monument, facing the road to Italy, stands firm. It can be seen by travelers from

[81] Le Corbusier, "Le destin de la peinture," in *La querelle du réalisme* (Paris: Editions Sociales Internationales, 1936), p. 85.

[82] Le Corbusier had decided to publish articles in the review *Europe*, edited by the left socialist intellectual Jean-Richard Bloch: Le Corbusier, "Elie Faure," *Europe* 18 (15 December 1937): 503–11; "Espoir de la civilisation machiniste: Le logis," *Europe* 19 (15 May 1938): 91–98.

[83] Maximilen Gauthier, *Le Corbusier ou l'architecture au service de l'homme* (Paris: Denoël, 1944), p. 233. For Le Corbusier's political peregrinations, see Jean-Louis Cohen, "Droite-gauche: Invite à l'action," in *Le Corbusier (1887–1965): Une encyclopédie*, pp. 309–13.

[84] For details concerning the contents of Plans, see McLeod, *Le Corbusier, from Regional Syndicalism to Vichy*, and "Bibliography: *Plans*, 1–13 (1931–32); *Plans* (bi-monthly), 1–8 (1932); *Bulletin des Groupes Plans*, 1–4 (1933)," *Oppositions* 19–20 (Winter–Spring 1980): 185–201.

[85] Le Corbusier, *Quand les cathédrales étaient blanches, Voyage au pays des timides* (Paris: Plon, 1937), pp. 263–64.

afar; it is like the first Paris milestone. After it, one enters Paris. From here, therefore, it can address a message.[86]

The "hand of the orator"—an essential element of the message—was the very hand that Maurice Thorez had held out in a speech to the Catholic workers—but also to the Croix-de-Feu—broadcast by Radio-Paris on 17 April 1936. Le Corbusier, who was henceforth more moderate in his commitment to technocratic circles, had touched the hand without grasping it, so to speak. The hand subsequently took on an "open" though more static form for Le Corbusier, who would use it to crown the enterprise of Chandigarh.

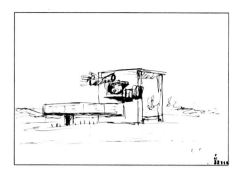

311. Le Corbusier, monument to Paul Vaillant-Couturier, Villejuif, 1938, sketch FLC 32115.

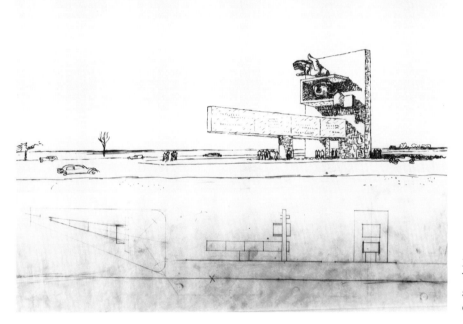

312. Le Corbusier, monument to Paul Vaillant-Couturier, Villejuif, 1938, perspective from highway no. 7, plan and elevation, FLC 32115.

POSTWAR HEARTBURN

Following the bitter episode of the Vichy government, Le Corbusier renewed his contacts with the French Communist party and the Confédération Générale du Travail and made serious attempts to profit from the past by seeking support for his schemes at Saint-Dié and Marseilles. Writing to his contact Jean Nicolas, former secretary of the Maison de la Culture, he now staked his claim to the role of "friend" of the Soviet Union:

I built Centrosoyuz in Moscow. I was the object of unspeakable accusations: capitalist architect and fascist individual. In 1928 (a little courage was required to do business with the Soviets at the time) I estimated my fees for this work as simply the reimbursement of my expenses (and these were practically zero, since my draughtsmen worked for nothing). Thus, in a spontaneous gesture, I reduced my fees to approximately *one-tenth* of what I would normally have charged. But I made no compromise for the Palace of Soviets, an example of architecture that I challenge anyone to match. No compromise, and no reinforced concrete in the Graeco-Latin style.

[86] Le Corbusier and Pierre Jeanneret, "Projet de monument à la gloire de P. Vaillant-Couturier, note explicative," December 1938, FLC.

In 1922, when I was in charge of *L'Esprit Nouveau*, Ozenfant and I announced, on page 1814, a raffle of art works in support of the USSR, which at the time had fallen prey to an appalling famine. But in 1934, as a result of a campaign waged by people known to me, I was unable to obtain permission to travel to Moscow in order to defend the architectural ideas for which I had been acclaimed in Moscow lecture halls and clubs in 1928.[87]

An active member of the Front National des Architectes and the Union Nationale des Intellectuels, and a signatory of the Stockholm petition against the atom bomb, Le Corbusier did not join the opponents of the Soviet Union in the postwar years. At the same time, his disillusion following the failure of his United Nations project intensified an anti-American sentiment to which he had already given voice on his return from the United States in 1935, and he steadfastly refused to resolve the "USA-USSR dilemma"—a fact that he stressed on several occasions. For the United Nations project, he even sought the assistance of Alexander Vesnin, and proposed that he be entrusted with one of the commissions.[88] In New York he also met Ilya Ehrenburg again. They lunched together, and Ehrenburg was talked into agreeing with Le Corbusier's view of Manhattan as a "magical catastrophe" (*catastrophe féérique*).[89]

In mid-1945, Le Corbusier was even commissioned to design a "monument to Franco-Soviet relations," which was to have been built in Moscow and financed "by national subscription." This project had the support of Francis Jourdain and, for a time at least, the minister of foreign affairs.[90] But on the Soviet side, the attacks went on regardless, and although Le Corbusier did not appear in official writings as one of those evil spirits who had led revolutionary architecture astray, this was because his very name was taboo.[91] In the course of the "anticosmopolitan" campaign that marked the early fifties, Lurçat took up the banner by attacking Chandigarh,[92] whereas in 1948 Hélène Parmelin wrote in the pages of *L'Humanité* that Le Corbusier's "most ardent supporters [were] to be found among the young and the workers."[93]

The 1953 edition of the *Great Soviet Encyclopedia* gives an idea of the then "official" position regarding Le Corbusier. He could not be completely ignored, but his work was now disposed of in fourteen lines (instead of the eighty published in the first edition), and none of his projects was named except the League of Nations. Yet although the author condemned the "leader" of "the new architecture" for his "formalism," he also cited Le Corbusier as one of "the representatives of the progressive French intelligentsia" who had signed the Stockholm petition.[94] On the other hand, Le Corbusier's own assessment of Soviet architectural production was devoid both of violence and indulgence:

In Moscow they build apartment houses and skyscraper hotels, for reasonable reasons. And in Gothic, for unreasonable reasons: "to please." (Showing off: "We too can make rich and beautiful things . . .")[95]

Following Khrushchev's 1954 denunciation of the "excesses" of Stalinist architecture, modernism was allowed back into the Soviet Union, but Le Corbusier was not "rehabilitated" until the early sixties—although functionalist urban planning became official doctrine as early as 1956.

In 1962, on the occasion of Le Corbusier's seventy-fifth birthday, Nikolai Kolli initiated the process with an article in which he evoked the "great master's globally positive record" in the Soviet Union; and although he failed to mention the Palace of Soviets project, he did full justice to Centrosoyuz and referred briefly to the "Response to Moscow."[96] In the same year Le Corbusier's former correspondent Victor Nekrasov, now a recognized author, again wrote

[87] Le Corbusier, letter to Jean Nicolas, Paris, 27 September 1945, Jean Nicolas archives. The "campaign" clearly refers to the attacks by Lurçat.

[88] Vesnin was included in Le Corbusier's scheme along with Wallace Harrison, Lucio Costa, and Walter Gropius or Mies Van der Rohe. See Le Corbusier, note concerning the hierarchy of commissions, 17 September 1946, FLC.

[89] Ilya Ehrenburg, *Retour des Etats-Unis* (Paris: Nagel, 1947), p. 18.

[90] See the correspondence with the publisher G. Frouin, FLC.

[91] Mikhail Tsapenko, *O realisticheskikh osnovakh sovetskoi arkhitektury* (Moscow: Gos. izd. Lit. po Stroitelstvu i Arkhitekture, 1954), p. 130.

[92] André Lurçat, "Essai sur la ville," *La Nouvelle Critique*, no. 52 (February 1954): 162–71.

[93] Hélène Parmelin, "L'homme qui veut construire des cités radieuses," *L'Humanité* (19 May 1948).

[94] "Corbusier Le," in *Bolshaia Sovetskaia Entsiklopediia*, vol. 22 (Moscow: Izd. Sov. Entsiklopediia, 1953), p. 565.

[95] Le Corbusier, open letter to the Préfet de Police, 7 February 1956, published in *Les plans de Paris 1956–1922* (Paris: Editions de Minuit, 1956), p. 9.

[96] Arkh. N. Kolli, "K 75-letiiu Le Corbusier (Le Corbusier v Moskve)," *Arkhitektura SSSR* 12, no. 8 (1962): 36–42.

to Le Corbusier, asking "if he might not propose his services to a nation that has buried Stalin and which, albeit rather late in the day, has abandoned columns and porticoes"; in reply, Le Corbusier simply said he had "other things to do."[97]

On Le Corbusier's death in 1965, Kolli contributed obituaries to *Pravda* and to *Trud*, the trade-union daily.[98] His work as a whole was now at last fully recognized, and his last projects—Chandigarh, Ronchamp, La Tourette— were brought to the attention of the Soviet public. In another article, Kolli now canonized him as a "friend" who "greatly appreciated the creative researches and advanced orientations" of the twenties, and who "could not ignore the enormous advantages of the Soviet system for the development of urban planning."[99]

AN INDELIBLE MARK

The traces of the period 1928–1936 had thus remained as fresh in Le Corbusier's mind as it did in Moscow, even if this was denied for a time; moreover, he obviously left a far greater mark than the German or Swiss architects who had devoutly fulfilled their roles as technicians or revolutionaries, but whose stay in Russia had not been surrounded by such an aura of controversy. How can we assess the "Moscow effect" on the conceptual vicissitudes of Le Corbusier's career wherever his architectural ideas encounter a solid political or ideological referent?

The "promised land for technicians," which Le Corbusier initially believed he had discovered in the new Russia, at first gave him immense narcissistic satisfaction, since it was there that he first succeeded in playing out the role of international "expert" to which he had aspired. But apart from this mutual recognition one has to admit that, all in all, the corpus of Soviet critical writing on Le Corbusier from the mid-twenties on is remarkable for the subtlety and perspicacity of its assessment, despite the occasions when it serves questionable ideological aims. Le Corbusier had to pay for these analyses as a "hostage" to internal struggles and conflicts; in his relations with Soviet politicians (Lunacharsky or Liubimov) and architects (Vesnin), he hung on stubbornly to positions whose significance he did not always grasp in this period of the great upheavals of Stalinist cultural policy. Here again, Le Corbusier manifested the same political naiveté that had marked his indifference to the transformations of the Muscovite political scene in 1928.

The intensity of the Soviet theoretical debate nonetheless forced Le Corbusier to sharpen his own positions vis-à-vis functionalism, and to articulate "technology" and "lyricism" more precisely. The scale of the industrial and territorial challenge linked to the Five-Year Plan inspired him to reflect on the problem of fluxes in architecture and urban planning, to dissociate his vision of the city from the specific instance of Paris and give it universal scope with the "Ville Radieuse," and to become quite simply a "technician of architecture and urbanism."[100]

Just as the Soviet theorists doubtless read Le Corbusier with greater attention than anyone else, he too was an efficient though discreet analyst of the mature (but doomed) constructivist production that emerged at the end of the twenties. He viewed the projects and rarely executed communal-housing designs as interpretations of his own architectural preoccupations, albeit linked to social demand quite unlike that of his own Parisian clientele, and, as we have seen, set about redefining the scale of housing units and infrastructure. The term *collective services* took on new significance in the "Response to

[97] Victor Nekrasov, introductory note to "Deux lettres de Le Corbusier à Victor Nékrassov," *Cahiers du Monde Russe et Soviétique* 21, no. 2 (1980): 201–2.

[98] Nikolai Kolli, "Genii Arkhitektury," *Trud* (31 August 1965); "Vydaiushchiisia master arkhitektury," *Pravda* (4 September 1965).

[99] Nikolai Kolli, "Arkhitektor Le Corbusier," *Arkhitektura SSSR* 15, no. 12 (1965): 51–63. Since 1970, several works on and by Le Corbusier have been published, e.g., Le Corbusier, *Tvorcheskii Put* (Moscow: Stroiizdat, 1970), translation from *Le Corbusier textes et planches* (Paris: Vincent et Fréal, 1960); *Modulor* (Moscow: Stroiizdat, 1976); and Ern, *Poslednie raboty Le Corbusier*.

[100] Le Corbusier, *The Radiant City*, p. 90.

Moscow" with its idea of fully equipped, collective roof terraces and "streets in the air," which found their ultimate expression in the "Unités d'Habitation de Grandeur Conforme."

In addition to this evolution in the housing sphere, the commissions given by the Russian "plan factory," together with Centrosoyuz and the Palace of Soviets, led him to redefine relations with the urban context and to anticipate the revitalization of plastic forms in his postwar architecture. Far from constituting a phase of stagnation in his architectural production (despite the frustrations), the Soviet episode on the contrary marks a point of inflection that enabled Le Corbusier to assert the unshakeable independence of his architectural inventiveness.

LIST OF MOST FREQUENTLY USED ABBREVIATIONS AND ACRONYMS

ARKOS: Anglo-Sovetskoe Torgovoe Obshchestvo (Anglo-Russian Trading Society)

ARU: Assosiatsiia Arkhitektorov-Urbanistov (Association of Architects-Urbanists)

ASNOVA: Assosiatsiia Novykh Arkhitektorov (Association of New Architects)

Centrosoyuz: Tsentralny Soiuz Potrebitelskikh Obshchestv (Central Union of Consumer Cooperatives)

CIAM: Congrès Internationaux d'Architecture Moderne

CIRPAC: Comité International pour la Réalisation du Problème Architectural Contemporain

FLC: Fondation Le Corbusier

ETH: Eidgenössische Technische Hochschule

GAKhN: Gosudarstvennaia Akademiia Kommunalnykh Nauk (State Academy of Artistic Sciences)

Gostorg: Gosudarstvennaia Importno-Exportnaia Torgovaia Kontora (State Trading Office for Import and Export)

gta: Geschichte und Theorie der Architektur

GUM: Gosudarstvenny Universalny Magazin (State Department Store)

INKhUK: Institut Khudozhestvennoi Kultury (Institute of Artistic Culture)

LEF: Levy Front Iskusstva (Left Front of the Arts)

MAO: Moskovskoe Arkhitekturnoe Obshchestvo (Moscow Architectural Society)

MOGES: Moskovskoe Obedinenie Gosudarstvennykh Elektricheskikh Stantsii (Moscow Union of State Electrical Power Plants)

MOKKh: Moskovsky Oblastnoi Otdel Kommunalnogo Khoziaistva (Department of Municipal Economy for the Moscow Region)

MSPO: Moskovsky Soiuz potrebitelskikh Obshchestv (Moscow Union of Consumer Cooperatives)

Mossoviet: Moskovsky Sovet Rabochikh, Krestianskikh i Soldatskikh Deputatov (Moscow Council of Worker, Peasant and Soldier's Delegates.

Narkomfin: Narodny Kommissariat Finansov (People's Commissariate for Finance)

NEP: Novaia Ekonomicheskaia Politika (New Economy Policy)

OBMOKhU: Obshchestvo Molodyh Khudozhnikov (Society of Young Artists)

OSA: Obedinenie Sovremennykh Arkhitektorov (Union of Contemporary Architects)

PROOUN or PROUN: Proekt Utverzhdeniia Novogo (Project for the Affirmation of the New)

RK(B)P: Rossiiskaia Kommunisticheskaia (Bolshevisticheskaia) Partiia (Russian Communist [Bolshevik] party)

RSFSR: Rossiiskaia Sovetskaia Federativnaia Sotsialisticheskaia Respublika (Russian Soviet Socialist Federative Republic)

SA: Sovremennaia Arkhitektura (Contemporary Architecture)

SADG: Société des Architectes Diplômés par le Gouvernement

SASS: Sektor Arkhitektorov Sotsialisticheskogo Stroitelstva (Sector of Architects for the Construction of Socialism)

Sinskulptarkh: Skulpturno-Arkhitekturny Sintez (Synthesis of Sculpture and Architecture)

Sovkhoz: Sovetskoe Khoziaistvo (State Farm)

SSSR: Soiuz Sovetskikh Sotsialisticheskikh Respublik (Union of Soviet Socialist Republics)

Stroikom RSFSR: Stroitelny Komitet RSFSR (Committee for Construction of the Russian Federation)

TsGALI: Tsentralny Gosudarstvenny Arkhiv Literatury i Isskustva (Central State Archive for Literature and Art)

UN: United Nations

Vkhutein: Vysshy Gosudarstvenny Khudozhestvenno-Tekhnichesky Institut (Higher State Artistic and Technical Institute)

Vkhutemas: Vysshie Gosudarstvennye Khudozhestvenno-Tekhnicheskie Master-skie (Higher State Artistic and Technical Workshops)

VOKS: Vsesoiuznoe Obshchestvo Kulturnykh Sviazei s Zagranichnoi (Society of Cultural Relations with the Foreign Countries)

VOPRA: Vserossiiskoe Obedinie Proletarskikh Arkhitektorov (Russian Union of Proletarian Architects)

Zhivskulptarkh: Kollektiv Zhivopisno-skulpturno-arkhitekturnogo Sinteza (Synthesis of Painting, Sculpture and Architecture Collective)

LIST OF ILLUSTRATIONS

Note: All the projects of Le Corbusier from 1923 to 1940 were designed in association with Pierre Jeanneret.

1919–1920, and Georgi Yakulov, Monument to the Twenty-six Baku Commissars, 1923, models exhibited at the Exposition des Arts Décoratifs et Industriels Modernes, Paris, 1925, in *Panorama Iskusstv*, no. 5 (1982).

20. El Lissitzky, title page of *Veshch*, no. 3 (Berlin, 1922) (collection of the author).

21. El Lissitzky, title page of *Veshch*, nos. 1–2 (Berlin, 1922) containing Le Corbusier's article "Contemporary Architecture" (collection of the author).

22. Le Corbusier, "Eyes which do not see," page of *Vers une architecture* (Paris, 1923) (collection of the author).

23. Le Corbusier, "3 Reminders to Mssrs. the Architects," page of *Vers une architecture* (Paris, 1923) (collection of the author).

24. Le Corbusier, "Voisin Plan" for Paris, 1925, perspective with Paris skyline, FLC 29721 (Fondation Le Corbusier/SPADEM).

25. Le Corbusier, "Voisin Plan" for Paris, 1925, partial axonometric view, FLC 29723 (Fondation Le Corbusier/SPADEM).

26. "The City of the Future according to the Project of the Architect Le Corbusier–Saugnier," in *Stroitelnaia Promyshlennost* 3, no. 2 (1925) (Lenin Library, Moscow).

27. Le Corbusier on a roof terrace of the Quartiers Modernes Frugès, Pessac, 1926 (Lucien Hervé archives, Paris).

28. Le Corbusier, Church villa, view through the glass wall, Ville-d'Avray, 1928–1929 (Lucien Hervé archives, Paris).

29. Le Corbusier, house in the Weissenhof *Siedlung*, Stuttgart, 1927; in N. V. Markovnikov, *Zhilishchnoe stroitelstvo za granitsei i v SSSR* (Moscow, 1928) (Lenin Library, Moscow).

30. Le Corbusier, project for League of Nations, Geneva, 1927, general axonometric view of second design, FLC 23185 (Fondation Le Corbusier/SPADEM).

31. Alexander Vesnin, dust jacket for Moisei Ginzburg's *Stil i Epokha*, 1924 (Shchusev Museum of Architecture, Moscow).

32. Alexei Gan, cover of *Sovremennaia Arkhitektura* 1, no. 3 (1926) (collection of the author).

33. Page of *Sovremennaia Arkhitektura* 1, no. 3 (1926) (collection of the author).

34. Le Corbusier, "Five Points of a New Architecture," in *Sovremennaia Arkhitektura* 3, no. 1 (1928) (Musée des Arts Décoratifs, Paris).

35. Le Corbusier, answer to *Bauwelt's* "inquiry on the flat roof," published in *Sovremennaia Arkhitektura* 1, no. 4 (1926) (Getty Center for the History of Art and the Humanities, Santa Monica).

36. Le Corbusier, Stein-de Monzie villa, Garches, 1926–1928, in *Sovremennaia Arkhitektura* 4, no. 5 (1929) (Musée des Arts Décoratifs, Paris).

37. Alexei Gan, poster for the First Exhibition of Modern Architecture, Moscow, 1927; in *Sovremennaia Arkhitektura* 2, no. 6 (1927) (Musée des Arts Décoratifs, Paris).

38. Works by the architects of the OSA at the the First Exhibition of Modern Architecture, Moscow, 1927; in *Sovremennaia Arkhitektura* 2, nos. 4–5 (1927) (Musée des Arts Décoratifs, Paris).

39. Alexander Rodchenko, "In the Streets of Moscow," photograph, 1929 (Alexander Rodchenko Archive, Moscow).

40. Le Corbusier in the offices of VOKS, together with Olga Kameneva (on his left) and Andrei Burov (on his right), Moscow, October 1928 (H. Roger-Viollet, Paris).

41. Le Corbusier lecturing at the State Academy of Artistic Sciences, Moscow, October 1928, (H. Roger-Viollet, Paris).

42. Le Corbusier in a group of Soviet architects, Moscow, October 1928; left to right: Andrei Burov, Le Corbusier, Alexander Vesnin (Fondation Le Corbusier/SPADEM).

43. Le Corbusier's lecture at the Polytechnical Museum, Moscow, 20 October 1928; left to right: Anatoli Lunacharsky, Le Corbusier, Andrei Burov, ?, ?, Nikolai Kolli, ?, Alexander Vesnin (Fondation Le Corbusier/SPADEM).

44. Sketch executed by Le Corbusier during his lecture at the Polytechnical Museum, Moscow, 20 October 1928 (Shchusev Museum of Architecture, Moscow).

45. Sketch executed by Le Corbusier during his lecture at the Polytechnical Museum, Moscow, 20 October 1928 (Shchusev Museum of Architecture, Moscow).

INDEX OF NAMES

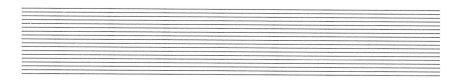